EXPISCATIONS IN CROSS-CULTURAL PSYCHOLOGY

Selected Papers from the
Sixth International Congress of the
International Association for Cross-Cultural Psychology
held at Aberdeen, July 20-23, 1982

Edited by

J. B. DERȨGOWSKI, S. DZIURAWIEC and R. C. ANNIS

Published for the International Association
for Cross-Cultural Psychology

Swets and Zeitlinger B.V., Lisse
1983

CIP-GEGEVENS

Expiscations

Expiscations in cross-cultural psychology : selected
papers from the Sixth International Congress of the
International Association for Cross-cultural Psychology
held at Aberdeen, July 20-23, 1982 / ed. by J.B.
Deregowski, S. Dziurawiec ... [et al.]. - Lisse : Swets
and Zeitlinger. - Ill.
Uitg. voor de International Association for Cross-cultura
Psychology. - Met index, lit. opg.
ISBN 90-265-0450-0
SISO 905.2 UDC 159.922.4
Trefw. : cultuurpsychologie.

EXPISCATIONS
IN
CROSS-CULTURAL PSYCHOLOGY

CONTENTS

PROBLEMS OF MIGRANTS AND REFUGEES

MUTUAL PERCEPTIONS

VIOLENCE AND AGGRESSION

WORK, INDUSTRY AND ORGANISATION

DIVERS ISSUES EXPISCATED

INTRODUCTION

J. B. Derȩgowski, S. Dziurawiec and R. C. Annis

This volume contains a selection from the papers presented at the Sixth International Congress of the Association for Cross-cultural Psychology held at Aberdeen between 19th and 23rd July 1982.

The present editors have departed somewhat from the procedure established in the earlier issues of the Proceedings. The practice followed hitherto was to print the selected papers almost exactly as delivered allowing only for minor emendations. This leads to publication of the maximum number of papers, but it also results in a rather disjointed text which does not do justice to the flavour of the discussions. The Editors have decided therefore to make room for comments on some of the papers. Accordingly a number of scholars with especial expertise and interest in the issues examined in the papers was invited to send brief comments (some thought too brief, since the editors have strictly limited the space). These comments follow the papers to which they pertain, and in the case of Professor Jahoda's invited paper are in turn followed by a reply. This practice obviously expands the space required and the number of papers contained in this volume is, consequently, less than the number in any of its predecessors. It can be plausibly argued, however, that the discussions which papers provoke are not merely a part of the deliberations but the very essence of the Congress and that their absence impoverishes the record. We hope that in diverging from an admittedly young tradition we have struck a balance which will be found pleasing.

You might have been surprised by a rather rare word, "expiscations", in the title of this book. The reasons for its inclusion are of a sociocultural kind. Traditionally, since the second congress in 1976, the volumes Selected Proceedings have had titles beginnning with the consecutive letters of the alphabet. "Advances in ...", "Basic Problems ...", "Cross-cultural ..." and so on. The title of the present volume had therefore to begin with an "E". There are of course obvious possibilities such as Explorations, Extrapolations ..., words devoid of any local flavour, which were thought by us to be bland and commonplace.

> **Expiscate** (ekspi·skeit), *v.* [f. L. *expiscāt-*, ppl.
> stem of *expiscārī*, f. *ex-* out + *piscārī* to fish,
> f. *piscis* fish.] *trans.* To 'fish out'; hence, to
> find out by scrutiny. Occas. with sentence as
> object.
> Chiefly in Sc. writers; elsewhere usually humorously, with
> distinct reference to the etymology.

Oxford English Dict. Vol. 3, 1933.

In despair, one of the editors (Sz. Dz.) opened a
dictionary and expiscated expiscations. A Scots word, it
appears, of plain etymological significance, and in what
numismatists would term Extra Fine condition -- not worn
out with use. This was the solution to our problem, a
solution made more attractive by the fact that although
drawn from three disparate cultures, none of the editors is
a Scot.

The figures which we have used as a decorative motif
throughout the volume are also of local provenance. These
are based on the ornamentation found on Pictish Standing
Stones. The patterns are thought, by some, to have been
used to denote social rank. However, the placement in this
volume is entirely arbitrary and in no way should be taken
as editorial comment on the standing of the authors whose
papers they embellish.

In editing papers we have tried to retain the flavour
of each author's style of English provided it did not
obscure the meaning. The extent of editing varies therefore
considerably. We have adopted an equally liberal attitude
to the style of references used. Again our criterion was
not that of uniformity but of comprehensibility.

In preparing this volume we have received much help
from a variety of sources. The Department of Psychology of
the University of Aberdeen permitted us the use of
facilities. Dr. J.R. Lishman guided us in the use of the
word-processor. The typing was cheerfully done by Ms. L.
Bell. We are especially grateful to Miss K. McPherson who
not only assisted with typing, proof reading and indexing,
but has also expertly conducted several successful library
searches when it seemed to the senior editor that all hope
had faded.

J. B. D.
Sz. Dz.
R. C. A.

Acknowledgement

We are grateful to the publishers of Punch for
permitting us to reproduce their cross-cultural cartoon.

Presidential address

CROSS-CULTURAL PSYCHOLOGY: A VIEW FROM THE THIRD WORLD

D. Sinha

A.N.S. Institute, Patna

Cross-Cultural Orientation

Cross-Cultural Psychology is one of the more recent branches of psychology. Its authenticity has been established for hardly two decades, and even now, some scientists do not ungrudgingly accept its claim as a separate branch. Its roots can be discerned in various studies done over a period of almost 80 years. It can be said that Wundt's treatise on folk psychology, heralded its origin. Studies of psychological processes like illusion in diverse cultures and observing certain cultural differences therein as early as 1901 (Rivers, 1901), noting peculiarities in memories of the Swazis of South Africa and of Indian and British students in Cambridge by Bartlett (1932) constitute some of the early researches which were cross-cultural in orientation. Moreover, researches conducted by cultural anthropologists, the earlier ones being that of W.H.R. Rivers and Malinowski, and of Ruth Benedict and Margaret Mead, and the work of those psychologists using anthropological approaches or anthropologists interested in the study of personality which constituted the culture-personality approach provided firm roots to this subject. The pioneering investigations pointedly challenged the "pan-human verities" of psychological theories which are implicitly conveyed but have sometimes been stated quite explicitly (Faucheux, 1976). Culture as an important factor in the variation of all behaviour has been recognised. Moreover, in recent years there has been a growing realization of the parochial and ethnocentric character of the discipline. It has sometimes been called an Euro-American product (Campbell, 1968; Sinha, 1977) based largely on the study of urban middle class adolescents constituted by the American sophomore population. It is even felt that most theories in psychology, especially those dealing with social processes, are the product of a specific social milieu that characterizes advanced industrial societies of the West (Jahoda, 1980), and as such are not applicable to the unstable environment of developing countries which are in a state of flux and rapid social change. The concern for universality of psychological theories, as Malpass (1977) points out, is the major overarching rationale for psychologists' venturing to obtain cross-cultural data. Though cross-cultural psychology can be defined in many ways, it can be regarded primarily as a convenient and useful methodological strategy for "expanding psychology to panhuman proportions" (Malpass, 1977, p.1069). This has been the main reason for the growing popularity of cross-cultural studies.

Western Theoretical Models and Research Tools in the Third World

Thus, psychologists in large numbers from the West started gathering data from newly independent countries of Africa, Asia, Latin America and other parts of the world which are often referred to as the Third World. The initial interest has been to focus on psychological differences between peoples of contrasting cultures, describing and analysing the processes involved and unravelling the mechanisms underlying these differences. For many psychologists, this was a serious academic pursuit having its origin in their deep rooted concern for the advancement of psychological theories. For some, however, this interest was only casual, enabling them to travel to foreign lands and encounter strange people with the help of grants received from research foundations. In a general way it led to the export of Western theoretical models and methodological strategies to the Third World countires. Its influence on psychologists working in the developing countries has not always been academically very congenial, because in many parts of the Third World the development of modern scientific psychology has not been a very systematic process. It does not have firm roots in historical and cultural traditions and has little relation to the needs of the country. This is amply reflected in the development of modern psychology in India which is characterised by uncritical dependence of research workers on the West for their concepts, ideas and instruments (Sinha, 1972, 1977). This dependence, which is typical in more than one way of many Third World countries, has resulted in indiscriminate borrowing. As a result, a large amount of psychological research has been replicative in character and far removed from the problems that really matter. Thus, one is not surprised at the uncritical way in which many psychologists working in this part of the world have been influenced by the American and European cross-cultural psychologists and have indiscriminately gone after finding differences among various sub-cultural groups without bothering to work out a proper rationale for making comparisons. The statement that "no such study has been conducted to study the second-order personality factors of tribals (Tharu) and non-tribal boys" (Srivastava, Saxena, and Saksena, 1979) typifies the reason advanced for such researches. To give a few examples from India: Nepali, Bhutia, and Lepcha tribal school-going adolescents are administered a 169-item multiphasic inventory to compare, among other things, the "psychological structure for social and personal adjustment" (Bose, 1971), or 500 tribal and 500 non-tribal children from Tripura have been compared for their intelligence on different performance tests (Chattopadhyay, 1961). Comparisons have also been made on different personality variables like need for achievement and anxiety (Gokulnathan and Mehta, 1972), authoritarianism (Srivastava, Saksena and Kapoor, 1979), adjustment problems and attitude towards child rearing and what not between tribals of sub-Himalayan regions or the Central India plateau with the non-tribals of other regions. One wonders at the rationale of these so-called cross-cultural comparisons. Two or more cultural groups have been compared on certain personality variables because it is convenient to get from them differences on scores on whatever tests that may have been used without ever considering their suitability, the relevance of concepts which underlie such measures for the population studied, and the theoretical justification for making comparisons. Most of such researches are simply meaningless comparisons and exemplify empiricism running riot and these psychologists are what Westerlund, the President of the International Association for Applied Psychology in his welcome address in Liege in 1971, termed as "helpless victims of their data".

The situation is not very much better with regard to intelligence and other cognitive variables. When I read such papers and find that the unsophisticated tribals have not done as well on these tests as the non-tribal population (Chattopadhyay, 1961), I feel pity for the lot of poor tribals. This raises a very important question of equivalence of concepts and tools, and comparability of groups in cross-cultural research. The investigators have not paid sufficient heed to the difficulties involved in the transfer of concepts and tools across cultures or have not cared to utilize the steps Frederiksen (1977), and Frijda and Jahoda (1966) have suggested for overcoming them. It is one of the major shortcomings of cross-cultural research that it has not so far generated much by way of methodological break-through in forging new tools, but has generally led to uncritical and blind adoption of tools developed in the West. Diaz-Guerrero's (1977) remark in this context is pertinent: "Cross-cultural psychology upto now has promoted a great deal of application of the instruments developed in the First World. It has done very little to stimulate the development of local instruments that will at least measure socio-economic characteristics in the Third World and has been completely blind regarding the development of measures sensitive to idiosyncratic cultural and personality dynamics."

Ethnocentrism in Cross-Cultural Research

If Western value-orientation in cross-cultural research characterizes the work of psychologists from the Third World countries, it is not at all surprising that many scholars from the West working in these countries tend to perceive and value other cultures in terms of their own and impose their own vlaues in their effort to understand a diverse culture. In either case, non-Western cultures and their psychological functioning tend to be viewed through the lens of Western psychological theories thereby displaying a kind of ethnocentrism.

Individualistic orientation that generally characterizes the Western psychology has been taken for granted and is freely used in formulating problems for research. To give only one instance, in tune with individualistic bias prevalent in the West, parent-child interaction has frequently been studied to assess its influence on children's linguistic, cognitive or social development. The special feature of the Indian family setting is ignored. Typical interactional pattern in the Indian system is rarely between individual to individual as such, but is group or collective-based (Sinha, 1980 p. 159), and "contextual", as Roland (1981) puts it. While distinguishing the traditional Indian healing techniques, Kakar (1982) characterizes the former as individualistic where the cure lies in cognitive restructuring of the past on the part of the patient while the latter is characterized by contextual (social) approach in which the entire family of the patient shares in the idioms of therapeutic procedure. There is involvement of the relatives in the total healing process and a kind of "public sharing" of illness. Viewed against this perspective, in the Indian and for that matter in many Eastern cultures, instead of analysing only the influence of parent-child interactions, it is more appropriate to take into cognizance the entire context or the "ecology" in which the development of the child takes place. That is, the roles of cousins, aunts and older relations who frequently act as parental surrogates cannot be ignored and probably constitute equal, if not more, potent influences. In other words, the total psychological climate of the entire family complex, if not of the community, in which the child grows has to be analyzed to understand the conditions of his development. The foregoing example would indicate that overawed under Western influence, many of our scholars have ignored these contextual factors and have thereby missed the important causative influence that the "collective" exerts on the growing child.

There are more obvious instances of ethnocentrism in our cross-cultural researches. As pointed out earlier, a model of Western personality is utilized as a measuring stick against which all other psychological development is assessed and such processes and factors have been studied which to such researchers seem to be of importance but are of little consequence to the people on whom the studies are conducted. Comparing populations from different cultures and pronouncing some of them to be "lower" or "higher" on factors like authoritarianism, anxiety and need for achievement, to mention only a few, whose applicability to preliterate and unsophisticated populations of the Third World is extremely doubtful, are examples of such ethnocentrism.

There is also a danger of "distorted and half baked interpretation of data" (Zaidi, 1979) by researchers who are not sufficiently careful about understanding genuinely the people and culture in which the study is conducted. The point requires emphasis because there are instances where research projects have been completed and papers have been written about certain phenomena pertaining to a foreign country without the author having taken care to encounter the reality at first hand. I have in mind a research on the concern expressed by "slow-moving" and "fast-moving" managers in India, Columbia and Venezuela (Doktor and Bass, 1974) which was presented to an international congress a few years ago. It was pointed out that the "fast-moving" managers were low in education and were more concerned about pollution and a host of other factors which to me did not collectively make much sense. When I queeried to find out details about the industries from which the sample had been drawn and other basic information, the famous investigator was not even aware whether the managerial sample hailed from modern steel mills, old-fashioned textile industries, or from eastern, western or southern India. The fact of the matter was that the investigator had an enormous research grant at his disposal and had gathered data from many countries with the help of a few local investigators. He had excellent competence but his interpretation lacked meaning because he had no first hand encounter with the reality. This is a frequent danger of a multi-national research project. I have used the expression purposely because it readily conjures up the dangers and suspicions which people in developing countries sometimes harbour against the "multinationals". I would only add that a truly cross-cultural research as distinct from a multinational research should be characterized by an earnest effort to understand the social reality, should be of relevance to the country where data are collected, and tempered by a belief that just by remaining an outsider, the reality would elude his grasp.

The researches that I have referred to in passing and
which claim to be cross-cultural are patent instances of
what has been termed an imposed etic or more appropriately
"Euro-American emics" (Berry, 1978). Despite the fact that
many of these studies have been conducted by local
scholars, they at best provide outsider's view of the
phenomenon in question, and do not display insider's
perspective. While the necessity of emic view is
emphasized, it is to be borne in mind that insider's view
by itself is not sufficient. For cross-cultural research to
be meaningful, the first essential step is to carry out
many emic studies from within the culture, and then
supplement the same with a comparative framework. If the
researcher confines himself only to emic approach, he would
simply be substituting one kind of ethnocentrism with
another. As Berry (1978) has pointed out, the advocacy of a
local view logically requires also the advocacy of an
outsider's view and vice versa. When emic understanding of
behaviour which reflects one's own societal base is
supplemented by a comparative analysis of these variations,
emergence of pan-cultural regularities and the
establishment of whatever universal features are found
becomes possible. In other words, attainment of what has
been called a derived etic can come about only after a wide
range of culture-specific phenomena and their relationships
have been observed and analysed, and their common features
are isolated. This would necessitate the modification of
our cultural framework and categories which have been
uncritically borrowed from the West by local scholars or
uncritically imposed by their Western counterparts. Only
when they are made applicable and appropriate to the
behavioural system under study and backed by culturally
appropriate tools for data collection is a true
cross-cultural investigation possible.

Nature of Partnership in Cross-Cultural Research

As has been said earlier, cross-cultural researches
have largely been initiated and conducted by scientists
from prosperous and developed countries of North American
and European continents in less developed countries of Asia
and Africa. By and large, there has been a kind of "one-way
traffic" and this has brought to the fore some very
delicate but important professional as well as ethical
problems. Tapp, Kelman, Triandis, Wrightsman and Coelho
(1974) in their report on cross-cultural ethics have hinted
at some of these problems. One of them concerns the nature
of collaboration which is worked out for the conduct of
studies in the developing countries. Three kinds of
collaborative relationships with the consultant counterpart
in the host country are possible. They are: exploitive,
subordinate and truly collaborative with various nuances of

each. The bulk of collaboration has been of the first two varieties where the reseachers from the developed countries, either intentionally or otherwise, have taken advantage of the "power of research funds". The exploitive relationship is that in which the outside researcher utilizes in data collection a number of junior scientists from the host country who hardly know what is going on. The advantage that they receive is a decent remuneration which is often so many times more than what they have been receiving in their own country or could expect to receive on the basis of their qualifications and experience. In subordinate relationships, the local consultant assumes a subservient role irrespective of his competence and status. This was more true in the fifties when funds in the developing countries for conducting research in psychology and most other social sciences were almost non-existent. Cross-cultural researchers from Western countries with enormous funds provided by various foundations took advantage of this "poverty" of the social scientists in the developing world and utilized the knowledge of local scientists and their competence in collecting data in a foreign land with which the principal investigator was unfamiliar. These scholars in the host country were just used for implementing the programme of the research which had been chalked out independently of them. When some distinguished scholars resented the subordinate role, they were given high sounding designations but in fact remained at best glorified investigators or field supervisors. They had little say in locating or formulating the problem, developing the research design, interpreting the results or writing the final report. To mention only one example, in the Harvard project on modernization, none of the local collaborators have featured as authors in the publication, Becoming Modern (Inkeles and Smith, 1974), which incorporates the results of investigations in six developing countries. Some of them were scholars of high academic competence and probably in no way inferior to their Western "collaborators". They have been content to accept the subordinate status readily because of the prospect of foreign travel and the prestige attached as a collaborator in a foreign research project. Even senior scholars of repute have found it difficult to resist the lure of the "fringe benefits" of foreign collaboration. This kind of relationship, exploitive or subordinate, hardly enhanced the status or position of the collaborator. What is more serious is that the advantages of having a scholar from the host country associated with research is lost. The value of his knowledge as an "insider" in his own culture in formulating the research problem and generating specific questions in the context of the social system of that culture, and selection and development of culturally appropriate tools for data collection are not fully utilized.

9

Both these kinds of relationships are at base
exploitive, and should be avoided. It is not possible to
have genuine collaborative research and a mature academic
relationship if the relationship between psychologists from
the developed and developing countries is one-sided. To
quote Tapp et al. (1974), "there should be a significant
involvement of colleagues from the cultures studied during
all project phases, particularly during formulation of the
problem and interpretation of the results." This is
possible only when there is convergence of interest between
scientists from the developed and developing countries. The
ideal relationship is one of collaborators in a common
endeavour, i.e., a relationship in which the two would
interact with one another at all stages of the research
process rather than simply helping in data collection.
Warwick (1980) asserts that cross-cultural research
projects should involve equal-status collaboration right
from the planning stage to its execution and eventual
publication. It is only when a relationship of equal
partnership is developed and there is participation in the
entire research process that this neo-colonialism in the
intellectual sphere can be avoided.

An excellent example of such international
collaboration and team work is provided by "International
Studies of Value in Politics" sponsored by the
International Social Science Council in which eight
institutions from India, Poland, U.S.A. and Yugoslavia
participated. By using the method of controlled comparison
and applying identical methodology, scholars with
specialised knowledge of particular countries were able to
combine the results of parallel studies to account for
differences and similarities that appear among nations. On
the organizational side, it piloted a pattern of
international collaboration in which research design,
execution and analysis were jointly determined by teams
from four countries. Each national team was mainly
responsible for carrying out its own fieldwork, analysis of
pooled data was assigned to cross-national groups working
face-to-face on specific phases of the programme, and
conclusions were submitted to successive international
roundtables, where progress was checked and further
guidelines agreed upon. On the financial side also, it was
a "cost-shared programme" from its inception. The
publication that emerged, Values and the Active Community
(1971), was not under the authorship of one or two project
directors but had the names of all the collaborators who
were mainly responsible for different sections and
chapters. It even included quite prominently the list of
all the principal participants. The project was truly an
"international joint enterprise based on equality of
participation by the respective institutions in each
country" (International Studies of Values in Politics,
1971, p. xxii).

Tapp et al. (1974, p. 246) have spelt out three
guidelines for the purpose which are laudable and deserve
to be carefully kept in mind while developing programmes of
cross-cultural research. They are: (a) collaborating as
full partners in the entire research enterprise, from
defining the problems to publishing reports; (b) sharing
with local colleagues the purposes of the research as well
as its sponsorship and sources of funds; and (c) selecting
local collaborators for complementing scientific skills and
knowledge, and also to balance cultural, historical and
socio-political perspectives. As Tapp et al. (1974) put it,
" a major function of local participants is to question
basic assumptions, correct for cultural biases, and bring
another cultural perspective and conceptual orientation to
the research ". (Italics are author's).

It is to be noted that the kind of collaboration that
has so far been visualised is likely to be a limited one.
The possibility of truly collaborative relationships at the
present juncture has been seriously doubted (Sinha, 1982)
because psychologists in the Third World countries have yet
to evolve indigenous conceptual models and theories
appropriate to their own socio-cultural setting. As a
result, they have been formulating their research problems
within the general framework of psychological theories
developed in and borrowed from the West. As such, they
still largely depend on their foreign counterparts. While
the local scholars have to be fully aware of the models and
theories prevalent in the West, it is essential that they
develop an indigenous social science in the Third World
having deep roots in the historical and social traditions
and in tune with the beliefs, values and social systems
that are characteristic of the people of these countries. I
would like to visualise a situation in which the initiative
for cross-cultural research comes not only from Western
scholars but also from those from the Third World countries
and on topics which the latter regard as important and feel
the necessity of a comparative study to find out
similarities and differences with patterns of behaviour
that prevail in Western societies. Till that happens, the
kind of collaboration that is likely to develop between
societies from the First and Third World countries is going
to remain a "partnership among unequals" (Sinha, 1982).

Impact of Cross-Cultural Research on Host Countries

The impact of the findings of cross-cultural studies
on the host country is another important point worth
considering. If continued collaboration of the developed
and the developing countries in joint research activities
is to be desired such an activity should maximise social as
well as scientific benefits to both sides. Theoretical
needs of the Western scientists as well as practical
relevance of such research to the host country of the Third

World are equally vital. This is an important question to be borne in mind while formulating research questions and in the execution of the project. The very process of cross-cultural research so far has been that the initiative for the study has come from scholars from the West who have their own interest in making comparative analysis of behaviour across countries with different cultural backgrounds. Warwick (1980) is right when he asserts that seeking help of local collaborators into research projects formulated outside the country might distort local research priorities. This frequently leads to a shift in the local scholar's focus of attention away from the country and its problem. As such, many of the studies are found to be remote and of little relevance to the problems of the countries where data have been gathered.

Through cross-cultural research, such knowledge should be generated which is likely to enhance the welfare of the community. Jahoda (1975) is justified when he asserts that there are strong indications that Third World countries will not indefinitely welcome or even tolerate the activities of psychological researchers without at least some prospects of tangible returns.

Problem-orientated approach, interdisciplinary perspective and a more macrocosmic orientation are essential prerequisites for psychological studies that are likely to have relevance to problems of developing countries (Sinha, 1977). Cross-cultural psychology is inherently suited for this task. Multi-disciplinary perspective and taking cognizance of structural variables are not at all alien to it because of its historical origin and the forces that have operated in its development. It is a branch of psychology which has been very strongly influenced not only by different areas of the subject itself, like experimental, social, clinical, and personality psychology, but has additionally been moulded by strong influences coming from anthropology and sociology. Therefore, it is multi-disciplinary from its very inception, not constrained by a single disciplinary stance, individualistic or systemic, or by methodological strategies which have been largely modelled after physics and the natural sciences. A cross-cultural psychologist is not afraid of investigating larger and complex social processes which others tend to avoid because the phenomena do not readily fit into their pet methodological framework and are alien to their individualistic orientations. With such a perspective, the subject is well suited to investigate topics that are socially relevant. What is required is that the selection of topics for investigation has to be made taking into account not only the interest of the scholar but also the needs of the country where the project is proposed to be carried out. Only through a blend of the two will cross-cultural studies be able to serve the

12

demands of theory and praxis and enhance the welfare of the community.

Appropriate Orientation for Cross-Cultural Research

The question of orientation and attitude of scientists who are suited for cross-cultural research is often raised. Heron (1975) has stressed the need for certain "attitudes" on the part of the psychologist if he is to be useful in his role in a developing country. Zaidi (1979) decries strongly the patronizing attitude of Western psychologists engaged in cross-cultural research and the misplaced sympathy at times shown by them for the lot of psychologists in developing countries who are overburdened with teaching loads, with inadequate laboratory and computer facilities and meagre research funds. Such a partonizing attitude will not at all be helpful in developing healthy collaborative relationships with scientists from the Third World. The latter do not lack in scientific competence. Despite the limitations of excessive work-loads and the necessity of operating not on too narrow and specialized areas but on a much wider field, many have produced excellent research work. Instead of an attitude of sympathy for their hard lot, a feeling of partnership in a common endeavour is required to generate cross-cultural collaboration.

On the part of the psychologist from the host country itself, there is also need for certain attitudes and sensitivity, if he is to be engaged in cross-cultural research. Apart from his general competence in the subject, he has to be highly sensitive to his country's problems so that his research effort has some relevance to the national needs. Das (1975) is very much to the point when he observes that "if you wish to do psychology in a developing country, you should not only be a competent psychologist, but a person who is sensitive to the needs and demands of the community in which your study is going to be based. Further, if you are a foreigner to that area of the country, you should be reasonably well versed in the socio-cultural history of the people. A mere knowledge of the socio-cultural history, however, would not suffice; you need to experience the culture of the society."

Benefits from Cross-Cultural Research

In his very thought provoking paper "Psychology and the Developing Countries", Jahoda (1973) has pointedly posed the question whether psychologists from the developed and developing countries needed each other. I would not go into all the facets of the problem that he has raised. But as a scientist from the Third World, I feel that he has perhaps unintentionally given the impression of a sharp dichotomy between the two. Cross-cultural collaboration

13

even to the extent that has occurred, despite distinct sets
of problems and orientations towards the subject and the
strategies for which they call, has demonstrated that there
is a lot of common ground among psychologists and there are
benefits to be derived from mutual exchanges. The developed
countries have served as a "crucible in which to put to
more rigorous test psychologist's tentative theories"
(Campbell and Naroll, 1972) which has helped to expand
psychology to panhuman proportions, so that, as Jahoda puts
it, psychologists from the developing countries "badly need
the developing countries".

But this is not all. There is another benefit to be
derived from mutual collaboration. Psychologists from
countries with different socio-cultural systems are likely
to bring in fresh perspectives and novel conceptual
frameworks for understanding psychological phenomena. These
new conceptual schemes and alternative approaches can be
utilised in gathering data and can expand our understanding
of various psychological processes. Many Western
psychologists have been conscious of the inadequacies of
their theories and methodology in studying personality
integration, mental health, emotion and other processes. As
such, a plea has been made for taking alternative models
and concepts from traditional Indian and non-Western
sources and for examinining them scientifically so that
some of the gaps in our psychological knowledge may be
filled (Sinha, 1969). Cross-cultural experience can be of
great use in this respect for enriching our psychological
knowledge and providing new directions to the subject. To
one of my colleagues I posed the problem of "the impact of
psychology on the Third World". Well, it has made an
impact. But what my friend said further is more important.
"We look forward to the impact of the Third World on the
development of psychology."

REFERENCES

Bartlett, F. C. Remembering. Cambridge: Cambridge Unversity
Press, 1932.

Berry, J. Social psychology: comparative, societal and
universal. Canadian Psychological Review, 1978, 19(2),
93-104.

Bose, S. A socio-psychological study of tribal adolescents
of Darjeeling hills. Journal of Psychological Researches,
1971, 15(2), 73-79.

Campbell, D. T. A cooperative multinational opinion sample exchange. Journal of Social Issues, 1968, 24(2) 245-256.

Campbell, D.T. & Naroll, R. The mutual methodological relevance of anthropology and psychology. In Hsu, F.L.K. (ed.) Psychological Anthropology, Cambridge, Mass: Scherkman, 1972.

Chattopadhyay, N. Psychological study of intelligence of tribal and non-tribal children of Tripura. Doctoral Dissertation in Psychology. Calcutta University, 1961.

Das, J.P. Psychology and the developing countries: the effect of malnutrition on cognitive ability. In J.W. Berry and W.J. Lonner (eds.) Applied Cross-Cultural Psychology. Amsterdam: Swets and Zeitlinger, 1975, 32-38.

Diaz-Guerrero, R. Editorial response. IACCP Cross-Cultural Psychology Newsletter, 1977, 11(3), 4-6.

Doktar, R., & Bass, B. Traditional values and career advancement in modern organizations in India, Columbia and Venezuela. Paper presented at the symposium on "Traditional Values and Modern Organizations" at the 18th Interational Congress of Applied Psychology, Montreal, 1974.

Faucheux, C. Cross-cultural research in social psychology. European Journal of Social Psychology, 1976, 6, 269-322.

Frederiksen, N. How to tell if a test measures the same thing in different cultures. In Y.H. Poortinga (ed) Basic Problems in Cross-Cultural Psychology, Amsterdam and Lisse: Swets and Zeitlinger, 1977, 14-18.

Frijda, N., & Jahoda, G. On the scope and methods of cross-cultural research. International Journal of Psychology, 1966, 1, 110-127.

Gokulnathan, P.P. & Mehta, P. Achievement motive in tribal and non-tribal Assamese secondary school adolescents. Indian Educational Review, 1972, 7 (1), 67-90.

Heron, A. Psychology and national development. The Zambian experience. In J.W. Berry and W.J. Lonner (eds.) Applied Cross-Cultural Psychology. Amsterdam: Swets and Zeitlinger, 1975, 13-17.

Inkeles, A., & Smith, D.H. Becoming Modern. Cambridge, Mass.: Harvard Univerisity Press, 1974.

International Studies of Values in Politics. Values and Active Community: A Cross-National Study of Influence of Local Leadership. New York: Free Press, 1971.

Jahoda, G. Psychology and the developing countries: do they need each other. International Social Science Journal, 1973, 25(i), 461-475.

Jahoda, G. Applying cross-cultural psychology to the Third World. In J.W. Berry & W.J. Lonner (eds.) Applied Cross-Cultural Psychology, Amsterdam: Swets and Zeitlinger, 1975, 3-7.

Jahoda, G. Has social psychology a distinct contribution to make? Paper presented at the Conference on "Social Psychology and the Developing Country", University of Lancaster, U.K., September 26-29, 1980.

Kakar, S. Personal communication, 1982.

Malpass, H.S. Theory and method in cross-cultural psychology, American Psychologist, 1977, 32, 1069-1079.

Rivers, W.H.R. Primitive colour vision, Popular Science Monthly, 1901, 59, 44-58.

Roland, A. The self in India and America: towards a psycho-analysis of sociocultural contexts. Unpublished paper, Centre for the Study of Developing Society, Delhi, 1981.

Sinha, D. Integration of modern psychology with Indian thought. In A.J. Sutich and M.A. Vich (eds.) Readings in Humanistic Psychology, New York : Free Press, 1969, 265-279.

Sinha, D. Industrial psychology. In a Survey of Research in Psychology. Chapter 5, ICSSR, New Delhi; Bombay: Popular Prakashan, 1972, 175-257.

Sinha, D. Orientation and attitude of the social psychologist in a developing country; the Indian case. International Review of Applied Psychology, 1977, 26, 1-10.

Sinha, D. Social psychology in India: a historical perspective. Psychological Studies, 1980, 25(2), 157-163.

Sinha, J.B.P. Personal communication, 1982.

Srivastava, R.K., Saxena, V. & Saksena, N.K. A study of authoriatarianism as a function of cultural practices. Indian Journal of Behaviour, 1979 (in press).

Srivastava, R.K., Saksena, N.K. & Kapoor, K.D. Differences in self-disclosure among tribals and non-tribal boys in India, Journal of Social Psychology, 1979, 109, 139-140.

Tapp. J.L., Kelman, H.C., Triandis, H.C., Wrightsman, L.S. & Coelho, G.V. Continuing concerns in cross-cultural ethics: a report. International Journal of Psychology, 1974, (3), 231-249.

Warwick, D.P. The politics and ethics of cross-cultural research. In H.C. Triandis (ed.) Handbook of Cross-Cultural Psychology, Vol. 1 to V1, New York: Allyn and Bacon, 1980.

Zaidi, S.M.H. Applied cross-cultural psychology: submission of a cross-cultural psychologist from the Third World. In L. Eckensberger, W.J. Lonner & Y.H. Poortinga (eds.) Cross-Cultural Contributions to Psychology, Amsterdam : Swets and Zeitlinger, 1979, 236-243.

"Still, it would be a dull world if we were all the same."

THE CROSS-CULTURAL EMPEROR'S CONCEPTUAL CLOTHES: THE EMIC-ETIC ISSUE REVISITED

G. Jahoda

University of Strathclyde, Glasgow

Since the early 1970s it has become fashionable in cross-cultural psychology to make use of the terms "emic" and "etic". In my view these terms were more often misapplied than employed correctly, and at our Tilburg meeting in 1976 I ventured to point this out. The response to my critique has been a deafening silence. When the paper was published (Jahoda 1977) I received a generous number of reprints which continue to fill my drawer, since the number of requests for copies can be counted on the fingers of one hand. Since then resort to the "emic-etic" terminology has become ever more popular, but the critique has been studiously ignored; the only exception of which I am aware is John Berry, who made at least passing reference to it. At any rate, when asked to give a talk here at Aberdeen I decided to get my own back by inflicting upon the assembled elite of cross-cultural psychologists yet another tirade on the same theme.

Just in case there may be people who take me to be entirely serious, I should add that there are other justifications for returning to the topic. It seems to me that the emic-etic issue is closely connected with some crucial theoretical, and perhaps epistemological, problems of the social sciences. Within psychology, the use of the terms has certainly spread beyond the cross-cultural field. I shall illustrate this by citing, without comment, from a recent book on social psychology:
"... the analysis of action in time must ... start from structuring the behaviour stream in a certain way. Such structuring may be "etic", involving only the investigator's point of view, or it may be "emic", relying on the ways in which people subjectively structure the behaviour of others." (Brenner 1980, p.22).

19

Although not confined to cross-cultural psychology, there is broad consensus that it is supposed to be of outstanding importance within that area. Thus Richard Brislin, who will figure prominently in my later discussion, wrote as follows:

"... the emic-etic distinction is one of the central concepts in current thinking about cross-cultural research" (1980 : 390).

Where we differ is in our evaluation of current thinking. Brislin is clearly very happy about it, while I regard it as at best somewhat misguided and at worst woolly and confused. Let me hasten to admit, lest I be regarded as even more arrogant than I really am, that the area is a difficult and complex one; many people, especially among anthroplogists, have wrestled with the problems and arrived at widely varying conclusions. My own views have undergone some modifications since I last wrote, though my fundamental stance remains unchanged. The object of my paper is not to come up with the right answer, and I suspect that in this sphere such an aim would be unattainable. My purpose is that of challenging the complacent belief shared by many cross-cultural emperors that they are wearing solidly made conceptual emic-etic clothes. I would maintain that, if not entirely naked, they are at most dressed in ill-fitting rags.

In order to be able to develop my argument it will be necessary to say something about the background of the emic-etic issue. For the reasons mentioned at the outset it would be rash for me to assume that everyone in the audience is familiar with what I have said before; hence it will mean going over some ground covered earlier, and I therefore crave the indulgence of those who might have heard or read me on the topic. In any case the approach will be somewhat different and treat the subject in rather more depth.

Thereafter the main part of the paper will break relatively fresh ground, by analyzing the use made of the emic-etic dichotomy within the six volumes of our authoritative Handbook.

In order to understand the origins of the notions of emic and etic, we must look to anthropology. From its inception in the 19th century it had a dual orientation which generated conflict. On the one hand the aim was that of discovering something about human nature in general as manifest in the numerous cultures around the globe, on the other that of understanding particular cultures with little or no concern for generalizations beyond their boundary. The latter approach gave rise to a debate as to how far it was possible to get, as it were, "inside the skin" of the

people one was studying. This issue became more prominent
with the advent of modern field methods in the 20th
century. Thereafter the emphasis shifted increasingly
towards comparisons between cultures, and then the problem
of how to deal with all manner of variations obtruded
itself. Ideally what was needed was a general theory of
behaviour transcending as well as accounting for cultural
variations. Almost a generation ago an anthroplogical
linguist, Kenneth Pike (1954, 1967), made an ambitious
attempt to meet such a need. The purpose of his grand
design was summarized by Pike (1966 : 54):

"The thesis which for the past seven years I have been
exploring is the following: that every purposeful activity
of man is structured, and that certain basic charateristics
are common to every such activity, so that it should be
possible to develop a theory and a technique which would
pass without jar from the study of the structure of one
kind of activity of man to that of any other kind. Ideally,
this would result in one basic theory of structure, one
basic set of terms, and one basic methodology which could
be applied to the analysis of ritual behaviour, and
analysis of sports, the analysis of occupational activity,
or even to the processing of thought itself."

The grand design itself has, for various reasons, not
met with any success. However, Pike has bequeathed to
social science a pair of terms that has gained wide
currency, namely emic and etic.

As is well known, the terms were coined by Pike from
the suffixes of the words phon<u>etic</u> and phon<u>emic</u>. Phonetic
studies of language concentrate on the physical aspects of
the production of utterances, relating the activities of
various body parts such as the vocal chords, tongue and
teeth to the resulting acoustic waves. The phonemic
approach to the sounds of a language, on the other hand, is
concerned with the smallest units of speech that enable a
native speaker to distinguish one word from another; this
depends on an implicit system of sound contrasts which such
speakers carry in their heads. This means that while in
phonetics physical measurements are appropriate, in
phonemics the critical test depends upon the response of
the speaker indicating that two phonemes are perceived as
being contrasting, in as much as they alter the meaning of
an utterance.

Pike took the audacious step of extending the
linguistic analysis, by analogy to the manner in which
phonemes, morphemes and other emic language units are
identified, to behaviour within particular cultures. Such
"behavioremes", as he called them, can be discovered within
the behaviour stream; for like language, behaviour consists
of orderly structures. Suggested parallels were offered in
some detail, as when Pike compared kinship groups with

21

phonemes and voluntary associations with morphemes. When approaching a new and unknown culture, an etic strategy is unavoidable, but the purpose is that of progressively advancing towards a purely emic account:
"etic data provide access into the system - the starting point of the analysis"...... "the initial etic description is gradually refined, and is ultimately - in principle, but probably never in practice - replaced by one which is totally emic." (Pike 1967 : 38 and 39).

A useful summary of the global distinctions between the etic and emic approaches has been provided by Berry (1969) and is shown below:

Emic approach	Etic approach
studies behaviour from within the system	studies behaviour from outside the system
examines only one culture	examines many cultures comparing them
structure discovered by the analyst	structure created by the analyst
criteria are relative to internal characteristics	criteria are considered absolute or universal

While these are all relevant criteria, Pike himself offered a concise formal definition: "Two units are different etically when instrumental measurements can show them to be so. Units are different emically only when they elicit different responses from people acting within the system." (Pike 1967 : 38).

It has been necessary to set out Pike's position in more than usual detail, so that subsequent developments can be understood against the background of the original version. The major focus of the debate among those anthropologists who attach importance to comparisons (and not all of them do) has been the relationship between emics and etics. There is a long tradition in anthropology which corresponds to Pike's conception that the aim of the study of culture should be emic description. This was implicit in Malinowski's famous phrase that the final goal is to "grasp the native's point of view." Similarly Boas (1943 : 314) stated: "If it is our serious purpose to understand the thoughts of a people the whole analysis of experience must be based on their concepts, not ours." One of the prominent contemporary exponents of this tradition is Clifford Geertz (1973) who borrowed the phrase "thick description" from Gilbert Ryle in order to characterize the anthropological endeavour as he saw it; moreover, according to Geertz, such description must be actor-oriented. Nonetheless, he insists upon the fact that such description involves interpretation and construction and therefore cannot be identical with the way people themselves experience their lives. Thus to the extent that anthropology entails scientific analysis, an inescapable etic appears to be tacitly conceded (though Geertz himself is reluctant to use this terminology).

Other anthropologists have addressed themselves directly to the emic-etic issue and I shall single out for discussion two notable ones, Ward Goodenough and Marvin Harris. Both are concerned with the interplay between emics and etics, and agree (contrary to Pike) that the final objective of anthropological study must be an etic formulation; in other respects they remain far apart. Harris (1979) takes pride in calling himself a "cultural materialist" and, unlike Goodenough (1970), wishes to establish the causes of cultural phenomena; his daring and fascinating efforts in this direction are most readily accessible in a semi-popular book characteristically entitled "Cows, Pigs, Wars and Witches" (Harris 1975). An example based on a monograph by Rappaport, one of his students, will illustrate the approach.

The study deals with a remote New Guinean tribe, the Maring, and it focuses on the relationship between these pig-loving people and their pigs. Note that "pig-love" is not treated as a peculiar psychological trait of the Maring, but as a problem-solving device for their society. Each clan holds a pig-festival about every twelve years involving many component rituals over a period of a year ending in a massive slaughter. In the following months warfare betwen clans ensues, during which there is more slaughter not merely of pigs, but also of men, resulting in gain and loss of territory. At the end of all this no adult pigs are left, fighting ceases and in a ritual addressed to the ancestors the Maring vow to devote all their energies henceforth to the raising of pigs, until the next cycle comes around.

Such a crude summary of course leaves out many important elements but after reading the full account one is still left with the impression that this is very odd behaviour. Not at all, protests Harris, and I quote:
"(it) is no mere psychodrama of pig farmers gone berserk. Every part of the cycle is integrated within a complex, self-regulating ecosystem, that effectively adjusts the size of the ... human and animal population to conform to available resources and production opportunities" (1975 : 41).

Thus the psychological features of Maring behaviour are regarded as mere epiphenomena, while the locus of causation is in the adaptive character of the social

23

system. While many anthropologists would not agree with aspects of Harris's theoretical approach, the emphasis on explanations in terms of social or ideological systems is almost universally shared by them. Let me now turn to Harris's position with regard to the issue of present concern, which is of course related to his "materialist" theoretical stance. For him the distinction between emic and etic depends upon whether the locus of an event, entity or relationship is inside or outside some actor's head (Harris 1976). This definition has important implications. First, Harris dissents from those who would locate the key distinctions between emic and etic in the fact that the former refers to particular cultures, and the latter is pancultural; such a view is taken by cross-cultural psychlogists and anthropologists like Naroll (1973). Secondly. it does not make sense, according to Harris, to talk about transformation from emic to etic constructs: "Once an eme, always an eme" (Harris 1976 : 343).

This usage of the terms contrasts with that of Goodenough (1970), in whose view one can and must develop etic concepts capable of describing the set of emic distinctions people make in cultures all over the world. He cites as an example his own ethnographic work on Truk, a Pacific island. In order to be able to describe the kinship terminology it was necessary to understand kinship organization; this in turn required the grasp of notions of property, since ownership of property was one of the salient attributes of the most important kind of kin group. Now the bundles of rights and obligations associated with property are very different from Euramerican ones. Hence Goodenough had to pinpoint distinctions quite unfamiliar to him in a manner corresponding to those made by the Trukese themselves. Goodenough called this a "kit of etic tools", which then became available to other anthropologists for analyzing other cultures, and was in fact so used.

It will be clear even from this sketchy account, glossing over many subtleties, that there are quite disparate interpretations of the emic-etic issue in anthropology. It is a highly contentious matter, hotly debated, so much so that one philosophical anthropologist was moved to write: "I am not at all sure that I understand what the emic-etic controversy is all about ....." (Vermeersch 1977 : 58). Needless to say, he went on immediately to give his version of what the issue really was. In spite of such differences anthropologists, including Harris and Goodenough, agree with Pike on one fundamental principle without which Pike's analogy between language and behaviour would become entirely pointless: namely that the object of study, be it emic or etic, is not concerned with isolated cultural elements but rather with structured systems.

Here, as I have argued previously (Jahoda 1977), lies the great divide between the anthropological approach to the emic-etic issue and that of cross-cultural psychologists. Let me therefore turn to the latter, noting that the kind of debate on the issue prevalent among anthropologists is conspicuously absent.

It will be best to begin with what is the most commonly cited exposition, that of John Berry (1969, 1980). After describing the emic approach as "internal" descriptions of behaviour, he singles out what he calls "the presence of universals in the system" (1980 : 12) as the defining feature of the etic approach. If such universals are simply taken for granted by the outside investigator they constitute an "imposed" or "pseudo" etic, being merely the ethnocentric attribution of Euramerican etics. On the other hand a "true" etic is one constructed empirically from initial emic anlysis, and Berry names this a "derived etic". The critical question is of course how such a derivation may be achieved in cross-cultural psychology. The suggested procedure, in Berry's own words, is as follows:

"... an emic description can be made by progressively altering the imposed etic until it matches a purely emic point of view; if this can be done without destroying the etic character of the entry categories, then the next step can be taken. If some of the etic is left, it is possible to note the categories or concepts that are shared by the behaviour system previously known and the one just understood emically. Now a derived etic that is valid for making comparisons between the two behaviour settings can be set up; thus the problem of obtaining a descriptive framework which is valid for comparing behaviour across behaviour settings has been resolved." (1980 : 12/13).

The passage goes on to say that the procedure can be iterated until one arrives at a universal for a particular behaviour.

Now at first glance this prescription might appear rather similar to the procedure employed by Goodenough in relation to kinship, but in fact it is quite different in two respects. One is that Goodenough has a clear and rather simple notion of the relationship between emic and etic. It is neatly summarized by Naroll et al. (1980, p.501) when they say that "Etic concepts are abstractions generated by social scientists from the analysis of emic definitions." Secondly, Goodenough illustrated his approach by a full description of the way in which his material from Truk was analyzed.

Berry obviously has a rather different view of the relationship between emics and etics, but what precisely is it? In my previous critique I merely registered a complaint about his remaining at a high level of abstraction; now I must go further and confess that I simply fail to understand it, even after having read through it many times and pondered over it. There is no time to go through the argument with a toothcomb, so I shall just pose a few questions to indicate the reasons for my perplexity. The starting point, we are told, are existing hypotheses; yet thereafter there is no further mention of them: where have they disappeared to? Have they been transmuted into etics? How can hypotheses lead to a "truly emic description"? What is the meaning of the phrase "if some of the etic is left"? Does this mean "if anything remains of the hypotheses?" or, if not, what else? What is the nature of the final goal described as a "universal for that particular behaviour"? A universal what?

Perhaps there are adequate answers to these and other questions one might pose, but I cannot see them. Thus it is a typical case of my not being able to see what many others apparently can see quite well: for surely they would not cite an article as an authoritative source unless they understood what it contained!

One of the distinguished cross-cultural psychologists who not merely subscribes to Berry's formulation but also made his own contribution is Harry Triandis (1980, p.7). Part of his general introduction to the Handbook is devoted to the emic-etic issue, and it does provide a specific example to consider. Here is what it says:
"It is appropriate to distinguish emic and etic constructs, as well as emic and etic measurements. Social distance is an etic construct that can be measured emically as well etically. On the other hand philotimo is an emic construct applicable only to Greece. It refers to the extent to which the individual conforms to the expectations of his ingroup. It is a dimension that is most salient among Greeks, and is defined in that culture. It can be used, then, only to understand Greek behaviour patterns, and is not useful for comparisons. Measuring social distance after careful definition of the meaning of the continuum, with items appropriate for each culture, is etic. Measuring it in one culture only, as was done by Bogardus, is emic. All these measurements are appropriate. What is not appropriate is taking an emic scale and using it as if it were etic."

This passage has every appearance of being straightforward and lucid. However, I would suggest that every cross-cultural psychologist needs a warning bell that rings whenever the terms emic and etic turn up, alerting him or her to look for logical traps and pitfalls that lurk beneath the deceptive surface. Let us therefore scrutinize the passage with more care.

It is stated that social distance is an etic construct
that can be measured emically as well as etically. What is
the difference between the two types of measurement? It
would seem that "etically" refers to measurement in several
cultures, "emically" to a single one. When Bogardus first
measured social distance, it was an emic measurement
because it was done in one culture only.

What, then, are the grounds for asserting that social
distance is an etic construct? How did it come to change
its nature when Bogardus' original measure was extended to
other cultures?

The claim that the difference between the two kinds of
measurement is merely a function of the number of cultures
studied is really a rather odd one. Can a given measure,
say the Rorschach, change from emic to etic as one applies
it to one or several cultures? I have deliberately chosen
this example to illustrate the amazing elasticity of the
terminology. One writer has claimed that the Rorschach
furnishes stimuli from outside the culture and also elicits
the subjective reality of the informants; therefore it is
both emic and etic (Spindler 1975, p.144).

After this brief digression we must get back to
Triandis, who would probably complain that I have paid no
attention to the crucial sentence where he spells out what
etic measurement consists of; here it is again: "Measuring
social distance after careful definition of the meaning of
the continuum, with items appropriate for each culture, is
etic".

In reply I would ask how the meaning of the continuum
comes to be defined, and the answer will have to refer in
some way or another to people's social behaviour, or their
ideas about social behaviour. Now all such elements form
part of a structured system within each culture, and in the
original sense of Pike, and in that of most
anthropologists, are therefore emic. Two further questions
can then be asked: the first is, once again, where does the
etic actually come from? (I shall suggest my own answer to
this later on.) Secondly, assuming this has been
satisfactorily answered, how do we manage the etic essence
from these various emics? It is no good merely asserting
that it can be done, for it is the disinguishing feature of
emic elements of culture that they only make sense within a
particular set of social relations or a culture-specific
idea system. We have Triandis' own word for this, when he
was at pains to stress that philotimo is defined uniquely
within Greek culture and thus useless for comparisons.

It follows that the mere slotting of items regarded as
culturally appropriate into a scale does not in itself
resolve the emic-etic dilemma. In fact, there is a

27

considerable risk that the very mode of construction of such a scale may largely pre-determine the outcome.

What has been said by no means exhausts the issues that could be discussed; for instance there is the problem of the relationship between emic and etic constructs and measurements. However, I have probably said enough to show that Triandis' single paragraph contains a host of statements and concealed assumptions that are, at the very least, highly controversial.

Both Berry and Triandis deal with the emic-etic issue rather briefly - perhaps too briefly; and one might imagine that the flaws in their explications could at least in part be due to the need for excessive compression. There is one place in the Handbook where the emic-etic distinction is treated at greater length, and that is the chapter by Richard Brislin (1980). Let me add parenthetically that this amounts to no more than half a dozen pages in a Handbook totalling more than 2500; this hardly fits in with Brislin's previously quoted statement that "the emic-etic distinction is one of the central concepts in current cross-cultural thinking." At any rate, he is clearly regarded as the emic-etic guru, to whom other contributors tend to refer when they make mention of the topic.

Let us therefore scrutinize this piece de resistance to find out the extent to which it provides conceptual enlightenment and advice on methods for dealing with the emic-etic dilemma.

The beginning is inauspicious, referring mainly to other writers. Brislin's own formulation of the emic-etic distinction is as follows:
"... the distinction relates to two goals of cross-cultural research. The first goal is to document valid principles that describe behaviour in any one culture by using constructs that the people themselves conceive as meaningful and important; this is an emic analysis. The second goal of cross-cultural research is to make generalizations across cultures that take into account all human behaviour. The goal, then, is theory building; that would be an etic analyis. The distinction may become clear after a few examples from cross-cultural investigations are discussed." (p.391).

I recall that when first reading this passage I could not believe it, but on second and third reading it was still there. "The first goal is to document valid principles" - that strikes me as mere empty verbiage; and to describe behaviour in any one culture in terms of the people's own category system is certainly an emic analysis. However, it is the kind of task, or rather part of it, that some anthropologists set themselves; and it is difficult to see how it could be regarded as the goal of cross-cultural psychologists.

The second alleged goal is almost equally odd. Admittedly, there are a few bold spirits among cross-cultural psychologists who have been engaged in "theory-building"; names that spring to mind are Berry, Dawson, Osgood and Triandis. Yet it certainly cannot be said to be the goal of the vast majority of cross-cultural psychologists.

Altogether, this is a distinctly discouraging beginning. Still, there is the promise that everything will be illuminated by some actual research examples.

Alas, this promise is not fulfilled, or at least not in the way intended. The first thing to note is the remarkable fact that not a single one of the studies cited by Brislin for the purpose of illustrating the emic-etic dichotomy was conceived in terms of that dichotomy; hardly any even mention it. What he did was to impose his own interpretation by applying these labels.

I shall spare you an exegesis of all but one of the examples given by Brislin. The one which I propose to discuss in some detail has been chosen because it is particularly instructive. It constitutes the main item under the rather odd heading "Methods for the emic-etic distinction." The first sentence under this heading is this: "Research methods meant to yield both emic and etic findings will not be reviewed." The meaning of this remains rather obscure to me, but it seems to contradict most of what follows. Let us go on to the next sentence:
"One approach is that suggested by Przeworski and Teune (1966, 1970), who gave special attention to questionnaire research, which is an etic since people in all cultures are not equally familiar with questionnaires."

Now if my argument so far has been sufficiently well presented to be at least moderately clear, this sentence ought to leave you really puzzled. You will have gained the impression that cross-cultural psychologists tend to equate emic with intra-cultural or culture-specific, and etic with culture-general or universal. Such usage recurs in the Handbook, e.g. Lonner (1980, p.167) states it quite explicitly. Yet here is Brislin saying that questionnaire research is etic because it is not universal, when it ought to be emic for that very reason: what should one make of that?

One possibility is that it might be simply a printing error, but this is unlikely since the substitution of "emic" would not make any better sense within the general context of the discussion. Let us therefore assume that

Chapter 3

"etic" is what Brislin intended to say and try to throw
some light on this.

In order to understand what probably happened here, it
will be helpful to go back for a moment to what Triandis
wrote about the social distance scale. It is implicit from
what he said that the truly rather than pseudo-etic scale
must always be emic. Perhaps he would also agree that the
scale as such is bound to be etic. If so, we arrive at the
paradox that a social distance scale is both emic and etic.
How did we get into this tangle?

The paradox arises from the fact that there is an
important ambiguity in the term "etic": on the one hand it
is used to refer to types of behaviour or social
institutions present in all human cultures; on the other
hand it is also used to denote scientific tools, and
generalizations of supposed universal applicability. The
snag is of course that science does not by any means form
part of all or even most cultures; thus, as pointed out by
Price-Williams (1975), within a framework of the sociology
of knowledge all etic systems become emic.

Going back to Brislin's remarkable statement, I trust
we can now see what has happened: he managed within a
single sentence to burden the term etic with both meanings
simultaneously, leading to self-contradiction!

We have not yet finished with Brislin - this was only
the preliminary to the account of the method. I shall cite
only sufficient extracts from the key passages to convey
the gist of the suggested approach, and while I quote it
you should look at Figure 1.

"Przeworski and Teune suggest that a core of items be
written that are meaningful and hence answerable by members
of each culture under study.... These items would be
relevant to all cultures. In addition, culture-specific
items would be written that are expected to tap emic
aspects.... interpretable statistical interrelations ....
computed separately for individual responses in each
culture would be expected between culture-general and
culture-specific items. No relationships would be expected
between the emic items for the different cultures .... From
the results of this procedure the investigator can
formulate general theoretical statements (etics) that
summarize the data. These statements can then be refined by
the results of the culture-specific questions (emics)"
(1980, p.393).
When you read this casually, it seems to make sense;
but once you start thinking about it the sense begins to
melt away into absurdity. But I am jumping ahead, so let us
take it step by step.

30

Figure 1

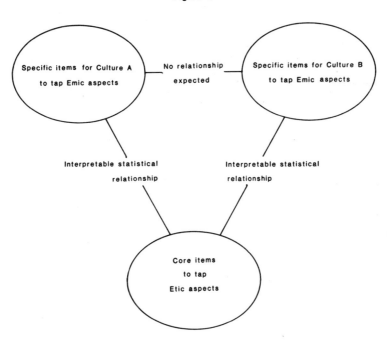

Etic core item

You start with etic core items meaningful everywhere, and add culture-specific emic items. You then go through a correlational procedure arriving at general theoretical statements that are etic; and then you refine these etics by taking the emics into account.

All kinds of questions obtrude themselves; what is the relationship between the initial etic items and the general theoretical etics one gets later? How can these theoretical etics be "refined" by means of emics? Remember also that one has to know in the first place what kinds of items are etics and what kind emic: so where does the theory come from and what does it consist of?

Perhaps you may regard my judgement as being too harsh, since it leaves out of account the neat diagram that you might find convincing. So I shall now take a closer look at the diagram. The first thing to note is that, like the description, it is entirely abstract. You may recall that I had occasion to complain about this in connection with Berry's exposition.

Now why did Brislin fail to provide any content, some concrete illustration? The reason, I submit, is because it would be extremely difficult to do so without exposing the threadbareness of the argument. It is possible to demonstrate this by taking material used by Brislin himself in an earlier work (Brislin et al. 1973) that deals with the same topic, drawn from the same source. There he presented some concrete examples, though the diagram is new. What I have done is to slightly condense the material, cast it into question form and enter it into the diagram. Please note that all the questions are addressed to a mother.

Looking first at the so-called "etic core item" at the bottom, one finds it to be utterly trivial; the two "emic" ones at the top are scarcely more exciting. It also becomes immediately evident that there is no reason why the correlations should turn out as predicted - in fact they could take any form whatsoever, depending upon content.

No doubt enough has been said to indicate that Brislin's expostion of the emic-etic issue, on which a number of Handbook contributors relied, falls somewhat short of the clarity and logic demanded by this exceedingly difficult problem.

Before moving on I wish to emphasize that this critique is in no way intended as a reflection on the work of Przeworski and Teune. They were writing about the methodology of cross-national survey studies, being totally unconcerned with the emic-etic problem as such; and these terms did not figure in their writings.

If one stands back to look at things from a broader perspective, it becomes apparent that many of the Handbook contributors were afflicted with a kind of collective illusion. They believed that they themselves and everybody else knew all there was to be known about the emic-etic dichotomy. If the reader was in any doubt, it was fully explained elsewhere. Let me just give you one instance: in a generally excellent chapter Altman and Chemers (1980, p.361) cited some anthropological evidence accompanied by the remark: "such cases must be considered in the light of the emic-etic issues discussed throughout this Handbook, especially in Brislin's chapter." Evidently they were totally unaware that the chapter in question, far from throwing any light on the matter, actually clouds and confuses it.

Figure 2

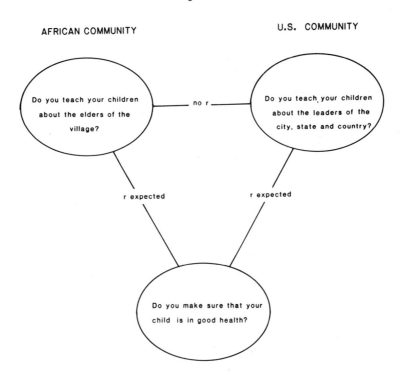

AFRICAN COMMUNITY

U.S. COMMUNITY

Do you teach your children about the elders of the village?

— no r —

Do you teach your children about the leaders of the city, state and country?

r expected

r expected

Do you make sure that your child is in good health?

If you are expecting at this stage a concise and authoritative statement as to what the emic-etic dichotomy is really about you are, as I warned at the beginning, in for a disappointment. All I can do is to suggest reasons why the emic-etic distinction is, in my view, a delusion and snare in cross-cultural psychology. One is that the distinction was originally designed for the analysis of systems and ceases to be meaningful when applied to variables. As you are no doubt well aware cross-cultural, like other kinds of psychology, is primarily concerned with the relationships among variables. The Handbook is replete with examples, and I shall merely cite one: Davidson and Thomson (1980, p.51) wrote about "an emic measure of an etic variable."

A second reason is that, as I have indicated repeatedly without actually spelling it out, psychological usage of the terms is mainly non-reflexive, so that when applied to the techniques of measuring as well as that which is being measured, contradictions result. This is because different levels of discourse are not kept separate, and one would need a meta-language to maintain the distinctions.

Lastly, the declared aim of cross-cultural psychology is to reach towards universals, and the language of etics is seductive for this purpose. Unfortunately, as I pointed out when discussing Berry's exposition, we are often far from clear what kinds of universals we are looking for in the emic-etic context. Lonner ended his chapter on this topic by asking the question whether the search for behavioural universals, other than blatantly obvious ones, is bound to fail. For reasons which there is no time to expound now, I would regard this view as somewhat too pessimistic. Nonetheless, I think that Lonner has asked a question which it would be unwise for us to ignore; and here again I believe that the recitation of the emic-etic formula has led to a great deal of obfuscation concerning our starting points and our goals.

Since this lies perhaps at the heart of the matter, I shall seek to clarify it in one particular context, namely that of social distance chosen by Triandis. The notion of social distance was in vogue among American sociologists during the early twenties. In an article published in 1924 and entitled "The concept of social distance", Park defined it as follows:
" ... an attempt to reduce to something like measureable terms the grades and degrees of understanding and intimacy which characterize personal and social relations generally."

Although Park was writing within an American cultural setting, and the concept was first operationalized in that setting, it is by no means confined to that; nor is this recognition any great discovery: the concept is based on ideas held about persons and societies not merely by social scientists, but by men and women in the street or indeed the bush path. Thus the universal, taken as axiomatic, is the starting rather than the end point in this case. From that it is only possible to move towards the particular, by dealing with types of relationships and their relative saliency in specific cultures, and the kinds of social personae with whom the relationship in envisaged. So you will see that, stripped of its emic-etic mystique, all this is perfectly straightforward.

My general message is thus much the same as before; but, alas, so is my position: I still remain the solitary little boy who shouts that the emperor's conceptual clothes are in tatters and that the nakedness shows through. I am not so naive as to imagine that my arguments will have the effect of eradicating what are by now well-established words from our vocabulary. They are perhaps quite useful in a vague kind of way, especially for corridor chats. However, my appeal is to steer clear of pontification about emics and etics.

Before finally concluding, I should like to add a brief kind of postscript. For quite some time now I have been wondering how it is that I am condemned to remain the lonely little boy, when everybody else either sees splendid and practical robes, or at least fails to voice his or her doubts. While preparing the talk I came across a report of the work of Dr. Armstrong at the University of Pennsylvania, which might throw some light on the reasons. He formulated and sucesfully tested the following hypothesis:
" ... work which is unintelligible will not necessarily be recognised as such by scholars, and ... in some cases the less intelligible a piece of prose the greater the respect it will earn from its readers or victims" (Leapman 1982, p.215).

By the same token, of course, this might apply to my presentation here; though I am consoled by the fact that if it was not intelligible, then you should be mightily impressed!

REFERENCES

(The abbreviation H.C.C.P. stands for Handbook of Cross-Cultural Psychology, General Editor H.C. Triandis, Boston: Allyn & Bacon)

ALTMAN, I. & CHEMERS, M.M. (1980). H.C.C.P., Vol. 5.

BERRY, J.W. (1969). On cross-cultural comparability. International Journal of Psychology, 4: 119-128.

BERRY, J.W. (1980). H.C.C.P., Vol. 2, Introduction.

BOAS, F. (1943). Recent anthropology. Science, 98: 311-314.

BRENNER, M. (Ed.) (1980) The Structure of Action. Oxford: Blackwell.

BRISLIN, R.W., LONNER, W.J. & THORNDIKE, R.M. (1973). Cross-Cultural Research Methods. New York: Wiley.

Chapter 3

BRISLIN, R.W. (1980). H.C.C.P., Vol. 1.

DAVIDSON, A.R. & THOMSON, E. (1980). H.C.C.P., Vol. 5.

GEERTZ, C. (1973). The Interpretation of Cultures. London: Hutchinson.

GOODENOUGH, W.H. (1970). Description and Comparison in Cultural Anthropology. Cambridge: Cambridge University Press.

HARRIS, M. (1975). Cows, Pigs, Wars and Witches. London: Hutchinson.

HARRIS, M. (1976). History and significance of the emic/etic distinction. Annual Review of Anthropology, 5: 329-350.

HARRIS M. (1979). Cultural Materialism. New York: Random House.

JAHODA, G. (1977). In pursuit of the emic-etic distinction: can we ever capture it? In Y.J. Poortinga (Ed.), Basic Problems in Cross-Cultural Psychology. Amsterdam: Swets & Zeitlinger.

LEAPMAN, M. (1982). Bulletin of the British Psychological Society, 35: 215-216. (A feature reprinted from the Times of 9 June 1980)

LONNER, W.J. (1980). H.C.C.P., Vol.1.

NAROLL, R. (1973). Introduction. In R. & F. Naroll (Eds.), Main Currents in Anthropolgy. New York: Appleton Century.

NAROLL, R., MICHIK, G.L. & NAROLL, F. (1980). H.C.C.P., Vol.2.

PARK, R.E. (1924). The concept of social distance. Journal of Applied Sociology, 8: 339-344.

PIKE, K. (1954; revised ed. 1967). Language in Relation to a Unified Theory of the Structures of Human Behaviour. The Hague; Mouton.

PIKE, K. (1966). Towards a theory of the structure of human behaviour. In D. Hymes (Ed.), Language in Culture and Society. New York: Harper & Row.

PRICE-WILLIAMS, D.R. (1975). Explorations in Cross-Cultural Psychology. San Francisco: Chandler & Sharp.

SPINDLER, L.S. (1975). Researching the Psychology of culture change. In T.R. Williams (Ed.): Psychological Anthropology. The Hague: Mouton.

TRIANDIS, H.C. (1980). H.C.C.P., Vol.1.

VERMEERSCH, E. (1977). An analysis of the concept of culture. In: B. Bernardi (Ed.), The Concept and Dynamics of Culture. The Hague: Mouton.

COMMENT

J. W. Berry

Queen's University, Kingston

My basic point in this discussion is that if we did not use the terms emic and etic, we in cross-cultural psychology would have to create two terms which reflect our dual interests: we cannot be "cultural" without being something like emic, and we cannot be "cross" without something like etic.

It seems to me that the intensive study of behaviour in one cultural setting is a well-established activity in psychology; in recent years we have become more and more aware of the sociocultural roots of such an enterprise, and in some cases, of the ethnocentrism of the discipline. Increasingly, the recognition of these cultural linkages has led us to work in other cultural settings: this activity in turn achieves both an increase in our awareness of other local psychological phenomena, and brings us to the act of comparison, with the resulting parade of group differences and similarities. Thus, in my view cross-cultural psychologists are already bound up in these joint activities, and we need some way, terminologically, to identify them.

It also seems to me that many of the problems raised by Jahoda in his two papers (Tilburg and Aberdeen) are due to the origin and development of the terms emic and etic in other disciplines. It may be that much of the conceptual baggage (such as the two issues of "systems" and "structure") may not be appropriate for psychology at the present time, and that without them, the importance of the fundamental distinction would become more clear to Jahoda. However, as cross-cultural psychology matures, I believe that even these two aspects will become relevant to our research activity.

There are two other points which need more attention. One is the relationship between the two concepts, and the other is their use at both the conceptual and empirical levels of our work. Jahoda indicates that he "fails to understand" (p.25) my 1969 discussion between emic and etic. The sequence is rather simple: one begins work in another culture armed with what one already knows, believes, etc.; this I have termed an imposed etic, a choice of words which indicates that it is an approach from

39

outside, which may or may not match the phenomena to be studied in the selected cultural group. If it corresponds at all with the local phenomenon (the emic), then some comparative analysis is possible; if not, then comparison is not possible. By a sequence of such entries and comparisons it may be that an etic phenomenon will emerge, corresponding to all the common emic phenomena; this I have termed a derived etic, indicating that it stems from a series of legitimate comparisons of common, local phenomena, and has an existence outside, beyond, any single culture.

Conceptual and empirical use of the terms also needs to be distinguished. At the conceptual level, cross-cultural psychologists should be concerned with the similarities and differences in how human behaviour is understood in the various cultural groups included in a study. To me it is obvious that if in one culture we have a notion of general ability that incorporates speed and precision, while in another culture the generally able person is one who is considered to be thoughtful and empathic, then despite the apparent etic notion of general ability, we have two very different emic conceptualizations of it. Similarly at the empirical level, that of observation and measurement, we should be concerned that our metric indicators (item analysis, factor structure, etc.) exhibit similarities which confirm that our data from the two cultural groups correspond to each other; if not then we have two different emic measurements.

To conclude, while I applaud Jahoda's attention to these key concepts in cross-cultural psychology, I must admit to a belief that his analysis reveals an idiosyncratic problem rather than a general one among cross-cultural psychologists. I think I also detect a slight twinkle in the eye, and a marginal tongue in cheek in his presentation, an approach more reminiscent of a Jester in the Court than of the solitary little boy in the crowd!

COMMENT

R. Brislin

East-West Center, Honolulu

If the exchanges concerning the emic-etic issue
encourage readers to study the original journal articles
and chapters cited therein, then the effort will be
worthwhile. If not, it will be an exercise "full of sound
and fury, signifying nothing."

One issue Jahoda raises can be dealt with immediately.
In quoting from my chapter in the Handbook of
Cross-Cultural Psychology (Brislin, 1980), Jahoda correctly
reproduced the printed word as "Research methods meant to
yield both emic and etic findings will not be reviewed." He
was then quite reasonably surprised when approaches were
immediately discussed. The problem stems from one letter:
the original "now" was typeset as "not" and this mistake
was missed in the proofreading (which was done by the
publishers and not the authors). This mistake is easy to
miss in proofreading, of course, since both sentences are
grammatically correct. I am happy to have this opportunity
to set the matter straight.

Much of the debate centers on opinions about the
usefulness of the emic-etic construct. What Jahoda calls
cloudy and confusing is to me a useful metaphor. Jahoda is
correct in stating that there is not total agreement among
anthropologists and psychologists regarding the meaning of
the construct, and to these I would add that there is not
total agreement among political scientists and linguists
who use the terms "emic" and "etic." Yet it is one of the
few constructs which allows people to sit down and discuss
cross-cultural methodological issues with each other across
disciplines. I have worked at the East-West Center for 10
years and interact on a day-to-day basis with more
linguists and anthropologists than psychologists. In my
experience, cross-disciplinary interaction is more
difficult and problem-prone than cross-cultural
interaction. I have observed that discussions of emics and
etics, as applied to a person's specific research
interests, often provide points of contact where
cross-disciplinary fertilization is possible. My judgment
is that the emic-etic distinction is a useful metaphor;
Jahoda's judgment is quite different. Again, readers can
study the references and draw their own conclusions.

Jahoda brings up the issue of specific examples. In my previous writings, I tried to point out the usefulness of the emic-etic construct by bringing in examples which were not formulated with the construct in mind but which are better explained by using it. These examples have included cross-cultural work on the need for achievement and technological change in the development of rangelands in East Africa. I thought that by showing how the approach could organize previous research data in a manner better than that of the original studies, this would show an additional strength of the construct. Research findings are often neglected because there are not good frameworks which incorporate them. This is still my opinion, but perhaps it is not as useful as a straightforward example in which the emic-etic approach was explicitly used.

Joanne Miller (a sociologist) and her colleagues employed the approach in a study of authoritarian -conservatism in the United States and Poland (Miller, Slomczynski and Schoenberg, 1981). She drew from the writings of the same people Jahoda cites as concerned with the emic-etic construct (Berry, Brislin, Pike, Przeworski and Teune, Triandis, others). She obtained etic indicators of conservatism, e.g.: "The most important thing to teach children is absolute obedience to their parents", and four other items. Emic indicators for the United States included the item, "Young people should not be allowed to read books that are likely to confuse them", and three others. The label given to these emic items was "the use of stereotypes and the endorsement of public intervention in matters ordinarily addressed elsewhere (p. 187)." The emic indicators for Poland included the item "You should obey your superiors whether or not you think they're right", and two others. The label for these items was "deference to hierarchical authority which is bureaucratically or legally legitimized (p. 186)." The etic and emic indicators were interrelated through the use of multivariate statistics developed by K.G. Joreskorg.

The labels for the emic items are complex, but this is not surprising. Items from culture A will be different, or will interrelate differently, than items in culture B. Consequently, unfamiliar aspects of culture A will be manifested from the point of view of people in culture B. Such unfamiliar aspects often demand long descriptions.

This example brings up one more use of the emic-etic construct which I have found useful in cross-cultural training programs designed to prepare people to live and work in a country other than their own. Emic aspects of a concept can be given special attention in training since these are the features of another culture which will seem most strange and which are likely to cause ethnocentric judgments if not fully understood.

REFERENCES

Brislin, R. Translation and content analysis of oral and written materials. In H. Triandis and J. Berry (Eds.), Handbook of Cross-Cultural Psychology, vol. 2. Boston: Allyn and Bacon, 1980, pp 389-444.

Miller, J., Slomczynski, K., & Schoenberg, R. Assessing comparability of measurement in cross-national research: authoritarian-conservatism in different sociocultural settings. Social Psychological Quarterly, 1981, 44, 178-191.

COMMENT

H. C. Triandis

University of Illinois, Champaign

Gustav Jahoda's paper is most welcome, because it gives us an opportunity to clarify the meaning of one of the most important constructs in cross-cultural psychology. However, I strongly suspect that the reason Jahoda's 1976 paper has met with "deafening silence" (p.18) is that it is "much ado about nothing".

It is quite clear that we need a term that refers to concepts and data (items, measurements) that reflect the famous Malinowskian statement, to "grasp the native's point of view". Logically these refer to one culture. We use the word emic to refer to such concepts or data. We also need a term that refers to the scientist's concepts and measurements. Such concepts will have to refer to more than one culture and the measurements should be appropriate for more than one culture. This is so because the purpose of science is to provide the most parsimonious, accurate, and general account of the phenomena under study. I am aware that one cannot hope to simultaneously maximize all three aspects of the scientific enterprise. But at least one should strive to do so. Clearly, "general" here means that the constructs would apply to more than one culture. Thus, when we refer to etic constructs we are stating that they account for some phenomenon in more than one culture.

An example of a scientist's variable is a "factor"; an example of a scientist's measure is a "factor score", obtained after factor analysis. Now suppose that in each culture the natives describe a phenomenon using entirely different words (e.g. in Osgood's study "good" and "beautiful" in one culture, "nectar-like" and "pleasing" in another culture). If the patterns of correlations among the emic measures is similar we have identified an etic variable and the factor scores based on the emic measures are etic measures.

In my opinion the reason Jahoda finds contradictions in the way cross-cultural psychologists have used the emic-etic construct is that he uses an Aristotelian logic that requires an entity to be classified in one or another category. Thus, he finds "tangles" and cannot approve of Davidson and Thomson writing about "an emic measure of an etic variable" (p.32). However, there is no reason why the native and the scientist cannot agree, some of the time! If that happens there is an overlap between emics and etics. Thus, there is no contradiction when a construct is found to be both emic and etic, and the Davidson and Thomson sentence makes sense.

Perhaps stating the case in a formal way will make it clear. Suppose we study a phenomenon, by exploring the "native's point of view" and find that the variables A, B, and C are involved in culture 1 and X, Y, Z in culture 2. The emic case occurs when the correlations among A, B, and C are quite different from the correlations among X, Y, and Z; furthermore, the correlations of variables that are antecedents of A, B, and C do not show similar patterns to the correlations of variables that are antecedent to X, Y, Z. The same is true for variables that are assumed to be consequents of A, B, C, X, Y, Z. The etic case is one where the correlations among the variables A, B, C are quite similar to the correlations among the variables X, Y, Z, and also, the antecedent and consequent variables show similar patterns of correlations in the two cultures.

Now suppose we studied A, B, and C in one culture and established that they are emic, but we did a study in a third culture with variables L, M and N and found the same patterns we had found for variables A, B and C. This new evidence changes our conclusion. We can no longer claim that A, B and C are emic. Of course, what is in the "native's point of view" has not changed. What has changed is what is in the scientist's mind. That, of course, happens all the time in science. We keep changing our viewpoint as new data become available.

What is "emic at time 1" is "etic at time 2". So, there is no contradiction if some variable is both emic and etic.

So, to answer only those points which correspond to Jahoda's critique of my statements: "What are the grounds for asserting that social distance is an etic construct?" (p.26). The pattern of correlations among some of the items is the same in each culture; the pattern of correlations with outside variables is the same (e.g. in all cultures those high in social distance have high scores on the F-scale). "How did it come to change its nature when Bogardus's measures were extended to other cultures?" (p.26). Bogardus used some measures that do not work in other cultures. For example, "to admit a person in one's neighborhood" does not have the same meaning in the U.S. and in Japan. "Can a measure of the Rorschach change from emic to etic?" (p.26). The answer is yes. Jahoda asks "... how the meaning of the continuum comes to be defined..." (p.26). The answer is through some form of construct validation, i.e. looking for similar patterns of correlation with antecedent and consequent variables.

REPLY

G. Jahoda

University of Strathclyde, Glasgow

All three of my critics stress that we need "two terms
which reflect our dual interests", in John Berry's words. I
share this view, a fact that I have evidently failed to
make sufficiently clear. My point is that the emic-etic
dichotomy is inappropriate, when used in a strict sense, at
the present time; though as Berry suggests, it may become
so in future. What he calls "the conceptual baggage" of
system and structure, as though it were peripheral, is
really central to the meaning of these terms; hence talking
about "emic variables" is analogous to expressions like
"linear cubes", which do not make sense. An unpretentious
alternative pair of terms at our disposal is already widely
used and less liable to create confusion, namely
"culture-specific" versus "general".

Berry summarizes his earlier discussion for my
benefit, but in spite of its alleged simplicity this does
not help me a great deal. It is obvious that one approaches
another culture with whatever intellectual equipment one
has at one's disposal - there is no other way! What I
cannot grasp are the empirical referents of such terms as
"match" or "correspond" in relation to something
intriguingly described as "the local phenomenon". Does it
mean whether or not my equipment allows me to understand,
or perhaps even explain, particular bits of behaviour of
the people in the culture? If it does mean that, then one
is either successful and there is no problem, or
"comparison is not possible". The latter would seem to
indicate coming to a full stop, but this cannot be meant
since there is said to follow "a sequence of such entries
and comparisons" from which somehow an "etic phenomenon"
might emerge. Now although Berry correctly diagnosed an
occasional tongue in my cheek, I want to assure him that
here my perplexity is entirely genuine.

As mentioned in my Tilburg paper, the difficulty lies
in the excessively high level of abstraction which
encompasses a wide range of possiblities. There is a vast
difference between such segmentary aspects of behaviour as,
on the one hand, spatial perception and, on the other,
beliefs, attitudes and personality characteristics tied up
with social relations. The emic-etic dichotomy is certainly
relevant to the latter, albeit not to the manner in which

these problems are typically tackled by psychologists. As for the remainder of Berry's comments I find myself in entire agreement, particularly welcoming his distinction between conceptual and empirical levels.

This distinction appears to be lacking in the comments by Harry Triandis. who transports us into an idealized psychometric world sanctified by science. It is idealized because in the real world patterns of correlations, especially in cross-cultural contexts, tend to be messy and their interpretations controversial. While worth remembering, this would not affect the principles advocated by Triandis, namely that emic and etic be defined in terms of similarities and differences in patterns of correlation. Unfortunately such a claim is not admissible because the correlational approach, while undoubtedly important, is by no means the only one in cross-cultural research. It predominates where research is done among literate populations, and workers in this sphere run the risk of forgetting that a large part of humanity is thereby excluded. Triandis falls into this trap when, trying to answer my question, he proposes that "in all cultures those high in social distance have high scores on the F-scale" as though that scale were universally applicable.

One of Triandis' points arises from a misunderstanding for which I am probably responsible through being insufficiently explicit: what I objected to in Davidson and Thomson's sentence was the inappropriate coupling of terms - I would be quite content with "a culture-specific measure of a general variable".

Triandis also accuses me of using an Aristotelian logic, and I must admit a penchant towards that when it helps to avoid the kinds of confusions liable to arise from questionable resort to the emic-etic language. Take the case of the scientist who "agrees" with the native, a most ambiguous statement covering at least two possiblities. One is that the scientist agrees on something like the fact that the beer is good, not qua scientist but qua native of another place. The other, more interesting one, is that he agrees qua scientist; now according to Triandis' definition this means that they must have "etic constructs" in common. Since such constructs are not part of ordinary language, the Aristotelian conclusion must be that they are both native scientists!

Let me now take my tongue out of my cheek and consider a more serious problem. This can be illustrated with reference to the second part of Triandis' formal exposition, where he supposes that "we studied A, B and C in one culture and established that it is emic". I shall mention briefly that it is not evident to me how that might be done, nor what the "it" could mean - but let that pass.

Then we take another culture and find a similar pattern of correlations, which leads us to switch the label to "etic".

There are several points to be made about this. First, it is possible to make a mistaken attribution that is subsequently corrected, but this does not imply "emic at time 1" and "etic at time 2". Admittedly one should differentiate here between empirical and conceptual issues. Empirically the categorization may often be problematic, but on the conceptual level I would regard the emic-etic (or according to my preference "culture-specific" versus "general") dichotomy as mutually exclusive. I would certainly agree that there are some tricky problems here, and perhaps it was Triandis' intention to draw attention to these.

Nonetheless, the previously mentioned switch from emic to etic on the basis of evidence from <u>one</u> other culture is, to say the least, rather puzzling. Unless I have misunderstood him, it would seem that Triandis is somewhat inconsistent in his use of the term "etic", which he has commonly in the past confined to <u>universal</u> dimensions. Lastly, the analysis of this example brings out the inadequacy of the inductive strategy apparently advocated here by Triandis which, I submit, would make our quest an endless and hopeless one. It is fortunate that, as evidenced by his distinguished contributions, Triandis has not really followed this path in practice.

Richard Brislin explains that one of my minor criticisms resulted from a typing error, and so I gladly withdraw it. He is also quite right that the emic-etic terminology can oil the wheels of conversation with colleagues from other disciplines; in that kind of context it may well be viewed as a useful, though vague, metaphor. It is quite another matter to say, as Brislin also does, that it is a "construct" that can serve to "organize" completed research and give it additional polish; he has certainly not demonstrated how the tacking on of emic-etic labels improves the product.

The additional example offered, which does to some extent employ an emic-etic conceptual framework, is therefore welcome. On the other hand it could be pointed out that it is a piece of cross-national, rather than cross-cultural, survey research. Moreover, the relevant paragraphs are headed respectively "Within-country (emic)" and "Cross-national (etic)", thereby supporting my view that the words within the brackets are there purely for effect, adding nothing to the meaning. However, I would concede that in his last paragraph Brislin may be using the term "emic" in its technical sense, for which it would then be wrong to substitute "culture-specific".

Finally, I would not agree that the discussion of these issues is "much ado about nothing", or that my paper is a mere "tale told by an idiot". Yet I am quite content that John Berry should promote me to Court Jester, since a major function of that role was to tell one's betters, with impunity, some unpalatable truths!.

NATIVE LANGUAGE AND COGNITIVE STRUCTURES
– A CROSS CULTURAL ENQUIRY

A. Z. Guiora and A. Herold

The University of Michigan, Ann Arbor

Introduction

In a series of papers written in the 1930's and 1940's Benjamin Lee Whorf, inspired by Edward Sapir, formulated the now well known Sapir-Whorf hypothesis linking the structure of native language to non-linguistic behavior. This "principle of linguistic relativity" stated that the structure of an individual's linguistic system influences both the manner in which he apprehends and constructs reality, and his behavior with respect to it. Whorf overturned the classical Greek understanding of language as an epiphenomenon that overlies a communication of pure reason, meshed approximately but ever-increasingly precisely with "reality", and which was equally accessible to all men. The ancient notion of the translatability of any thought from one language to another without loss of meaning was, by corollary reasoning, also put in doubt. Instead, Whorf saw all higher levels of thinking dependent on language so that different languages with specific groupings of semantic categories offer and are limited to correspondingly different sets of possible ideas. Different languages provide different "segmentations of experience". This idea while not exactly new, (a statement from classical Hebrew literature of the second century, for example, claimed Latin was best suited for war, Greek for poetry, Persian for grief, and Hebrew, of course, for speech), aroused the interest of linguists, psychologists, philosophers, sociologists, and anthropologists to name but a few. Evidence for the hypothesis has, to date, been meager and despite current efforts to revive the theory, it has been criticised on a priori and on methodological grounds.

51

Empirical criticism centers on the failure to find consistent, unequivocal evidence for such an effect. In the realm of science, such criticism has a curious and highly utilitarian epistemological function - it "disproves" the hypothesis by asserting it has not been shown to correctly predict "expectable" results. The hypothesis itself, however, does not state where one should look for such proof. These areas are determined by linking together domains which would "sensibly and intuitively" exhibit the hypothesized phenomena. Two palpable responses to criticisms of the Whorf hypothesis are that investigators have been searching in the wrong places in the wrong ways. It is posssible that the effects may be too small (or conversely, the instrument too clumsy), too subtle (the influence is seen less directly than assumed), or both.

Background

Since 1968, the University of Michigan Personality and Language Behavior Research Project has been studying the reciprocal, co-existing effects of personality on language behavior and language structure on personality (e.g. Guiora and Acton, 1979; Guiora, 1982). This effort grew out of a desire to reformulate certain psychological constructs (such as empathy and intuition) in measurable behavioral terms. The theoretical rationale for this "transpositional research" paradigm can be found elsewhere (Guiora, 1970). Successive efforts have uncovered, over the years, distinct and measurable personality parameters that affect language behavior. More importantly for the present concern, 1974 saw our first published study examining the reverse relation: language structures that affect personality, i.e. an empirical investigation of the so-called Sapir-Whorf hypothesis (Beit-Hallahmi et al., 1974). These studies, summarized elsewhere (Guiora, et al., 1982), have looked at the effect gender markings within a particular language have on the timing of attainment of gender identity. Languages vary widely in gender prominence, and gender marking in many languages applies only to nominal categories, such as pronouns and adjectives. In other languages gender marking applies also to verbs, and may in certain cases be directly related to the gender of the human participant in the speech situation. There are yet other languages, such as those of the Finno-Ugrian group, in which gender plays practically no grammatical role at all. Furthermore, languages differ not only in the extent to which they employ grammatical gender (manifested in pronominal and sometimes verb agreement in the third person) but also in the rules which govern gender-related grammatical constructs. For example, those of us who grew up referring to a male friend's mother as "his mother" (the agreement of the pronoun is with the sex of the friend) might stumble over sa mère (the agreement of the pronoun is with the gender assignment of the word mère). Conversely, if one grew up saying <u>son</u> p\`ere he might have occasional difficulty with <u>her</u> father. This is to to say that for the mature speaker of French learning English (as in the last example) there is no way to communicate and understand that the person in question is the daughter of the father, but simply that the understanding that it is the daughter and not the son is communicated through different grammatical structures. We suggested that if the structure of language has an effect on the way we experience and process the world around us, then the differences in gender-loading might provide a productive arena for inquiry.

On a more systematic level, we set out to explore what effect grammatical gender loading in the native language has on the development of gender identity. One would expect the exposure to gender differentiation in language to create an awareness of gender differences in the objects of language, especially the self and other humans. Thus, the child's awareness of gender loading and its uses becomes a part of the materials that go into his construction of the social world and his own place in that world.

The empirical question we asked was: will there be a relationship between the <u>amount</u> of linguistic emphasis on gender and the <u>average age</u> of attaining gender identity in children, in a specific linguistic environment.

To answer this question, we have tested three groups of children between the ages of 16 and 42 months, reared in three different language environments, on a measure constructed for this purpose, the Michigan Gender Identity Test (MIGIT). Eighty-nine toddlers in Israel, seventy-two in Finland, and one-hundred-and-one in the United States constituted the research samples. All children came from monolingual families, Hebrew, Finnish and English respectively. In terms of gender-loading, Hebrew can be said to have maximum gender-loading, English minimal, Finnish zero. (Since these data have been reported elsewhere, they will only be summarized here.)

The findings indicate a direct relationship between gender loading in the language and gender identity attainment. The Hebrew-speaking sample of children showed the highest (earliest) level of gender identity attainment, while the Finnish-speaking group showed the lowest (latest) level. It appears that the Israeli children have a significant, albeit <u>temporary</u>, advantage over their American and Finnish counterparts in the <u>timing</u> of gender identity development. What we may see then is a difference in the growth curve, apparently attributable to differences in the native language. The results suggest a possible confirmation of the Sapir-Whorf hypothesis.

Since these earlier gender studies examined possible

consequences native language may have in three different countries, the objection of non-linguistic cultural determinants responsible for the perceived differences may be raised. In the last of the series of gender studies, data bearing directly on this objection have been collected and analyzed. In the Finnish portion of that study (Guiora et al., 1982), two culturally similar yet linguistically dissimilar Finnish subgroups have been compared: Swedish-speaking Finns and Finnish-speaking Finns. Even though the socio-cultural environments were similar, the difference in language structure relative to gender marking is pronounced, with Swedish more approximating English. The results were in the expected direction with Swedish-speaking Finns scoring better on the MIGIT than Finnish-speaking Finns. These results are all the more impressive when one considers that in follow-up questionnaires given to both groups, it was discovered that even though the socio-cultural parameters were similar for the two groups, they were not identical. It was found that attitudinal and behavioral sex-role stereotyping differences between the two groups would operate in the direction of earlier gender identity attainment for the Finnish Finns. This suggests that the role of the linguistic structure not only predisposes the Swedish Finn group to earlier gender identity development but actually overturns other socio-cultural factors that would tend to favor earlier development for the Finnish Finn group.

The validity of the construct under study would be strengthened if some other linguistic structure could be shown to have similar impact on some other developmental template. This has been successfully attempted by Sinclair de Zwart (1967) who showed that children who can perform Piagetian conservation tasks use different linguistic forms than children who can not, and this finding was further refined by Sevinc and Turner (1976). Demsey (1971) found experimental evidence for differential performance of Piagetian time conservation tasks across cultures, though a link with specific linguistic structures was less convincing than with general cultural world-views concerning time experience segmentation.

One of the more difficult developmental tasks children have to master is a correct perception of time: past, present, and future. Piaget (1969) has suggested that the young child struggles in separating two distinct components of time: succession and duration. Lovell and Slater (1960) have demonstrated that spatial factors, extrinsic to time factors, can mislead the child into incorrect judgments about the duration of events since he cannot coordinate duration with succession. For example, if two toy cars move down a track at different velocities and the faster car stops first, even if the slower car stops before it has reached the mark of the faster car, the child will judge the faster car to have been in motion longer since it moved faster. Refinements in experimental design (c.f. Levin, 1977) have modified the stages involved in learning to accurately perceive time duration and succession, yet the basic interconnection between the two components and an inability to use succession to modulate perception of duration remain in the young child.

One of the Piagetian tasks measuring succession, or order of events, is to demonstrate to a child the siphoning of water from a beaker into a cylinder and then present a series of cards showing the various stages of the beaker being emptied and the cylinder being filled, (Piaget, 1966; Lovell and Slater, 1960). The child is asked to arrange six sets of cards in the right order so that the first set shows a picture of a full beaker placed next to an empty cylinder, the second set a picture of a partially emptied beaker next to a partially filled cylinder, and so on.

It can be seen that the cognitive capability necessary for such a task is more than an accurate perception of the succession component of time. What is additionally involved is the ability to divide into portions a single experimental unit, in this case the pouring of water into a cylinder. Moreover, the act of portioning is such that a relation is established in an overall cognitive schema organizing the experiential unit in such a way that the child is able to say: this portion occurs first, then this portion, etc. A more sophisticated analog would state the mental operation as: of and when event "a" occurs then event "b" can or may occur, if and when event "b" occurs then event "c" can or may occur, etc. An example using a slightly more complicated experimental unit than the pouring of water may prove instructive. Consider the following single experiential unit divided into three portions: a person walking toward a house, opening the door, and going inside. If the child were shown three pictures corresponding to each portion and asked to place them in order recreating the experiential unit, he would be exercising cognitive operations additional to time succession, namely: causal understanding that the first portion must precede the second poption in order to conform to experience. In such an analysis, it can be stated with equal correctness that the judgment of the proper sequencing can be either on temporal or logical grounds. That is, the child may say that one will open a door first before entering a house (temporal justification), or that one must open a door first before entering a house (logical justification). At this point, we do not make any assumptions concerning whether or not one or both of these justificatory systems are being used, and have simply named this cognitive operation the "segmentation of experience." Segmentation means not merely to split up but to divide relationally, i.e., concurrently, partially overlapping,

At this level of mental operation (rather than at the
level where segmentation is seen as a compound mental
function), there is at work a remarkable, morphologically
similar, linguistic structure: verb tense and all related
markers such as aspectual and modal auxiliaries. An
analysis of verb tense and related markings shows that its
principal function is to coordinate and place events within
a sentence or larger semantically related structure into
causal and/or temporal relation: i.e., to segment
experience. As an example, consider the following different
sentences: "He said he saw the dog" and "He said he has
seen the dog." The differing tenses and markers of the
second verb-form in each sentence place the act of seeing
the dog in a different relation to the time of telling of
the act. The first sentence can be reworded as "He spoke in
the past of the following event: He sees the dog as he is
speaking." The second sentence can be reworded as "He spoke
in the past of the following event: He saw the dog prior to
speaking."

It is important to keep separate the linguistic
verb-form from the psychological experience of it. For
example, in the sentence "He said he saw the dog," the
second verb "saw" is in the past tense but refers and
creates a psychological interpretation of an event in the
present. The speaker of the sentence is indicating that he
is seeing a dog. However, the time at which he is
indicating he is seeing the dog has already happened. It is
the first verb in the sentence ("said") that surrounds the
second verb with a context that, in essence, goes beyond
the past verb-form of the second verb. We are not
maintaining that there is a direct correspondence between
verb-form and the psychological experience of it but rather
that the richness in relationships with which a language
can employ verb-forms promotes a psychological richness
with which to experience relations among the occurrence of
events.

Present Study

In the remainder of this paper we shall present data
tentatively confirming the Sapir-Whorf hypothesis in the
area of "segmentation of experience", and thus, indirectly
strengthen the effect found in our gender studies described
earlier.

English is a language with a diversity of verb-forms
indicated by either a present or past tense together with
varying aspectual and modal auxiliaries. Consider some of
the possible variations on the preceding example: he sees,
he saw, he was seeing, he has been seeing, he had been
seeing, he will have been seeing, etc. Each of these forms

offers intricate variations on the relations between
events. It is conceivable that a language such as English
with its relative richness of grammatical structures to
identify discrete events will offer an advantage in
segmentation of experience just as a language with
pronounced gender loading offers an advantage in gender
identity attainment. The evident availability of verb-forms
offering a profusion of differing relations means that the
segmentation operation is not a simple division of events.
We have found it useful to consider first order and higher
order segmentation defined by the following. First order
segmentation means: event "a" starts and stops, then event
"b" starts and stops, etc. Higher order segmentation refers
to all other relations: e.g. "a" starts before "b" but
continues as "b" continues, etc.

Languages differ in the way they provide structures
for segmenting experience, past, present, or future.
English, as suggested, like most Indo-European languages,
has a number of grammatical forms to indicate different
moments in the past as they relate sequentially to one
another. This segmenting of the past can be accomplished
with great ease, without any paraphrastic effort, because
of the ready availability of these grammatical forms, as in
this example: "For some time now my sister has been telling
me that there was this man she had known in her youth who
has now returned to town and whom she was going to marry."
The five distinct grammatical forms used in this sentence
to identify discrete moments in the past are simply not
available in languages like Hungarian or Hebrew. Both these
languages, and possibly others, have only one grammatical
form to mark the past. Surely, speakers of these languages,
by the time they have reached linguistic maturity, will
have compensated for these structural deficiencies by
developing paraphrastic strategies; however, it is
conceivable that the availability of, and exposure to, a
multiplicity of forms to order events, (in this case past
events), in a proper sequence and segmenting them with
precision might have an effect on specific growth curves
and accelerate the development of segmentation of
experience in children. As stated earlier, if this were so,
the findings emerging from our gender study would represent
a more powerful explanatory principle.

There are many possible tasks that could be devised to
assess this, the simplest being a test of first order
segmentation. Fortunately, data have already been collected
to allow such a preliminary check. One of the subtests of
the well-known Wechsler Intelligence Scale for Children
(WISC) is the so-called Picture Arrangement Test. In this
test, subjects are shown several single pictures, and told
that properly arranged these will yield a story. There is
only one possible way to arrange the pictures in the right
sequence and get a coherent story. If the prevalence of

relative abundance of past tense forms in the native
language has an effect on the development of segmentation
of experience, American children should show a performance
superior to that of their Israeli counterparts. The WISC is
widely used in Israel, but more importantly its Hewbrew
version has been standardized and the norms have been
published. Thus we can compare an American data base (based
on thousands of subjects) with an Israeli data base
established in the same manner. The findings are
potentially of great consequence.

Because of comparability of scoring in the English and
Israeli systems, eight of the twelve subtests can be
directly compared in a post hoc analysis for percent
difference in performance. It is expected that the percent
difference in performance in Picture Arrangement will be
significantly higher, favoring Americans, in contrast to
other subtests since the remaining tasks are either
relatively equivalent in terms of cultural biases, (i.e.,
Arithmetic, Coding, Digit Span, etc), or involve language
skills where a prima facie functional and structural
equivalent between Hebrew and English exists (i.e.,
conceptual reasoning in Similarities, Information).

The subtest data were analyzed in the following way.
For each eight comparable subtests, (Picture Arrangement,
Information, Picture Completion, Similarities, Coding,
Digit Span, Comprehension, and Arithmetic), four different
intelligence levels varying in numbers of standard
deviations from the mean were considered: $-\sigma$, μ, $+\sigma$, $+2\sigma$.
At each intelligence level, a comparison of raw scores
across ages 6 to 16 was made between Israeli and American
children and a "% Difference" was found. For example, on
the Information subtest, scores qualifying for $+\sigma$ on
Israeli and American norms were compared from 6 to 16 and
"% Difference" was obtained for each age by calculating the
difference between American and Israeli raw scores
pertaining to $+\sigma$ and dividing by the total possible score
for that subtest. (Positive %'s indicated Americans were
scoring higher at $+\sigma$, negative %'s indicated Israelis were
ahead at $+\sigma$). For each of the four intelligence levels,
curves were drawn reflecting this "% Difference" in scoring
of Americans over Israelis.

Figures 1-4 show two curves. The solid line represents
the % Difference values for Picture Arrangement, the broken
line represents the mean of the % Difference values for the
remaining seven subtests.

As seen in Figures 1-4, the Picture Arrangement curves
for $-\sigma$, μ, $+\sigma$, and $+2\sigma$ reflect a larger "% Difference" in
performance compared to other subtests. When compared to
the other subtests individually, Picture Arrangement is
greater than all other subtests at μ, $+\sigma$, and $+2\sigma$, and at

FIGURE 1

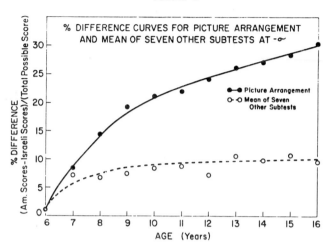

FIGURE 2

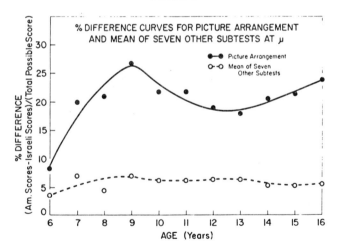

FIGURE 3

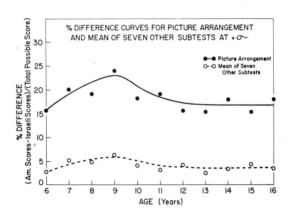

FIGURE 4

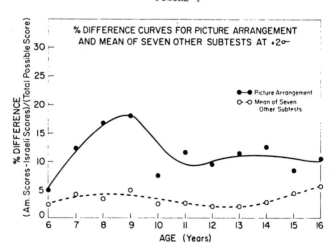

-σ Picture Arrangement is second only to Picture Completion but from age 14 on assumes the highest value.

To determine the statistical significance of these values, 44 "z" values were computed corresponding to each age group across the four intelligence levels. This statistic measured the probability level of finding the "% Difference" value for Picture Arrangement among a theoretical population among which the other subtests served as a representative sample of N = 7. These "P" values (one-tailed) are reproduced in Table 1.

TABLE 1

% Difference 'p' values one - tailed

("% Difference" of Picture Arrangement compared to sample of remaining 7 subtests)

Age	Intelligence Level			
	-σ	μ	+σ	+2σ
6	.47	.26	.02	.29
7	.43	.08	<.01	.07
8	.16	.02	<.01	<.01
9	.09	<.01	<.01	.04
10	.10	<.01	<.01	.16
11	.08	<.01	<.01	.05
12	.02	<.01	<.01	.09
13	.04	<.01	<.01	<.01
14	.03	<.01	<.01	.02
15	.01	<.01	.02	.20
16	.01	<.01	<.01	.17

As expected, most "% Difference" values of the Picture Arrangement subtest were highly statistically significantly different from the values of the other seven subtests, suggesting that the differentially better performance of Americans on this particular subtest was significantly higher than their generally superior performances on the remaining subtests.

An additional area of interest was the relationship, if any, between the size of the differentially better performance on Picture Arrangement across intelligence levels. We hypothesized that for children of modest intellectual achievement ($-\sigma$), the inherent richness or poverty of linguistic structures would manifest itself in a larger effect than for children of greater intellectual achievement. Our reasoning was that brighter children using a less rich language system would be able to compensate more easily for its deficiencies, i.e., in this study the brighter Israeli children would have an easier time developing, internalizing and utilizing paraphrastic strategies to cope with complex segmentations of experience.

We checked for this effect by grouping within each age level the "% Difference" scores of all subtests exclusive of Picture Arrangement and computing a "Median % Difference." This use of a median for a measure of central tendency was used to minimize the effects of the different and unknown variances corresponding to each subtest. Then, the "Difference Value from the Median" was computed by subtracting the "Median % Difference" from the "% Difference" of Picture Arrangement. This was tabulated for each age group across the four intelligence levels and the values are shown in Table 2.

Six groups of comparisons were made between the four intelligence levels ($-\sigma/\mu$, $-\sigma/+\sigma$, $-\sigma/+2\sigma$, $\mu/+\sigma$, $\mu/+2\sigma$, $+\sigma/+2\sigma$) to determine the probability from age 6 to 16 of the $-\sigma$ scores being statistically significantly lower or higher than μ scores, $-\sigma$ scores being lower or higher than $+\sigma$ scores, etc. A non-parametric nature of the curves was inferred to guard against a possibly unwarranted assumption about the normality of the distributions, and a simple binomial expansion was employed. "P" (one-tailed) values are reported in Table 3 for each comparison of pairs of intelligence levels.

It can be seen that with the exception of the $-\sigma/\mu$ comparison (in which an equal probability existed for $-\sigma$ scores to be lower rather than higher than μ scores), near significant to highly statistically significant values were obtained suggesting that "Difference Values from the Median" are greater for the $-\sigma$ group than $+\sigma$ group, $-\sigma$ group than $+2\sigma$ group, μ group than $+\sigma$ group, μ group than $+2\sigma$ group, and $+\sigma$ group than $+2\sigma$ group.

In abbreviated form, the magnitudes of the "Difference Values from the Median" follow a pattern of :
$$-\sigma = \mu > +\sigma > +2\sigma$$
and suggest a confirmation of our hypothesis.

TABLE 2

Difference Value from the Median (Percentage points)

("% Difference" of Picture Arrangement –
"Median % Difference" of remaining 7 subtests)

Age	Intelligence Level			
	$-\sigma$	μ	$+\sigma$	$+2\sigma$
6	1	6	14	2
7	0	17	17	7
8	9	18	13	14
9	15	20	17	11
10	16	18	13	5
11	17	15	14	9
12	19	13	13	7
13	18	13	13	9
14	23	17	16	11
15	19	16	14	6
16	21	18	18	8

TABLE 3

Paired Intelligence Level 'p' values (one – tailed)

	$-\sigma$	μ	$+\sigma$	$+2\sigma$
$-\sigma$	–			
μ	.50	–		
$+\sigma$	.27	.11	–	
$+2\sigma$	.11	< .006	.006	–

To summarize, two hypotheses were suggested and confirmed: it was assummed that the differential linguistic structure of English and Hebrew would manifest itself in a significantly better performance by Americans on Picture Arrangement over the other subtests (as measured by "% Difference") across ages and across levels of intelligence. Additionally, this better performance by American children would show a decline across the four intelligence groups since the brighter Israeli child would be more capable of adopting compensatory paraphrastic linguistic strategies.

An objection might be raised that our analysis will produce artificially inflated levels of significance since we have used the percent difference between means of the various subtests, and the use of means does not take into account a measure of the deviation or spread of scores. If it is the case that the standard deviation for Picture Arrangement is significantly larger than for the other subtests, a large measure of the significant difference between Picture Arrangement and the other subtests could be due simply to this large variance. While it was impossible to gain direct measures of the standard deviation of all the eight subtests since these raw data were already standardized, we performed another check. For a particular age level and intelligence level, say μ, we found what the Israeli scores would represent as scaled scores on the American norms. We now had a direct comparison of two different scaled scores: the American scaled score at μ and the American scaled score that corresponded to the Israeli raw score at the Israeli scaled score of μ. These two values now represented a difference among scaled scores along one distribution of scores, i.e., the American scores. Since the values being compared were along the scaled dimension of the American population, it allowed us to determine how many standard deviations below or above the Americans the Israelis scored. We calculated such values for each subtest and found that though there was a slight decrease in the level of significant difference between Picture Arrangement and the other seven subtests, it still remained significant. For example, using differences between means gave a $p < .01$ for age 9 at μ between Picture Arrangement and the other subtests, while calculating the difference between Picture Arrangement and other subtests using standard deviations gave $p = .02$.

Naturally, any post hoc analysis as this is open to criticism on the grounds that the particular subtest (in this case, Picture Arrangement) may not be measuring a segment skill or that the elevated differential performance is the result of other confounding factors. Nevertheless, these findings seem to suggest at least a possible growing confirmation of our working hypothesis and should prompt the development of a more rigorous design testing both first and higher order segmentation processes.

Discussion

This study has described a putative causal link between linguistic structures and developmental growth curves for specific psychological processes. In the developmental psychological literature, accounting for differential performance on growth curves within cultures currently centers on three possible explanations: cognitive, academic ("cumulative deficit"), and linguistic. These theories have been advanced to account for retarded learning of a number of cognitive tasks, as well as for an understanding of the progressive acquisition of conceptually distinct mental functions, such as progressing from a Piagetian level of concrete operations to formal operations.

In the cognitive explanation, it is assumed that different tasks are handled by different cognitive strategies. For example, to memorize three or four digits one need use only rote memorization. But to memorize a larger group of numbers, or a group of numbers backwards, one must employ a different cognitive strategy such as chunking or semantic associations. A comparison of how one learns the two types of strategies by looking at their storage and retrieval within memory might show the difference between paired-associates learning and hierarchical learning.

The academic explanation, also known as the "cumulative deficit hypothesis," is an elaboration upon the cognitive explanation. It assumes that different academic tasks, distinguished by the age at which they are introduced to the child (e.g., learning letters as opposed to learning the multiplication table), are handled by different cognitive strategies which develop in an unfolding maturational pattern and work in conjunction with earlier developed strategies. Thus, academic tasks requiring the most elementary cognitive strategies (which might be found in kindergarten or 1st grade) will not distinguish between learning-disabled, mildly retarded or normal children. But upon the introduction of an academic task in second grade, calling for a cognitive strategy distinct from those previously used, the normal children may show a differentially better performance than retarded or disabled children. This notion of compound parallel strategies (or, in some cases, the domination of a later more advanced strategy over an earlier one) stresses key developmental points at which there are discontinuities of style of mental functioning because new, structurally dissimilar and advanced cognitive strategies emerge.

Finally, the linguistic explanation was initially directed to the political issue of the consistent lower

scoring of black compared with white children on standard
IQ tests. This position states that the lower black scores
do not reflect an inherently lower IQ but children's
struggling to take a test based on standard "white" English
coming from a native "black" English environment. The
conclusion is that black English is sufficiently different
from standard white English so that some tasks on the IQ
tests cannot be adequately dealt with by thinking in black
English, (a process theory). Notice that this is a more
powerful and far-reaching statement than saying that
children raised in a black environment will not know
informational items belonging to a standard white English
environment, (a content theory). For example, this position
is not simply saying that a black child raised in an inner
city will probably less often know the meaning of "donkey"
than a white child raised in the suburbs (a WISC question)
but that a black child will not be able to think in the
same way about how, for example, a bicycle and a car are
alike (another WISC item).

These three explanations, cognitive, academic, and
linguistic, attempt to account for observed develomental
differences among different populations (learning-disabled,
retarded, normal, white, black). We feel that the
Sapir-Whorf hypothesis can provide a face validity
framework within which it is possible to make these
explanations more comprehensible. Considering the cognitive
and academic theories together, the important element is
the introduction of a "cognitive strategy" which is
morphologically similar to the different "sets of ideas" or
"interpretation schemas" suggested by differing linguistic
structures. In the academic explanation, developmental
process is measured at precisely that point of
discontinuity where a distinct and more powerful cognitive
strategy ("interpretation schema") is developed. Our
contention is that these cognitive strategies, in some
degree, are isomorphic to the overall liguistic structure
used by the child. The psychological process which the
cognitive strategy directly shapes is thus, on some level,
connected to the linguistic structure. The degree of
isomorphism will determine the degree to which the
linguistic structure participates in the cognitive
strategy, either in an immediate or remote way. Thus, in
the gender identity study, the psychological process in the
attainment of gender identity and the cognitive strategies
are those mental organizations which schematize and present
for the child a sense of gender identity. The heavy gender
loading of Hebrew facilitates and promotes the uses of
cognitive strategies dealing with gender identity whereas
English does not.

In the linguistic theory, the Sapir-Whorf hypothesis
is sympathetically invoked to account for "cultural
deprivation" of native speakers of black English on

standard English testing. It is noteworthy that this
mismatching of native language and testing language is not
unidirectional. The Sapir-Whorf hypothesis would
accommodate explanations of equally poor results of
standard English speakers on black English tests. In this
sense, the Sapir-Whorf hypothesis is a more general
statement than the linguistic theory, which is to date
limited to a cultural bias (deprivation?) perspective.

Verification of the Sapir-Whorf hypothesis, by looking
at robust, longstanding, and radically different perceptual
or cognitive processes, has been mostly negative to date,
though some possible important exceptions exist for
circumscribed phenomena, such as cross-cultural differences
in color perception (Brown and Lenneberg, 1954). This does
not necessarily mean that the hypothesis is incorrect. The
phenomena studied by us constitute a different order of
investigation in that significant effects have been found
which are, for the most part, temporary.

The effect that exists is a more subtle and
unobtrusive one than previously predicted. We have found,
for instance, that the linguistic structures seem to act as
catalysts for the onset of naturally occurring
psychological processes, rather than creating the processes
themselves ex nihilo. The significance of this is twofold:
firstly, it appears likely that the onset of particular
processes does not occur in a vacuum, but is linked to an
already ongoing psychic process in such a way that timing
will affect the final "outcome matrix" in which all
processes intermingle. As an example, consider the process
of gender identity formation. The early first years of
child development see the emergence and maturation of
manifold cognitive structures and content and it would be
important to establish when gender identity first
crystallizes during this period.

Secondly, one can assume, not unreasonably, that
certain psychological processes occur as a consequence of
general cognitive maturation regardless of the specific
linguistic environment, (e.g., the ability to segment the
past). Given this assumption, our modified Sapir-Whorf
position suggests that the linguistic structures will give
added shape to this process by promoting or retarding its
onset. This retardation or promotion does not simply push
ahead or leave behind the same process, but by the very act
of affecting onset it interweaves with the structure of the
process itself, leaving it permanently altered. This is to
say no more than that while a comparison of English- and
Hebrew-speaking subjects may show equal ability to reach an
identical level of proficiency beyond a certain age, the
process of performing this function is not necessarily
identical.

67

It would appear from our various studies that in terms of cognitive development the linguistic component does not have a uniform effect. In certain instances, like recognition of gender, and perhaps segmentation of experience, native language has an accelerating effect on cognitive growth. In other instances, such as for example in the assignment of sexual connotation to essentially asexual words, differences in the gender loading of native language have no apparent effect (Guiora et al., 1980). In sum, native language does have an effect, accelerating or retarding, on the development of certain cognitive structures and no apparent effect on others. It is a matter of a particular combination of timing <u>and</u> the affected cognitive structure.

A repeated theme in Whorf's linguistic studies was to create a sound scientific basis from which to understand differing world-views delineated by differing linguistic communities. His contention was that English, along with the other Indo-European languages, did not offer a superior "hold" on reality relative to the native American languages he studied, but rather that each language group offered that world-view best suited to the cultural and environmental requirements of its inhabitants. It was his hope that communication between cultures could be facilitated through the recognition of the principle of linguistic relativity, since this principle would enhance the need to understand other cultures through their language. The end result was to be an understanding of the diversity of linguistic forms leading to a "brotherhood of thought".

The results of our gender studies and preliminary interpretation of the time perception study indicate that linguistic structures do have at least a temporary effect on the developmental growth curves of certain psychological functions and may have a permanent effect on others. Moreover, the direction of the findings indicates that a list can be composed of what languages facilitate which psychological process. In this research, the evidence suggests that a language structure similar to Hebrew (heavy gender loading) promotes earlier age of onset of gender identity comparable to English. In contradistinction, preliminary evidence suggests that English promotes the age of onset of the ability to segment the past into meaningful relationships compared to Hebrew. Thus we might have the first two entries in a "lexicon" of linguistic structures which enhance specific psychologic processes.

An <u>a priori</u> critical position would argue that the natural ordering effect of the world would impress itself upon language in such a way that all languages would necessarily have to take account of certain features of reality, (space, time, causality, will, etc.). Essentially,

68

different languages say the same thing in different ways. A weak response to this criticism of the Sapir-Whorf hypothesis would be to admit that those features of reality which are "sufficiently salient" would find themselves represented in every language while perhaps the idiosyncratic (and dispensible as far as survival) aspects may come under the rubric of the Sapir-Whorf hypothesis. While it can certainly be argued in some quarters, it is our belief that the two psychological processes we have investigated are important ones. Thus, this research raises anew, on an empirical basis, the metaphysical argument as to what attributes necessarily comprise reality across cultures and how that reality is made manifest to individuals of differing linguistic communities.

It should be evident that the political consequences of such a view are potentially quite flammable, (to use a Whorfian term), for we are suggesting that specific linguistic communities have a "headstart" in mastering certin processes. The logical conclusion is that second language instruction in a language which enhances specific desirable psychological processes relative to one's native language is advisable. Should the modified Sapir-Whorf hypothesis, as described here, be upheld in future studies, the setting of priorities in foreign language instruction could have an empirical basis in addition to other, political or cultural, considerations.

<h2 style="text-align:center">REFERENCES</h2>

Beit-Hallahmi, B., Catford, J.C., Cooley, R.E., Dull, C.Y., Guiora, A.Z., & Paluszny, H., (1974). Grammatical gender and gender identity development: cross-cultural and cross-lingual implications. Am. J. Orthopsychiat. 44:3, 424-431.

Brown, R., & Lenneberg, E., (1954). A study in language and cognition. J. Abnorm. Soc. Psychol. 49: 454-462.

Dempsey, A.D., (1971). Time conservation across cultures. Int. J. Psychol. 6:2, 115-120.

Guiora, A.Z., (1970). Transpositional research in the clinical process. Compr. Psychiat. 11:6, 531-538.

Guiora, A.Z., (1982). Language, personality and culture, or the Whorfian hypothesis revisited. In Mary Hines (ed). On Tesol '81. Washington, D.C.

Guiora, A.Z. & Acton, W.D., (1979) Personality and language behavior: a restatement. Language Learning. 29:1, 193-204.

Guiora, A.Z., Beit-Hallahmi, B. & Sagi, A. (1980). A cross-cultural study of symbolic meaning. Balshanut Shimushit. 2:27-40.

Guiora, A.Z., Beit-Hallahmi, B., Fried, R. & Yoder, C., (1982). Language environment and gender identity development. Language Learning. In press.

Levin, I., (1977) The development of time concepts in young children: reasoning about duration. Child Development. 48:435-444.

Lovell, K. & Slater, A., (1960). The growth of the concept of time: A comparative study. J. Child Psychol. & Psychiat. & Related Disciplines. 1: 179-190.

Piaget, J., (1966). Nécessité et signification de recherches comparatives en psychologie génétique. Int. J. Psychol. 1:1-13.

Piaget, J., (1969). The mechanisms of perception. New York: Basic Books.

Sevinc, M. & Turner, C., (1976) Language and latent structure of cognitive development. Int. J. Psychol. 11:4, 231-250.

Sinclair de Zwart, H., (1967). Acquisition du langage et développement de la pensée. Paris: Dunod.

COMMENT

R. Brislin

East-West Center, Honolulu

Studies in the complex area of proposed links between the language people speak and some aspect of their behavior should be welcome for their boldness, in general, and their willingness to grapple with incredibly difficult conceptual issues, in particular. The Sapir-Whorf hypothesis summarizes an idea which won't go away, although hopefully what keeps returning is a good rather than a bad penny. There are too many compelling anecdotes about how speaking one language contrasted to another affects people's behavior to allow complete dismissal of Sapir-Whorf. This lack of dismissal is the wisest decision researchers can take despite the admitted difficulties in specifying process (exactly how language structures affect behavior); and difficulties in untangling a host of variables which may be contributing to any one researcher's results. For example, speakers of English have commented on their emotions and thoughts when using another language. Females talk about feeling as if they were in a straightjacket when speaking Japanese. Scientists talk about the relative ease discussing theoretical physics when working in Chinese; anthropologists argue that sensitivity to contextual cues becomes necessary when speaking Pacific Island languages which do not have a long written history. Some of these effects have been studied, as in Ervin-Tripp's (1964) study of the personalities of French-English bilinguals and perhaps Enriquez and Brislin's (1977) study of translation from English to Filipino and vice-versa. Sussman and Rosenfeld (1982) demonstrated that Spanish-English and Japanese-English bilinguals kept a predictable distance from others based on whether they believed they would be speaking English or their native language. The fact that all these examples involve cultural factors which can be reflected in language, a plausible rival explanation to the proposed direct causal link between language structure and behavior, is exactly the issue which has plagued widespread acceptance of Sapir-Whorf analyses.

A research area as complex as this one will depend upon the contributions of many investigators working in many different parts of the world. Individuals will be made wise by their peers. In the paper by Guiora and Herold, I found the earlier research on gender markings and age of attaining gender identity more compelling than the later study on past tense forms and the segmentation of experience. Some reasons are methodological: it is always wiser to study <u>more</u> than two languages, and this was the case in the <u>gender</u> study. Plausible rival hypotheses brought on by examination of any two languages (and two cultures) are often weakened since they cannot also take into account data from a third language. The other reason is that the link between language structure and the dependent variable of gender identity is well argued by the authors.

In the case of (a) past tense forms and (b) segmentation of experience, the exact processes to identify why languages involving variations in (a) would have an effect on (b) remain unspecified. The fact that only two languages are compared, Hebrew and English, compounds the problem. However, it should be noted that comparisons of multiple test scores on which there should <u>and should</u> <u>not</u> be predicted differences was a wise methodological decision, as was the comparison of children who performed at various levels across the range of total test scores. Opportunities to discuss issues which would have led to more confidence in the author's reasoning went untaken. "Paraphrastic strategies" were brought up but examples were not given. Several examples of how English-speaking, as opposed to Hewbrew-speaking children, went about their tasks, as well as what they told the experimenter, would have been welcome. I agree with the author's conclusion that an intriguing finding has been identified but more rigorous research designs are necessary to confirm the proposed underlying cause.

A number of ideas brought up by the authors were underdeveloped. Permanent effects on psychological functions were mentioned but not a shred of evidence was presented to explicate the issue. The important concept that "the very act of affecting onset interweaves with the structure of the process itself, leaving it permanently altered," is mentioned but not developed and no data are presented to show the possibility of the effect. The meaning of what the authors call the "modified Sapir-Whorf hypothesis" is unclear. A treatment here would have benefitted from Miller and McNeill's (1969) analyses of strong, weak, and weakest versions of Sapir-Whorf. The materials on Black English and how it possibly relates to others' ideas of cultural deprivation seems part of another paper and accidentally included here. Links between arguments about Black English and the present data set are tenuous at best.

Even with these reservations I applaud the efforts of Guiora and Herold to sort out the intricate issues which will inevitably be part of any investigation of culture, language, and behavior.

REFERENCES

Enriquez, V., and Brislin, R. The measurement of affective content in American English and Filipino. Philippines Journal of Psychology, 1977, 10(1), 55-69.

Ervin-Tripp, S. Language and TAT content in bilinguals. Journal of Abnormal and Social Psychology, 1964, 68, 500-507.

Miller, G., and McNeill, D. Psycholinguistics. In G. Lindzey and E. Aronson (Eds), Handbook of Social Psychology, 2nd. ed., vol. 3. Reading, Mass: Addison-Wesley, 1969, pp. 666-794.

Sussman, N., and Rosenfeld, H. Influence of culture, language, and sex on conversational distance. Journal of Personality and Social Psychology, 1982, 42, 66-74.

COMMENT

J. Edwards

St. Francis Xavier University, Nova Scotia

The Guiora and Herold paper is an interesting and stimulating one, and my overall view of it is very favourable. Perhaps its most general contribution is the part it plays in a fairly recent revival of interest in the Whorfian hypothesis (see Edwards, 1979). We should note here that the authors' findings -- on gender identity and on the segmentation of experience -- do not deal with the difference between the "weak" and "strong" forms of Whorf's linguistic relativity hypothesis (i.e., "language determines cognitive functioning" versus "language determines customary or habitual ways of thinking"). Guiora and Herold state that the Whorfian hypothesis casts doubt on the "ancient notion of translatability of any thought from one language to another without loss or embellishment". "Loss or embellishment" are important qualifiers here since, as Steiner (1975) has pointed out, translation is obviously possible at some level. Steiner is also in agreement with weak Whorfianism inasmuch as he makes a strong case for different languages providing different perspectives on reality -- thus, the old suspicion of translators betraying group secrets.

At a more specific level, Guiora and Herold report on a study of Israeli, Finnish and American children's gender identity attainment. Hebrew-speaking children showed the highest (earliest) attainment, Finnish speakers the lowest. This accords with the fact that Hebrew has maximum gender loading while Finnish has none. Two points here: (1) the Israeli children's advantage is temporary (see below); (2) why should these languages differ in the first place? If it is true that languages differ because sociocultural environments do, the findings here offer one interesting approach for further cross-cultural, sociolinguistic studies.

In Guiora and Herold's present study, we again see a
difference in children's performance. American speakers of
English -- which can segment the past in great detail --
outperformed Israeli speakers of Hebrew, which is much less
detailed here. The measure was the WISC Picture Arrangement
subtest, and the differences in favour of the American
children were most marked at the lower intelligence levels.
As with the gender identity study, the present
investigation appears to support at least the weaker
version of the Whorfian hypothesis. Two points may be made
here. First, the advantage that the English speakers have
should be a temporary one; Guiora and Herold say that
speakers of Hebrew will have learned to compensate for
"structural deficiencies" once they have reached
"linguistic maturity" (a definition of this term is
obviously required in order to obviate circularity of
argument). However, decreasing American superiority over
age is not evident here. Why? Is it because the Israeli
children, by age 16, have still not reached linguistic
maturity? This would still not explain why differences are
actually greater at higher ages (see Guiora and Herold's
discussion section). Second, the fact that the American
children also do better than their Israeli counterparts on
the other seven WISC subtests is interesting. Could this
indicate problems with the Israeli standardisation of the
WISC? At the least, it should suggest caution in
interpretation of the Picture Arrangement subtest findings.
The authors themselves note, in this connection, that it is
possible that the subtest does not measure segmentation
skill; it is also possible that the test does not, in
itself, mean the same thing to Israeli children as it does
to Americans.

In their discussion, Guiora and Herold mention three
possible explanations for differences in developmental
curves -- cognitive, academic and linguistic. With regard
to the last, the authors confuse somewhat the linguistic
"difference" position and the linguistic "deficit" one (see
Edwards, 1979). The former tends to support weak
Whorfianism, while the latter (now generally discredited)
might, it could be thought, support the stronger version --
"might", because Whorf himself would see linguistic
"deficit" as a relative concept itself.

Finally, Guiora and Herold suggest that their studies
have implications for second language learning; choice of a
foreign language could be based upon a desire to acquire
features which are given more emphasis in the second
language than in the maternal variety, rather than upon
political or cultural grounds. This is not, perhaps, a
likely possibility if differences between languages are not
crippling, and if differences are only temporary.
Sociocultural determinants are likely to remain

pre-eminent. This does nothing, however, to vitiate Guiora and Herold's provocative paper.

REFERENCES

EDWARDS,J. Language and Disadvantage. London: Edward Arnold (New York: Elsevier), 1979.

STEINER, G. After Babel: Aspects of Language and Translation. London: Oxford University Press, 1975.

SEMANTIC RETRIEVAL: AN INVESTIGATION IN THREE LANGUAGES

M. M. McM. Deines and K. E. Nelson

Pennsylvania State University, University Park

The rapid retrieval from memory of a single very specific item from among numberless other items stored makes some effective form or forms of organization of memory a certainty. Several general models have been proposed to describe semantic retrieval and the dimensions of memory storage, each leading to predictions concerning the relative efficiency of long-term memory. A popular technique for testing such predictions has been the sentence verification task. If a model predicts, for example, that attributes of a catagory are more closely associated with the category name (that birds <u>fly</u>, for example) than are some of its instances (e.g., that a <u>duck</u> is a bird), then the time required to verify a sentence should be shorter when an attribute-category relationship is to be verified, than when an instance-category relationship is to be confirmed. Predictions from models of memory considered here have employed sentence verification tasks requiring confirmation of category-instance ("an X is a Y") or noun-attribute ("an X has/can Y") relationships to obtain different kinds of information about memory processes.

Collins and Quillian (1969) proposed a memory model in which information is stored as units and properties within a network of associations, a hierarchical network model. Storage of information in this model is efficient, not redundant, with only more specific attributes ("properties") stored with a noun ("unit"), while more general attributes are stored with the noun's direct or more remote superordinate. For example the relatively general attribute "eats", might be stored with "animal", rather than "goat". This kind of storage model would lead to the prediction that more general properties should take longer to retrieve in sentence verification tasks than more

77

specific ones. Collins and Quillian cite sentence verification reaction time data in support of their model of memory organization. Subjects were required to verify that, e.g., "a canary is an animal" or "a canary is a bird", and to verify "a canary is yellow" or "a canary can sing". Longer reaction times occurred to the sentences presenting relationships (e.g., of canary) to more remote superordinates and to less specific or defining attributes.

Rather than assuming, as Collins and Quillian's model does, that information is stored in a particular manner in long term memory, e.g., least specific attributes stored with higher-order superordinates, Meyer's (1970) approach to formulating memory structures was to identify processes involved in retrieval and stimulus dimensions that affect retrieval time, and to infer structure from them too. Size of category, or specificity, appeared to be an important stimulus dimension in retrieval, with the direction of effect of category size relatively consistent for a fixed kind of subject-predicate relationship.

The hierarchical storage model has been challenged also by studies such as those by Conrad (1972), Rips, Shoben and Smith (1973) and Nelson and Kosslyn (1975) which control for strength of relationship between a superordinate category and its instances or members. Supported by their studies which indicate an effect of rated association strength upon retrieval time, Smith, Shoben and Rips (1974) propose a semantic feature alternative to a hierarchical network model for long term memory. Smith et al. propose that information is stored in memory as concepts and features of concepts. A concept is defined by a set of features or attributes. Concepts are related to other concepts in a multi-dimensional semantic space, in which the distance or closeness of concepts depends upon the number and importance of their features in common, rather than subordinate-superordinate relationship. Highly associated features (salient) might be stored with the noun, even if of low specificity (see also Conrad, 1972). For example, the attribute "sleeps" is very low in specificity and should be stored, perhaps, with "animates" in a hierarchical model of storage; however, this attribute might have high associative strength for a given noun such as "bear", and might therefore be verified more quickly than a more specific but less salient attribute, such as, "has a tail". Knowledge of the relative salience of an attribute would lead to more accurate prediction of response time than knowledge of the attribute's specificity alone.

A semantic feature model can also be used to make predictions concerning shared features' effects upon reaction times to true versus false sentences in a verification task. A number of common features between

78

concepts proposed in a sentence would increase the probability of occurrence of a prompt match of some features between concepts, and therefore of a positive decision concerning a relationship between them. A greater number of features in common should also tend to delay a negative decision because of the probable occurence of a number of positive feature matches likely to impede identification of the mismatch that would lead to a judgment of "false". One might expect that falsification would require longer reaction times when the false attribute to be assessed is a true attribute of a related concept.

The present study employed a sentence verification task to investigate the generality of two stimulus dimensions, salience and specificity, that have evoked consistent patterns of response in studies of true sentences with English speaking adults and children (Nelson and Kosslyn, 1975). Our interest was in acquiring evidence that dimensions of salience and specificity are, or are not, relevant dimensions of memory organization in languages other than English. It is possible, for example, that the pattern of response evoked in English by varying salience of attributes presented for verification appears only in English, and that this dimension is either not as relevant to organization of semantic memory in other languages, or that its effects are somewhat different. The languages chosen to test the effects of varying predicates upon these two dimensions were German and Spanish. A further interest was the exploration of systematic differences in organization between first and second language systems of fluent bilinguals. Specifically, the relevance of salience or specificity to semantic retrieval in the secoond language was questioned. To test these dimensions' relevance in second-language organization, the bilingual German- and Spanish-speakers were also tested in English. A final subject of interest was the alterations in processing that might occur when material to be retrieved has been recently accessed. In addition to these central questions for semantically correct (true) sentences, false sentences across languages were also examined.

Method

Subjects

Native-language trials. Sixteen native speakers of Spanish and thirteen native speakers of German, aged 24-43, served as volunteer subjects. Two Spanish-speaking subjects were excluded because of error rates in excess of 20%.

English trial. A bilingually proficient subgroup of the above subjects, 9 Spanish-speakers and 12 German-speakers, was subsequently administered the sentence verification

task in English (Trial 3). The criteria for bilingual
proficiency for this study were: a pre-test rating by an
experimenter of completely bilingual (1) or nearly
bilingual (2); and an error differential score of 1 or 2,
reflecting low native-language versus English error-rate
difference. Error differential scores were obtained by
subtracting the subject's English trial errors from his or
her average number of errors for the two native-language
trials, and assigning weighted scores to the obtained
difference; a score of 1 corresponded to fewest additional
errors in the second language (English), and a score of 4
to greatest number of additional errors. Negative numbers
occurred for some subjects, indicating fewer errors on the
English trial than on the native-language trials, and these
negative numbers were also assigned a score of 1. Degree of
match beetween error differential scores and experimenter
ratings was 83%; that is, mismatch occurred for three
subjects. In the case of a mismatch (which never exceeded +
or - one rating point) the error differential score was
decisive. Data for one bilingual Spanish-speaking subject
were forfeited because of an equipment failure.

Procedure

The experimental task was essentially that of Nelson
and Kosslyn (1975). They constructed a set of 36 true and
36 false sentences describing animals. True sentences
paired 12 animals each with 3 attributes previously rated
for salience by an independent group of subjects. Each
attribute corresponded to a different level of salience,
from high to low, for example, from "spots" for a leopard
(high) to "neck" for a peacock (low). Animal attributes
were further classified by specificity, again with three
levels: high (characteristic of the animal's direct
superordinate, e.g., a lion's fur); and low (an attribute
of virtually any animal, e.g., a leopard's eyes). By use of
both salience ratings and specificity levels, a 3 x 3
matrix was constructed to permit independent assessment of
effects of specificity and salience.

The structure of the set of false sentences
necessarily differed, but again class relationships and
verbs were varied. False sentences paired the same 12
animals each with 3 false attributes representing a
characteristic of another animal of the same superordinate
class ("same superordinate"), or of a different direct
superordinate class ("different superordinate"), or of an
inanimate or a non-animal entity, such as a plant
("anomalous"). For each kind of false attribute category,
an equal number of verb ("active", e.g., "can trot") and
noun ("static", e.g., "has stripes") predicates was used.
Three random presentation orders, one for each trial, were
established, each with the constraint that no animal occurs
twice within any four-sentence sequence.

Spanish and German sentence sets were direct translations of the English sentences. Back translations to check for incorrect or ambiguous items were obtained for each set from native speakers who did not serve as subjects in the study.

In each trial subjects heard 6 tape-recorded practice sentences, using 3 animal subjects, followed by 72 recorded test sentences, using 12 other animals as subjects. A one-minute pause followed presentation of the first 36 terms of each trial. Reaction time was measured from the time the last word of each sentence was played, initiating the reaction time clock, until the subject pressed a "true" or "false" button, which concluded the timing interval. For example, the correct response to "A lion has a mane", is "true". Subjects were requested to respond as quickly as possible, but correctly.

Every subject first received a trial of 72 sentences in his native language. After a 3-minute pause, these same 72 sentences were again presented, but in a new order. This second trial thus assessed any shifts in retrieval times that could be attributed to a recent prior accessing of the same information. Bilingually proficient subjects (see above) were given a third trial, in English, scheduled as close as possible to one week after the first session.

Analyses

Analyses of variance were performed. Data were analyzed separately by language group for the two native-language trials together, and for the Englich language trial alone. Only correct items were included in the analyses. Maximum error rates of subjects included in the analyses were 12% (native-language trials) and 19% (English trial). Higher error rates were admitted for the English trial because of the considerably greater difficulty of the second-language task. Average error rates for subjects whose data were analyzed were 7.2% (native-language trial 1), 5.9% (native-language trial 2), and 8.8% (English trial).

Results

True Sentences

German-speaking subjects.

Native-language trials (T1 and T2). Across trials, the designated degree of salience of an attribute affected retrieval time, $F (2,24) = 27.57$, $p <.001$. Reaction times differed among levels of salience in the direction observed by Nelson and Kosslyn with their English-speaking monolinguals, reaction time increasing from high salience to low. An interaction of salience with trials, F (2,24) = 7.03, p < .005, results from a smaller reduction across the two trials in reaction time to highly salient attributes than to attributes of medium and low salience. Table 1 shows the mean reaction times for the three salience levels on each trial.

Attributes of low ($\bar{x}$ = 1.192) and medium ($\bar{x}$ = 1.205) specificity were also more quickly verified than high specificity ($\bar{x}$ = 1.262) attributes, F (2,24) = 4.10, p < .03. Specificity of attributes, unlike salience, did not interact with trials: the effect of practice was a uniform reaction time reduction at all salience levels.

TABLE 1

For True Sentences Reaction Times (in seconds) by Salience Level for German-speaking Subjects (non-significant differences underlined)

Salience level	High	Medium	Low
Trial 1	1.278	1.368	1.521
Trial 2	1.016	0.991	1.145

The effects of practice, the reaction time reductions between the first and second native-language trials, were significant not only for German-speaking subjects, and for true sentences, but for both language groups and both true and false sentences. Significance in all these cases was at the .001 level (Table 2).

English-language trial (T3). The performance pattern in the third trial, the English-language trial, differs somewhat from that of the first two, native-language trials. Salience effects were not shown; only specificity of attributes significantly affected reaction times, F (2,22) = 9.03. p < .002. Highly specific attributes were verified significantly more slowly than the least specific attributes, as in the native-language trials. A significant interaction of specificity with salience, F (4,44) = 3.47, p < .02, primarily reflects effects of specificity that are strong at only high and medium salience levels. Table 3 shows the interaction between specificity and salience for English-language trials of both German and Spanish speakers.

TABLE 2

Practice Effects: Mean Reaction Times, dfs, and Fs,
By Language Group, Item Type, and Trial
(p < .001 for all differences)

	German-speakers		Spanish-speakers	
	True	False	True	False
Trial 1	1.389	1.486	1.168	1.427
Trial 2	1.051	1.122	0.966	1.072
df	1,12	1,12	1,13	1,13
F	55.03	25.82	23.43	49.82

Spanish-speaking subjects.

Native-language trials. The pattern of response shown
in these trials is similar to those of German-speaking
subjects and of Nelson and Kosslyn's (1975)
English-speaking monolinguals. The degree of salience of an
attribute also affected the verification times of
Spanish-speaking subjects in the Spanish-language trials, F
$(2,26) = 9.24$, p <.002. Specificity effects upon reaction
time were also indicated, $F(2,26) = 6.67$, p <.006.
Interpretation of these effects is complicated by a
significant interaction of salience with specificity, F
$(4,52) = 10.17$, p <.001, as shown in Table 4. Relatively
lower verification times are consistently associated with
very high salience of an attribute or with very low
specificity. The key to the interactions between salience
and specificity rests in the upper right-hand cells of
Table 4, and particularly with the elevated reaction times
to high-specificity-medium-salience (cell 2) and
medium-specificity-low-salience items (cell 6). With regard
to the remaining cells, however, specificity level does not
appear to affect reaction times at the highest level of
salience, with low reaction times even at the highest level
of specificity; and, similarly, salience appears to have no
effect at the lowest level of specificity, with
verification items equally low at the lowest level of
salience.

83

TABLE 3

Specificity-Salience Interaction
English-language Trial
(non-significant differences underlined)

A German-speaking subjects		Specificity		
		High	Medium	Low
	High	1.206	0.994	1.151
Salience	Medium	1.461	1.020	1.061
	Low	1.255	1.217	1.170

B Spanish-speaking subjects		Specificity		
		High	Medium	Low
	High	1.350	1.015	1.169
Salience	Medium	1.501	1.211	0.983
	Low	1.183	1.316	1.115

TABLE 4

Spanish-speaking Subjects, T1 and T2,
True Sentences: Salience by Specificity Interaction
(non-significant differences underlined and sidelined)

Cells:			Salience		
			High	Medium	Low
1-3		High	1.059	1.268	1.052
4-6	Specificity	Medium	1.002	1.043	1.136
7-9		Low	1.032	0.977	1.038

English-language trial (T3). The significant pattern
of responding to the true sentences presented in English
was a greater delay in verifying sentences with attributes
of high specificity compared to sentences employing low- or
medium-specificity attributes, F (2,14) = 5.11, p < .025. As
for the German-speaking subjects, a significant interaction
of specificity occurred with salience, F (4,28) = 5.61, p
<.003, with no significant specificity effects at the
lowest level of salience (Table 3).

False Sentences

No predictions had been made prior to testing
concerning the judgment of false sentences in either of the
two primary languages or in English by this group of
subjects. The results shown in Table 5, were remarkably
consistent with Nelson and Kosslyn's (1975) findings with
English monolinguals. Active (verb attribute) reaction
times were shorter than static (noun attribute) across
trials for both groups; F (1,12) = 64.46, p < .001, for
German-speaking subjects, and F (1,13) = 7.79, p < .02, for
Spanish-speaking subjects. Also for both language groups,
the anomalous (e.g., "a lion has a chair") category showed
a marked practice effect, while the different superordinate
category (e.g., "a goat can sing") changed least with
practice. The longest search times, for both groups, were
required to judge same-superordinate attributes as false, F
(2,24) = 6.79, p < .006, for German-speaking subjects; F
(2,26) = 7.23, p < .004, for Spanish-speaking subjects.
Static-same-superordinate attributes, e.g., "an anteater
has tusks", were particularly difficult to judge as false
(category by active/static interaction): mean reaction time
= 1,706 for this cell, F (2,24) = 4.63, p < .03 for
German-speaking subjects; and mean reaction time = 1.616, F
(2,26) = 13.51, p < .001 for Spanish-speaking subjects.

Central effects found for German-speaking subjects in
the English-language trial were an effect of category,
reflected by means of 1.267, 1.375 and 1.484 for sentences
with anomalous, different superordinate, and same
superordinate predicates, respectively, F (2,22) = 3.80, p
<.04, and an interaction of category and activity level, F
(2,22) = 4.62, p< 0.25. Static attributes of animals of the
same superordinate class were judged false more slowly ($\bar{x}$ =
1.654) than static attributes from other categories, or
than active attributes of any category. Reaction times
across categories and active-static levels were not
significantly different for Spanish-speaking subjects in
the English trial, although the highest response time for
Spanish-speakers also occurred to the static-same
superordinate attributes. The lower power of the test for
Spanish-speaking bilinguals (N = 8, versus N = 12 for the
German-speaking group) may have been responsible for the

TABLE 5

Category by Level (active/static)
Mean Reaction Times, Trials 1 and 2,
For False Sentences in Subject's Native Language

		Anomalous		Same superordinate		Different superordinate	
		Active	Static	Active	Static	Active	Static
Spanish	T1	1.438	1.451	1.381	1.616	1.333	1.340
	T2	1.032	0.965	0.998	1.243	1.055	1.140
German	T1	1.557	1.432	1.454	1.706	1.244	1.525
	T2	0.996	1.125	1.117	1.185	1.047	1.263

non-significance of this trend. Over trials and across first and second languages, such judgments appeared harder to make for subjects of both language groups.

Referring again to Table 5, it may be seen that, on the first trial, the same-superordinate category, both active and static, and for both German-speakers and Spanish-speakers, shows longer reaction times than the different-superordinate category. The position of Smith, Shoben and Rips (1974) concerning effects of shared features in sentence verification tasks for false sentences is that increasing similarity should produce increased reaction times, while low similarity should produce decreased reaction times. This position fits well with the observed reaction times for both groups. The present data further show that after recent access of items on Trial 1, the Trial 2 same-superordinate reaction times are markedly reduced.

The negation task presented in this study appears to differ in difficulty by category on both trials; and practice effects are of different magnitude for different categories. Level of activity has a nearly constant effect, with verb (active) judgments typically faster than noun (static) judgments, with the exception of the anomalous category, where results were mixed. For the anomalous category only, active attribute judgments were made less

quickly than static judgments by the Spanish-speaking
subjects, and there was no time difference between the
anomalous verb and noun judgments by German-speaking
subjects. It seems that a decision regarding anomalous
attributes, particularly verbs, was harder to reach, and
perhaps involved some consideration by the subject of
alternative meanings or of possible special contexts in
order to decide. Once a decision was made, however, it was
more quickly reiterated in Trial 2, producing marked
reductions in reaction time. This interpretation is
suggested by the report of a number of subjects of both
language groups that their reaction to anomalous verbs, in
particular (although they were unaware of any of the
stimulus category designations), was to try to think of a
context in which these statements might be true. Whether
their reports indicate a positive response bias or greater
ambiguity of the anomalous verb category is not certain. In
the absence of other indications of any positive bias, the
latter possibility seems likelier.

Nelson and Kosslyn (1975) report that significantly
longer reaction times to false than to true sentences
occurred for their adult subjects, and for their two groups
of older children (11-year-olds and 13-year-olds), but not
for their youngest group of children (8-year-olds). (As a
possible explanation for the departure, it was proposed
that the younger subjects were responding more slowly to
the true items because of a failure to search efficiently,
that is, to end their search when sufficient information
had been reviewed to make a judgment.) In this context, it
is interesting to note that the German- and
Spanish-speaking subjects in this study also gave slower
responses to the false statements borrowed from Nelson and
Kosslyn (Table 2) and that the bilinguals showed this same
effect when the language of testing shifted to English.
German-speaking subjects' mean reaction time for false
sentences in English was 1.376 seconds, while for true
sentences, mean reaction time was 1.170 seconds.
Spanish-speaking subjects responded to false English
sentences in an average of 1.451 seconds but to true
English sentences in only 1.205 seconds.

Discussion

The most interesting outcome is the significant effect
of specificity of attributes in the direction shown by the
English-speaking subjects of Nelson and Kosslyn, and
directly opposite to that predicted by Collins and
Quillian's (1969) hierarchical storage model. With salience
approximately controlled, higher-specificity attributes
were associated with higher verification times, and
lower-specificity attributes with lower times, regardless
of language group or language of administration (Table 6).
Specificity effects were also robust to practice, remaining

TABLE 6

Specificity: Mean Reaction Times
by Language-group and Trial

			Specificity		
			High	Medium	Low
Native	German	T1	1.417	1.391	1.360
		T2	1.107	1.020	1.025
	T1 and T2		1.262	1.205	1.192
	Spanish	T1	1.227	1.177	1.101
		T2	1.026	0.943	0.930
	T1 and T2		1.126	1.060	1.016
English	German	T3	1.307	1.077	1.127
	Spanish	T3	1.344	1.180	1.089

marked in the second presentation of the true sentences, and showed no interaction with trials, unlike salience, for the German-speaking subjects. The results for specificity of attributes accord well with the findings of Conrad (1972) and of Nelson and Kosslyn (1975) and support an organization of long term memory that is other than, or in addition to, a straightforwardly hierarchical one.

Salience of attributes also affected retrieval times, although in a somewhat less consistent or simple way, for both language groups. Highly significant salience effects shown by German-speaking and Spanish-speaking subjects in the native-language trials were clearly in the direction of higher reaction times for attributes of low salience and low reaction times for highly salient attributes. For both groups, the interpretation of these significant main effects is qualified by their involvement in interactions. For German-speaking subjects, the interpretation of the interaction with trials is unambiguous: practice effects differed with level of attribute salience, with highly salient attributes, associated with low reaction times in the first trial, undergoing less subsequent reduction in Trial 2. For the Spanish-speaking subjects, the interaction involved specificity. Salience (high association of noun and attribute) effects were apparent at the high and medium levels of specificity, while reaction times were uniformly low at the lowest level of specificity, independent of salience value. For each group in the native-language trials salience effects are similar to those observed by Nelson and Kosslyn in testing in English, suggesting that both a salience dimension and a dimension of specificity in semantic organization are not first-language-specific.

The finding of salience effects in the German- and Spanish-language trials is particularly striking, given that salience could only be approximately controlled in these tests and with the present stimulus sets. Ratings were not established independently within the language of testing for the German and Spanish sentence sets, for which English-language salience ratings were employed. Despite possible differences in attribute salience resulting from translation, however, the salience effects were observed, and were in the direction suggested by Anderson and Bower (1973) and observed by Nelson and Kosslyn.

Effects of attribute salience were neither strongly demonstrated nor clear in the English-language trial for either language group. There are probably several ways to account for the non-occurence of unambiguous effects of attribute salience in English for the bilingual subjects, only two are considered here. The first of these is that attribute salience is acquired by frequency of pairing of an attribute with a noun within a specific language; that is, that frequency of use in English, not only in the first language of our bilingual subjects, would be required to establish salience of an attribute in English. If the retrieval test uses a category of content seldom used in the second language, salience of the attributes within that language may not be a meaningful dimension.

The second possibility is that practice effects increased the salience of low and medium salience attributes so that, by Trial 3 (the English-language trial), salience of all attributes tested was roughly equivalent. With the exception of the nature of the interaction observed between salience and Trials 1 and 2 for the German-speaking subjects, discussed above, only anecdotal evidence supports the latter interpretation. A number of subjects of both language groups reported spontaneously, following testing, that they had formed images of the animal-attribute pairs, and that these images persisted to the last trial (and beyond). If imaginal encoding is involved in semantic memory, as Rummelhart et al., (1972) and Kosslyn (1975) propose, persistent image encoding attributes at all of the levels of salience might mediate test performance in both languages and contribute to reduced salience effects in Trial 3, which would,

89

although in another language, simply be another practice trial. However, this explanation cannot be complete, since specificity effects should be attenuated also, as the particular attributes used to represent varying specificity levels should also have become more salient over trials.

Practice effects deserve brief comment. The clear savings in retrieval time shown in the second native-language trial strongly supports a reordering of retrieval lists for each noun based upon recency of use (Anderson and Bower, 1973).

A number of interesting consistencies in performance of the two language-groups in the present study and of the monolingual English-speakers of Nelson and Kosslyn have been identified. Despite the absence of salience effects in the English-language trial (T3) in this study, the overall patterns of retrieval show considerable similarity across groups and languages and lend additional support to the "reality" of salience and specificity as dimensions of semantic memory. Failure to obtain salience effects in the English-language trial have been very tentatively interpreted as in part the result of practice effects. This interpretation could readily be tested with a group of subjects given their second-language trial or trials first. This was not done in the present study chiefly because of the limited pool of completely bilingual subjects available. A further study might do so with profit.

REFERENCES

Anderson, J. R and G.H. Bower (1973) Human Associative Memory. New York: Winston.

Collins, A. M. and M.R. Quillian (1969) Retrieval time from semantic memory. J. of Verbal Learning and Verbal Behavior. 8: 240-247.

Conrad, C. (1972) Cognitive economy in semantic memory. J. of Exper. Psych. 92: 149-154.

Kosslyn, S.M. (1975) Information representation in visual images. Cognitive Psych. 7: 341-370.

Meyer, D.E. (1970) On the representation and retrieval of stored semantic information. Cognitive Psych. 1: 242-299.

Nelson, K.E. and S.M. Kosslyn (1975) Semantic retrieval in children and adults. Developmental Psych. 11: 807-813.

Rips, L.J., E.J. Shoben, and E.E. Smith (1973) Semantic distance and the verification of semantic relations. J. of Verbal Learning and Verbal Behavior. 12: 1-20.

Rumelhart, D.E., P.H. Lindsay, and D.A. Norman (1972) A process model for long-term memory, pp. 198-246 in E.Tulving and W. Donaldson (eds.) Organization of Memory. New York: Academic Press.

Smith, E. E., E.J. Shoben, & L.J. Rips (1974) Structure and process in semantic memory: a featural model for semantic decision. Psych. Rev. 81: 214-241.

CHILDREN'S PERCEPTION OF EMOTION:
THE INFLUENCE OF LANGUAGE IN A MODIFIED CROSS-OVER DESIGN

B. J. Starr and A. Razafharilala

Howard University, Washington

The ability of children to accurately perceive or infer the emotional reactions of others has been of theoretical and empirical interest for some time. Piaget and others (e.g., Dymond, Hughes, and Raabe, 1952) note that empathic ability increases with age. Piaget's notions, which are nearly paradigmatic for many researchers, suggest that children's emotional perceptions are too egocentric to accurately empathize prior to age seven. Egocentrism refers to the inability to perceive the world from another's perspective.

Grove and Keating (1979) define empathy in terms of the ability to know about or understand the feelings of another without any necessary concomitant affective state in the observer. The subtle definitional differences may go some distance toward explaining conflicting interpretations of research findings. The Piagetian approach implies that identification with the other may be necessary for an accurate empathic response. There is no such inherent assumption in the Grove and Keating definition. Thus, a child may accurately perceive an emotional reaction simply on the basis of how s/he feels in that situation. This would qualify as an empathic response under the Grove and Keating definition but not under the Piagetian. In any case, the subtle differences alluded to here are rarely separated experimentally.

Empirical findings are equally conflicting. Results of studies by Burns and Cavey (1957) and Flapan (1968) generally support Piaget's stance. Younger children give significantly more egocentric responses than older ones. Borke (1971) and Green (1977), on the other hand, both find evidence for empathy in younger children. Chandler and

Greenspan (1972) suggested that the findings of the Borke (1971) study were due to the participants' projection of their own feelings. Those authors also conclude, on the basis of their own study, that the ability to adopt a different perspective arrives relatively late developmentally. Green (1977) did, however, find data supporting the notion that preoperational children were able to understand the causes of emotion in others.

Perception of emotion in a cross-cultural context can be an immensely complex endeavor. Although there seems to be strong evidence bolstering the Darwinian position that the facial expression of many emotions is innate and universal (Izard, 1980), the studies reviewed here do not involve the assessment of facial expression. Rather, more complex stimuli involving verbal descriptions of interpersonal situations are evaluated. Cultures do vary on socialization with regard to emotion and these variations are reflected in measures related to empathy ability (Borke, 1972; McCluskey, 1974). Moreover, there are findings which indicate cultural differences in attitudes toward various emotions (Izard, 1971).

Language is a major aspect of culture. It forms a primary vehicle for socialization and enculturation practices and often reflects features of the unique adaption of human beings and their cultures to their particular environment. Recent research shows clearly that language mediates interpersonal distancing (Sussman and Rosenfeld, 1982). In addition, it also mediates other expressive, emotion-related behavior not reported in the article (Sussman, Note 1).

Recently, the senior author (Starr, Note 2) offered a modified cross-over design for studying cognitively -mediated behaviors. The design should allow researchers to begin to tease apart the effects of language and the effects of aspects of culture which are less directly influenced by language.

Thus, the purpose of this study was three-fold. First, we wanted to investigate, again, the developmental aspects of empathy. Second, we were interested in the effects of culture on the empathic process. Finally, we sought to field test, at least in part, the modified cross-over design.

Method

The study was conducted in two phases. The purpose of the first phase was to gather data to be used in constructing culturally distinct stimulus materials for Phase II of the investigation. Each phase is described separately below.

93

Chapter 12

Phase I

Subjects. Children from a private French-speaking and a private English-speaking school in the Washington, DC area were used in this phase of the study. At each school 20 children, equally divided as to sex, participated. The French school has a school life and curriculum characterized as typical of France.

Procedure. The children were assembled in a classroom where they informally interacted with the experimenter (the junior author) for about 15 minutes. The experimenter then asked the children three kinds of questions as part of a "game":

1. Tell me, what would an adult person do to you to make you feel happy (sad, angry, afraid)?
2. Tell me, what would a child do to you to make you feel happy (sad, angry, afraid)?
3. Tell me, about something that could happen to make you feel happy (sad, angry, afraid)?

Both groups were tested in their native language in the order specified, each question being asked, in turn, for each of the four target emotions. This procedure had been revealed to be satisfactory in a pilot study with second-grade children. The children were asked to raise their hands when they had an answer. The experimenter then went over to the child and tape recorded his or her response.

Two bilingual graduate students examined the (approximately 400) responses given by each of the two groups. Their task was to isolate any themes that differentiated the two groups for each emotion. These culturally distinct themes were later used to structure the stimulus materials (stories) to be used in Phase II. There was 90% agreement between the two raters in selecting such themes.

No culturally distinct themes emerged for the emotion of anger. Consequently only three emotions (happiness, sadness and fear) were studied in Phase II. The culturally distinct themes were used to structure four stories (two French in origin and two English in origin) for each of the three emotions. The two bilinguals back-translated all of the stories in order to create English-language versions of the French origin stories and French-language versions of the English origin stories. Thus, there were matched sets of 12 stories in both French and English. The few problems that arose during back-translation were resolved after discussion between the bilinguals.

Phase II

Subjects. Students from grades Kindergarten 3, inclusive, aged 4-8, from the schools used in Phase I participated in this phase of the study. The French school yielded 28 boys and 25 girls while the American school had 38 boys and 36 girls who participated. In addition, 8 boys and 10 girls who were native English speakers but attended a public school where the curriculum is taught in French formed a bilingual sample. These children were about 8 years of age. All participating schools can be characterized as being clearly middle class.

Procedure. Children were interviewed individually in a vacant room at their schools during Phase II. A lottery porcedure determined the (random) order of presentation used with each child. A child was read a story and then asked the following two questions:

1. How do you think the child (name of child in story is inserted) feels?
2. Why do you think he or she feels that way?

Responses to the first question were awarded points according to a scoring scheme modified from Green (1977). A child received a score of 4 when he provided the correct answer without prompting. Three points were awarded if the child was able to select the correct emotion from a list following an answer that was generally in the right direction. Thus, for example, if a child indicated that the person in the story felt "good" and selected "happy" from the list, he was awarded three points. Two points were awarded if the child selected the target emotion from the list following an incorrect (or no) answer. One point was awarded for incorrect answers or "I don't know" responses.

Results

Because the validity of our analyses hinged on the accurate depiction of emotional states, additional data were collected from samples of graduate students, French-speaking elementary school children, and English-speaking elementary school children. These data bore on whether or not the target emotion was depicted, in a salient manner, in the stories. Table 1 summarizes the results of the data collection with these samples.

Scanning Table 1 suggests that there are clear problems in depicting fear on the basis of the American-origin stories. Data not presented here suggests that there are also problems with one of the French-origin fear stories. For these reasons, subsequent analyses examined only the data on happiness and sadness.

Data on Bilinguals

Mixed mode analyses of variance with Language of Test (LT) as the between groups factor and Culture of Origin (CO) as the repeated measures factor were applied to the data for happiness and sadness. For happiness, only the Culture of Origin factor proved to be significant ($F = 4.706$; $df = 1,16$; $p = .046$). This result reflected the children's ability to discern happiness better in the stories of American origin ($M = 11.722$) than in those of French origin ($M = 11.167$).

Table 1

Summary of Data Indicating the Adequacy of the Stories in Depicting

the Targeted Emotions (H = Happiness, S = Sadness, F = Fear).

Story[1]	Grad. Students (Rating)[2]	Grad. Students (ID)[3]	French Children (ID)[3]	American Children (ID)[3]
FrH	2.495	13	14	18
AmH	2.56	13	14	17
FrS	3.39	9	13	17
AmS	4.12	8	13	15
FrF	2.745	13	14	13
AmF	5.625	1	3	7
Sample N	8	8	7	9

[1] Fr = French origin, Am = American origin

[2] Ratings were on an eleven-point scale, 1 indicating that the story portrayed the emotion "very much" and 11 indicating "very little".

[3] This column indicates the number of subjects out of 2N who identified the appropriate emotion for each story from a list of eight emotions. Because there were two stories for each target emotion, the maximum number in a column would be 2N.

The data on the sadness variable revealed a significant CO factor ($F = 19.332$; $df = 1,16$; $p<.001$) and a significant LT x CO interaction ($F = 5.304$; $df = 1,16$; $p = .036$). Again, children perceived the emotions in the American stories ($M = 10.722$) better than they did in the French ones ($M = 8.389$). The LT x CO interaction was ordinal and showed that bilingual children tested in French perceived sadness better on the American-origin stories and that this differential was superior to the same differential for the children tested in English.

Data on Monolinguals

Mixed mode analyses of variance were also applied to the happiness and sadness data gathered from monolinguals. For these analyses, CO was a repeated measure factor while LT, Age and Sex were between groups factors. An unweighted means analysis was used.

The analysis of the data on happiness revealed significant main effects for LT ($F = 12.823$; $df = 1,107$; $p .001$), Age ($F = 7.535$; $df = 1,107$; $p <.001$), and CO ($F = 4.596$; $df = 1.107$; $p = .035$). There were also two significant interactions involving Age. These were LT x Age ($F = 2.507$; $df = 4,107$; $p = .047$) and Age x Sex ($F = 3.478$; $df = 4,107$; $p = .011$). The main effect for LT showed that English speakers ($M = 10.686$) were more accurate than French speakers ($M = 9.601$) on the perception of happiness. The age effect revealed a gradual increase in accuracy with age among 4- through 8-year olds. The R for age revealed that age accounts for 16% of the variance in accuracy. The CO effect revealed that stories of American origin ($M = 10.382$) were more accurately perceived than those of French origin ($M = 9.905$).

The LT x Age interaction is accounted for by the fact that English speakers were more accurate in all age groups except among 5-year olds where the performance of the French speakers was superior. The Age x Sex interaction displayed superior performance among younger females (aged 4 and 5) and older males (aged 6, 7, and 8) on the perception of happiness.

When the same type of analysis was applied to the data on sadness, main effects due to LT ($F = 8.043$; $df = 1,107$; $p = .006$), Age ($F = 8.347$; $df = 4,107$ $p < .001$), and Sex ($F = 4.738$; $df = 1,107$; $p = .032$) emerged. The English speakers ($M = 9.405$) perceived sadness more accurately than the French speakers ($M = 8.446$). The gradual increase in accuracy with age accounted for 18% of the variance. Males ($M = 9.293$) also perceived sadness more accurately than females ($M = 8.557$).

Several interactions were also statistically

97

significant in the analysis of sadness data. The LT x Age interaction (F = 2.712; df = 4,107; p = .032) showed English speakers to be more accurate at all age levels except among 8-year-olds where the French speakers were superior. An important LT x CO interaction (F = 14.816; df = 1,107; p < .001) was also found. This confirmed a hypothesis of the investigators in that French speakers perceived sadness more accurately in stories structured from the French and English speakers perceived more accurately in stories from American children's repsonses. This cross-over interaction had been anticipated.

An Age x CO interaction (F = 2.640; df = 4,107; p = .038) resulted from the finding that 6- and 7-year olds were more accurate on stories from the American culture whereas other age groups performed better on the French-origin stories. A triple interaction was also found to be significant. The LT x Sex x CO interaction (F = 4.191; df = 4,107; p = .044) indicated a uniformly greater accuracy for the English-speaking males and the presence of a disordinal (cross-over) interaction depending on CO for females. Thus, among females (unlike the males) French-speakers were more accurate on French-origin stories. Therefore, our initial anticipated cross-over was, in truth, due to the performance of the females.

Discussion

Although age and sex effects were not the primary thrust of this study, such effects were found. The age effects were present for both emotions analyzed here (happiness and sadness). The results confirm the general finding (e.g., Burns & Cavey, 1957; Flapan, 1968; Chandler and Greenspan, 1972; Green, 1977) of a developmental effect for empathy. The sex effect emerged only for sadness with males perceiving it more accurately. This finding is somewhat puzzling.

More germane to this study were the tests of the CO and LT factors. Culture of Origin was a significant effect in both analyses with bilinguals and with the happiness data for monolinguals. In all three cases, stories of American origin were accurately perceived. This is a tantalizing finding in light of the data summarized in Table 1. These data, it will be recalled, bear on concensus indices of the degree to which the stories depict the target emotion. The data are interesting in that they indicate that, if any effect of story structure is discernible, that effect would bias against these findings. Thus, although the effect is very likely a real one, several alternative explanations suggest themselves. More obvious (and probably correct) is the notion that the children are all resident in the U.S. culture and are therefore quite sensitive to the cultural milieu. Moreover,

98

two of the positive results were obtained with the
bilinguals who are virtually uniform in the fact that they
are U.S.-born and raised. Further information on this
alternative would emerge by using the full modification of
the cross-over design suggested by the senior author
(Starr, Note 2). Another explanation deals with the
cultural origin of the bilinguals who structured the
stories. Neither of them is likely to share a great deal in
common (other than language) with either the culture
represented by the French school or the American
bilinguals. Thus, the French stories, while they might be
technically accurate (i.e., in depicting emotion), might
contain distractors. This refers to a similar problem that
exists when one attempts to translate materials for use in
other cultures, the problem of readability as opposed to
technical accuracy (Starr & Wilson, 1977).

Among monolinguals, English speakers were more
accurate than French speakers. This may be due to a
combination of factors. The English speakers would be more
familiar (due to cultural origin) with the American-origin
stories and less affected by distractors in the
French-origin stories.

These findings, in addition to the finding of several
interesting LT & CO interactions, which we cannot discuss
here due to time constraints, suggest the usefulness of the
approach in this modification of the basic cross-over
design.

The two LT x CO interactions do, however, merit
discussion. Among bilinguals, children perceived sadness
better on the American-origin stories, but the greater
accuracy on the the American-origin stories was more
pronounced among children tested in French. This is a
direct disconfirmation of one of our hypotheses. One
possible explanation might be that the testing of these
(American) children in French made salient both cultural
factors in all stories and any distractors present in the
French stories. Also, these children probably have a
somewhat greater familiarity with French-Canadian as
opposed to French culture.

The LT x CO interaction for sadness among the
monolinguals was as predicted. French speakers perceived
sadness more accurately in the French-origin stories and
English-speakers perceived this emotion better in the
American-origin stories. The weight of this particular
finding is carried by the females in the story as shown by
the LT x CO x Sex triple interaction. In addition, males
perceived sadness more accurately, overall. Thus, the
findings are complex and suggest the utility of further
research employing the full design put forth by Starr (Note
2).

In sum, the first and third purposes of this research were fulfilled. The developmental trend for empathy, was confirmed and the suggested design, although only partially implemented, indicated fruitfulness via several suggestive findings. The second purpose, to assess the effect of cultural factors on empathy, awaits further research while at the same time indicating that the answers may be quite complex.

NOTES

1. Sussman, N.M. Personal Communication, June 19, 1982.

2. Starr, B.J. A modified cross-over design to study cognitively mediated behavior. Paper presented at the 11th Annual Meeting of the Society for Cross-Cultural Research, Minneapolis, February, 1982.

REFERENCES

Borke, H. Interpersonal perception of young children: Egocentrism of empathy? Developmental Psychology, 1971, 5, 263-269.

Borke, H. Chandler and Greenspan's "Ersatz Egocentrism": A rejoinder. Developmental Psychology, 1972, 7 107-109.

Burns, N & Cavey, L. Age differences in empathic ability among children. Canadian Journal of Psychology, 1957, 11, 227-230

Chandler, M. & Greenspan, S. Ersatz egocentrism. Developmental Psychology, 1972, 7 104-106.

Dymond, R.F., Hughes, A. S., & Raabe, V.L. Measurable changes in empathy with age. Journal of Consulting Psychology, 1952, 16, 202-206.

Flapan, D. Children's understanding of social interaction: New York: Teachers College, Columbia University Press, 1968.

Green, S.K. Causal attribution of emotion in kindergarten children. Developmental Psychology, 1977, 13, 533-534.

ove, F.L. & Keating, D.P. Empathic role-taking precursors. Developmental Psychology, 1979, 15, 594-600.

:ard, C.E. The face of emotion. New York: Appleton-Century-Crofts, 1971.

:ard, C.E. Cross-cultural perspectives on emotion and emotion communication. In H.C. Triandis & W. Lonner (Eds.). Handbook of Cross-cultural Psychology, vol. 3. Basic Processes. Boston: Allyn and Bacon, 1980.

:Cluskey, K.W. Cross-cultural differences in the perception of the emotional content of speech: A study of the development of sensitivity in Canadian and Mexican children. Journal of Cross-cultural Psychology, 1974, 11, 551-555.

tarr, B.J. & Wilson, S.F. Some epistemological and methodological issues in the design of cross-cultural research. In B.J. Starr (Ed.), Cross-cultural empirical research: Investigative strategies. Topics in Culture Learning, 1977, 5 (Pt. 2): 125-135.

ussman, N.M. & Rosenfeld, H.M. Influence of culture, language, and sex on conversational distance. Journal of Personality and Social Psychology, 1982, 42, 66-74.

BLACK SOUTH AFRICANS' REACTION TO WHITE ACCENTS

G. A. Tyson and M. C. Mzinyati

University of Witwatersrand, Johannesburg

Inherent in any conflict situation are attitudes relating to the other group and it seems highly probable that if we are to successfully deal with conflict we need to know these attitudes.

The major area of conflict in South Africa is between peoples of different racial groups and yet relatively little is known about racial attitudes in this country even though, as Mann (1971) points out, South Africa is, from a coldly scientific point of view, very nearly the perfect laboratory in its potential for the study of race attitudes" (p.51). Unfortunately this potential has not been realized. Certainly some studies have been carried out but these are often simplistic in terms of their design and analysis, and sometimes even in the interpretation of their results. Furthermore, most of these studies have used White university students as subjects. Relatively little is known about the racial attitudes of Blacks and more specifically about their attitudes towards Whites. The few studies which have been carried out on Black attitudes to Whites have tended to indicate that Blacks have far more positive attitudes towards English speaking South Africans than towards Afrikaans speaking South Africans (Bloom, 1960; Brett & Morse, 1975; Edelstein, 1972; MacCrone, 1947; and Vorster & Proctor, 1976), and according to Brett and Morse (1975) this difference is mediated by alleged kindness i.e. English speaking South Africans are seen as kinder.

Despite this apparent consistency amongst these findings, care must be taken in interpreting them and more especially in trying to apply them to the present. There are two reasons for this. First, as Biesheuvel (1955), Edelstein (1972), and MacCrone (1947) have all pointed out, the study of Black attitudes is sometimes complicated by

the Blacks' strong, deep-rooted suspicions of what motives
are prompting such investigations and such suspicions could
easily lead to unreliable results. Secondly, in recent
years it appears that Blacks' attitudes have undergone
drastic changes as is manifested in the emergence of the
Black militant movements and the voices of the militant
Black leaders.

Consequently, the aim of the present study was to
obtain an indication of the attitudes of Black Sowetonians
to the two major White groups in South Africa. However, in
view of what was said earlier about the contamination
effects of suspicion, we considered that the use of a
direct attitude measure would be inadvisable. We thus
decided to use response to accent as an indirect measure of
attitude as it has frequently been shown that stereotypes
and evaluations of the speaker's group are elicited in
response to language stimuli (Lambert et al., 1960;
Anisfeld et al., 1962). Such a technique has in fact been
used successfully in S.A. before by Vorster & Proctor
(1976). They played eight tape-recorded passages -- four in
English and four in Afrikaans -- to Black university
students, who were required to rate the speaker and his job
status. The subjects were not aware that the eight
performances that they heard came from only four people,
each of whom spoke in both English and Afrikaans, this
being done to control for the effect of other linguistic
factors. The results of this study showed a bias towards
English.

However, Vorster & Proctor's study suffers from the
same defect that is apparent in almost all the "matched
guise" experiments, viz., that they are rather simplistic
and artificial and hence very susceptible to the effects of
demand characteristics.

In order to overcome this problem in the present
study, a more sophisticated, and hopefully less artificial,
technique was developed. Essentially this required the
subject to respond to a film, which had a spoken commentary
and the accent of the voice speaking the commentary was
varied. Exact details of the method will be given later.

METHOD

Subjects

Over 700 students at 14 night schools in Soweto
participated in the experiment. These night schools were
used in the study because their student bodies comprised
both young and old people and hence the attitudes of
different age-groups could be compared. About 80% of the
subjects were people who were employed in the nearby
Johannesburg industrial area while the remaining 20% were

103

students who dropped out of school after the 1976 Soweto riots. The medium of instruction at all the schools was English.

The level of education of the volunteers varied from standard one to standard ten. However, to control for the possible effects of education, only the data from students in standard seven or higher were used in the present study. This resulted in a sample of 605 students - 214 males and 391 females. The ages of the subjects ranged between 13 and 62 with the mean of 24,1 (S.D. = 6,89).

Apparatus

(a) The Film

A film on family planning which was obtained from the Family Planning Association of Rhodesia was used in the present experiment.

The film has a spoken commentary and tells, very simply, the story of two girls - Mary and Janet - who grew up together in the same township in Rhodesia and attended the same school. Both had a lively intelligence and planned to be teachers when they grew up. However, Mary came from a small family and had only two brothers. Her parents decided to plan their family in accordance with their income. On the other hand, Janet was one of nine children. Her parents did not think about planning their family. The film shows how, as a result of the small family, Mary's parents were able to take a real interest in her and help fulfill her ambitions, whereas Janet, as a result of her unstable family background, dropped out of school and became an unmarried mother.

For this experiment, four copies of the film were made. Each of these copies had the same English commentary except for the fact the each commentary was spoken with a different accent. The four accents used were an English-speaking South African accent, an Afrikaans accent, an African accent and an American accent. Ideally, all four commentaries should have been made by the same person to control for paralinguistic cues, but no person capable of doing this could be found. Hence a black male university graduate spoke the African accent commentary and a white male professional actor made the other three commentaries.

(b) The Questionnaire

The questionnaire comprised four major areas. The first section dealt with biographical questions e.g. age, sex, education, etc. The second section contained twelve questions which were designed to assess the subjects' attitudes toward family planning and also to assess whether they had understood the film and commentary. In the third and fourth sections, the semantic differential technique was used to rate the film and the subjects' attitudes tpwards the commentator. These adjective pairs were arranged in such a way as to avoid response set. The final question asked the subjects to indicate the commentator's ethnic group.

Procedure

The principals and teachers in the night schools were approached beforehand by the investigator about the project and were asked to co-operate. The teachers were requested to tell the students that they were to see a short educational film.

The investigator at the testing session, who was black, introduced himself as coming from the School of Psychology, University of Witwatersrand. The subjects were told that they were to see a short film of about 10 minutes. They were asked to pay attention to the film as they would be required thereafter to fill in questionnaires. The subjects were assured that their replies would be anonymous. One of the films was then shown after which the subjects filled in the questionnaires. Each subject saw only one version of the film.

Statistical Design

In the present study, multiple regression analysis was used to explore the nature of the relationships between the independent and dependent variables. Multiple regression embraces, in general, analysis of variance but is more flexible due to the fact that correlations between independent variables pose no special problem for it, and it is designed to allow for this. Thus it is ideally suited to the present study.

In all the analyses the independent variables were accent (in the form of dummy variables), sex, age and all their interactions, and they were entered into the equation in that order. In order to assess the relative importance of the predictor variables, the increase in explained variance method suggested by Kerlinger and Pedhazur (1973) was used.

RESULTS

Factor Analysis of the Ratings of the Film.

Inspection of the data indicated that there was a certain consistency in the subjects' ratings of the film on the semantic differential. In order to establish the exact nature of this consistency, a factor analsyis of these

ratings was performed. A principle factoring method was
used to extract the initial factors and it produced two
factors, the first of which accounted for approximately 74%
of the variance and the second the remaining 26%. The two
factors were clearly defined, the first consisting of the
adjectives Good, Enjoyable and Interesting and the second
consisting of the adjectives Unrealistic, Political and
Worthless. The interpretation of these factors is not
obvious but it would seem that factor 1 involves
entertainment value whereas factor 2 is more concerned with
practical value.

Factor scores based upon this factor analysis were
generated for use in further analysis.

Factor Analysis of the Rating of the Commentator

As was the case with the ratings of the film, there
appeared to be a certain degree of consistency in the
ratings of the commentator on the 14 rating scales. Thus a
factor analysis was also performed on this data and only
one main factor emerged accounting for approximately 89% of
the variance. This factor was clearly an evaluative factor.

Multiple Regression Analysis

1. Entertainment Value

The only independent variable which significantly
increased the explained variance was sex, and this was due
to the fact that females rated the film more favourably
than males (M = -0,1226, SD = 0,7697 vs. M = 0,2533, SD =
0,9641).

2. Practical Value

In this analysis only age contributed significantly to
the explained variance. This was due to the fact that there
was a tendency for the perceived practical value to
increase as age did (r = 0,182).

3. Rating of commentator

Here too age was found to contribute significantly to
the explained variance, but more importantly a significant
interaction between age and sex was found. This interaction
is shown in Figure 1 and it can be seen that for males age
did not affect the rating of the commentator (r = 0,01),
whereas for females there was a tendency for the
commentator to be evaluated more favourably with increasing
age (r = 0,19).

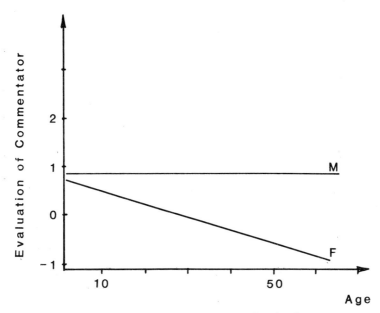

Figure 1 - Interaction of Age by Sex

Ratings of Commentary

The subjects were asked three questions regarding the commentary. Although these questions were not related directly to the aims of this study, the responses to them were analysed in order to provide additional information to assist with the interpretation of results. The same independent variable and procedure of stepwise regression used in the previous analysis were used.

Significant group differences were found in response to all three questions. The responses to the question, "Could you understand the commentary?" are shown in Table 1 and it can be seen that while the level of understanding was generally high, the understanding of the African accented commentary was highest.

A similar pattern of results was obtained in response to the question "Did the commentator speak too quickly?" (Table 2). Here it can be seen that almost 40% of the subjects in the Afrikaans, English and American accent groups thought that the commentator spoke too quickly, whereas only 17% of the African accent group thought that the commentator spoke too quickly.

107

TABLE 1

Responses to the Question 'Did you understand the Commentary ?'

Group

	African	Afrikaans	English	American
Yes	124 (91,9%)	126 (78,8%)	113 (75,8%)	111 (76,0%)
No	11 (8,1%)	34 (21,3%)	36 (24,2%)	35 (24,0%)

In response to the final question which concerned the evaluation of the commentary, over 82% of all the Ss rated the commentary favourably, but the African accented commentary was rated more favourably than the other three commentaries (Table 3).

The Perceived Accent

The results reported above indicate that, contrary to expectation, accent has no effect on the ratings of either the film or the commentator which implies that racial attitudes did not influence the subjects' perception of either the commentator or the film. However, it is possible that this finding is due to the fact that the subjects did not recognise the accent. This interpretation is supported by an inspection of the answers to the final question on the questionnaire in which the subjects were asked to indicate to which group the commentator belonged (Table 4).

It can be seen from the Table that over half of the subjects thought that the commentator was African and relatively few perceived the commentator to be Afrikaans or American.

As the stereotype elicited by an accent may depend on the group membership label assigned to the accent rather than the actual group membership, the analyses performed above on the ratings of the film and the commentator were repeated using perceived group membership rather than the actual group membership of the commentator as an independent variable. All the other independent variables remained the same. The same procedure of stepwise regression as used in the previous regression equation was used to enter the independent variables in the following regressions.

TABLE 2

Responses to the Question 'Did the Commentator Speak too Quickly ?'

| | Group | | | |
	African	Afrikaans	English	American
Yes	23 (17,2%)	60 (37,3%)	55 (37,2%)	59 (39,9%)
No	111 (82,8%)	101 (62,7%)	93 (52,8%)	89 (60,1%)

TABLE 3

Responses to the Question 'On Goodness of Commentary'

| | Group | | | |
	African	Afrikaans	English	American
Good	124 (93,2%)	126 (82,9%)	105 (73,9%)	120 (81,6%)
Bad	9 (6,8%)	26 (17,1%)	37 (26,1%)	27 (18,4%)

TABLE 4

Perceived Group Membership of Commentator

Group	Actual Group	Perceived Group
African	140	328
Afrikaans	164	33
English	151	153
American	150	52
Did not answer	-	44
Total		610

The results of these analyses were almost identical to those already reported. There were only 2 major differences. The first was that in the rating of the entertainment value of the film there was a significant interaction between accent and sex. This interaction is shown in Figure 2 and it seems that, in general, females tended to rate the film favourably when the perceived group membership of the commentator was African, English or Afrikaans, but it was rated unfavourably for the American commentary. In all groups, however, females rated the film more highly than males. The second major difference was that there were no significant differences between the groups when evaluating the commentary.

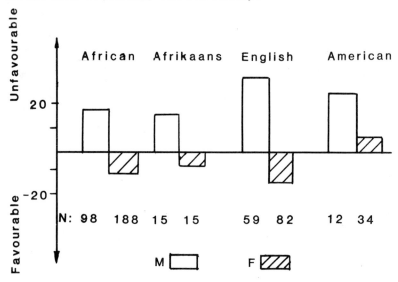

Figure 2 - Interaction of Accent by Sex

DISCUSSION

Overall, the results suggest that the subjects' perception of the commentator's group membership did not really influence their ratings of the film or the commentator, which was contrary to our expectations and the existing literature.

The simplest explanation is of course that the Ss do not evaluate the four groups differently, i.e. they have the same relatively positive attitude towards each group. This however does not seem likely.

A more likely explanation for the results is that the impact of the film or commentary outweighed the effect of the source. In most of the matched guise experiments, one finds that in addition to the possible existence of demand characteristics the content of the message has been rather trivial and hence unlikely to nullify the effects of the speakers' linguistic characteristics. The same probably holds for the experiments done on source effects on attitude change.

While the accent of the commentator did not affect the rating of the film or the commentator, there were however significant differences between the groups on the evaluation of the commentary. It appears that most subjects rated the commentary fairly favourably but the African accented commentary was rated more highly than the other three commentaries. This difference may have been due to the subjects' ability to understand the commentary, for the African accented commentary was rated as easier to understand than the other three commentaries. This in turn may have been due to the speed at which the commentator spoke, for group differences also appeared in response to the question, "Did the commentator speak too quickly?" The commentator in the three white accented commentaries was rated by the subjects as speaking too quickly, which would hamper understanding, whereas only a few rated the African accented commentator as speaking too quickly.

Another purpose of the study was to investigate how young and old Blacks in South Africa differ in their reaction to English- and Afrikaans-speaking South Africans. It was hypothesized in this study that young Blacks would differ from older Blacks in their reactions to the speakers, as young Blacks seem to be more politically conscious, demanding an immediate change in South Africa, whereas older Blacks are conservative about the current state of affairs.

However, the results did not support this hypothesis, that age would interact with accent, but they did show that age did affect the subjects' general response to the film and commentator. Age was highly significant on the ratings of both the practical value of the film and the commentator. This effect was due to the fact that as the subjects' age increased, the tendency was to rate the film and commentator more highly. This suggests that older people saw the film as having more practical value – perhaps because they are more experienced in rearing children and they know the consequences of having a big unplanned family unlike younger people who are not so experienced. This in turn probably caused them to view the commentator in a more favourable light, although as the age by sex interaction shows, this was only the case for female subjects.

The results of this study also indicated that the subjects' sex affects the rating of the film's entertainment value, with females showing greater favourability towards the film than males, as it has been previously pointed out. There was no sex effect on the rating of the practical value of the film or the commentator. The fact that the information involved in the film (family planning) was more familiar and more relevant to females than males might have influenced them to rate the film more favourably. It is also possible that the sex effect was due to the fact that the vocal stimulus was a male voice and this may have evoked a feeling of effeminity for male listeners (Giles, 1970). In addition, talking and teaching about family planning to males may be counter to the customs in certain communities, in which in order for a person to prove his real masculinity he must be able to produce many children.

To conclude, the results of the present study would suggest that when the content of a message is perceived to be important, then the source of that message becomes less important.

REFERENCES

Anisfeld, M., Bogo, N., & Lambert, W.E. Evaluational reactions to accented English speech. Journal of Abnormal and Social Psychology, 65, 223-231, 1962.

Biesheuvel, S. The measurement of African attitudes towards European ethical concepts, customs, laws and the administration of justice. Journal of the National Institute for Personnel Research, 6, 5-17, 1955.

Bloom. L. Self concept and social status in South Africa. Journal of Social Psychology, 51, 103-112, 1960.

Brett, E.A. & Morse, S.J. A study of the attitudes of middle class Africans. In S. J. Morse and C. Orpen (eds.) Contemporary South Africa: Social Psychological Perspectives, Johannesburg: Juta and Company Ltd., 1975.

Edelstein, M.L. What do young Africans think? An attitude survey of urban African matric pupils in Soweto with special reference to stereotyping and social distance; a sociological study. Johannesburg: South African Institute of Race Relations, 1972.

Giles, H. Evaluation reactions to accents. Educational Review, 22, 211-227, 1970. Kerlinger, F.N & Pedhazur, E.J. Multiple regression in behavioural research. New York: Holt, Rinehart and Winston, 1973.

Lambert, W.E., Hodgson, R.C., Gardner, R.C. & Fillenbaum, S. Evaluational reactions to spoken languages. Journal of Abnormal and Social Pscyhology, 60: 1, 44-51, 1960.

MacCrone, I.D. Reaction of domination in a colour-caste society: A preliminary study of the race attitudes of a dominated group. Journal of Social Psychology, 26, 69-98, 1947.

Mann, J.W. Attitudes toward ethnic groups. In Adam, H. (ed.): South Africa: Sociological Perspectives. London: Oxford University Press, 1971.

Vorster, J. & Proctor, L. Black attitudes to "White" languages in South Africa: a pilot study. Journal of Psychology, 92, 103-108, 1976.

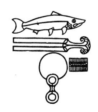

AN EXAMINATION OF CONSERVATION PERFORMANCE BY CHILDREN FROM CONTRASTING SOCIAL AND CULTURAL BACKGROUNDS

M. R. Chung

University of Edinburgh

This study concerns some problems of the interpretation of cognitive ability in relation to contrasting social and cultural contexts and to child language.

There has been increasing interest in wider applications of Piagetian theory and this is due to the interdisciplinary nature of the theory: biological analogy in cognitive development, psychological aspect of child development, nature of knowledge and its development, and related disciplines. Researchers specializing in these disciplines have studied the theory which has consequently created dissentient opinions to as well as agreement with Piaget.

This enquiry focuses on an aspect of child psychology, with data collected from cross-cultural observations. It is in a way controversial by reason of Piaget's insufficient attention firstly to the children's real ability and secondly to child language.

Piaget has been considered as an epistemologist and not a developmental psychologist, and his theory is epistemological. Why then should psychologists bother about his theory? It has been suggested that he takes as much of child development as he needs for epistemological theory, which is so far legitimate, but that he does not give sufficient attention to the nature of children's language and to the social and cultural contexts in which the child's mental experience is based. Elliot and Donaldson (1982) indicate the weakness of Piaget's theory with regard to child language and argue that "Piaget's views of language appear to be largely offshoots of his epistemological position. That is, he does not seem to ask

what is known about language and then see what this can
contribute to epistemology".

In the Piagetian theory, successes and failures in
solving conservation tasks of liquid, substance, etc. are,
for example, taken as confirmation of the way in which a
child gradually acquires the ability to think logically. In
his experimental paradigm, cognitive ability is seen as
"logico-mathematical" ability and forms the basis of
scientific knowledge; this is because scientific knowledge
has to be logico-mathematical. In the Piagetian theoretical
framework it is difficult to explain children's diverse
abilities, as they appear in their everyday life in
different ethnic groups. Regardless of cultural background
and different usages of language between various cultural
groups in the world, Piaget suggests the use of the same
questions (or directly translated tasks) to assess the
cognitive ability of all children. Such universal
consideration becomes particularly problematic when
considering the intellectual skills displayed by people in
non-Western cultures.

A concern with the influence of social context has
been discussed in the work of Dasen (1972). He carried out
an experiment wih Aborigines in Australia to assess the
relative development between logico-mathematical operations
and their spatial operations. The hypothesis was that
because Aborigines depend traditionally on hunting in
groups, travelling long distances in a barren environment,
they would develop spatial operations earlier than
logico-mathematical operations. He did find that the
Aboriginal children acquired spatial concepts earlier than
logico-mathematical concepts, compared with a control group
of European children who acquired logico-mathematical
concepts earlier than spatial concepts. In conclusion,
Dasen suggested that environmental factors can influence
not only the rate of development, but also the "homogeneity
of the operational structures within each stage". Cole,
Gay, Glick and Sharp (1971) have also shown how contextual
factors are influential in general performance. They
compared the performance of Kpelle rice farmers from
Liberia with American University students in standard
reasoning tasks. While the performance of the university
students was as good as anticipated, that of the farmers
was far worse. Not satisfied that the farmers' test
performance was representative of their real ability, the
authors used anthropological techniques in an attempt to
discover the kinds of reeasoning used in the daily life of
the Kpelle. On the basis of their observations, they were
able to rework the tests using more familiar materials and
situations. When the tasks involved estimating of
quantities of rice, the performance of the Kpelle farmers
improved dramatically whereas that of the American students
declined. They, therefore, suggested an observational

methodology which examines the role of situations.

The Experiment

This enquiry is to examine how young Korean and British children from various social and educational backgrounds express their conservation ability. It attempts to find answers to a series of questions:

1. Is the way of expressing the possession of the conservation principle consistent among young children from different social and cultural groups?

2. Is the children's language sufficiently consistent for adults to be able to judge adequately their ability to reason?

3. Is the performance level in solving conservation tasks influenced by familiarity?

Samples

In selecting samples, the social and educational backgrounds of children were taken into account. There was a total of 410 children who were divided into nine groups. However, in this paper there are four groups chosen for discussion. The age range of the British and Korean children was from five to nine years. There were 50 children in each sample consisting of ten in each age group. Boys and girls were evenly balanced in number.

Sample-1 comprises Korean children residing temporarily in Britain. Their parents are professionals or diplomats who have lived in Seoul where the life style and education are very much Westernized. These children have a great deal of opportunity to utilize what they learn from school in everyday life situations by using the metric system at home, shopping in modern supermarkets, watching television etc.

Sample-2 comprises Korean children attending a state school in a remote rural area. The parents of the children were mainly engaged in farming and fishing on a small scale. Television is rarely available. These children, however, use the same textbooks as city children since the Korean Ministry of Education provides them to all primary schools in the country. In the real life situation they have hardly any opportunity to make use of what they learn at school. They learn mathematical measurements in the class, but use traditional measurements in real life situations, for example, the size of a farm field is measured by the number of bags of rice produced, not in hectares.

Sample-3 comprises British children attending an independent school where substantial fees are paid. These children have been educated in a privileged school environment and have grown up in upper-middle-class families in Britain.

Sample-4 comprises British children attending a state school in a rural area. In rural areas in Britain, the parents who are farm workers usually have a lower standard of pay than the industrial workers and their children may have a poorer intellectual environment compared to the middle class children, but they have access to television and community centres where they can enjoy out-of-school activities.

Tests used

The experimental procedure proposed here is to test what and how young children think logically, and also to generate new hypotheses, if necessary, to substantiate the initial results. Therefore, the experimental design and the tests used and the testing procedures were different from those of Piaget and many other researchers of Piagetian studies. The tests used in this study are described in the following section.

1. Standard Piagetian Test

Conservation of liquid

Procedure: The same amount of juice was initially prepared in beaker A-1 and beaker A-2. The investigator poured a little juice from one beaker to the other so that the child was presented with uneven amounts of the juice before the experiment started. As soon as the child sat down in front of the desk where the two beakers of juice were on display, s/he was asked to describe the amount of orange juice and to make them equal in both beakers. Any child who could not discern the difference was excluded from the experiment. After this preliminary session, juice from beaker A-1 was poured into taller beaker B and then the child was asked to compare the relative amount of juice in A2 and B.

Question: Which glass has more juice in it? Or is there the same amount of juice in A-2 and B? (or vice versa) Why do you think so?

The juice was poured back into beaker A-1 from beaker B. From beaker A-2, the juice was poured into beaker C-1 and beaker C-2 in equal amounts. The child was then asked to compare the amounts of juice in beaker A-1 and beaker C-1 and C-2 combined.

Question: Is there the same amount of juice in glass A-1 as is in glasses C-1 and C-2 combined? Or which, this or those two have more juice? Why do you think so?

Conservation of substance

Procedure: The child was presented with two pieces of the same amount of plasticine, P-1 and P-2, and assured by the investigator on each occasion that there was actually the same amount of plasticine in both pieces. The child was asked to make a sausage with plasticine P-1 and a ball with plasticine P-2. The child was then asked to determine whether there was the same quantity of plasticine in the sausage and the ball.

Question: Which one has more plasticine, or is there the same amount in the ball and the sausage? Why do you think so?

The altered forms of the ball and sausage of plasticine were returned to their original shapes. The child was asked to make two balls with plasticine P-1 and a thin square piece of blanket with P-2. The child was asked to compare the amount of plasticine in the blanket and the two balls.

Question: Is there the same amount of plasticine in the blanket and the two balls combined, or which one has more? Why do you think so?

Conservation of discontinuous quantity

Procedure: There were two packets of the same amount of sweets, S-1 and S-2. The sweets in packet S-1 were transferred to a wider glass A-1 and the sweets in packet S-2 were transferred to a taller glass B. The child was asked to determine whether there was the same amount of sweets in the taller or wider glasses.

Question: Which glass has more sweets in it, or is there the same amount in them? Why do you think so?

The sweets in glass B were returned to glass A-2 and the child was assured that the amount of sweets in both glasses was the same. The sweets from A-1 were transferred to two smaller glasses, C-1 and C-2, in equal amounts by counting them one by one. After doing this, the child was asked to determine whether there was the same amount of sweets in glass A-2 and glass C-1 and C-2 combined.

Question: Is there the same amount of sweets in this or those together, or which glass has more sweets? Why do you think so?

2. The Revised Test

The term "Revised Test" was used for the revised

version of the standard Piagetian Test (Piaget, 1952). As a result of observing children, it was noticed that the terms "more" or "less" in questions seem vague to children and confuse them. Therefore the Revised Test was designed to prevent children from misunderstanding the language used in the question forms and also the purport of the questions. It also aimed to question the child's point of view, not by imposing the adults' intention on the child answering the question.

Conservation of liquid, substance and discontinuous quantity

The tasks in the Revised Test were exactly the same as they were in the standard Piagetian Test. However, three toy animals (a teddy bear, a rabbit, and a dog) were introduced, one of which was credited with the right to answer. The child had to point to the animal which s/he believed to have made the correct response. We may call it, "Let us find out situation" and the procedure was as follows.

The child was presented with three toy animals, such as a Teddy Bear, who had a taller beaker B, a Rabbit who had a wider beaker A-2, and a Dog who had nothing. The experimenter said, "These three animals are going to drink orange juice, and before drinking they had a chat. The Teddy Bear said, "I have more juice than the Rabbit", the Rabbit said, "I have more juice than the Teddy Bear", and the Dog said, "You both have the same amount of juice". The animal who answered correctly was varied by the investigator.

Question: Which animal's answer is correct? Why?

3. The New Test

The children from a remote rural area (sample-2) seemed to be totally confused by the presentation of the Standard Piagetian experiment and their consequent performance was extremely poor. It is also observed that these children have mathematical conceptual experience, but an experience different from that of the city children, as described earlier. The investigator, therefore, sought for tasks which were part of their everyday experience. In order to make tasks meaningful, it was necessary to find conceptually familiar tasks for them. In this case, tasks related to outdoor activities were considered to be more appropriate because the children actually help their parents with farm work and play on the beach or in the fields. Therefore the tasks incorporating children's familiar activities, and leading gradually to understanding the principle of conservation, were devised by the present investigator and are called "New Test".

Conservation of liquid

The children were taken to a well. The following water containers were available: Daeya is a mobile washing basin, hamjipak is used for washing vegetables and is wider than a bucket which is used to convey water.

Procedure: The investigator said, "Let us give the calves their water. They are both young calves, therefore we must not forget to provide each of them with the same amount of water". The child was helped in drawing water from the well. The child was then asked to pour one daeya-ful of water into hamjipak A-1 and two daeya-fuls of water into the identical hamjipak A-2. Similarly, one daeya-ful of water was poured into tall bucket B-1 and two daeya-fuls into the identical bucket, B-2.

It was noted here that the water containers and drinking bowls were not transparent so that the level of water in each container has to be guaged from the top. In this situation the use of "daeya" as a measuring unit was useful to make clear to the child the equivalent amount used in each transfer.

Procedure: The investigator said, "Please give the calves their water now. Don't forget to give the same amount of water to each calf". The child was expected to choose a correct water container. The child was then asked to determine whether both calves had the same amount of water.

Question: Do both calves have the same amount of water to drink or not? Why?
(One drinking bowl is smaller than the other so that the smaller bowl is fuller than the other.)

Conservation of substance

Children were taken to a beach nearby where clay and shells were to be found. Two lumps of the same amount of clay were prepared by the children.

Procedure: The investigator said, "Use the clay in front of you and make two houses. We need to build a small house and a big house but each house has to be made from the same amount of clay". Each child used his hands to shape a bowl of clay, holding it inverted, following which he moulded the clay on the back of one hand. For a small house he made a small empty space with his hand, and for a big house the space became bigger and the clay walls thinner.

Question: Do both houses have the same amount of clay in

121

them or the bigger house has more clay? Why?

Conservation of discontinuous quantity

The children collected shells from the beach and divided them into two equal piles by counting them by means of one to one correspondence.

Procedure: The investigator poured one pile by hand into a wider glass A and another identical pile of shells into a taller glass B. While pouring shells into the tall glass B, the investigator dropped some shells and said, "I dropped some shells". Therefore in glass B, there were fewer shells than in glass A although the level of shells in glass B was higher than in glass A.

Question: Of the shells in glass A and glass B, which will make the longer necklace? Why?

Summary of the New Test

It is emphasized here that the New Test is not equivalent to the Standard Piagetian Test in terms of the normative level of knowledge required by the technically advanced Western World. One might wish to point out some unresolved problems involved in evaluating children's ability to reason by using two different tests which require a different kind of knowledge and way of thinking. What justification could one make for the administration of such different tasks then? First of all, fair grounds for the assessment of reasoning ability of children from extreme groups was not to be established by using the Standard Piagetian Test only since their conceptual experiences are vastly different from one another. The only way to achieve a fair assessment, if it is the aim, is to provide them with tasks appropriate for each group, and they are not necessarily the same tasks. The second point is that the main aim of the study is not to compare the children's level of ability to solve certain problems but to find out how and in what context the children could think logically. The reasoning behind this is that the ability to solve certain logical or mathematical problems is not necessarily the yardstick of the ability to think logically for some cultural groups of people. Therefore, the present study is different from those which administered only the Standard Piagetian Test in non-Western cultures to gain a comparative ability to solve the Western type of logico-mathematical problem.

The results

All the children tested performed better in the Revised Test than in the Piagetian Test, with varying degrees of differences. The British children from an

independent school (sample-3) and the Westernized Korean
children (sample-1) performed similarly with a clear age
trend, that is, 5-6 year-olds performed significantly
better in the Revised Test than in the Piagetian Test
(p<0.01), whereas 7-8-9 year-olds performed well (85-100%)
in both tests, so the difference is not significant. This
trend was less obvious for the British children from the
rural area (sample-4) and their better performance in the
Revised Test was seen in all age groups. It is also seen
that the Korean children from a remote rural area
(sample-2) were exceptional to the extent that they
performed poorly in both tests in all age groups in
comparison with the other three groups, and the significant
improvement in the Revised Test is seen at the later stage
of their development.

Table 1 shows the number of conservation responses in
each sample and the significance of differences of
performance between the Piagetian and the Revised Test in
the younger (5-6) and the older (7-9) age groups.

TABLE 1

Conservation responses and significant levels of performance between
Piagetian and Revised Test for 5-6-year olds and 7-8-9-year olds.

		5-6-year-olds (N=20)			7-8-9-year-olds (N=30)		
		Piaget	Revised	Prob.	Piaget	Revised	Prob.
Sample-1	Liq.	3	17	.01	26	30	NS
	Sub.	6	14	.05	26	30	NS
	D.Q.	4	15	.01	26	30	NS
Sample-2	Liq.	1	3	NS	6	15	.01
	Sub.	1	3	NS	6	15	.01
	D.Q.	1	2	NS	6	14	.05
Sample-3	Liq.	7	17	.01	28	30	NS
	Sub.	6	16	.01	29	30	NS
	D.Q.	7	17	.01	29	30	NS
Sample-4	Liq.	2	8	.01	12	22	.05
	Sub.	2	8	.01	17	27	.05
	D.Q.	3	9	.01	16	21	NS

Chapter 14

Figure 1

Comparison of the performance in the Piagetian, Revised and the New Tests

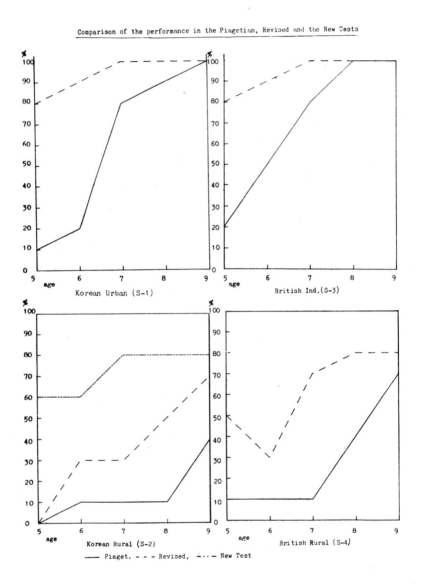

Korean Urban (S-1)

British Ind.(S-3)

Korean Rural (S-2)

British Rural (S-4)

—— Piaget, - - - Revised, –··– New Test

124

TABLE 2

Conservation responses in the New Test and the Piagetian Test
and the significant levels of performance by remote
rural Korean children (sample-2).

Age		New Test	Piaget Test	Prob.
5	Liquid	6	0	.01
(N=10)	Substance	5	0	.05
	D.Q.	6	0	.01
6	Liquid	6	1	.05
(N=10)	Substance	6	1	.05
	D.Q.	6	1	.05
7	Liquid	8	2	.01
(N=10)	Substance	7	1	.01
	D.Q.	8	1	.01
8	Liquid	8	1	.01
(N=10)	Substance	7	1	.01
	D.Q.	9	2	.01
9	Liquid	8	4	NS
(N=10)	Substance	8	4	NS
	D.Q.	9	4	.05

The results demonstrated, in general, that the younger age children are affected by the Revised Test in their successful performance whereas for older age groups the degree of influence is less obvious, except for the Korean children from a remote rural area.

It is noted that the experimental design adopted here was firstly to test initial hypotheses and then to generate new hypotheses at the later stage so that the sequence of administering tests was: Piagetian, Revised, New. In consideration of possible effects caused by the sequence a control group received the tests in a different order. The details of the results of the control group are not included here due to the limited space and in consideration of the focus of the present report. However, it is necessary to mention that the performance pattern and the differences of performance between the tests in the control group were not so great as to alter the general trend of the results mentioned above.

Figure 1 shows the development of the performance by

125

children (5-9 years) in each sample in the conservation of
liquid test in the Piagetian, the Revised and the New Test.

The results of the New Test

As described earlier, the performance by remote rural
Korean children was considerably poorer in relation to
their city counterparts. However, they performed
significantly better on the New Test than on the Piagetian
Test in all age groups. The result of the performance by
this group on the New Test together with the significance
of differences ("Sign-Test" used) between the New Test and
the Piagetian Test is shown in Table 2.

Discussion of the findings

The British and Korean children in all samples and all
age groups performed better in the Revised Test than in the
Piagetian Test. These differences do, however, vary. It is
therefore argued here that successful performance by
children in cognitive tasks is affected by the appropriate
usage of child language since the Revised Test was designed
to prevent children from misunderstanding the language
used.

Korean children from a remote rural village who failed
in the Piagetian tasks showed significant improvement in
the New Test in all age groups. It is therefore evident
that familiarity in the ways of handling materials becomes
highly relevant to cognitive performance. This demonstrates
that these children could express their logical thinking
ability only when they were provided with tasks
conceptually familiar to them. Let us call this
"logico-practical" ability. In the present study, however,
it has not been possible to give details of the
relationship between "logico-practical"(1) and
"logico-mathematical" ability. For example, whether all
children who have "logico-mathematical" ability also
possess "logico-practical" ability remains to be seen.

How are these findings connected to the Piagetian
theory? Piaget's epistemological constructionism of
cognitive development is in no way confirmed or refuted by
the empirical data so far gathered here or elsewhere since
Piaget observed children's ability to solve mathematical
tasks on the one hand and then on the other hand claimed
the existence of an internal cognitive structure. The
problem of testability of his theory is well described in
the work of Desforges and Brown (1979) who argue that
"Piaget is claiming that it is necessary to adopt a
constructivist theory. But the presence of the processes
and regulations at the core of this account has to be
inferred from the behaviour they are used to explain.
Hence, once again the account is untestable ...".

It is however, possible as a result of the present study to suggest what may have been wrong with Piaget's use of his observation to assess a child's ability to solve the conservation problem:

1. The way in which children use their language and thinking in various ethnic groups and age levels is not seriously taken into account,

2. The level of cognitive performance seems to mean very little when there are extreme differences in the physical and logical backgrounds of the children being tested. It might be impossible to make a valid judgement concerning the children's cognitive ability by administering the Piagetian tasks if the children in one group are familiar with that kind of task and the others have no idea what it is all about. In the Piagetian view the latter children have to be considered as failures as they have been unable to coordinate concepts strange to them. However, the results of the present study suggest that the failure to coordinate strange concepts is not necessarily the result of cognitive inability.

Conclusion

All the children tested in this study, regardless of their ages (5-9) and of their social, cultural and educational backgrounds, could think logically in solving conservation tasks, but the ways of manipulating the problems varied between groups and individuals.

Piaget's interpretation of children's ability to reason is in a way contradictory to the opinion of the present investigator, because Piaget's theory of the development of children's logical thinking rests entirely upon the ground of children's performance of certain logico-mathematical tasks, whereas the investigator argues that children's ability to think logically in a real life situation has to be taken into account.

NOTE

1. "Logico-practical" ability is a new term used initially by the present investigator to describe the ability of rural Korean children who were successful in solving logical problems when the problems were practical and part of their familiar conceptual framework. The term "logico-practical" ability is therefore used by contrast with "logico-mathematical" operation as used by Piaget.

127

Chapter 14

REFERENCES

Cole, M., Gay, J., Glick, J. and Sharp, D. (1971), The Cultural Context of Learning and Thinking. N.Y. Basic Books.

Dasen, P.R. (1972), Cross-cultural Piagetian Research: Journal of Cross-Cultural Psychology, 13, 23-40.

Desforges, C. and Brown, G. (1979), Piaget's theory: A Psychological Critique, London, Routledge and Kegan Paul.

Elliot, A. and Donaldson, M. (1981), Consensus and Controversy, in Modgil, S. and Modgil, C. (Eds.), Jean Piaget, Holt Rinehart and Winston, 157-166.

Piaget, J. (1952), The Child's Conception of Number, London, Routledge and Kegan Paul.

SOME IMPLICATIONS OF THE EMERGENCE OF REGIONAL PSYCHOLOGIES FOR A PIAGETIAN APPROACH TO THE DEVELOPMENT OF COGNITION

M. F. Davids

University of Cape Town

An evaluation of the significance of cross-cultural contributions to Piagetian theory, and hence of the relevance of Piagetian psychology to the cross-cultural enterprise, is problematic from a number of points of view. However, when the theoretical model is used as a base to inform cross-cultural research (as has been the case) it becomes essential to pay particular attention to delineating the central theoretical constructs in the theory, and to demonstrate the gains to be made from their cross-cultural application. There are at last two reasons why such an exercise has become necessary.

Firstly, it is widely recognised that the Piagetian oeuvre not only contains different levels of theorising (Brown and Desforges, 1979), but also addresses questions located in a number of different domains. While eschewing the approach of philosophy, Piaget remains concerned with epistemology, which is located within the philosophical terrain (Venn and Walkerdine, 1978); but his experimental work directly addresses the development of cognition, hence his reception in psychology and education. This is compounded by the fact that, as a self-conscious theorist, Piaget is well aware that in addressing knowledge, the theory has to account not only for an external object, but also for itself as a theory of knowledge par excellence.

The ensuing body of work thus comprises a rich fabric of interwoven strands. However, when "Piaget's theory" is used by others, it is often not clear whether the theoretical constructs drawn upon are central to his work, or rather more peripheral. Thus, particular difficulties arise when the significance of experimental findings for the theory itself are evaluated. To determine the centrality of concepts in the theory is difficult because

Piaget himself does not provide crisp, precise definitions
(Vuyk, 1981). It appears that he remains true to his
constructivist bias in preferring to develop a concept
throughout the course of a text, thus apparently violating
the rules familiar to Anglo-American psychology (Brainerd,
1978). In addition, not only central concepts, but the
theory itself undergoes progressive elaboration (Riegel,
1979). This necessitates an attempt at delineating the
central thrust of Piaget's work as a basis for both an
evaluation of the cross-cultural contributions in this
paradigm, and for determining the utility or otherwise of
the approach for cross-cultural psychology.

Secondly, a number of critical studies of Piaget have
recently levelled strong attacks against those operating
within the Piagetian framework, not from the framework of a
positivist epistemology, but from a structural one.
Generally, Piagetian research has been accused of
capitalising on the rich number of ideas in Piaget's
writings, while ignoring the central import of his
approach:

> Piaget's essential insights, and the critical
> potential residing in the more original parts of his
> thinking, have been systematically eclipsed. The
> "structure" of Piaget's theory has been dismantled
> in the rush to appropriate particular empirical
> techniques, replicate specific studies, develop test
> items or curricular materials, and produce piecemeal
> critiques. The whole conception of "genetic
> epistemology" has been laid waste by bevies of
> hyperkinetic researchers who resemble nothing more
> than ardent rummagers in a bargain basement
> (Broughton, 1981a : 79).

Greenfield's (1976) call to cross-cultural researchers
to pay greater attention to Piaget's theory rather than his
"procedures" thus receives renewed support not from the
cross-culturalists, but from those rather more concerned
with theoretical concepts themselves.

The present paper attempts to do just this. Piaget's
theoretical constructs are examined with a view to
specifying his metatheoretical stance, and showing how the
central concepts derive from this. In separating the
essential from the incidental, a criterion for evaluating
existing cross-cultural data is generated, as well as
future directions within the thrust of the theory outlined,
taking into account some of the difficulties encountered in
Piagetian cross-cultural research.

Piaget's metatheory

An attempt to identify aspects of the theory that are

open to empirical verification demands a prior distinction between the metatheoretical and the theoretical. The metatheory usually explicates the assumptions upon which the theory is based, as well as the direction in which the theory is intended to move. It thus pinpoints the problematic within which the theoretical constructs are inserted, and as such constitutes the a priori of the entire theoretical body. It follows, then, that metatheoretical concepts are twice removed from reality – theoretical propositions concerning the nature of phenomena lie between these orienting principles and the real world – and hence are not amenable to empirical verification or refutation. Theoretical propositions themselves, on the other hand, constitute the concrete accounts of the phenomena in question. These accounts may of course be modified in the light of empirical findings, although such modifications would take place within the conceptual space delimited by the metatheory.

From a metatheoretical perspective, Piaget's work falls within the structuralist paradigm (Piaget, 1971; Brown and Desforges, 1979; Welton, 1980). Broughton locates the rise of structuralism within the social sciences in "a growing awareness of the limitations of traditional empiricist thinking and an at least half complete revolt against positivism" (1981a : 82). The structuralist quest aims at illuminating the structural order that underlies and unites divergent surface forms (Wozniak, 1975). From this it follows that the thrust of any structuralist theory is to illuminate the structures or forms that underlie the diverse observations, to discover the order beneath apparent randomness.

Formalisation of the order that unites apparently divergent surface phenomena is thus the central focus of structuralist theory. While the formal description of the structure is based on, and refers to, specific events in the external world, the emphasis is on the process by which the various events come to stand in a particular relation to one another. The task of formalisation becomes one of codifying the rules by which these relations between events or elements become possible, such that the actual relation may be viewed as one of a class of possible relations permitted by the ordering structure.

Such a characterisation of structure is necessarily abstract (Brainerd, 1978), and assumed to have a formative role in producing the observed relations. As such, explication of structure renders observed relations comprehensible. Piaget himself goes one step further in maintaining that structures have a "real" existence quite independent of the formalisation of the theorist (Piaget, 1980). Nevertheless, despite this empiricist tendency, Piaget does not attempt to validate structures directly

against concrete criteria in external reality; he avoids
the Popperian criterion of falsifiability for validation of
his constructs. Instead, structures are accorded a
conceptual status that remains abstract, with rigour as the
primary criterion of validity. Levi-Strauss, with whose
views Piaget is essentially in agreement, clarifies the
problem of validation within structuralism in the folowing
way:

> In the human sciences, no work can be scientific in
> the traditional sense. What annoys me most about
> criticisms directed at me... is that the defect of
> my work (according to the criteria of Karl Popper)
> is this: what you say is not scientific, because an
> acceptable scientific hypothesis must be
> "falsifiable" (that is, the nature of theory is such
> that one can construct tests that could refute it).
> Perhaps this is true in physics or biology, but it
> is a completely senseless requirement in the human
> sciences... (where) nothing is falsifiable. The only
> possible criterion of truth is that our way of
> explaining things allows us to account for more
> elements than we could account for with other
> explanations... (Levi-Strauss, 1972 : 79).

From this point of view, it becomes apparent that the
assumption of external structures in the real world is not
essential to Piagetian theorising. Since the structure can
only be known through its formalisation, any attempt to
validate such a formalisation against some definitive
external structure becomes tautologous. Elsewhere, Piaget
shows that it is the formalisation, rather than the pursuit
of external reality, that is the theorist's prime task:

> The limits of formalisation are not laid down one
> and for all... but, instead, are "moveable" or
> "vicarious"... (Piaget, 1971 : 35).

which rules out the possibility of validation against an
external, definitive structure.

If Piaget is not alone in the search for a deep level
of order that underlies apparent randomness, there are two
aspects of his work that distinguish him from other
structuralists. These are the specific object of his theory
and his particular approach to diachronic transformations.

Piaget's main interest is an epistemological one (Venn
and Walkerdine, 1978; Vuyk, 1981); the object of his
science is the knowing or epistemic subject. In line with
the structuralist approach, his interest lies in uncovering
the structures which permit the individual to make sense of
his world, and to function in accordance with such
knowledge. The assumption is that all activity on the part

of the knowing subject is lawful, and throughout his empirical odyssey, Piaget's emphasis is on finding instances of "knowing activity" that are codifiable, and hence demonstrate the assumption of underlying order. Given Piaget's familiarity with and interest in the explanatory possibilities of formal mathematics (rather than, say, structural linguistics) it is not surprising that his actual demonstrations of structure take a mathematical form. However, from a metatheoretical perspective, it is the demonstration of order itself that is central; the actual language in which that demonstration (formalisation) is couched is, from this vantage point, purely idiosyncratic.

Piaget's second distinguishing feature is his unshakable belief in evolution (Scott, 1980). This leads him to the notion of constructivism, whereby structures undergo diochronic transformations into increasingly sophisticated and adaptive forms. Here the concern is not the reductionist one with ultimate origin or destination:

> A phenomenon is always biological in its roots, and social at its end point. (Piaget, 1973 : Quoted in Broughton, 1981b : 336).

Rather he is concerned with the processes by which the active organism constructs successively more adaptive structures that facilitate increasingly adaptive forms of thought and action. On the empirical level, this again leads to a selection of observations that demonstrate the evolution of structures into more sophisticated ones, capable of handling ever more complex relationships.

Given the quest after structures of knowledge that are ontogenetically constructed (Gruber and Voneche, 1977), the theory emerges against a metatheoretical backdrop that provides fertile ground for the search for universals of human thought. Yet, although Piaget's metatheory provides a context within which universal structures of thought may be formalised (Gruber and Voneche, 1977), it is at the theoretical level that the adequacy (rigour) of the structures as explanatory concepts must be evaluated. As Gellner (1981) recognises, an adequately defined universalist metatheory does not guarantee that the structures formulated do adequately account for the observations. Equally, an unsatisfactory theoretical account may reflect the limitations of the theorist rather than a shortcoming of the paradigm. It becomes important, then, to evaluate the extent to which the actual structures proposed i) are able to account for cross-cultural evidence, and ii) to consider whether the paradigm permits alternative structures that take account of the various difficulties that have emerged in the cross-cultural arena.

Structure and transformation

Because of the complexity of Piaget's theory, his cross-cultural followers have found it necessary to group the constructs in various categories. Dasen (1977), for example, proposes a distinction between qualitative and quantitative aspects of the theory, while the competence-performance and content-process distinctions have also enjoyed some currency in the literature. The problem which such distinctions, however, is that they are invariably post hoc attempts at making sense of empirical findings, and relating these back to the theory. As such, these categories do not enjoy a priori theoretical primacy, which makes it difficult to evaluate the findings with respect to the theory itself. There is a growing recognition that, despite a preponderance of cross-cultural data, the potential of the theory to illuminate universal principles that govern human thought has not been fully exploited.

> If Piaget has, in the past, led the cross-cultural enterprise astray, it is because researchers have followed his procedures rather than his theory. (Greenfield, 1976 : 333).

Following Greenfield's suggestion, an evaluation of the cross-cultural findings with reference to central theoretical concepts might well prove productive, both in terms of enriching the theory itself (Piaget, 1974), and generating a theoretically informed direction for future research. Such an attempt has to start with the central metatheoretical concerns of structure and constructivism in order to explicate their relationship to concepts at the theoretical level.

Piaget's boldest definition of a structure is "as a system of transformations" (1971 : 34). Transformation involves action on elements; the latter including objects in the external world, perceptions, memories and concepts (Vuyk, 1981). Although elements form part of a structure, it is not the nature of the elements themselves that are of primary theoretical importance. For example, in infancy the concern is not so much with the range of objects with which the baby interacts, but rather with what she does with the objects. Thus,

> It is (not) the elements... but the relations among elements that count. In other words, the logical procedures or natural processes by which the whole is formed are primary, not the whole, which is consequent on the system's laws of composition, nor the elements. (Piaget, 1971 : 9, parentheses added).

From this, it is clear that although structure, law and elements are indissociable in Piaget's work (Gruber and Voneche, 1977), the major focus of theorising is not the elements, but what is done to them. Given the definition of structure as a system of transformations, and that transformations are actions performed on elements, it becomes clear that the task of the Piagetian theorist revolves around formalising the rules by which transformations take place.

> We are concerned with a system, which... presents laws of totality distinct from the properties of its elements. The term "structure" remains vague, however, so long as the laws of totality are not specified. (Piaget, 1980 : 143).

> ... the elements of a structure must be differentiated from the transformation laws that apply to them... (Piaget, 1971 : 12).

In describing the processes of intelligence Piaget makes extensive use of the biological metaphors of assimilation and accommodation. Rigorous theorising requires that these concepts be incorporated into the central notion of structure in a way that transcends the merely metaphorical. If knowing a structure permits action on (transformation of) its elements, it is possible to argue that these laws in fact demonstrate the operation of assimilation.

Piaget, however, recognises the dialectical relationship between accommodation and assimilation. This means that every action on elements incorporates both processes. To account for the relationship between transformation and the accommdation process, the above argument thus needs to be expanded.

> Because it is the former (elements of a structure) that undergo transformation or change, it is easy to think of the latter as immutable... (This raises) the central problem... of the construction (of structures), of the relation between structuralism and constructivism. (Piaget, 1971 : 12/13; parenthesis added).

Piaget's constructivism is an attempt to establish the genesis of a structure in the preceding structure, "motivated" by increasing adaptation (progressive equilibration). He argues persuasively against both the pre-formist and gestalt viewpoints on the grounds that the former posits genesis without structure, while the latter posits structure without genesis. Constructivism, on the other hand, holds that structures are progressively constructed through the actions of the subject (Piaget,

1980).

In addition to furnishing evidence of a structure's transformation laws, action on elements thus also provides the focus for the progressive elaboration of sophisticated structures from their ultimate root in the reflexes. In this way, the dialectical nature of equilibration (assimilation/accommodation) is established in each action of the subject. Moreover, by applying the principle of underlying order (read: structure) to constructivism itself, Piaget argues that diachronic change of the structure (read: transformation laws) should also be ordered. That is, there are transformation laws that govern the transformation of structures themselves. Since all of this is rooted in action performed on elements, the formalisation of such transformation laws is synonymous with a rigorous theoretical description of the accommodation process.

Piaget's own definition of transformation is a general one:

> I call transformation an operation which transforms one state into another. (Piaget, 1977; quoted in Vuyk, 1981 : 55).

A more precise explication, aimed at clarifying the problematic of the Piagetian theorist, ties the definition of transformation to any interaction with elements that results in lawful change, either of the elements, or of the laws themselves. The theoretical task is thus one specifying two varieties of transformation law:

> i) Laws which govern synchronic action on the elements of a stucture, and

> ii) Laws which govern the process themselves take place.

Transformations are thus the central theoretical constructs in Piagetian theory. They are inferred directly from the actions of the subject, and serve as the link between the "vague" (i.e., metatheoretical) stucture and the elements of cognitive activity. The formalisation of the laws by which transformations are carried out is focussed around the dialectic of assimilation and accommodation. The long term goal of the Piagetian theorist is to uncover these transformation laws (Gruber and Voneche, 1977). Formalisation of such transformation laws is dependent on observation, and is thus not definitional (Brown and Desforges, 1979) in the sense that verification is inevitable due to the metatheoretical stance. It is entirely possible that a given transformation law does not adequately account for the observed relations between elements, and hence is in need of modification or replacement.

Universality in cross-cultural psychology

Since the content of thought is culturally variable, the structuralist focus on form (laws that govern relations) rather than content (elements) suggests the possibility of uncovering universal rules by which thought is organised. Since the theoretical focus in Piagetian psychology is on formalising transformation laws, it is appropriate to expect that these laws should be universal. The cross cultural setting with its diversity at the manifest level thus provides an ideal laboratory for the stucturalist enterprise.

Piaget's conviction is, of course, that he has discovered aspects of the development of thought that conform to precisely this universalist ideal. Consequently he views the contribution of cross-cultural data primarily in terms of ascertaining the relative importance of different factors in development (Piaget, 1974). However, before this thrust in cross-cultural studies can be evaluated, it is important to critically examine the underlying assumption that Piaget's theoretical formulations conform to the structuralist ideal.

"Piaget's theory" has come to be associated with the stages of cognitive development (Pinard and Laurendau, 1969). While a number of writers recognise that stage is not a central concept in Piaget (Brainerd, 1978; Vuyk, 1981), there is considerable appeal in the successive stage descriptions as a "psychological theory" quite distinct from the more metatheoretical concern with structures, constructivism and the processes of intelligence. The metatheoretical constructs cause a great deal of exasperation on account of their "definitional" status (Brown and Desforges, 1979), while the stage theory has the advantage of opening a direct route to the empirical. Cross-cultural Piagetian practice has followed the trend of directing attention predominantly at concepts deriving from the stage theory (Dasen, 1974; Ashton, 1975).

The above argument has been that the structuralist aim and method in Piaget are well suited to the cross-cultural enterprise. In the light of the emphasis placed on stage related concepts in cross-cultural research, it is appropriate to consider whether the stage theory is equally well suited to cross-cultural work.

The end-point towards which development veers is perhaps the most problematic aspect of the stage theory from the cross-cultural perspective (Greenfield, 1976). Piaget's well documented epistemological interest leads to

an end-point which focuses on the thought of the scientist;
he wants to explain how scientific knowlege is possible.
The entire stage theory proceeds retrospectively from this
aim; his constructvist assumption leads him to identify
aspects of the thought activity of the child that can be
constituted as logical building blocks towards this goal.
That Piaget has done the task well is borne out by the fact
that wherever the stages do occur, they follow the same
sequence (Dasen, 1974).

However, the possibility that the selection of this
particular end-point is not immune to ideological influence
(Foucault, 1972) is worthy of consideration. Some writers
(Buck-Morss, 1975; Buss, 1977) have specifically pointed to
bias of this nature in Piaget's theory, and linked the
value attached to scientific thought to the
"culture-specific" position that this type of knowledge
occupies in technologically advanced societies. Since this
assumption underlies the entire stage theory, this aspect
of Piaget's work is thus far more susceptible to bias
against both technologically unsophisticated cultures, and
the less privileged classes in "advanced" societies.

In this respect, the developmental lag frequently
encountered in non-western cultures (Ashton,1975; Dasen and
Heron, 1980) is important. Piagetians generally take the
view that since the qualititative aspects of the theory are
more important than the quantitative, these lags are of
limited significance. As there are numerous difficulties in
conducting cross-cultural research in a satisfactory way,
methodological problems are seen as a large source of error
variance (Kamara and Easley, 1977; Price-Williams, 1978).
Consequently, a number of studies have demonstrated a
greater likelyhood of accepting the null hypothesis when
such problems are adequately controlled for.

However, it is an almost impossible task to render two
cultures equally comparable in the experimental situation;
this opens the way for permutations of the methodological
shortcomings argument. And it is possible that an
exaggerated concern with methodological issues may conceal
basic conceptual difficulties that underlie recurrent
methodological ones (Brown and Desforges, 1979).

Of importance from the conceptual point of view is the
recurrent finding that European contact and schooling
appear positively related to performance on Piagetian
measures (Greenfield, 1976; Dasen, 1974). This suggests
that these Piagetian tasks require skills associated with
western, technologically advanced societies. From the point
of view of universal forms that govern human thought, they
may thus be artifactual. This raises questions in
cross-cultural work regarding the nature of skills and
abilities that operate within native cultures

uncontaminated by contact with European ideological formations.

A constructivist alternative

An alternative approach to those current in the cross-cultural Piagetian literature would be to apply the principle of constructivism to genetic epistemology itself. This implies that Piaget's own stage theory should be viewed as heuristically important, but in no way theoretically definitive of cognitive development. Instead, the ongoing risk of the theory itself would be to develop a stage theory that could be shown to incorporate divergent forms of cognition in different cultural settings. Piaget's own stage theory would thus be an important necessary but by no means sufficient requirement for this exercise. Thus, testing the generality of this theory in different cultural settings would be discouraged since it leads to the unsatisfactory implications of cultural retardation (Ashton, 1975; Dasen, 1977). Instead, the universalist potential of this theory, which has been shown to be tied to the specification of transformation laws, should ideally be incorporated into the stage theory. Such a stage theory cannot be the one proposed by Piaget, although it would incorporate the latter. A two-step procedure might be useful in this regard.

Firstly, taking cognisance of the problems highlighted in the emic-etic debate, an attempt should be made to generate culture appropriate stage theories in non-Western societies. These would take into account the end-point socially sought in that society, and attempt to construct appropriate stages that lead in that direction. Due to the complex relationship between ideology and cognition, determining whether the mode of cognition in two cultures is likely to differ does pose problems. A partial solution would rely on the known occurrence of a developmental lag, since adherence to a cognitive difference rather than a deficit view (Dasen, 1977) would suggest that the apparent lag is a result of a difference between the cognitive activity measured, and that generally utilised in the person's life situation. This would account for the general observation that those who fail on Piagetian tasks are no less competent in their life situations than those who don't (Brown and Desforges, 1979).

When the limitations of Piagetian stage theory are recognised in this way, cross-cultural reliance on nomothetic methods also become problematic. Since the focus is placed on the rules that govern how people construct knowledge of their world, rather than whether what Piaget says about this process is correct, the idiographic approach seems more appropriate. This follows Piaget's own method at a comparable stage of his research into the way children construct knowledge of the Genevan world (Opper, 1977). The clinical method would dominate this stage of theorising, where the focus would be on generating first the rules of synchronic transformation that characterise the structures that emerge in the cultural setting concerned, followed by the rules of diachronic transformation of the structures themselves.

The second stage in the constructivist procedure proposed here is central to the theoretical propositions of genetic epistemology. When a number of presumably different "stage theories" have emerged, it becomes possible to test the usefulness of Piaget's structuralist approach. This approach holds that it is possible to arrive at formalisations that unite surface divergencies at a deeper level of structures. Having arrived at a number of different emic stage theories, the theorist's task becomes one of formalising superordinate laws of transformation that subsume the variety of forms that these laws assume in the different cultural settings. An appropriate "test" of Piaget's theory would be to demonstrate that such laws are possible (although Gellner's remarks concerning negative results are important here). Such a demonstration would formally incorporate the philosophical assumption of cultural differences into the fabric of the theory itself. Universality, then, would be sought at the abstract level rather than in empirical observations; in fact, observational variation would be an important pre-requisite for deriving these superordinate transformation laws; such demonstrations would lend strong support to Piaget's basic assumptions.

The argument presented in this paper is that a distinction between the structural and stage theory in Piaget is necessary in the cross-cultural arena. While the structural theory contains the potential for universality, the stage theory is likely to contain a "Geneva-centric" bias. It is, therefore, ironic that components of the stage theory sould have featured so prominently in Piagetian cross-cultural research. However, the problems generated in this area, focused around the emic-etic dabate, provide impetus for a renewed examination of the possibility of generating culture-specific stage theories. These would provide the basis for theorising at the structural level; this, in turn, is seen as the central problematic in genetic epistemology. Working towards culture-specific stage theories seems perfectly compatible with the idea of developing regional psychologies. In the context of Piagetian psychology, such regional psychologies would provide the essential ways of discovering the unity of the form that governs human thought in its cultural variety.

REFERENCES

ASHTON, P.T. Cross-cultural Piagetian research: An experimental perspective. Harvard Educational Review, 1975, 45, 475-506.

BERRY, J.W. and DASEN, P.R. (Eds.) Culture and cognition: Readings in cross-cultural psychology. London: Methuen, 1974.

BRAINERD, C.J. Piaget's theory of intelligence. Englewood Cliffs, N.J.: Prentice-Hall, 1978.

BROUGHTON, J.M. Piaget's structural developmental psychology: I. Piaget and structuralism. Human Development, 1981, 24, 78-109 (a).

BROUGHTON, J.M. Piaget's structural developmenal psychology: IV. Knowledge without a self and without history. Human Development, 1981, 24, 320-346 (b).

BROWN, G. and DESFORGES, C. Piaget's theory: A psychological critique. London: Routledge and Kegan Paul, 1979.

BUCK-MORSS, S. Socio-economic bias in Piaget's theory and its implications for cross-cultural studies. Human Development, 1975, 18, 35-49.

BUSS, A. Piaget, Marx and Buck-Morss on cognitive developmennt: A critique and reinterpretation. Human Development, 1977, 20, 118-128.

DASEN, P.R. Piagetian cross-cultual research: A summary. In J.W. Berry and P.R. Dasen (Eds.) Culture and cognition. (Op. cit.)

DASEN, P.R. (Ed.) Piagetian psychology: Cross-cultural contributions. N.Y.: Gardner Press, 1977.

DASEN, P.R. and HERON, A. Cross-cultural tests of Piaget's theory. In H.C. Triandis and A. Heron (Eds.) Handbook of Cross-Cultural psychology. Vol. 4. Boston: Allyn and Bacon, 1980.

FOUCAULT, M. The archeology of knowledge. London: Tavistock, 1972.

GELLNER, E. General introduction: relativism and universals. In B. Lloyd and J. Gay. Universals of human thought: Some African evidence. London: Cambridge University Press, 1981.

141

Chapter 15

GREENFIELD, P.M. Cross-cultural research and Piagetian theory: Paradox and progress. In K.F. Riegel and J.A. Meacham (Eds.) The developing individual in a changing world. Vol. 1. The Hague: Mouton, 1976.

GRUBER, H.E. and VONECHE, J.J. The essential Piaget. London: Routledge and Kegan Paul, 1977.

KAMARA, A.I. and EASLEY, J.A. Jr. Is the rate of cognitive development uniform across cultures? - A methodological critique with new evidence from Themne children. In P.R. Dasen (Ed.) Piagetian psychology. N.Y.: Gardner Press, 1977.

LEVI-STRAUSS, J. The father of structural anthropology takes a misanthropic view of lawless humanism. Psychology Today, May, 1972.

OPPER, S. Piaget's clinical method. J. Children's Mathematical Behaviour, 1977, 1, 90-107.

PIAGET, J. Structuralism. London: Routledge and Kegan Paul, 1971.

PIAGET, J. The need and significance of cross-cultural studies in genetic psychology. In J.W. Berry and P.R. Dasen (Eds.) Culture and cognition: Studies in cross-cultural psychology. London: Methuen, 1974.

PIAGET, J. Six psychological studies. Sussex: Harvester Press, 1980.

PINARD, A. and LAURENDAU, M. "Stage" in Piaget's cognitive developmental theory: Exegesis of a concept. In D. Elkind and J.H. Flavell (Eds.) Studies in cognitive growth. London: Oxford University Press, 1969.

PRICE-WILLIAMS, D.W. Cognition: Anthropological and psychological nexus. In G.A. Spindler (Ed) The making of psychological anthropology. Berkeley: University of California Press, 1978.

RIEGEL, K.F. Foundations of dialectical psychology. N.Y.: Academic Press, 1979.

SCOTT, C.E. Structure and order. In H.J. Silverman (Ed.) Piaget, philosophy and the human sciences. Sussex: Harvester Press, 1980.

VENN, C. and WALKERDINE, V. The acquisition and production of knowledge: Piaget's theory reconsidered. Ideology and Consciousness, 1978, 3, 67-94.

VUYK, R. Overview and critique of Piaget's genetic epistemology, 1965-1980. Vol. 1. N.Y.: Academic Press, 1981.

WELTON, D. Introduction: Concept of structure in Piaget's genetic epistemology. In H.J. Silverman (Ed.) Piaget, philosophy and the human sciences. Sussex: Harvester Press, 1980.

WOZNIAK, R.H. Dialecticism and structuralism: the philosophical foundations of Soviet psychology and Piagetian development theory. In K.F. Riegel and G.C. Rosenwald (Eds.) Structure and transformation. N.Y.: John Wiley and Sons, 1975.

A PROPOSED AMENDMENT TO PIAGET'S THEORY OF CAUSAL REASONING

H. Poole

Dalhousie University, Halifax

The Problem

A great deal of cross-cultural research into cognitive development has relied heavily on Piaget's theory. In this paper I shall challenge the validity of a major aspect of that theory. Although the chief concern will be with the adequacy of Piaget's attempt to explain the development of causal reasoning, the results of the analysis will be applicable to other areas of Piaget's theory. Certain general weaknesses in Piaget's system will be identified, and their implication for cross-cultural psychologists briefly examined.

There are two aspects of Piaget's theory which need to be distinguished for present purposes. First, there is the Stage Theory - the claim that there are four biological stages in intellectual development. These stages are defined in terms of characteristic systems of mental ability, each of which supports a qualitatively different experience and understanding of the world. Second, there is the quite distinct theory which attempts to explain what makes individuals pass from one stage to the next. According to Piaget, the growth of intelligence is essentially a process of interaction between organism and environment, a form of adaption and the inevitable result of living in an orderly universe in which action must gradually produce the categories of understanding. This process is said to be governed by the mechanisms of assimilation, accommodation, and equilibration, and is described in the idiom of efficient causation; at least, it is not clear what part is played in intellectual development by the subject's own intentional rational activity. This organism-environment theory will be referred to as the Autoregulative Theory (1).

As other writers have argued, it is difficult to see how the autoregulative theory can be successfully maintained (2). It cannot, for example, give a satisfactory account of the influence of the social environment on mental development. Piaget seems to think of society as acting on the individual in essentially the same way as the material environment does (3). This view is clearly in error because intellectual activity is at least partly shaped and governed by norms, by considerations of what is correct. And, of course, norms presuppose society; they cannot be generated in the process of solo interaction with the environment. These facts call for an alternative interpretation of Piaget's data which will take account of the norm-governed nature of intellectual development. The ensuing argument must therefore establish the following positions.

1. The autoregulative theory cannot be a valid account of causal or any other sort of reasoning because reasoning is governed by norms, which are of social origin (4).

2. Because reasoning is normative, stages in development are to be understood as successive approximations to an adult norm. Cognitive stages are distinguished by reference to the norm.

3. Piaget, therefore, must have started his theorizing, albeit unwittingly, with the idea of mature causal judgement, thence working backwards and establishing stages as the discrepancies with adult judgement become wider with increasing age. These stages, however, reflect normative differences.

4. If Piaget's stages can be shown to be sufficiently explained as a normative progression, this explanation will be more acceptable on grounds of parsimony than Piaget's preferred autoregulative alternative. A brief review will now be given of Piaget's characterization of stages in the development of causal reasoning.

II Piaget's Description of Stages in the Development of Causality

In this rendering of Piaget's views I shall restrict myself to those aspects of Piaget's account which are especially relevant to the argument which is to be developed in the next two sections. In attempting to be selective, I shall strive to represent Piaget faithfully and not omit any of his views which might invalidate my criticisms.

Piaget's interest is essentially limited to efficiently causal reasoning. There are two kinds of causality: agent causation, which is embodied in action and explained teleologically, and efficient causation which is typically explained in terms of laws. These are logically distinct ways of accounting for change and constancy in the world. Because Genetic Epistemology is concerned with the evolution of scientific thought, Piaget is primarily interested in efficient causation. Consequently, the idea of purposeful agents as causes receives attention from Piaget only insofar as it is an inappropriate concept for dealing with problems which are known to lie within the province of efficient causality. The stages of causal reasoning proposed by Piaget therefore have to be understood as stages in the development of efficiently causal reasoning.

Ignoring the sensory-motor period, causal reasoning is claimed by Piaget to develop in three main stages. In the first, the pre-operational child's causal thinking is often transductive, citing reasons which seem either irrelevant to adults or adduced on the basis of association of contiguity (5). One aspect of this kind of causal thinking noted by Piaget is the child's inability to formulate general rules for understanding causation in the empirical world (6). There is also a tendency to explain all happenings in the language of action and purpose (7).

At 7 or 8 years of age begins the second, concrete operational phase. Children now distinguish between teleological and efficient (or mechanical) causation and acquire the notion of causal necessity (8). These changes are accompanied by what Piaget reports as being a new concern for generality in explanation (9). The reversible character of the child's thinking which is fundamental to operativity provides the foundation for the logic of classes and relations which is required for generality- or regularity-based causal explanation (10).

Finally, the stage of formal operations is attained, and with it the ability to deal with second-order causal relationships. Formal thinking is hypothetico-deductive; the adolescent proposes hypotheses and tests for the presence of each causal factor separately while holding other factors constant (11). This strategy of examining various possibilities systematically is the essence of critical thinking in science because the special error of uncritical empirical reasoning consists in overlooking or improperly evaluating competing alternative explanations.

The aim of the succeeding pages will be to decide whether this sequence of development can be sufficiently explained in normative terms. The next task therefore is to determine the normative structure of causal judgement.

III The Structure of Causal Judgement

The question now is, "What conditions must be present before a person's causal judgement can be considered procedurally correct (as opposed to true)?" The answer must specify epistemological conditions, that is, conditions which are assumed to be present when a modern educated adult makes a claim to causal knowledge.

The first of these conditions is a generality requirement. It is assumed that in making a causal claim the speaker has backing for his judgement in the form of a statement which asserts a necessary and general connection between the causally related events (12). There have been societies in which this generality assumption has not always been made, as when certain specially gifted persons were believed capable of apprehending causes directly in an act analogous to seeing and without any need for evidence or inference. This belief is, however, no longer widely accepted by educated people.

The second condition assumed to be present in efficiently causal judgement is empirical support for the general statement. It is important to be clear about the meaning of "empirical". It does not mean merely "what is checkable by sense experience". The sense experience at issue here must be such as to make possible public or intersubjective consensus; and this requirement presupposes fairly regular patterns of sense experience which in turn presuppose regularity and uniformity in nature. The notion of empirical is not therefore distinct from that of generality because empirical evidence makes no sense apart from generality.

The final ingredient of correct causal judgement is criticalness. General empirical statements can be adduced to support practically any theory. This sort of evidence only has scientific value, however, when it is critical, that is, when hypotheses are rigorously tested against the full range of plausible logical possibilities.

These three conditions: the general, the empirical and the critical, constitute the epistemological basis of correct efficiently causal judgement. It must now be shown that the Piagetian stages can be equated with different patterns of epistemological conditions. Accordingly, a decomposition of the correct pattern of causal judgement will be effected. In this procedure, the epistemological conditions will be removed one at a time to create a number of "epistemic sets", i.e. different frameworks within which causal judgements can be made. The aim is to show that the Piagetian stages can be produced by changes in normative conditions.

IV Epistemic Sets

By decomposing and recombining the elements of correct causal judgement a number of epistemic sets can be generated, three of which are consistent with the abilities and disabilities attributed to children at various stages by Piaget. Table 1 identifies the epistemological structure of the three Piagetian stages in causal judgement, together with some others which, though of some importance, are not included in Piaget's account (13).

TABLE 1

EPISTEMIC SETS FOR CAUSAL JUDGEMENT

Possible Combinations of Epistemic Conditions

(∼ denotes the absence of a condition)

Critical	General	Empirical	
A	∼B	C	Not a meaningful combination
∼A	∼B	C	Not a meaningful combination
A	B	C	PIAGET'S FORMAL OPERATIONS (also critical teleological Level II)
∼A	B	C	PIAGET'S CONCRETE STAGE (also pseudo-sciences)
∼A	∼B	∼C	PIAGET'S PREOPERATIONAL STAGE (also divinatory/magic)
A	B	∼C	Medieval "Science"
∼A	B	∼C	Magic (Frazerian)
A	∼B	∼C	Not a meaningful combination

Commencing with the notion of mature judgement, there appears to be an exact correspondence between the epistemological configuration created by the triad of critical, general and empirical conditions and the formal operational stage in causal judgement. By then removing the critical condition, a set is produced which is governed by

the general and empirical criteria which were earlier
identified as providing the basis of empirical causal
reasoning. This set appears to be consistent with Piaget's
description of the concrete stage.

Finally, the removal of all three conditions is
consistent with pre-operational causal thinking as
characterized by Piaget. He repeatedly describes the young
child's thought as lacking in generality and, as we have
seen, the empirical condition presupposes generality. In
terms of the three epistemological conditions, therefore,
there is no organization or constraint on the causal
judgements of pre-operational children. Since teleological
and efficient causality are the only two available ways of
explaining contingent change, the child must explain
teleologically if he is unable to master the generality
necessary to efficiently causal explanation. Explaining
something as the deed of an agent implies no commitment to
generality (14). Consequently, we may view the child's
animism as being the only kind of explanation which could
have any internal consistency for someone who has not yet
learnt to formulate general inference rules.

V An Amended Perspective on the Theory

Whereas the Autoregulative Theory maintains that
stages emerge as a result of a causal interaction between
the organism and the environment, it has been argued that
Piaget's stages of causal reasoning are most plausibly
regarded as successive stages of conceptual mastery which
entail an increasing normative regulation of thought. On
this view, the development of causal reasoning, or any
other form of social activity, is the result of social
interaction working through previously learnt concepts,
beliefs and attitudes in a continuous process of
socialization--a process, incidentally, which cannot be
entirely explained in efficiently causal terms as Piaget
wishes to suggest (15).

Causality has been chosen for examination in this
paper because causal judgement is a relatively simple
operation to decompose and examine. But the considerations
detailed above apply equally to other domains of Piaget's
theory. Whereas failure to operate at the adult level is
usually explained in Piagetian literature in a manner which
hints at qualitative differences in the child's perception
or cerebral integrative capacity, the conservation
experiments seem also to be sufficiently explained by the
child's lack of an adult concept (16). The child simply
might not have the adult concept of "water", "plasticine",
"more than", "less than", and so forth. His concept may
have only some of the attributes of the adult concept, as
when a child points to a hippopotamus and says "horse" or
uses the words "right" and "wrong" with quite different

149

meanings from adults.

The foregoing analysis has implications for cross-cultural psychology. First, it seems clear that the development of causal reasoning must be described as a logical rather than as a causal sequence. Consequently, the most that can be said about the role of age, the degree of maturity of the brain and general characteristics of cognitive processes is that these factors _might_ be necessary conditions for learning a concept. This revised perspective clearly has implications for the possible acceleration of the stages, though not necessarily to the extent of denying that teachability is limited by the maturity of the central nervous system. Second, the dangers of parochialism are drawn to our attention with the firm realization that Piagetian stages are the articulation of epistemic sets which are the standard sequence in Europe. Because of this western bias and Piaget's preoccupation with the history of science, certain possible epistemic sets which are prominent in non-western cultures find no place in the Piagetian scheme.

This sort of admonition has been voiced frequently enough, but it still goes largely unheeded. Thus, many psychologists persist in testing attainment cross-culturally on a variety of instruments which embody the Piagetian epistemic sets. Yet it shows a misunderstanding of the concept of culture to imagine that sampling performance on western norms can licence valid general abilities of its members. After all, part of what is implied in distinguishing between different cultures is that their conceptual systems are distinct. Causal thinking in a society must therefore be regarded as a network of epistemic sets, uniquely balanced and interrelated. Not to see this is to ignore the possibility of different standards of rationality, where the criteria for what is rational are internal to each cultural system. Admittedly, it is important for developing societies to acculturate to western forms of scientific thinking, and cross-cultural investigations using the Piagetian tasks can do something to determine the rate and pattern of this change. But it is all too easy to slip into the assumption that these data are indicative of degrees of mental inferiority, and this betrays a great disrespect for and misunderstanding of cultural forms. Any application of Piagetian tasks cross-culturally for any other than diagnostic purposes should be supplemented by an ethnographic appreciation of the unique significance of the relevant concepts and categories within each culture. A large part of the problem for cross-cultural Piagetians is that the Great Man did not produce a viable concept of culture.

NOTES and REFERENCES

Frequently cited works of Piaget will be abbreviated as
follows:

CCPC: The Child's Conception of Physical Causality
London: Kegan Paul, Trench, Trubner and Co., 1930.

GLT: The Growth of Logical Thinking from Childhood to
Adolescence
(Trans. Parsons, A. and Milgram, S.) New York: Basic
Books, 1958.

(1) The regulating principle is equilibration, which
is defined "very broadly as the compensation resulting from
the activities of the subject in response to external
intrusion". J. Piaget, Six Psychological Theories, ed, D.
Elkind, N.Y. Random House, 1967, p.101. For a critical
evaluation of the notion of equilibration see Theodore
Mischel "Piaget and the Nature of Psychological
Explanations" in The Impact of Piagetian Theory ed. F. B.
Murray, Baltimore University Park Press, 1979, pp.89-107.

(2) As for example D.W. Hamlyn "Epistemology and
Conceptual Developments" in Cognitive Development and
Epistemology, ed. T. Mischel, N.Y. Academic Press 1971,
pp.3 - 24; M.W. Wartofsky "From Praxis to Logos: Genetic
Epistemology and Physics", Mischel op cit pp.129 - 416.

(3) Piaget has an extremely limited view of social
influence on cognitive development. This follows from the
theory that the basic categories of understanding are
constructed by the child himself, leaving little room for
social enrichment of the basic repertoire. Indeed,
"society", with its logically related idea of norms, hardly
features at all in Piaget's account. Instead, "other
people" are viewed as having a limited effect on the
mainstream of development, though this influence seems to
be entirely non-rational. Thus, children are supposed to
accept social norms in order to escape the criticism of
others (GLT 243). And again, the abandonment of egocentrism
and the acceptance of the relativity of one's own viewpoint
is said to result from the mere fact of conflict with the
viewpoints of others (CCPC 296-7). This sort of change
cannot be regarded as rational unless the child also comes
to believe that these incompatible viewpoints are worth
taking into account, which would seem to presuppose norms.

(4) Against the autoregulative view put forward in

the name of Genetic Epistemology to account for the evolution of scientific concepts is the less startling but more tenable idea being advocated here that shared public modes of understanding are created out of basic epistemological units by a social dialectic which expresses mankind's continuing search for truth. Piaget rejects the social genesis of basic scientific concepts (Biology and Knowledge, Chicago: University of Chicago Press, 1971, p.98 and pp. 360-369).

(5) The Child's Conception of the World, London: Routledge and Kegan Paul 1929, passim.

(6) "There are certainly laws, but the exceptions are as frequent as the rule" (CCPC, p. 276).

(7) One can distinguish between two levels of teleological explanation. At the first, happenings are explained as acts of purposeful agents whereas at the second level, which appears to require more complex abilities, such as the use of rules and generalizations, action is explained (in terms of reasons, motives and so forth). The pre-operational child's special preference -- and the occasion of his animism -- is for teleological explanation at the first level.

(8) CCPC pp.274 - 7.

(9) As noted in CCPC p.276. There is empirical support for the operational focus on generality in Siegler, R.S, and Liebert, R.M. "Effects of Contiguity, Regularity and Age on Children's Causal Inferences", Developmental Psychology, 1974, 10:4: 574 - 579.

(10) GLT passim. esp. pp.XVII -83; also p.139 and 279.

(11) GLT passim

(12) "Necessary" and "General" are related concepts in the context of efficient causation, in the sense that what is necessary must always apply. The claim that A caused B implies that A will always cause B ceteris paribus.

(13) Some societies, having not developed methods for critically evaluating empirical evidence, use other strategies for diagnosing causes which fall short of the western norm. Nevertheless, non-empirical causal inferences may still be critical. Piaget alludes to this sort of case when he observes that the Ancient Greeks failed to progress beyond deductive reasoning (GLT p.347). If so, mature or correct causal reasoning from the Greek point of view would consist in conforming to the epistemic set A.B.~C Piagetian

guidelines for researching intellectual development completely ignore the development of epistemic sets which do not feature in the western "scientific" sequence.

(14) This generality expresses a law-like necessity (Note (12) above) which does not apply to either level of teleological explanation (as distinguished in Note (7) above). This was firmly demonstrated by W. Dray, Laws and Explanation in History, Oxford University Press, 1957, in opposition to the views of Carl G. Hempel, who maintained that the explanation of conduct relies tacitly on law-like general statements. The correct patterns for explaining action on the one hand, and events on the other, are logically different.

Piaget misconstrues this logical difference. He takes the view that teleological explanation is favoured by younger children because the relationship between an action and the reason for that action is not reversible (CCPC 270)--and the mental operations of pre-operational children are, by definition, not reversible. Reversibility, especially in Piaget's later work, e.g. Understanding Causality New York, W. W. Norton, 1974, is held to depend upon the ability of the child to conceptualize a chain of causally efficacious events between cause and effect. This account, however, begs the question by taking for granted the older child's possession of distinct concepts of "events" and "action". Conceptualizations presuppose concepts, and although the abilities which Piaget associates with reversibility may very well be necessary conditions for learning how to use public concepts correctly, reversibility--understood as a general characteristic of the workings of cognition--is certainly not sufficient of itself to guarantee the learning of these or any other concepts.

(15) To ask whether these accounts--the normative and the Piagetian--might not both and jointly be correct, betrays a misunderstanding. As pointed out earlier, intentional behaviour and events are each explained in a logically different way. These different discourses correspond to the two main areas of human interest--social activity on the one hand, and natural processes on the other. Piaget's error was to try to explain intentional behaviour--that which can be performed more or less carefully or correctly--in terms of causal processes. Standards of correctness cannot, however, be logically inferred from causal processes. Unfortunately, Piaget overlooked this constraint on psychological theorizing.

This is not only a matter of the limits of science in Piaget's own time. Someone might, for example, suppose that in some future epoch it will be possible to correlate correct performances with (for example) the underlying

electrical and chemical causal activity of the brain. But
this would involve establishing a one to one correspondence
between states of the brain and stages in a correct
performance, and there are so many ways of getting
something done correctly, and so many ways in which each
person might go about getting them done, that the prospects
for a unified science of behaviour look very bleak.

(16) This question is raised by D. W. Hamlyn, _ibid_
p.12.

COMMENT

P. R. Dasen

University of Geneva

Is cross-cultural Piagetian research reaching a new stage? When I first reviewed the literature (Dasen, 1972) the initial, exploratory phase was nearing its end; most of the early research had consisted of taking some Piagetian tasks, usually only one or two from the same conceptual area (usually conservation), and trying them out in some exotic context. In the second stage, the research designs became more quasi-experimental, usually comparing two or more sub-groups differing on some variables, these being often related to acculturation (schooling, urbanization, adoption into Western families, etc.). Stage 2 also has the following features: 1) a wider choice of tasks, including conceptual areas such as classification, space, time, speed, and so on; 2) a greater attention to methodological problems, the use of adapted tasks and local materials, or more care given to ensuring adequate communication; 3) more research being carried out by psychologists of developing countries working in their own culture. Most of the cross-cultural Piagetian research published in the last decade (exemplified by the volume I edited in 1977) is of that type. It has produced a large amount of data, showing mainly that the impact of culture really is much more important than Piaget had thought.

But ontogenesis occurs through conflict, and the first important criticisms against this line of research were voiced at the 1973 ISSBD (International Society for the Study of Behavioural Development) meeting in Ann Arbor. B. Whiting (1976) called attention to the need of "unpacking" the global environmental or cultural variables, and Greenfield (1976) voiced the following three criticisms of cross-cultural Piagetian research:

1) The standard Piagetian tasks are not sufficient to yield an unambiguous diagnosis of the subject's reasoning; additional methods are required, such as the use of training techniques.

2) Piaget's developmental endpoint, the stage of formal operations, really reflects the reasoning of a Western scientist; but this form of thought is not necessarily the one in other cultures, or even in some subcultures within our own society. Thus, in each culture to be studied, the ideal developmental endpoint should first be specified and then the ontogenetic changes leading to this endpoint

155

should be studied. This would lead to "a Piagetian
psychology for each culture" (Dasen, 1977).

3) The basic concepts in Piaget's genetic epistemology,
adaptation as an equilibrium between assimilation and
accommodation, structuralism and constructivism, have
received little attention in the cross-cultural literature.
"In conclusion, if Piaget has, in the past, led the
cross-cultural enterprise astray, it is because researchers
have followed his procedures rather than his theory"
(Greenfield, 1976, p.333).

The first criticism is mainly a methodological one. In
some of the stage 2 research, attention has been paid to
training techniques, and to models distinguishing
competence from performance (see Dasen & Heron, 1981, for a
summary). The other two criticisms, if they were truly
answered, would lead us into a third stage of
cross-cultural Piagetian research. The papers presented
here are particularly interesting because they represent
clear attempts to break away from the second stage; are
they the pioneers of stage 3?

Both Poole and Davids, implicitly or explicitly,
expand on Greenfield's second and third points. They both
remind us that Piaget was not primarily a developmental
psychologist, but an epistemologist, rejecting philosophy
per se (Piaget, 1971), while trying to explain the
development of knowledge through studying the child on the
one hand, and the history of science on the other. Piaget's
last manuscript, a collaborative effort with R. Garcia
about to be published, deals specifically with the history
of science, and shows that Piaget has remained true to his
programme (Piaget, 1918) throughout his life's work.

Within this context, Poole is right to say that "the
Great Man did not produce a viable concept of culture".
This is indeed a problem to cross-cultural psychologists,
but was of little concern to Piaget himself and to what he
meant to achieve. His epistemology is enculturated in
Western paradigms, his history of science goes back to
Aristotle more than to Chinese or Arab sciences, and Poole
reminds us of the debate about the universality of science
(UNESCO, 1974). We are starting to recognize that Western
science and its technological applications are leading not
only to "progress" but also to enormous ecological and
human disasters. It has become easier to admit that this
science may not be the ideal model for mankind, that indeed
there are different standards of rationality. The
popularity of Carlos Castaneda's writings shows us that
reality as a social consensus is becoming a possible
epistemic set even to those unfamiliar with some of the
modern philosophers (see for example Silverman, 1975). Of
course, it is a similar line of reasoning that leads the
fundamentalists, supported in part by the president of the

most powerful Western nation, to place the scientific
theory of evolution on the same level as a religious belief
(Thuillier, 1981).

Poole's criticism of the Piagetian endstate and his
alternative model of a norm-governed intellectual
development is very stimulating. The scheme of epistemic
sets for causal judgement is, I would say, very Piagetian;
both neat and cryptic. The paper gives only a cursory
explanation of the three conditions, and some additional
information may have been helpful on the difference between
Frazerian magic and divinatory magic, or between medieval
science, pseudo-science and a "critical teleological level
II"; no doubt clarity has here suffered from conciseness.
More importantly, Poole does not give us any specific
example drawn from a non-Western context of such a
culturally specific network of epistemic sets. Would these
sets be drawn from those labelled "not meaningful" in Table
1? Are we left with an implicit equation between Piaget's
pre-operational stage and magic, supposedly typical of
"primitive thinking"? This is obviously not Poole's
intention. Alas, neo-Levy-Bruhlian extrapolations of
Piagetian developmental psychology are not uncommon in the
recent literature (see for example Mangan, 1978; Hallpike,
1979; Hippler, 1980). Should we reject developmental
theories wholesale because of such possible misuses (Cole &
Scribner, 1977) or is it possible to use a developmental
model without an implicit value scale? (Dasen, Berry &
Witkin, 1979)

Using a standard Piagetian task may not necessarily be
"sampling performance on Western norms", as Poole puts it,
because the conceptual areas that Piaget has studied may
also be valued in some other cultures, such as spatial
concepts in nomadic hunting and gathering societies (Dasen,
1975). Finding a difference in the rate of development of a
particular concept does not necessarily mean ascribing
"mental inferiority", firstly because a particular concept
cannot be taken as an indicator of a general level of
reasoning, and secondly because the interpretation can just
as well be phrased in terms of a difference- rather than a
deficiency-model. However, Poole is quite right to caution
against too easy and frequent ethnocentric slips.

Both Poole and Davids draw attention to the
distinction between Piaget's stage theory and his
structural theory. Both agree that the stage theory is at
least partly culture-specific. Poole rejects the structural
or autoregulative theory because it neglects the influence
of the social environment. Indeed it is only with the work
of Doise & Mugny (1981) and Perret-Clermont (1980) that the
Piagetian school has paid real attention to social
psychology. Davids, on the other hand, sees in the
structural aspect of the theory a possibility of deriving

common laws underlying different surface contents. His programme follows Greenfield's second point: in each culture one would devise a "regional psychology", that could be a culture-specific stage theory. A comparison of these theories would then allow us to test the hypothesis of a universal deep structure.

Greenfield, Davids and Poole each tells us that cross-cultural research should become both more structural and more "emic" (2). The problem is that they tell us WHY, quite convincingly, but they do not tell us HOW.

Greenfield & Childs (1977) and Price-Williams et al. (1977) have studied children's use of kinship terms; Greenfield & Lave (1982) have taken the valued endstates of being a weaver in Mexico or a tailor in Liberia, and have studied the traditional educational settings surrounding these achievements. These studies are most interesting, but they are mainly descriptive and do not provide what could be called "regional structural theories". Is it at all possible to devise purely "emic" theories? Can it be done by a foreigner? Can it be done by local psychologists, as long as they are trained in Western institutions? Are we waiting for indigenous Piagets to arise? Or could it be that psychology is nothing but a Western paradigm anyway?

The difficulty of devising a culture-specific study of children's thinking is exemplified by Chung's interesting attempt to break away from standard Piagetian tasks. But first we may ask: What is a "standard" Piagetian task? For the techniques Chung calls standard are not the ones used by the Geneva school and described, for example, by Inhelder, Sinclair & Bovet (1974). In the second part of the conservation of liquids, for example, Chung pours the juice from one beaker into two smaller ones, while the equilavent step in the Genevan technique is to use a single wide glass; in the conservation of substance, Chung uses a double transformation, a problem that is surely more difficult than the single transformation used classically. As long as one is only interested in epistemology, such procedural differences may be of little import. Also there is no reason, except historical, to take the Genevan procedures as the "standard" ones. The trouble is that "the conservation of liquids" does not mean the same thing to different investigators, and this becomes a problem when the results of different studies are to be compared. Concrete operations are, by definition, dependent upon content, context and procedure. This is shown, quite strikingly, by Chung's "revised" tasks: quite a simple change in the tasks' context produces a marked change in results. The difficulty with Chung's design is that the revised tasks were always presented second, thus at least part of the change may be attributed to order-effects that may be particularly strong when the subjects are not familiar with the testing situation.

The "new tests", Chung emphasized herself, are not
equivalent to the standard tests. Indeed, they are not
tests of conservation at all, and should not be called
that, nor placed on the same graph (3). The new liquids
task can be solved quite simply by counting units (one or
two). It is not clear why, in this field situation, it
would not have been just as natural to use a truly
equivalent task. In the new substance task, the requirement
of equality is stated in the instructions, and therefore
is, again, not a conservation task. In the new
discontinuous quantity task, we are confronted with a
complex situation in that glass B contains fewer shells,
some having been dropped. If it is an emic characteristic
of Korean culture to pour shells into glasses, then the
standard procedure would have done just as well.

We are thus told that Korean children from a remote
rural area possess "logical-practical" abilities, while
urbanized and British children would have
"logical-mathematical" skills. But were the rural children
given a chance to express culture-specific logico-
mathematical skills? I do not think that Chung's conclusion
is warranted from the data presented. Her attempt to "go
emic" has failed. But at least she has tried, which is more
than can be said of many others. And the data on the new
tests are interesting in themselves, even if it is not
clear what they measure.

Also successful is the part that is a classical stage
2 study, comparing urban and rural samples. For the Korean
rural children, the results of both the standard and the
revised tasks indicate either of two possible
interpretations: 1) the conservation concepts tested do not
start to develop in most of the children before the age of
8 or 9; 2) the younger children do "have" these concepts,
but they do not usually display their ability in these
particular task situations. One would need much more
information, on how they react to training techniques, on
how older children perform on the same tasks, to what
extent quantitative comparisons are valued in the
community, etc., to decide between the alternative
interpretations. Since rice is produced (and we are told
its quantity is used to evaluate area) how is it measured
out? Is it sold on markets? Do children participate in
selling it?

As to the urban Korean children living in Britain,
they show an exceptionally early acquisition of the
conservation concepts tested, much earlier than the rural
British children; since the latter are also "Westernized",
there must be something in urban living beyond
acculturation that favours the development of these

concepts, or renders the tasks more adequate. But urbanization, we have been reminded by B. Whiting, is a "packaged variable".

Maybe the next step in cross-cultural Piagetian research, less ambitious but possibly more readily attainable than the one suggested by Greenfield, Davids and Poole, should be to unwrap some of these packages. For example this could mean paying greater attention to the environments in which concept development occurs: "cognitive ambience" suggested by Heron & Simonsson (1969) has still not been thoroughly investigated, nor language, child rearing practices or daily routines.

No, cross-cultural Piagetian psychology has not reached a new stage in Aberdeen, but even in a stage theory development may occur in small increments rather than in big leaps. The papers presented and the ones published here largely contribute to this ontogeny.

NOTES

1) Partial support for attending the conference came from grant 1.048-0.79 of the Fonds National Suisse de la Recherche Scientifique. Author's address: F.P.S.E., University of Geneva, CH-1211 Geneva 4, Switzerland.

2) After Jahoda's lecture this term has fallen into disrepute. However, "culture-specific" could mean specific to Western culture; if the theory is applied to other cultures it becomes an "imposed etic". Davids suggests that we need many indigenous theories specific to each culture; it may be possible to reach a "derived etic" at the level of a structural theory. This is of course Berry's scheme, but I agree with Jahoda that it is phrased in a very abstract mode and it is difficult to see how this grand programme will work in practice.

3) Several of the supposedly early attainments of conservation that have been reported recently can be explained by such a lack of attention to task equivalence.

REFERENCES

COLE, M. & SCRIBNER, S. (1977) Developmental theories applied to cross-cultural cognitive research. Annals of the New York Academy of Sciences, 285: 366-373.

DASEN, P.R. (1972) Cross-cultural Piagetian research: a summary. Journal of Cross-Cultural Psychology, 3: 23-39.

DASEN, P.R. (1975) Concrete operational development in three cultures. Journal of Cross-Cultural Psychology, 6: 156-172.

DASEN, P.R. (Ed.) (1977) Piagetian Psychology: Cross-Cultural Contributions. New York: Gardner Press (Wiley).

DASEN, P.R. (1977) Cross-cultural cognitive development: the cultural aspects of Piaget's theory. Annals of the New York Academy of Sciences, 285: 322-337.

DASEN, P.R. & HERON, A. (1981) Cross-cultural tests of Piaget's theory. In H.C Triandis & A. Heron (Eds.) Handbook of Cross-Cultural Psychology, Vol. 4. Boston: Allyn & Bacon. pp. 295-342.

DASEN, P.R., BERRY, J.W. & WITKIN, H. (1979) The use of developmental theories cross-culturally. In L. Eckensberger, Y. Poortinga & W. Lonner (Eds.) Cross-Cultural Contributions to Psychology. Amsterdam: Swets & Zeitlinger. pp. 69-82.

DOISE, W. & MUGNY, G. (1981) Le développement social de l'intelligence. Paris: Intereditions.

GREENFIELD, P. (1976) Cross-cultural research and Piagetian theory: paradox and progress. In K. Riegel & J. Meacham (Eds.) The Developing Individual in a Changing World, Vol. 1. The Hague: Mouton. pp. 322-333.

GREENFIELD, P.M. & CHILDS, C.P. (1977) Understanding sibling concepts: a developing study of kin terms in Zinacantan. In P.R. Dasen (Ed.) Piagetian Psychology: Cross-Cultural Contributions. New York: Gardner Press. pp. 335-358.

GREENFIELD, P.M. & LAVE, J. (1982) Cognitive aspects of informal education. In D.A. Wagner & H.W. Stevenson (Eds.) Cultural Perspectives on Child Development. San Francisco: W.H. Freeman. pp. 181-207.

HALLPIKE, C. (1979) The Foundations of Primitive Thought. London: Oxford University Press.

HERON, A. & SIMONSSON, M. (1969) Weight conservation in Zambian children: A non-verbal approach. International Journal of Psychology, 4: 281-292.

HIPPLER, A.E. (1980) Editorial. I.A.C.C.P. Cross-Cultural Psychology Newsletter, 14: 2-3.

INHELDER, B., SINCLAIR, H. & BOVET, M. (1974) Learning and the Development of Cognition. Cambridge, Mass.: Harvard University Press.

MANGAN, J. (1978) Piaget's theory and cultural differences: the case for value-based modes of cognition. Human Development, 21: 170-189.

PERRET-CLERMONT, A.-N. (1980) Social Interaction and Cognitive Development in Children. London: Academic Press.

PIAGET, J. (1918) Recherche. Lausanne: La Concorde.

PIAGET, J. (1971) Insights and Illusions of Philosophy. New York: The World Publishing.

PRICE-WILLIAMS, D., HAMMOND, O.W., EDGERTON, C. & WALKER, M. (1977) Kinship concepts among rural Hawaiian children. In P.R. Dasen (Ed.) Piagetian Psychology: Cross-Cultural Contributions. New York: Gardner Press. pp. 296-334.

SILVERMAN. D. (1975) Reading Castaneda. London: Routledge & Kegan Paul.

THUILLER, P. (1981) Bible et science: Darwin en proces. La Recherche, 12: 710-719.

UNESCO (1974) La science et la diversité des cultures. Paris: P.U.F.

WHITING, B.B. (1976) The problem of the packaged variable. In K. F. Riegel & J.A. Meacham (Eds.) The Developing Individual in a Changing World, Vol. 1. The Hague: Mouton. pp. 303-309.

THE GOUGH-HEILBRUN ADJECTIVE CHECK LIST AS CROSS-CULTURAL RESEARCH TOOL

J. E. Williams and D. L. Best

Wake Forest University, Winston-Salem

Cross-cultural psychology is a burgeoning enterprise. The six volumes of the recently published Handbook of Cross-Cultural Psychology (Triandis, 1980) document the increasing importance of this area of psychological theory and research. In view of the many difficulties encountered in cross-cultural work, it is impressive that the field has developed so far in such a relatively short period of time.

Among the problems faced by the cross-cultural researcher is that of developing research instruments that may be used appropriately in a variety of cultural settings. The knowledgeable researcher is sensitive to both emic and etic considerations in cross-cultural studies (Berry, 1969). Regarding the former, the researcher knows that human behavior often must be understood in the context of local culture and that methods developed in one culture may not be appropriate for use in others. On the other hand, the researcher recognizes that cross-cultural psychology is intrinsically comparative and, thus, continually seeks methods which permit valid cross-cultural comparisons.

Psychologists, cross-cultural and otherwise, are always searching for general methods which can be applied across a broad range of research topics. The advantage of such methods is obvious; one does not have to develop a new method every time one wishes to address a new problem. The semantic differential of Charles Osgood and his associates (1957, 1975) is a prime example of a general research tool. This method, which assesses the affective meanings associated with particular words or other stimulus objects, has been applied successfully to a remarkable variety of research questions.

163

Chapter 18

In this paper. we propose that the Gough-Heilbrun (1965, 1980b) Adjective Check List is another broad-range instrument with considerable promise as a general cross-cultural research tool. The argument is based on: the nature of the task, which seems appropriate in many cultural settings; the versatility of the method in addressing a variety of research questions; the fact that the instrument has been translated into many different languages; and the successful use of the method in recent cross-cultural studies.

The Nature of the Task

The item pool of the Adjective Check List (ACL) consists of 3000 English adjectives selected to be representative of terms used to characterize persons. Stated most broadly, the ACL provides a method for describing "what people are like," a topic of central concern in much psychological research. A representative sample of ACL items is shown in Table 1.

Table 1

A Sample of Items from the Adjective Check List

absent-minded	egotistical	mild	sharp-witted
affectionate	evasive	nagging	silent
anxious	feminine	obnoxious	sly
artistic	foresighted	original	sophisticated
bitter	friendly	peaceable	stable
capable	gloomy	planful	strong
cheerful	hard-headed	practical	superstitious
cold	helpful	progressive	talkative
confident	hurried	quiet	thoughtful
contented	impulsive	reasonable	tough
cowardly	infantile	reliable	unconventional
deceitful	insightful	restless	unfriendly
dependent	inventive	sarcastic	unscrupulous
disorderly	lazy	self-pitying	warm
dreamy	mannerly	sentimental	wise

The adjective list was developed by Harrison Gough and his associates at the Institute of Personality and Research at the University of California (Berkeley). Initially, the check list was devised as a method for staff members to record their impressions of persons who were being studied in assessment programs. Subsequently, the adjective pool was used to develop a self-descriptive, personality assessment procedure. While the latter use has become most widely-known, the item pool can be employed for a variety of other research tasks in which subjects are asked to describe persons, real or imaginary, or various personified constructs.

The basis for the use of the ACL method in cross-cultural studies is that all modern languages have an adjectival class of descriptors, including terms applied to persons (Gough & Heilbrun, 1980b, p.46). Thus, to ask subjects to describe persons by the use of adjectives should be a familiar and psychologically meaningful task in most, if not all, cultural settings. Furthermore, the checklist format avoids some problems which may occur in the cross-cultural application of psychological scaling formats, such as variations among groups in the use of extreme categories on rating scales of the 1-to-7 variety (Triandis, Vassiliou, Vassiliou, Tanaka, & Shanmugam, 1972, pp. 53-54). The simple format also permits the researcher to gather a large amount of data in a relatively short period of time.

One must, of course, be cautious in assuming that the particular set of adjectives employed in Gough and Heilbrun's standard 300-item list is adequate for the description of persons in all cultures. We will return to discuss this question later in the context of a cross-cultural study in which the item pool was used in a 25-country, 13-language study of sex stereotypes.

The Versatility of the Method

The item pool of the Adjective Check List can be applied to a great variety of research problems. This versatility is illustrated by the fact that the recent bibliography of ACL studies (Gough & Heilbrun, 1980a) has a total of 701 entries. The following taxonomy of ACL applications illustrates the variety of research uses of the method.

1. Descriptions of Individual Persons. A frequent application is one in which subjects are asked to describe self, significant others (spouse, parent, child, etc.), or persons whom the subjects have observed in particular settings (e.g., therapists describing clients; teachers describing pupils; supervisors describing employees, etc.).

The method could be used, for example, to compare the manner in which well-known politicians are perceived by the public.

2. Descriptions of Groups of Persons. Another common use is to ask subjects to consider groups of persons with whom they have had extensive experience and to indicate the traits which characterize them collectively (e.g., successful employees). A variation of this use is to compare two or more groups and to indicate the traits which are considered differentially characteristic (e.g., clinical type A vs. clinical type B, etc.).

3. Social Stereotypes. Related to the foregoing are applications in which subjects are asked to describe their beliefs concerning the psychological characteristics of persons classified into broad social groups: ethnic group A vs. ethnic group B; men, in general vs. women, in general; etc.

4. Historical Figures. The item pool can be used in psychobiographical studies in which subjects are asked to describe their impressions of historically important persons; e.g., Nehru, Stalin. Roosevelt, Churchill, etc.

5. Hypothetical Persons. The method may be employed to delineate the characteristics of various sorts of hypothetical persons. Illustrative here is the use of the item pool to characterize various ideal types such as ideal self, ideal mate, ideal physician, etc.

6. Personified Concepts. Subjects may be asked to use the item pool to characterize a variety of non-person concepts which, nevertheless, can be meaningfully personified. Illustrative here are the studies reported by Gough and Heilbrun (1980b, p. 40) comparing the cities of Rome and Paris, and Fiat and Volkswagen automobiles. The ACL would appear to have many other such applications in the areas of environmental and advertising psychology.

Another aspect of the versatility of the ACL method is the variety of ways in which the results from a particular study may be summarized. One can deal with the findings at the individual item level determining, for example, which individual adjectives are more frequently associated with group A or group B. In addition, there are three theoretically-based scoring systems, developed in the United States, which can be used to summarize findings. Best known is the original system devisd by Gough and Heilbrun (1965, 1980b) in which the findings are summarized in terms of 15 psychological needs. Another recently developed system, based upon Osgood's (1957) three-factor theory of affective meaning, summarizes findings in terms of Favorability, Strength and Activity (Best, Williams &

Briggs, 1980; Williams & Best, 1977). A third system (Williams & Williams, 1980) summarizes ACL findings in terms of the five functional ego states of Berne's (1961) Transactional Analysis theory: Critical Parent, Nurturing Parent, Adult, Free Child and Adapted Child. While all three of these systems have been found useful in cross-cultural research, one must bear in mind that since they are American based, they may possibly be American biased. A critique of this and other methodological matters is provided by Williams and Best (1982), who also provide further information concerning the three theoretically-based scoring systems. The revised ACL Manual (Gough & Heilbrun, 1980b) describes additional scales (e.g., creativity, military leadership, etc.) which may be useful in cross-cultural studies.

Illustrative Cross-Cultural Applications

We will describe two major cross-cultural applications of the ACL: one just completed and the other currently in progress. References to additional cross-cultural studies may be found in the ACL Manual (Gough & Heilbrun, 1980b) and Bibliography (Gough & Heilbrun, 1980a).

We have just completed a project in which we compared sex stereotypes among adults and young children in 30 nations (Williams & Best, 1982). The ACL item pool served as the basis for our adult studies with full 300-item data obtained in 25 countries.

The aim of the investigation was to study beliefs concerning differences in the psychological makeup of men and women in different countries. In the adult studies, university students served as cultural reporters. In each country, approximately 100 men and women students individually considered the 300 items of the ACL pool and identified the characteristics which, in their culture, were more frequently associated with one gender or the other. The items were presented in English, when appropriate, and in other languages as required. In all, 13 different languages were employed. A listing of these 25 countries is shown in Table 2.

In each country, the collective responses of the students were examined to identify sets of adjectives which were associated with one sex at least twice as often as the other. These sets of male-associated and female-associated adjectives were viewed as defining the sex stereotypes in the particular country. The findings from this project, which have just been published (Williams & Best, 1982), revealed some interesting variations in sex stereotypes among the countries studied. More dramatic, however, was the high degree of pancultural generality in the traits which were differently ascribed to women and men. For

example, in all countries women were said to be more
sentimental, submissive and superstitious than men, while
men were said to be more adventurous, independent and
forceful than women. The pancultural similarity in
stereotypes is summarized in Table 3 in terms of the three
theoretically-based scoring systems described earlier. The
Affective Meaning Analysis indicated that, in all
countries, the items associated with men were stronger and
more active than those associated with women. On the other
hand, there was no consistent difference in favorablility
which, in some countries, was greater for the
male-associated items and, in others, greater for the
female-associated items. The Transactional Analysis
ego-state findings indicated that, panculturally, the
Critical Parent and Adult functions were more
characteristic of men while the Nurturing Parent and
Adapted Child functions were more characteristic of women.
The Psychological Needs analysis indicated that certain
needs were more highly associated with men (i.e.,
dominance, autonomy, aggression, exhibition, achievement
and endurance) while others were more highly associated
with women (abasement, deference, succorance, nurturance,
affiliation and heterosexuality). It should be emphasized
that any or all of these scoring systems can be used to
summarize ACL findings from any of the various applications
described earlier.

Table 2

The 25 Countries in the Study

Africa	Asia
Nigeria	India
South Africa	Israel
	Japan
Europe	Malaysia
	Pakistan
England	
Finland	North America
France	
Germany	Canada
Ireland	United States
Italy	
The Netherlands	South America
Norway	
Scotland	Bolivia
	Brazil
Oceania	Peru
	Trinidad
Australia	Venezuela
New Zealand	

It is of methodological interest to note that in the project just described the 300 items of the ACL pool were viewed by the researchers and subjects in all countries as adequate for the task of describing men and women. Thus, the earlier question concerning possible American bias in the composition of the item pool did not seem important in the context of this study.

Table 3

Summary of Pancultural Similarities in

Sex-Trait Stereotypes

Characteristic of Men	Characteristic of Women
Affective Meanings	
Active	Passive
Strong	Weak
Ego States	
Critical Parent	Nurturing Parent
Adult	Adapted Child
Psychological Needs	
Dominance	Abasement
Autonomy	Deference
Aggression	Succorance
Exhibition	Nurturance
Achievement	Affiliation
Endurance	Heterosexuality

Findings from our sex-stereotype project are being used as the basis for another cross-cultural study, now being organized, in which we will study the degree to which sex stereotypes are represented in the self concepts of women and men in a subset (12 to 15) of our 25 countries. Subjects will be men and women university students each of whom will use the 300 ACL items to describe himself of

herself, followed by a description of his or her ideal
self. In a particular country, each self and ideal self
description will be scored for its sex-stereotype loading
using the findings from the sex-stereotype study in that
country. The degree to which the self or ideal self
description incorporates the local male- and
female-associated stereotype characteristics will be taken
as an index of the masculinity-femininity of the
description. Since the descriptions in each country are
scored in terms of the local stereotypes, the study will
permit the assessment of relative degrees of
masculinity-femininity in different countries. It will be
possible to determine, for example, whether the men's self
descriptions in country A are more or less masculine than
in country B, or whether women's ideal self concepts are
more feminine in some countries than in others. We feel
that the application of this derived-etic approach (Berry,
1969) to the cross-cultural study of masculinity and
femininity will prove more fruitful than previous efforts
which have not defined these concepts in culture-specific
terms.

The use of the ACL in the two projects described
illustrates the versatility of the method. By means of a
simple change in instructions to the subjects, the item
pool was used for the definition of the sex stereotypes,
for the description of self, and for the description of
ideal self. Had we wished to, we could easily have assessed
still other concepts; for example, ideal mate. The ease
with which the ACL is adapted to different research
questions is a distinct advantage over other questionnaire
methods which are designed for a specific purpose (e.g.,
self-description) and which require extensive modification
if they are to be used for a variety of research purposes.
While space does not permit a cataloging of other possible
cross-cultural applications of the method, the following
sample of research topics to which the ACL has been applied
on a unicultural basis may be provocative: aging,
creativity, alcoholism, student activism, vocational
interests, drug addiction, physical disability,
homosexuality, physical fitness, pregnancy, crime and
delinquency, child-rearing practices, mental retardation
and aesthetics (Gough & Heilbrun, 1980a).

Available Translations of the ACL Item Pool

The translation of the ACL items from English to a
second language is a difficult process, for several
reasons. Among these are the fact that word-to-word
translation is required which is a more difficult task than
translations of phrases, sentences, etc. (Brislin, 1980). A
second difficulty is due to the existence in the ACL pool
of many words with closely related meanings (e.g.,
adventurous, courageous, and daring) which the translators

must attempt to differentiate with appropriate words in the second language. Despite these problems, translations have been made to several other languages and still others are currently in progress.

Excellent translations exist in French and Italian and extensive work has been done in France and Italy in norming the ACL as a self-descriptive personality assessment method (Gough & Gendre, 1982; Gough, Heilbrun, & Fioravanti, 1981). Additional translations, adequate for research applications, are available in at least 10 other languages. Table 4 lists the translations currently available and provides information as to where they may be obtained.

Table 4

Available Translations of ACL Items

Bahasa Malaysia	Italian
Dutch	Japanese
Finnish	Norwegian
French	Portuguese
German	Spanish
Hebrew	Urdu

Note: Information concerning these translated versions
       may be obtained from the authors at Box 7778,
       Department of Psychology, Wake Forest University,
       Winston-Salem, N. C., 27109, U.S.A.

Conclusions

The Gough-Heilbrun Adjective Check List is a useful cross-cultural research tool. The nature of the method makes it applicable to a broad range of research topics. The several scoring systems available enable researchers to examine findings in a variety of different ways. The thirteen different language versions currently available make possible the immediate application of the method in many countries.

REFERENCES

Berne, E. Transactional analysis in psychotherapy. New
York: Grove Press, 1961.

Berry, J.W. On cross-cultural comparability. International
Journal of Psychology, 1969, 4, 119-128.

Best, D.L., Williams, J.E., & Briggs, S.R. A further
analysis of the affective meanings associated with male and
female sex-trait stereotypes. Sex Roles, 1980, 6, 735-746.

Brislin, R.W. Translation and content analysis of oral and
written materials. In H.C. Triandis & J.W. Berry (Eds.),
Handbook of cross-cultural psychology (Vol. 2). Boston:
Allyn and Bacon, 1980.

Gough, H.G. & Gendre, F. Une introduction à l'édition
française de l'Adjective Check List. Paris: Les Editions du
Centre de Psychologie Appliquée, 1982.

Gough, H.G. & Heilbrun, A.B.,Jr. The adjective check list
manual. Palo Alto, CA: Consulting Psychologists Press,
1965.

Gough, H.G. & Heilbrun, A.B., Jr. The adjective check list
bibliography. Palo Alto, CA: Consulting Psychologists
Press, 1980. (a)

Gough, H.G. & Heilbrun, A.B., Jr. The adjective check list
manual. Palo Alto, CA: Consulting Psychologists Press,
1980. (b)

Gough, H.G., Heilbrun, A.B., Jr., & Fioravanti, M. Manuale
della versione Italiana del' Adjective Check List. Firenze:
Organizzazioni Speciali, 1981.

Osgood, C.E., May, W.H., & Miron, M.S. Cross-cultural
universals of affective meaning. Urbana: University of
Illinois Press, 1975.

Osgood, C.E., Suci, G.J., & Tannenbaum, P.H. The
measurement of meaning. Urbana: University of Illinois
Press, 1957.

Triandis, H.C. (General Editor) Handbook of cross-cultural
psychology. Volumes 1-6. Allyn and Bacon: Boston, 1980.

Triandis, H.C., Vassiliou, V., Vassiliou, G., Tanaka, Y., &
Shanmugam, A.V. The analysis of subjective culture. New
York: Wiley, 1972.
172

Williams, J.E. & Best, D.L. Measuring sex stereoypes: A thirty nation study. Beverly Hills, CA: Sage Publications, 1982.

Williams, J.E. & Best, D.L. Sex stereotypes and trait favorablility on the Adjective Check List. Educational and Psychological Measurement, 1977, 37, 101-110.

Williams, K.B. & Williams, J.E. The assessment of Transactional Analysis ego states via the Adjective Check List. Journal of Personality Assessment, 1980, 44, 120-129.

SOME APPLICATIONS OF AN ITERATIVE METHOD TO DETECT BIASED ITEMS

H. van der Flier

Free University of Amsterdam

In conditional item bias models, an item is considered biased if the probability of a correct answer, given a certain ability level, differs for the groups distinguished. Ability level can be operationalised as the estimated latent trait position (Lord, 1977), or, more simply, as the observed test score (Scheuneman, 1979; Mellenbergh, 1982). A serious weakness of these models is that if the test contains a large number of biased items, the measure of ability level used in classifying subjects into ability categories will also be biased. This can mean that some biased items are not identified as such, and that some unbiased are erroneously classified as biased. The results of a recently completed study by Van der Flier, Mellenbergh, Ader, and Wijn (1982), using simulated data, show that in many cases better results can be obtained using an iterative method. Briefly, this method involves removing biased items from the test (or, more accurately, not counting them in determining the total score) so that the number of items removed increases by one with each successive iteration. At the end of the first iteration the most biased item is removed from the test, at the end of the second iteration the two most biased items, etc. Items which are eliminated at an early stage may be included again at a later stage.

A log linear model is applied to each item (i.e. per Score x Group x Response table) in the form of

$$\ln F_{ijk} = u + u_{1(i)} + u_{2(j)} + u_{3(k)} + u_{12(ij)} + u_{13(ik)}$$

where i is the score category, j the subgroup, and k the response category (see Mellenbergh, 1982). The fit of the model is expressed in a likelihood ratio χ^2 value. The L.R. χ^2 value indicates to what extent the parameters not

included in the model - Group x Response
interaction $(u_{23(jk)})$ and Score x Group x Response
interaction $(u_{123(ijk)})$ - are not equal to zero.

Figure 1 is a graphic presentation of part of the
results from the simulation study (for a more extensive
description, see Van der Flier, Mellenbergh, Ader, and
Wijn, 1982). It comprises the results of two groups of 500
simulated subjects on a test consisting of 29 items. For
both groups, the subject parameters were randomly selected
from a standard normal distribution. Item responses were
generated using the three-parameter normal ogive model
(Lord, 1980). Item bias was introduced by multiplying by
one-half the portion above chance level of the item
characteristic curves of the uneven numbered items from
group two. The items are arranged in order of difficulty
for group 1.

The outcome is clear: after iteration 1 (or using a
non-iterative method) the differentiation between biased
and unbiased items is far from perfect, particularly for
the more difficult items. By applying the iterative method,
the L.R. χ^2 values of the biased items increase and the
L.R. χ^2 values of the unbiased items decrease, thus making
it easier to distinguish the two. In other words, the
problem of biased ability estimates can, at least in
certain cases, be overcome by making use of iterative
procedures.

The present paper deals with the application of the
iterative item bias method to cross-cultural data. Two
studies are discussed, the first of which tests a
hypothesis, while the second one is more exploratory.

Item bias and command of language

This study was carried out to discover if the item
bias method discussed above can make a contribution to
identifying items with a different psychological meaning.
Use was made of test data collected in connection with the
project "Intelligence and Developmental Tests for East
Africa". The aim of this project is to develop test series
for use in the educational systems in Tanzania, Kenya, and
Uganda. For more detailed information on the backgrounds of
the IDEA project, see Drenth, Van der Flier, and Omari
(1979). The results discussed here are those from the test
series for end of primary school level.

In Tanzania, this test series was administered to a
nationwide sample of 892 pupils at the end of 1975. It was
given in Kiswahili. This was the obvious choice; Kiswahili
is the official language of Tanzania, and primary education
all over the country is given in this language. In Kenya,
it is not quite so simple. In the first three forms of

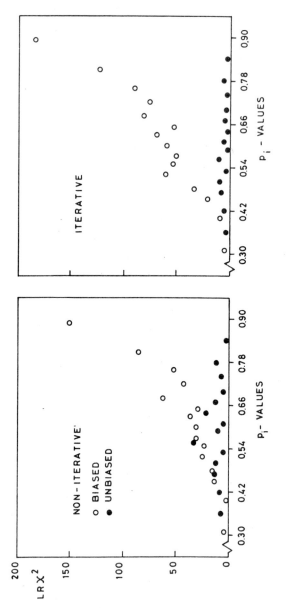

Figure 1. L.R. χ^2 values of biased and unbiased items; non-iterative and iterative procedure.

primary school, the medium of instruction often is one of
the local languages, while English is used in the higher
forms. On the other hand, Kiswahili is relatively close to
most local languages, and in fact acts as a lingua franca
for the various tribes. Besides, Kiswahili is presently
taught as a separate school subject, even though it is not
a subject on the school leaving examination. Because it was
expected that the command of Kiswahili would be less
dependent on factors such as degree of urbanisation,
socio-educational level of the parents, and quality of the
primary school, it was decided to administer the Kiswahili
version originally constructed for Tanzania to a limited
sample of 280 Kenyan pupils. (An English version of the
tests was administered to another sample of 571 pupils).
Testing took place in June 1976.

Of course, the question remains whether pupils
educated under the present system in Kenya have a
sufficient mastery of Kiswahili to be able to do all the
tests properly. Comparison of the test results from the
Tanzanian and the Kenyan samples shows a pattern of
differences which clearly points to a language handicap in
the Kenyan sample. On the verbal tests, the Kenyan pupils
obtain lower scores than the pupils from Tanzania, while
they do better on the non-verbal tests. Furthermore, in the
Kenyan sample the verbal tests appear to have higher
loadings on one and the same factor. The largest shifts are
found for the verbal reasoning tests, Word Exclusion and
Word Analogies. In the Tanzanian sample these tests,
together with other inductive reasoning tests such as
Figure Exclusion and Symbol Exclusion, form part of a
general reasoning factor, while in the Kenyan sample, along
with two fluency tests (Word Beginnings and Endings, and
Thing Categories) they have the highest loadings on a
general language factor (for a more detailed discussion see
Van der Flier, 1982).

The question now is whether it is possible, using the
iterative item bias method, to identify those items where
the language handicap has had the greatest influence on
test results. We will limit our discussion to the two
verbal reasoning tests, Word Exclusion and Word Analogies,
both of which were administered under power conditions.
Both tests consist of 40 items.

In applying the iterative item bias detection
programme to the results, five ability levels (score
categories) were distinguished. The critical L.R. χ^2 value
was set at 15.086 (corresponding to a significance level of
.01). This implied that the iteration procedure would stop
when for none of the remaining items an L.R. χ^2 value of
above 15.086 would be found. The maximum number of
iterations was fixed at 25, to guarantee that the
classification into ability categories would be based on a

Chapter 19

sufficient number of items.

To remove from the test all items with L.R. χ^2 values above 15.086, 16 iterations were required for Word Exclusion and 18 for Word Analogies. This means that the two tests, respectively, contain 16 and 18 biased items, and 24 and 22 unbiased items. Comparison of this classification with the classification which would have been obtained from the results of the first iteration (that is, using a non-iterative procedure) shows a fairly high degree of concurrence. The percentages of items which the two methods would classify in the same way are 87.5 and 80.0 respectively.

Table 1 shows the mean p_i and r_{it} values of the biased and unbiased items in the two samples.

TABLE 1

Word Exclusion and Word Analogies; mean p_i and r_{it} values

of biased and unbiased items in the Tanzanian sample

and in the Kenyan sample

		Biased items		Unbiased items	
		$\bar{p}_i$	$\bar{r}_{it}$	$\bar{p}_i$	$\bar{r}_{it}$
Word Exclusion	Tanzania	.617	.278	.465	.280
	Kenya	.453	.274	.405	.243
Word Analogies	Tanzania	.568	.406	.463	.369
	Kenya	.445	.346	.460	.324

A number of conclusions can be drawn from this table. First of all it appears that, on average, the biased items in the Tanzanian sample have higher p_i values than the unbiased items. Such a difference was to be expected: if there is a language handicap, it will show up most clearly in items where reasoning causes few difficulties (items with high p_i values in the Tanzanian sample). Comparison of the mean p_i values in the two samples supports this explanation. For both tests, the mean p_i values of the biased items in the Kenyan sample are markedly lower than in the Tanzanian sample, while the differences on the unbiased items are quite small. This last fact has an important practical implication: by eliminating biased items, the difference in test performance between the

178

Tanzanian and the Kenyan samples is considerably diminished.

For the r_{it} values, the differences between biased and unbiased items are much less pronounced. On the whole, the biased items seem to have somewhat higher r_{it} values, but the differences are quite small. It may be concluded that the mean r_{it} values in the Tanzanian sample are somewhat higher than in the Kenyan sample.

We now need to find out if the items classified as biased and unbiased also differ in what they measure. Here we will consider only the Kenyan sample. The assumption is that individual differences in the command of Kiswahili in this sample primarily played a role in answering the biased items. Based on this assumption, it is to be expected that the total scores on the biased items will show higher positive correlations (or lower negative ones) with variables which can be considered to reflect the command of Kiswahili, while the total scores on the unbiased items will show higher positive correlations with criterion measures for reasoning ability.

Actually there is no really good measure available in the study for the command of Kiswahili. The most obvious variable is the school mark in Kiswahili at the end of the seventh school year. But since this mark shows very high correlations with the other school marks, it is quite likely that it will not only reflect differences in the command of Kiswahili, but also in the overall level of school performance.

A second direct measure of the command of Kiswahili which comes into consideration is the total score on the subtest Word Beginnings and Endings. The task in this test is to write down in a limited time as many words as possible that begin and end with a certain letter. The psychological meaning of the test, in accordance with French et al. (1963), may be designated by "word fluency". One advantage of this criterion measure over the previous one is that it is comparatively independent of reasoning ability.

Besides these direct criterion measures, the regional location of the school is also included as a variable. In the coastal area of Kenya, more and better Kiswahili is spoken· than inland. For pupils from schools in the coastal area (51.6%) the variable has a value of 2 and for pupils from inland schools a value of 1.

Lastly, the replies to the question what language is generally spoken at home give information on the language background of the pupils. For the pupils who answered in Kiswahili (22.0%) the variable has a value of 2, for the

179

Chapter 19
others, 1.

    Three measures are used as criteria for reasoning
ability: the total score on the end of primary school
examination (which is taken in English and which does not
include the subject of Kiswahili) and the scores on the two
non-verbal reasoning tests from the IDEA test series,
Figure Exclusion and Symbol Exclusion.

    The intercorrelations of the criterion variables are
shown in Table 2.

TABLE 2

Intercorrelations of criterion variables for command
of Kiswahili and reasoning ability (N = 280)

		1	2	3	4	5	6	7
1.	Kiswahili P7 schoolmarks	-						
2.	Word Beginnings and Endings	.51	-					
3.	Region	.15	.20	-				
4.	Linguistic background	.18	.13	.32	-			
5.	P7 examination total score	.44	.14	-.36	-.16	-		
6.	Figure Exclusion	.28	.06	-.03	.01	.46	-	
7.	Symbol Exclusion	.34	.07	-.22	-.08	.61	.60	-

    The correlations of the total scores on the biased and
unbiased items in Word Exclusion and Word Analogies with
the criterion variables are presented in Table 3. To
facilitate comparison of the correlation patterns, the
correlations corrected for unreliability of the
combinations of biased/unbiased items are shown in italics.
(1)

    The table shows that the expectation that the biased
items will reflect to a greater degree differences in
command of language, and that the unbiased items will
reflect to a greater degree differences in reasoning
ability is supported by the results. If we take only the
correlation coefficients corrected for unreliability, then
we see that the biased parts of the two tests show stronger

180

positive relationships to three of the four criterion
variables for command of Kiswahili, and the unbiased parts
of the tests correlate higher with the three criterion
variables for reasoning ability. The strongest shift in
test meaning is observed for Word Exclusion. The difference
in predictive value of the biased and unbiased parts of
this test with regard to a criterion such as the total
score on the end of primary school examination is certainly
remarkable.

TABLE 3

Word Exclusion and Word Analogies; correlations* or biased
and unbiased parts of the tests with criterion variables

| | Word Exclusion | | Word Analogies | |
	Biased	Unbiased	Biased	Unbiased
Kis. P7 schoolmarks	.49 .70	.50 .68	.51 .60	.57 .67
Word Beg. and End.	.45 .64	.41 .55	.39 .47	.37 .43
Region	.25 .36	.04 .06	.11 .13	-.07 -.08
Linguistic backgr.	.15 .22	.14 .19	.17 .20	.10 .12
P7 Ex. total score	.23 .33	.45 .61	.44 .52	.54 .63
Figure Exclusion	.17 .24	.30 .41	.30 .35	.31 .37
Symbol Exclusion	.19 .26	.41 .55	.35 .42	.43 .50

* The correlation coefficients in italics are corrected for
unreliability of the biased/unbiased parts of the tests.

Item bias and western test skills

The study to be described in this section is mainly
exploratory. The results of a nationwide sample of 571
Kenyan pupils at the end of primary school who took the
English version of the IDEA test series are compared with
the results of a sample of English school children from the
London suburbs. The English sample consists of 447 pupils
(222 boys and 225 girls), all of them in the highest form
of primary school. The comparison is restricted to the four
reasoning tests from the test series: Figure Exclusion,
Word Exclusion, Symbol Exclusion and Word Analogies.
Administration of these tests in England took place in 1979
and 1980. (2)

Although the English pupils were on average two years

younger than the pupils in the Kenyan sample, they obtained much higher scores on all four tests (Table 4), particularly on Figure Exclusion and Word Exclusion.

Reliability estimates (according to the KR-20 method) and intercorrelation matrices for the four subtests are shown in Table 5. In both samples, Word Analogies and Symbol Exclusion appear to be the most reliable. In general, the subtest reliabilities for the Kenyan sample are somewhat lower than for the English sample. The intercorrelation matrices of the subtests in the two samples show strong correspondence. In both cases, the highest correlation is that between the verbal subtests, Word Exclusion and Word Analogies, while Symbol Exclusion is more strongly related to these two tests than Figure Exclusion is. Testing the equality of the matrices using the test described by Jennrich (1970) does not lead to rejection of the null hypothesis (χ^2=.285, df=6, p=.999).

In applying the iterative item bias detection programme, five ability levels were distinguished, just as in the previous study, and the critical L.R. χ^2 value was again set at 15.086. For Figure Exclusion, which consists of 26 items, the maximum number of iterations was fixed at 11; for the other three tests (40 items each) at 25.

The numbers of biased items turned out to be quite high. For Figure Exclusion, 11 iterations were not sufficient to remove from the test all items with L.R. χ^2 values above 15.086. Based on the results from the 11th iteration, this test contains 19 biased items. The number of biased items is higher than the maximum number of iterations for Word Exclusion as well. The results of the 25th iteration show a total of 27 biased items. For Symbol Exclusion and Word Analogies, the maximum number of iterations was sufficient; 22 and 24 items respectively were classified as biased.

Comparison of the classifications in biased/unbiased using the iterative procedure with the classifications using the non-iterative procedure (iteration 1) shows that the items are classified in the same way in 53.9, 82.5, 82.5, and 52.5% of the cases for the four tests.

Comparison of the mean p_i and r_{it} values of the biased and unbiased items in the two samples (Table 6) yields the same picture as the first study: in the English sample the biased items have, on the average, higher p_i values than the unbiased items, and the difference in mean p_i value between the English and the Kenyan sample is a good deal larger for the biased than for the unbiased items. Again in this case, eliminating the biased items would yield a considerably smaller difference in test scores between the two samples.

TABLE 4

Means and standard deviations of the
tests in the English and Kenyan samples.

Test	London (N=447)		Kenya-E (N=571)		t
	M	S	M	S	
1. Figure Exclusion	17.73	4.25	13.99	4.54	13.52**
2. Word Exclusion	25.38	5.27	20.75	5.12	14.09**
3. Symbol Exclusion	24.14	6.79	21.64	6.20	6.06**
4. Word Analogies	25.70	8.27	21.78	7.63	7.76**

**Difference significant at .01 level.

TABLE 5

Subtest reliabilities[1] and intercorrelation matrices
in the English and Kenyan samples

	London (N=447)				Kenya (N=571)			
	1	2	3	4	1	2	3	4
1. Figure Exclusion	(.79)				(.77)			
2. Word Exclusion	.49	(.78)			.47	(.75)		
3. Symbol Exclusion	.58	.54	(.88)		.56	.52	(.82)	
4. Word Analogies	.52	70	.59	(.92)	.51	.69	.57	(.88)

[1] The reliability estimates are in parentheses on the diagonal of
the intercorrelation matrices.

TABLE 6

Mean p_i and r_{it} values in the English sample and
and in the Kenya-E sample

		Biased items		Unbiased items	
		$\bar{p}_i$	$\bar{r}_{it}$	$\bar{p}_i$	$\bar{r}_{it}$
Figure Exclusion	London	.732	.388	.653	.344
	Kenya	.525	.390	.601	.364
Word Exclusion	London	.685	.323	.591	.232
	Kenya	.505	.316	.572	.264
Symbol Exclusion	London	.862	.384	.696	.309
	Kenya	.500	.360	.650	.332
Word Analogies	London	.745	.437	.566	.389
	Kenya	.556	.422	.556	.388

A content analysis of the items which are most clearly non-equivalent yields the following picture:

1. **Figure Exclusion**. In this test, subjects are shown a series of five geometric figures, four of which correspond in some way; the figure which does not follow the principle must be indicated. Five of the 7 cases where the L.R. χ^2 value found is higher than 40 involve items in which the first of the five figures does not belong in the series. In all, six such items occur in the test. It would seem that the Kenyan pupils allow themselves to be influenced more by the order in which the figures are presented, and that they have more trouble giving up a hypothesis formed on the basis of the first figures in the series.

2. **Word Exclusion**. With this test, it is not a clear-cut question of one particular cause of non-equivalence. For some of the items, the lower scores of the Kenyan pupils seem to be a result of their lesser acquaintance with certain words and objects. In other cases, it is primarily the different way of life which plays a role, which means that things are interrelated in a

different way. Finally, it appears that the Kenyan pupils tend more to classify objects in terms of quantitative physical categories (high-low, long-short, large-small). To illustrate this, we give below a few examples of non-equivalent items and indicate what percentages of the English and the Kenyan pupils chose the various alternatives.

item 15)	sculptor	driver*	author	poet	musician
English sample	6.7	79.5	1.9	4.5	7.5
Kenyan sample	17.8	28.6	9.4	18.1	26.1

item 33)	drum	flute	dance*	music	song
English sample	.9	5.1	75.1	5.1	13.9
Kenyan sample	11.4	53.9	18.1	7.7	8.9

item 39)	minute	year	hour	time*	month
English sample	11.0	16.9	2.0	59.8	10.3
Kenyan sample	11.3	48.3	4.0	27.2	9.2

We also give a few examples of non-equivalent items where the Kenyan pupils obtained higher scores.

item 35)	flour	rice	bread	meat*	maize
English sample	6.8	2.1	5.4	38.6	47.1
Kenyan sample	26.1	3.1	6.5	53.9	10.3

item 36)	Africa	Australia	Europe	England*	Asia
English sample	.5	2.9	60.8	23.8	12.1
Kenyan sample	29.2	6.9	7.1	51.3	5.5

The responses of the English pupils to the last item perhaps reflect a somewhat distant attitude towards (the rest of) Europe.

   3. Symbol Exclusion. In this test, it must be indicated which of five number or letter combinations does not belong in the series. This involves aspects such as symmetry, numerical relationships, order relationships

between letters, etc. As it turns out, on items with number combinations, the Kenyan pupils comparatively often select the alternative with the highest or lowest number, and on items with letter combinations, they select alternatives with letters from the beginning of the alphabet. This is true of 10 of the 13 items which most clearly show non-equivalence (L.R. $x^2 > 40$).

4. Word Analogies. In this test, too, factors such as unfamiliarity with certain concepts and differences in life style seem to play a role in the relatively low p_i values for some of the items in the Kenyan sample. Furthermore, the Kenyan pupils often seem to choose a synonym for the third term as the fourth term in the analogy. A few examples illustrate this:

item 14) poem - story

poet -	book	writer*	art	studying	read
English sample	16.8	69.7	4.9	3.2	5.4
Kenyan sample	10.6	24.9	24.3	21.8	18.4

item 15) morning - day

evening -	sleep	dark	night*	moon	afternoon
English sample	2.3	1.8	80.3	2.0	13.8
Kenyan sample	4.9	11.4	53.4	4.5	25.8

item 19) remember - forget

stay -	lose	refuse	live	come	leave*
English sample	5.0	2.9	9.5	10.6	72.0
Kenyan sample	9.0	19.2	34.7	10.9	26.3

On some of the items, the Kenyan pupils do better. However, the differences between the p_i values in the two samples are slight, and no clear cause can be pointed out for this. The following item forms an exception:

item 28) right - left

east -	south	distance	direction	journey	west*
English sample	27.1	1.5	2.0	1.7	67.8
Kenyan sample	12.2	1.3	6.8	2.0	77.7

The distinction between East Africa and West Africa is so much a part of life in the East African countries that this item causes fewer difficulties for the Kenyan pupils.

Conclusion

The results of the two studies described in this paper illustrate the usefulness of the iterative item bias detection method. The first study shows that the method can be used to identify items which measure something different in one of the samples. In the second study, there was less reason to assume that a shift in test meaning would occur, but the results of a content analysis of the non-equivalent items are quite easy to interpret. In both studies, eliminating biased items leads to a smaller difference in test scores between the samples — a result which was expected for the first study in particular.

In closing, a few remarks:

1. Whether differences in test meaning are also expressed in the score patterns on individual items primarily depends on the diversity of the items. One condition seems to be that the items are sensitive in varying degrees to the possession of certain skills. This means that homogeneous tests have less to offer in this direction than tests which are relatively heterogeneous in content.

2. Elimination of biased items of course does not always lead to decreasing the score differences between the groups distinguished. Items can also be biased against the group with the highest total scores on the test. However, the results of the studies discussed here raise the question whether the power of the iterative item bias method in this kind of bias is just as great as its power in detecting bias against the lower-scoring group. To answer this question (and the rather obvious question at what point, or what amount of bias, the iterative prodedure starts to work in the wrong direction) will once again require simulation studies.

NOTES

(1) The Homogeneity indices (according to the KR-20 formula) of the biased and unbiased parts of the tests are, respectively, .496 and .543 (Word Exclusion) and .709 and .719 (Word Analogies).

(2) The author is grateful to Elke Kroeger-Radcliffe for administering the tests.

REFERENCES

Drenth, P.J.D., Flier, H. van der and Omari, I.M. The use of classroom tests, examinations and aptitude tests in a developing country. In: L. Eckensberger, W. Lonner and Y.H. Poortinga (Eds.), Cross-Cultural Contributions to Psychology. Lisse: Swets and Zeitlinger, 1979.

Flier, H. van der. Deviant response patterns and comparability of test scores. Journal of Cross-Cultural Psychology, 1982, 13, 267-298.

Flier, H. van der, Mellenbergh, G.J., Ader, H.J. and Wijn, M. The iterative item bias detection method. Amsterdam: Psychologisch Laboratorium, University of Amsterdam, 1982.

French, J.W.,Ekstrom, R.B. and Price, L.A. Kit of reference tests for cognitive factors. Princeton, N.J.: Educational Testing Service, 1963.

Jennrich, R.I. An asymptotic "Chi-square"-test for the equality of two correlation matrices. Journal of the American Statistical Association, 1970, 65, 904-912.

Lord, F.M. A study of item bias using item characteristic curve theory. In: Y.H. Poortinga (Ed.), Basic Problems in Cross-Cultural Psychology. Amsterdam: Swets and Zeitlinger, 1977.

Lord F.M. Applications of item response theory to practical testing problems. Hillsdale, N.J.: Erlbaum, 1980.

Mellenbergh, G.J. Contingency table models for assessing item bias. Journal of Educational Statistics, 1982, 7.

Scheuneman, J. A method of assessing bias in test items. Journal of Educational Measurement, 1979, 16, 143-152.

A STUDY OF SOCIAL DYNAMICS IN JAPAN:
AN ANALYSIS OF STRESS ON THE SELF-CONCEPT OF THE
BLIND ADOLESCENT

D. Harries

Goldsmiths' College, London

This study reports the findings of an in-depth
analysis of Japanese society and of the major psycho-social
influences on an individual's achievement levels and
behaviour. It provides a useful working model which could,
I believe, afford a basis for a variety of empirical work.
It grew out of a four-year programme of research with blind
young adults, and it is to this field I shall relate it
today.

The research took place at a critical time in Japan's
educational development when most universities and
professions operated a "closed door" system towards the
blind. The research and resultant scholarship which I
helped establish with the Mainichi Shinbun, founded by the
CWAJ (1) and with the approval of the Ministry of
Education, opened the door just a little for blind
intellectuals whose needs for professional training were
hindered by a traditional system of entry regulations and
social attitudes which dissuaded many blind students from
seeking higher education.

The reason I attribute such importance to this
research is that there are 40 million blind in the world
today and yet there are very few psychologists indeed who
understand the range of the prolonged stress that families
suffer.

To situate the work within the framework of this
congress, I should point out that although congenital
blindness and ocular disease are generally on the decline,
the number of blind people all over the world is on the
increase. In many areas their numbers are outstripping
available facilities (Table 1).

TABLE 1

AREA STATISTICS

	TOTAL BLIND	TRAINING/EMPLOYMENT
World	40,000,000	?
India	9,000,000	Rural Training
Bangladesh	100,000	Under 1 in 100
Caribbean	25,000	600 employed
England	107,000	Employment Difficult

In some industrialised European countries, 6% of the blind population received eye injuries in car or industrial accidents. It is this category of blindness among the skilled and educated which is of particular concern to developing countries, where new machines may have inadequate safety guards, operators may not be using available guards correctly, and treatment of eye injuries is sometimes delayed – for example if the medical centre is at some distance from the place of work. Industrialisation may mean that the kind of traditional counselling for the rural blind may no longer be sufficient for people in this fast-growing category of the educated blind. Peru, Nigeria, Mexico and Indonesia have all specifically mentioned the need for psychological counsellors (2). In other countries, the problem exists, but is not yet even recognised. In 1972, the United Nations sent out a questionnaire on rehabilitation services for the blind covering many areas of education and employment but there was not a single question about the availablity of psychological counselling services. As the study shows, many of the newly-blinded and their families are in profound need of psychiatric help and it is essential that the helping professions and psychologists understand the inter-relationship of social and personal factors in adjustment to this kind of loss. As empirical studies by Bauman (1954) and by Cowen et al. (1961) have shown, adjustment may ulitimately depend on factors which are secondary to the loss of vision alone.

There is a brief review of some sample case studies in Table 2:

TABLE 2

CASE STUDIES

Case Study	Age Blinded	Cause	Qualification (+ = Univ. Degree)
A Female	Birth	Congenial	Eng. Literature +
B Female	16	Congenial	Human Science +
C Male	15	Accident	Law +
D Male	9	Accident	Massage
E Male	4	Disease	Acupuncture +
F Male	25	Disease	Nuclear Physics +

There is an ongoing study of the informants' level of personal adjustment and a ten-year follow-up study is planned to see how they finally adjust, both personally and socially, when their professional status is established.

For ease of presentation, I think the main factors influencing the development of their self-image could be represented diagrammatically:

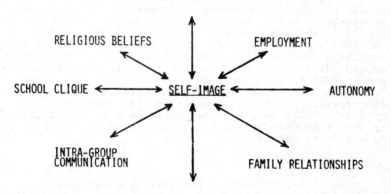

LEVEL OF ASPIRATION

RELIGIOUS BELIEFS   EMPLOYMENT

SCHOOL CLIQUE ←→ SELF-IMAGE ←→ AUTONOMY

INTRA-GROUP COMMUNICATION   FAMILY RELATIONSHIPS

RANGE OF RECIPROCITY

The model represents the interaction of the dynamic forces bearing on the formation and re-formation of the self-image in the day-to-day process of social living. A breakdown in interchange through any one of the channels can leave the self-image isolated at that point. That is, if the channels of positive and negative influences which are normally experienced by the sighted person are not getting through, then there will be a modification imposed on the development of the self-image.

Levels of Aspiration

It is not unusual for a blind adolescent to set him or herself virtually unrealisable goals. The problems facing a newly-blinded adolescent who seeks to become professionally qualified are quite different from those of the congenitally blind for whom there has been a constancy of expectations and social status. The newly-blinded adolescent has to adjust to a different scale of education and employment as well as to change in relationships and behaviour patterns. Age at onset of blindness plays an important role in subsequent development, especially in the consistency of the image the blind person has of him or herself. Respondents B, C and F spoke of family tension engendered by these secondary effects of blindness. All respondents mentioned their own temper tantrums, depression, feelings of rejection, an attitude of harshness on the part of the parents or of overprotection. They emphasised that their problems were beyond the understanding of the average parent. The interaction of frustration and stress between family members appears to increase the pressure on the young person, either to give up previously cherished ambitions or to cling to them even more tenaciously.

In addition, level of aspiration is severely affected by the policy of educational segregation which tends to contribute, at least at the higher levels, to the professional and social isolation of the blind. All informants showed strong rejection of the conflict in working at menial tasks while holding high professional aspirations. Part of the difficulty in reconciling ideal with actual self is that, if a young person is a candidate for the Bar or a nuclear physicist and his family are rice-growers, can he reasonably be expected to be psychologically well-adjusted going back to the family farm tc spend the rest of his life carrying water, stacking wood or winnowing grain?

Employment

The traditional prestigious occupations of acupuncture, moxacautery and massage were the protected occupations of the blind. Protection may not directly have hindered the development of new occupations, but it has excluded them from equal consideration for jobs using new technology. In other words, the traditional jobs are losing status and yet the blind are not being trained for the computer-based jobs and high technology, for much of which they are eminently well-suited. Protected occupations have been seen as jobs the blind should take up for harmonious living, an important principle in Japanese social relations. As already noted, with industrial expansion, the prestige of traditional occuapations is losing ground and taking with it the self respect that is concomitant with financial independence. Sighted masseurs apply for and get the top jobs - in hotels for example; similarly with acupunture, for which a four-year course of training is necessary. Mr E. stated that a sighted acupuncturist with his own means of transport has the advantage of being able to visit clients in their own home. Successful goal attainment is therefore difficult, and marriage and social status is affected.

Autonomy

In many relationships in Japan, the principle of "sweet dependency" ("amaeru") is fostered by parents and employers alike. "Amaeru" dependency relates back to the mother-child relationship. It is comfortable, secure. If the adolescent rejects this in favour of self-determination, then a fundamental aspect of Japanese society cannot function for him. In psychiatric circles in Japan it has been customary to give treatment principally with the aim of adjusting individuals to the obligations expected of them towards their social group. This is not restricted to psychiatry but is a general principal of education. One must lose individuality in order to be fully integrated into society. It is difficult to rationalise self-interest. Violation of prescribed codes of behaviour, morality and custom exposes one to ridicule or even exile from the community or family. Mr C. stated that there arose the possibility for him to file a claim for compensation for his school accident - money which would have provided much needed funds for his university text-books. However, his family are of modest status and pressured him not to file the claim so that the other villagers would not consider their behaviour unseemly. This clearly demonstrates the relationship of the Japanese household in community interaction. Dependency is culturally acceptable and autonomy perceived as a threat to the social order.

Family Relationships

It is difficult for parents of a handicapped child always to handle their problems as they see fit, especially when at times their ideas may contradict the traditional wisdom of the elders in matters of medicine and spiritual explanations. Because of the importance of filial duty towards elders and the fact that the extended family is still quite common in Japan, the wishes of the elders may delay the seeking of modern medical care. In the case of Mr. C. the grandmother refused to allow the child to see an ophthalmologist. When a medical examination routinely took place at school, she so frightened the child with stories of "men in white coats" that the child ran from the test room screaming. He was not examined and finally lost the sight of that eye. In adolescence, with a reduced field of vision, he lost the sight of the other eye in a school accident. In the case of Mr. F. he dared not tell his family that he was going blind having contracted a rare disease just before completing his Ph. D. qualification, and in the case of Miss B. the grandmother religiously blamed the blindness of the child on the mother after a previous male child had been stillborn. The parents of Miss B. subsequently left the grandmother's home to live and bring up their child on their own.

Reciprocity

Studies by the Maretzkis (1966) in Okinawa and by Harries and Shimamura (in press) show that the grandmother retains control over the daughter-in-law and thence of her son, by insisting on the dependence of the small child on the mother. Thus pinned down by maternal duties, the daughter-in-law is effectively dependent upon the son of the old mother and he owes his mother filial obedience. He finds himself between his wife's wishes - which he may share - and his mother's, but it is to his mother that he owes obedience.

However, not all wives want their children to be independent. The low status of rural women in general is to some extent mitigated by being responsible for a child. Thus, for different reasons both males and females tend to enourage dependency. To do otherwise makes family harmony difficult.

For the sighted as for the blind adolescent, problems of being accepted, of being rejected or ignored by peers are major concerns. Nevertheless, in the societies of many Third World countries, it is likely that age mates of the blind adolescent will also be faced with changing family patterns - fathers away as migratory workers, mothers or sisters working in towns. Rural families and age mates may be struggling with the reality of diminished status incurred by illiteracy. In this, at any rate, the blind may actually have the advantage: if they have been taught Braille they may be able to read English. Much of the world's Braille literature is in English. Their language ability may be relatively high, but while one may expect this to bring social recognition and acceptance, there may be jealousy instead. For example, Miss A. an English literature graduate, was offered a job in the town library - not a traditional occupation for the blind. She was given no work to do and no-one spoke to her. The humiliation of silence and denial of work finally caused her to resign and seek a job away from the community. I would suggest that her colleagues did not know how to relate to her because she was outside the traditional role accorded to young women and outside, also, the traditional role accorded to the blind. It seems that most girls stay at home doing domestic chores whatever their intellectual ability and some, according to several informants, become "pleasure hostesses" in travellers' hotels.

Another, vital, aspect of social relations is that which requires that one repay any favour of which one is even a passive recipient, and the fullest debt - that is, having been nurtured as a child - cannot be discharged with the passage of time. For the blind intellectual, there is no way to repay these favours except by obedience to the community. For people of exceptional ability, such as those reviewed by the case studies, such demands may be seen as repressive and unacceptable.

Intra-group Communication

The unusual nature of Japanese patterns of communication requires that we also examine its role in the dynamic process of forming a self-image. There is a saying in Japanese that "the person who goes away becomes more distant day by day". The absenteeism of an adolescent at residential school renders him or her less familiar to the remaining community members and as a "stranger", on return, the young person is likely to experience more difficulty in attracting the same sort of proximate communications that are projected amongst other members. As Kunihiro (1973) has clearly stated, distal communication is difficult for Japanese, and the blind person may well find him or herself left out of the group-sharing situation. His experience of the group will therefore be different.

The School Clique

This is a phenomenon peculiar to Japanese society and well documented by Chie Nakane (1970). It is a cross-cutting social mechanism, rather as an age-set is or the English public school system. However, there are differences. In Japan, the school clique ("gakku batsu") creates more effective relationships and in-group consciousness than any other social network. The school clique is vital to the aspiring intellectual, particularly at the level of the organisation man for obtaining introductions at the right level and the exchange of favours. The scope and availability of suchrelationships

are founded on the shared experience of a common university
background and facilitate social mobility at the
professional level especially. A measure of the bond which
joins same-status group members is frequency of contact,
and it is not unusual for 90% of old alumnae members to
meet once a month, even 30 years after leaving college. The
study revealed that in the case of the blind, they never
met with their school clique other than on an occasional
basis. The segregation of blind students implies that the
advantages of the system are no longer available to them.
School members are dispersed and of low status. They have
no effective group membership and as a consquence are
handicapped in the development of their careers.

Religious Beliefs

The informants in case studies C., E. and F. (as well
as others who contributed to the larger study) spoke of
being infuenced by the family's embarrassment within the
village at having "lost" one of its members. Within
Japanese religious beliefs, respects are paid to ancestors
if someone can actually remember them. One owes a debt to
the lineage and a member who becomes "lost" is thus not
fulfilling traditional obligations to the ancestors.
Obligation ("gimu") to the family is in some ways easier to
discharge through reciprocal favours. The blind
intellectual cannot repay "gimu" in any way that is
meaningful to the rural family. Other village families may
see academic pretensions as an escape from obligation. This
is a potentially shaming situation for the head of the
house.

Finally, all the informants stated that many blind
school residents have real psychological problems to work
through, and these are not necessarily met by the family or
a specially trained counsellor. There are few such
counsellors in Japan, the usual means of help is through
the college student counsellor whose knowledge may not
extend to the specific difficulties mentioned in this
paper. Some univeristy administrators feel they are doing
the blind a favour by refusing them entry to university
presumably in order to avoid their being disappointed
later. The blind intellectual speaks of the need for
achievement on his terms and of this being poorly
understood by the family or community. The counsellor
advising on psychological rather than on vocational matters
therefore, in Japan as elsewhere, has to be aware of the
fact that he or she is treating not just a blind person
with adjustment difficulties, but a person and a family who
may not be communicating at the same level.

Conclusions

From evidence drawn from the informants to the study,

196

it is possible to say:
1. Blind adolescents experience prolonged conflict between
   family and social roles on the one hand and the goals
   they set for themselves;
2. They are required to be dependent, although they may
   wish to seek self- determination;
3. Discrepancy between ideal self and reactions to actual
   self may be a major cause of frustration;
4. Age at onset and suddenness of blindness may damage
   consistency in development;
5. Stress and behavioural problems may be beyond the
   understanding of the family;
6. Distancing from the community and school clique
   contributes to isolation;
7. Isolation from proximate communication may lead to
   exclusion from a relevant point of reference.

A look to the future

    As cultural patterns of child rearing, traditional
medicine, family and social roles are influenced by
progressive industrialisation, the counselling psychologist
has a crucial role to play in the education of the
community. A project for the restructuring of the
environment is taking place in India and consists in
sending a counsellor back into the community with the blind
person to educate the community towards an understanding of
the tangible contribution the blind member can make if
allowed to do so. It is hoped that many other countries
will follow this example. World Council member states have
expressed the need for more trained psychologists to handle
the expanding number of newly-blinded adults. Research
procedures, comprehensive definitions of blindness and
statistics that are comparable, together with measurements
capable of locating the problems of the individual within
the larger social scheme, are urgently required.

NOTES

(1) CWAJ (College Women's Association of Japan) Committee
for the Blind. Tokyo. Matarai, M. 1982. (personal
communication)

(2) International Labour Office, Information on the
Rehabilitation and Employment of the Visually Handicapped.
October 1981.

REFERENCES

Bauman, M.K. (1954) <u>Adjustment to Blindness</u>: A Study as Reported by the Committee to Study Adjustment to Blindness. Harrisburgh: Pennsylvania State Council for the Blind, 1954.

Cowen, E.L. et al. (1961) <u>Adjustment to Visual Disability in Adolescence</u>. New York: American Foundation for the Blind.

Harries, D.C. and Shimamura, M. Fujin ni kan suru yushikishi chosa, Yuri International, Tokyo, Japan, in press.

Kunihiro, M. (1973) <u>Indigenous Barriers to Communication</u>. International College of Commerce & Economics Monographs.

Maretzki, T.W. and Maretzki, H. (1966), <u>Taira: An Okinawan Village</u>. New York: John Wiley.

Statistics have been drawn from:
International Labour Office, Info. Service on the Rehabilitation & Employment of the Visually Handicapped. October 1981.

Itayama, K. <u>Journal of General Rehabilitation</u>, Vol. 8 (12) 1980 Translated by the Canon Company of Japan, Nagato, Audio-Vis. Div.

Matsui, H. Vocational Development for the Japanese blind, Tokyo 1982. World Council for the Welfare of the Blind, published for the United Nations. <u>Rehabilitation Services for the Blind in Developing Countries</u>. 1977.

Nakane, C. (1970) <u>Japanese Society</u>. Berkeley: University of California Press.

World Council for the Welfare of the Blind: Desai, H.J.M. <u>Planning Employment Services for the Blind in Developing Countries</u>. 1981.

CULTURAL VARIATION IN THE MEANING AND USES OF CHILDREN'S "INTELLIGENCE"

C. M. Super

Judge Baker Guidance Center, Boston

Western psychology has tried for many years to understand, even measure, the intelligence of non-Western peoples. As usual in this sort of endeavor, we have made considerable progress in learning what not to do; and we also have come up with some useful and informative approximations of what we should do to reformulate the issue. The present work examines cognitive growth in a broader context than has been usual in the past, with the expectation that by observing the development of what other peoples value and indices of cognitive competence we will understand better the growth of intelligence in Western as well as non-Western children.

Efforts to date to examine "intelligence" in non-Western settings fall into four groups. The first, historically as well as logically, consists of the straightforward application of IQ tests (and related tasks) to children and adults in foreign lands. Such studies may now be regarded as telling us more about qualities of the IQ test than about qualities of the subjects.

A second kind of effort has examined the connotative as well as denotative meanings of the word "intelligence", or its common translation. Wober's often cited study in Uganda, applying the semantic differential to the English and Luganda terms for "intelligence", is an important contribution of this sort (Wober, 1974). As Serpell (1974) has pointed out, however, the results speak more to methodological issues of translation and learning the meaning of words than to the function of intelligence in traditional settings.

The third group of studies shares a related problem. Klein, Freeman, and Millett (1973) demonstrated that

199

Guatemalan women can use a Spanish word <u>listura</u> to rate children in a way that correlates with the children's cognitive test performance. A relationship was also found by Nerlove, Roberts, Klein, Yarbrough and Habicht (1975) in a similar population between children's test performance and their naturally occuring behavior outside the laboratory (see also Irwin, Klein & Townsend, 1982). While these studies provide a useful exploration of the validity of the North-American tests in this other environment, they depend on a particular cultural notion of cognitive performance to identify differences in children from a separate culture. Hence they really inform us about local aspects of the American-urban-academic idea of intelligence, not about how universal aspects of intelligence are expressed and used in other cultural contexts.

Ethnographic approaches favored by anthropologists constitute a fourth category of research, but there are few, if any, examples that focus primarily on intelligence and its growth. Interesting and relevant discussion, however, can be found in the work of Briggs (1970), Gladwin (1970), Blurton-Jones and Konner (1976), and Fortes (1938), among others. Such ethnographic examples point to different systems for conceptualizing some aspects of intellectual behavior.

The work of Serpell (1974) combines elements of the last two approaches, with provocative results. He asked Chewa adults, in rural Eastern Zambia, to rate village children on how they would perform on locally relevant tasks, such as carrying a message. Their responses, he found, did not relate to the children's cognitive test scores, even using carefully adapted and culturally appropriate tests. He concluded that the rural Chewa criteria of judgment were not related to the European notion of intelligence.

A limitation common to the first three kinds of investigation, and to Serpell's to some degree, is the emphasis on the Western notion of intelligence as the salient marker for cognitive growth in childhood. The work presented here starts instead with the more general question of indigenous concepts concerning children, and then proceeds to explore within that context how cognitive maturity is expressed by children and noticed by adults.

The study was carried out in a rural farming community in Western Kenya, called Kokwet. The people of Kokwet are Kipsigis, members of the larger Kalenjin grouping of Highland Nilotic peoples. The families of Kokwet are connected to the modern economy of Kenya through agricultural co-ops for maize, milk, and pyrethrum, and through small shops within walking distance. They are aware of the larger national scene through personal travel to the towns and cities. Daily life in Kokwet, however, remains isolated and traditional in many ways. It is centered on the cows and the maize fields, on family and community life and the passage of seasons. A minority of the male heads of household, and virtually none of the adult females, has any formal schooling, and the traditional initiation rites at adolescence are almost universally followed for both males and females. At the time the present data were collected (1973-1975), very few of the children under age 9 attended school.

Study 1

Exploration of local concepts about the differences among children was begun in a discussion and advisory group organized with six women of Kokwet. Meeting sporadically over the course of my three years' residence, the group served as counsellor and guide for the design of research and for understanding local customs, values, and beliefs concerning child rearing and child development. One topic presented to the group and discussed over several occasions was what words and ideas they used to note differences among children between 3 and 10 years of age. Further clarification of the meanings of the 20 or so words and phrases identified was obtained through detailed inquiry with eleven particularly helpful informants, including three men.

Results

Seven conceptual clusters were identified from this ethnographic inquiry:

(1) There is a large group of concepts referring to a child's helpfulness and obedience. Important root words are ngekonda ("disobedience," often used in the negative: Ma mi ngekong lakwet, or "The child is obedient"); kiptekīsiot ("respectful"); and ingeleliot ("rude"). There are also several phrases derived from words relating to domains we might separate more in English, such as: Kararon ngalekyik, literally "Nice (are) his words," indicating politeness; kaseit, derived from the word gase, to understand, meaning a child who understands quickly what is to be done and does it, hence translated by native speakers as "obedient"; and several other cognitively-orientated phrases. Also belonging in the helpful-obedience cluster is ne toche cho tugul, or "who welcomes or entertains everyone". While in literal translation this sounds like a social skill, it is often said to mean "respectful and obedient".

(2) Second in both number of phrases and in discussion generated is a cluster of concepts close to Euro-American notions of cognition and intelligence. Ngom is the central word when referring to children. Although ngom is

universally translated as "intelligent", elaboration of its
use reveals a strong component of "responsibility" as well.
One informant illustrated the word as follows:

> For a girl who is ngom, after eating she sweeps the
> house because she knows it should be done. Then she
> washes dishes, looks for vegetables, and takes good
> care of the baby. When you come home, you feel pleased
> and say: "This child is ngom." Another girl may not
> even clean her own dishes, but just go out and play,
> leaving the baby to cry. For a boy, if he is ngom, he
> will watch the cows, and take them to the river without
> being told. He knows to separate the calves from the
> cows and he will fix the (thorn) fence where it is
> broken. The other boy will let the cows into the maize
> field and will be found playing while they eat the
> maize.

A few informants distinguished a separate meaning of
gnom ngom for the child who gets good marks at school. This
could be specified as ngom en sukul rather than ngom en ga
("intelligent at home"). The informants stressed, however,
that the two meanings (domestic and academic) were not
necessarily related, and that a child may do well in school
while often forgetting to do chores at home.

Ngom is not normally used to refer to adults. Rather a
native speaker is more likely to use utat, which has a
stronger connotation of inventive and clever, or sometimes
wise and unselfish. Kwelat may also be used, meaning
"smart" or "sharp." A man who is kwelat dresses smart and
is clever in dealing with his family, though not
necessarily educated or even potentially successful in
school.

(3) A third cluster of considerable importance
centered on the term iyanat meaning "trustworthy" or
perhaps "honest", and related words.

(4) Most informants preferred to make a separate
category for mie mukulel, literally "good-hearted" and
usually translated as "loving". A child who is this way, in
the words of one informant, "will smile even when you say
she must wait a little for food, even though she is hugry."

(5) Ngololin is derived from the word for "word", and
means talkative, often with a connotation of playful or
cheeky. "You leave a visitor in the house for a little time
while you go to cook; when you return, the child is sitting
there and the visitor says "Oh, he is ngololin, for he has
told me such and such". All four-year-olds are seen to be
this way, but if a child is still ngololin at 9 years, when
he is also ngom then he will use nice words (Kararon
ngalekyik) and be polite as well.

(6) Bravery is an important quality in children as well as adults. Two slightly different meanings of "brave" (nyigan) were pointed out. In one case, the child is brave to go outside the house at night, or to walk two miles to the neighboring village with a message. Secondly, a child can show bravery when he is physically punished, or when his front teeth are ceremonially removed.

(7) A final and less important concept identified in these discussions is "shy", or yubat.

In order to obtain more objective information on the meanings and relationships of these words, two kinds of scaling exercises were undertaken. In Study 2 several key concepts were compared for their similarity, and in Study 3 the importance of a smaller set was rated for several social roles. Finally, the emergence with age of one quality particularly relevant to "intelligence" is traced in Study 4.

Study 2

Twelve adjectives were chosen from the results of Study 1, with the goal of representing the first six areas. The 12 words were prepared in a balanced set of triads according to the work of Burton and Nerlove (1976). For example, one triad consisted of ngom, kaseit, kiptekisiot (intelligent, obedient, respectful). Twenty-three adult residents of Kokwet (10 female, 13 male) were asked to indicate for each triad which two words were most similar in meaning. The similarity ratings were collected through individual interviews, and the pooled results were submitted to the KYST multidimensional scaling porgram.

Results

The most reasonable scaling solution was found in three dimensions. Figures 1 and 2 present the results. The first dimension, where kiptekisiot, ma mi ngekong, and kaseit ("respectful," "obedient," and "understanding/ obedient") are at one extreme and nyigan and ngololin ("brave" and "talkative") are at the other, appears to contrast characteristics of individual expression with social submissiveness. Dimension II reflects a verbal component, with ngom and ngololin ("intelligent" and "talkative") at one end, and nyigan and iyanat ("brave" and "honest") at the other. The third dimension (Figure 2) might be labelled cognitive quickness vs. positive interpersonal attributes, where kwelat, utat, ngom and kaseit ("smart," "clever," "intelligent," and "understanding/obedient") are opposite kararon ngalekyik and mie mukulel ("polite" and "good-hearted").

FIGURE 1

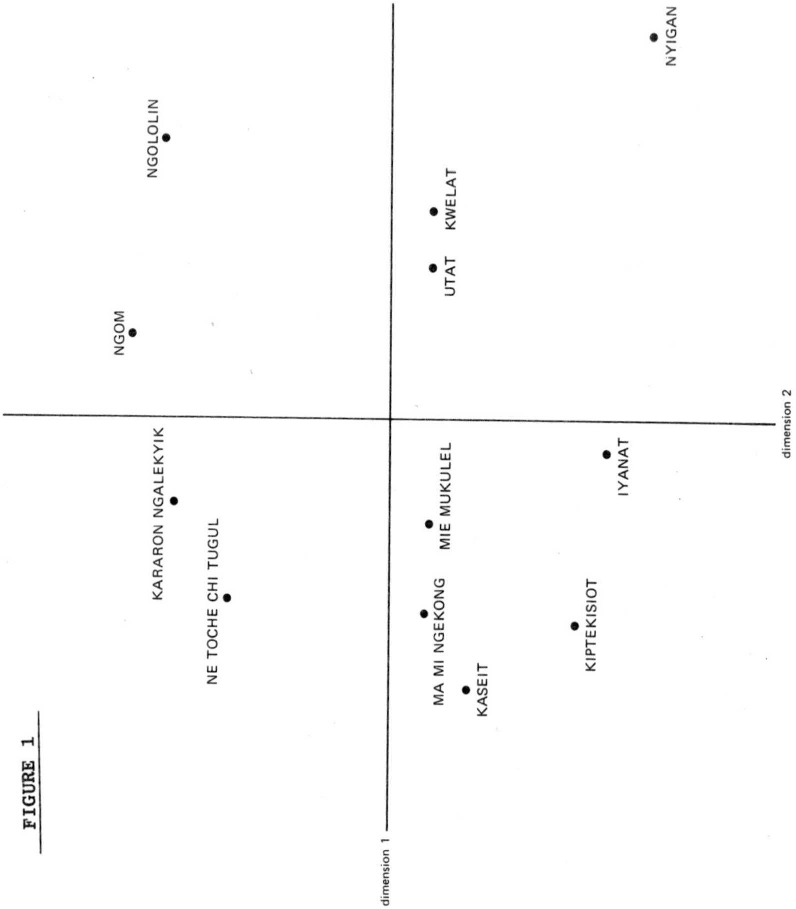
dimension 1
dimension 2
NYIGAN
NGOLOLIN
KWELAT
UTAT
NGOM
IYANAT
KARARON NGALEKYIK
MIE MUKULEL
NE TOCHE CHI TUGUL
KIPTEKISIOT
MA MI NGEKONG
KASEIT

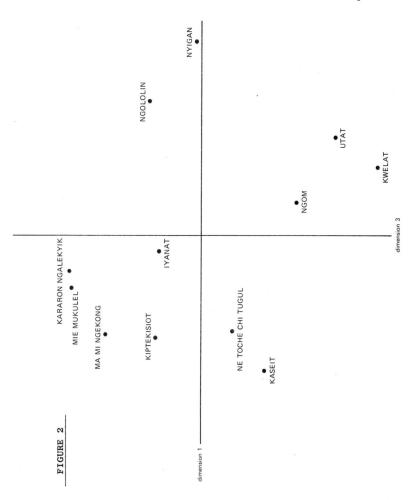

FIGURE 2

Study 3

Further insight into the denotations and connotations
of the adjectives used to describe children can be gained
by asking about their relative importance for various
social roles. Seven of the most common words were presented
to 26 adults (12 women and 14 men, overlapping with the
subjects in Study 2), who were asked to rank order them for
their importance to proper fulfillment of the following
roles: mother, father, husband, neighbor, fundi (skilled
mechanic or general repairman), assistant chief, teacher,
trader (who visits local markets to buy and sell maize,
etc.), businessman (store owner), employee, and advisor
(counsellor, one who is called to mediate disputes). The
average ranking of each role on each adjective was then
computed, and these data were processed by the MDPREF
program for scaling simultaneously the roles and
adjectives.

Results

The results are presented in Figure 3. It can be seen
that the roles are spread around the outside in three
general groupings: male roles, female roles, and
commercial/neutral roles. Alternatively, there is a
separate axis (from upper left to lower right) contrasting
family and dyadic roles on one hand with community roles in
larger social groups on the other.

Of particular interest, of course, is the distribution
of adjectives relative to the roles. As in all scalings of
this sort, physical closeness of the items in the figure
indicate greater association, so that nyigan is
particularly associated with the male roles of fundi,
husband, and advisor; and gnom is more important for roles
of social leadership and negotiation (trader, teacher,
etc.) than it is, for example, for functioning as father.
For the latter role, the differentially important qualities
are respectfulness (kiptekisiot), which is characteristic
of those who act in a manner worthy of respect (see
Harkness, Edwards, & Super, 1981), understanding/obedience
(kaseit), and lovingness (mie mukulel).

Study 4

A questionnaire was given to all mothers in Kokwet and
in a neighboring community whose children (between 3 and 9
years old) participated in a study of cognitive
development. Their mothers were asked, among other items,
for each child: (1) Is this child ngom? (2) Can you now
know this child's personality, that is, do you now know
what he/she will be like as an adult? (3) Can this child be

FIGURE 3

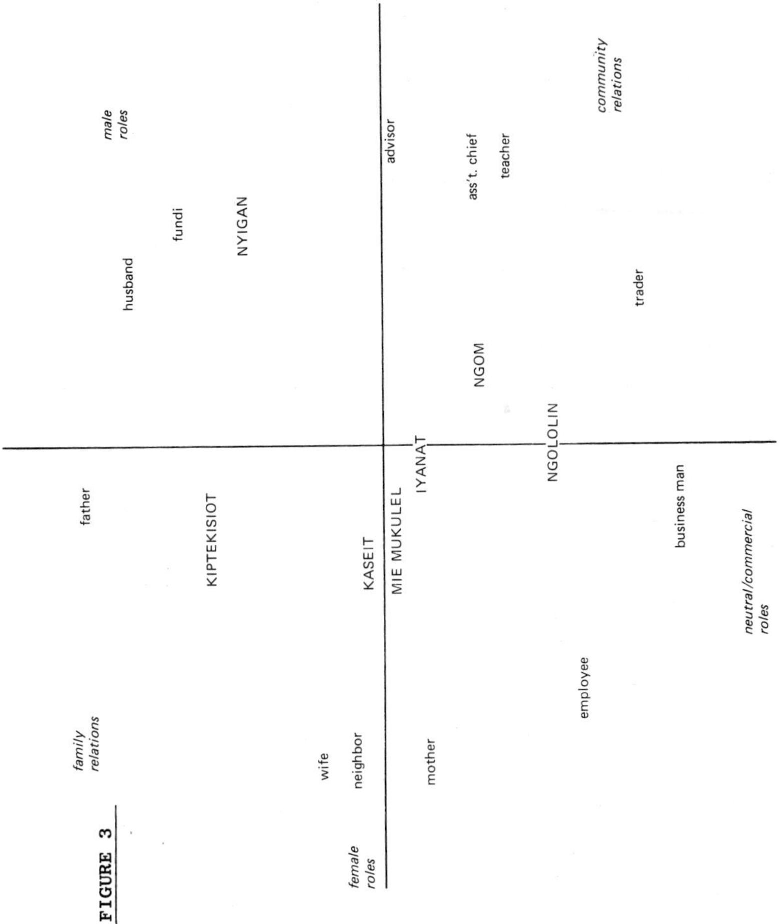

female roles

family relations

father

wife
neighbor

KIPTEKISIOT

mother

KASEIT

MIE MUKULEL

IYANAT

employee

NGOLOLIN

business man

NGOM

husband

fundi

NYIGAN

advisor

ass't. chief

teacher

trader

male roles

community relations

neutral/commercial roles

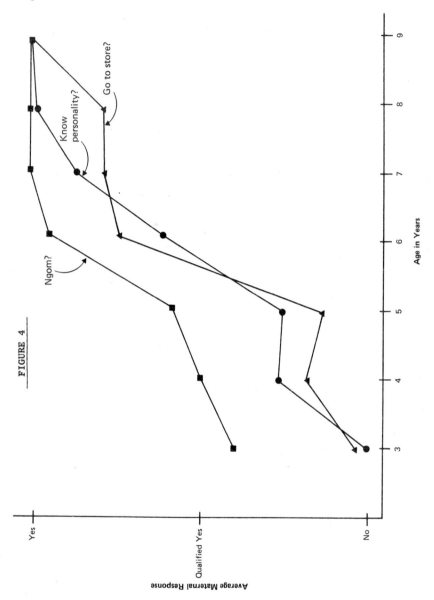

FIGURE 4

given a few shillings and told to go to the shops (about 2 miles away) to purchase a small pack of tea or sugar? Can you be sure he/she will return promptly with the goods and the change? The data presented here are for 79 children whose ages were reasonably certain (Super, 1982) and who demonstrated good nutritional and physical status (World Health Organization, 1978).

Results

The mother's responses are presented in Figure 4, as the percent of children at each year who are judged to be ngom, trustworthy for an errand, and whose personalities are knowable. It can be seen that all three curves increase most between 5 and 6 years.

Discussion

If we accept the common opinion of bilinguals that ngom is the closest Kipsigis word for the English "intelligent", then it would appear from these results that the Kipsigis notion of intelligence is a highly verbal cognitive quickness, neutral on the expression-submission dimension (see Figures 1 and 2). It is a skill particularly valuable for politicians, teachers, market traders, and social mediators (Figure 3). Thus intelligence is seen as the ability to quickly comprehend complex matters, and to use that comprehension in verbal interaction and the management of interpersonal relations.

As with the English "intelligent" or "smart", ngom is recognized by native speakers as describing variations among adults as well as a developmental universal. Unlike the way most Europeans and Americans commonly use "intelligent" for children - a relative concept operationalized in IQ - the Kipsigis adults look for something fairly specific in their children's behavior to indicate absolute acquisition of the quality ngom. The most striking aspect of the growth of the developmental curves in Figure 4 is that all three curves show similar progression with age. As the child becomes about 6 years old, the Kipsigis mother (who probably does not know the child's actual chronological age) feels that she can trust him/her on the shopping errand (and other similar tasks); she can know the child's personality, and the child is now ngom. Upper-middle class American mothers have been shown to make similar judgments about some task responsibilities but do not relate task competence so directly to "personality" or to central developmental phenomena (Harkness & Super, in press; Super, 1981).

The cluster of changes in behavior focused on by the Kipsigis mothers is found to occur around age 6, an age when Western society has institutionalized formal instruction in intellectual skills central to its economic functioning and value structure. It is also the age, as White (1970) has pointed out, when Western psychological theories place the beginnings of mature cognitive functioning: the onset of concrete operations for Piaget; completion of Freud's psychic triad of id, ego, and super-ego; emergence of Pavlov's second signal system; and the onset of verbal mediation and control in American mediation theory and in Russian models developed by Luria and Vygotsky. Rogoff et al. (1976) have shown that most cultures make some important changes in their view of the child around this age.

The data presented here are compatible with the theory that important, indeed critical, aspects of intellectual functioning emerge around age 6. The particular use of the emerging competence is channeled by the developmental niche, and similarly parental conceptualization of the changes reflect the needs and values of the community. The present data do not indicate that developmental changes occur without any structural constraints, but they do suggest viewing the intelligence found and fostered in urban Western society as only one structural manifestation of universal developmental events. Characterisation of the underlying competencies is a more complex task than looking for either culture-free or culture-specific manifestations of the existing Western notion of "intelligence".

REFERENCES

Blurton-Jones, N. & Konner, M.J. !Kung knowledge of animal behavior. In R.B. Lee & I. DeVore (Eds), Kalahari hunter-gatherers. Cambridge, Massachusetts: Harvard University Press, 1976.

Burton, M.L. & Nerlove, S.B. Balanced designs for triad tests. Social Science Research, 1976, 5, 247-267.

Briggs, J.L. Never in anger: Portrait of an Eskimo family. Cambridge, Massachusetts: Harvard University Press, 1970.

Fortes, M. Social & psychological aspects of education in Taleland. Supplement to Africa, 1938, 11 (4), 1-64.

Gladwin, T. East is a big bird: Navigation & logic on Puluwat atoll. Cambridge, Massachusetts: Harvard Unversity Press, 1970.

Harkness, S., Edwards, C.P. & Super, C.M. Social roles & moral reasoning: a case study in rural Africa. Developmental Psychology, 1981, 17, 595-603.

Harkness, S. & Super, C.M. The cultural construction of child development. Ethos, in press.

Irwin, M., Klein, R.E. & Townsend, J.W. Indigenous versus construct validity in cross-cultural research. In L.L. Adler (Ed.), Cross-cultural research at issue. New York: Academic Press, 1982.

Klein, R.E., Freeman, H.E. & Millett, R. Psychological test performance & indigenous conceptions of intelligence. The Journal of Psychology, 1973, 84, 219-222.

Nerlove, S.B., Roberts, J.M., Klein, R.E., Yarbrough, C. & Habicht, J.P. Natural indicators of cognitive development: an observational study of rural Guatemalan children. Ethos, 1975, 3, 265-295.

Rogoff, B., Sellers, M., Pirotta, S., Fox, N. & White, S.H. Age of assignment of roles & responsibilities to children: A cross-cultural survey. Human Development, 1976, 19, 99-107.

Serpell, R. Estimates of intelligence in a rural community of Eastern Zambia. Human Development Research Unit Reports, 1974, 25. Lusaka; University of Zambia (mimeographed).

Serpell, R. Strategies for investigating intelligence in its cultural context. Quarterly Newsletter of the Institute for Comparative Human Development, 1976, 11-15.

Super, C.M. The cultural construction of behavior problems in infancy. Paper presented at meetings of the Society for Research in Child Development, Boston, Mass., March 1981.

Super, C.M. Application of multi-dimensional scaling techniques to the estimation of children's ages in field research. Manuscript in preparation, 1982.

White, S.H. Some general outlines of the matrix of developmental changes between five and seven years. Bulletin of the Orton Society, 1970, 20, 41-57.

Wober, M. Towards an understanding of the Kiganda concept of intelligence. In: J.W. Berry & P.R. Dasen (Eds.), Culture and cognition: Readings in cross-cultural psychology. London: Methuen, 1974.

World Health Organization. <u>A growth chart for international</u>
<u>use in maternal and child health care;</u> <u>Guidelines for</u>
<u>primary health care personnel.</u> Geneva; World Health
Organization nonserial publication, 1978.

THE ASSESSMENT OF MODERNITY AMONGST BLACK WORKERS ON THE WITWATERSRAND

C. Thompson

Chamber of Mines of South Africa, Johannesburg

INTRODUCTION

The last 250 years have seen the spread of a revolution which has influenced and changed the lives of people throughout the world. I refer to the Industrial Revolution. The historians Lyon, Rowen and Hamerow (1969) note that the Industrial Revolution is more than simply "the application of mechanical energy to production" (p.575). It is a multifaceted process which revolutionizes economies, traditional social arrangements and political institutions.

Social theorists have written at great length about the changes which have resulted from this revolution, and particular attention has been paid to the social consequences. Giddens (1971) makes the point that "if Renaissance Europe gave rise to a concern with history, it was industrial Europe which provided the conditions for the emergence of sociology" (p.xi).

Early sociologists such as Marx (1818-1883), Durkheim (1858-1917) and Weber (1864-1920) recognised that the change from rural-agrarian life to urban-industrial life was bringing about changes in the nature of the "social bond" and that modern industrial society is a new kind of social species". The application of a Modernity Scale is but one attempt to understand and explain the attitude and values of this "new type of social species".

The "industrial revolution" in South Africa began with the discovery of diamonds in 1866, and was given further impetus twenty years later by the extraction of gold from the newly discovered Witwatersrand Main Reef. These developments created a demand for labour which was supplied

213

mainly by South Africa's rural/agrarian black population. The subsequent growth of secondary industry has increased the demand for labour and in the first seventy years of this century the urban black population has grown from 524,000 to 4,5 million (Dubb, 1974; South African Population Statistics, 1978).

The result of this massive move to urban centres has been ever increasing interaction between black South Africans and the urban, industrial environment. This contact has given rise to significant changes to, and adaptations of, traditional black culture. A Modernity Scale was used to assess the extent to which black attitudes and values have changed in response to contact with the urban-industrial environment of the Witwatersrand.

The word modern is used to characterize that which is characteristic of present or modern times. Social scientists give the word a more specific meaning and use it to describe the social, economic and political conditions which prevail in the industrially advanced nations of the world. Inkeles (see Brode, 1969) defines modern as "...a term for characterizing the tone or ethos of relations in the contemporary world" (p.vi).

Modernization theorists operationalize their conception of individual attitudinal modernity in an ideal-type definition of modern man. Some of the more frequently mentioned characteristics of a modern man are his openness to new experience, a rational and objective outlook on life, and a positive valuation of science and technology. The less modern, or traditional, man would be conservative in his attitude to new experience, less rational and objective and would place little faith in science and technology.

The problem addressed by the two studies was:

Do black South Africans living in the Witwatersrand tend to approximate the ideal of a modern man as a result of increased contact with the urban-industrial way of life.

The studies were undertaken to test two hypotheses:

Hypothesis 1.
The attitudes and values of blacks who live and work on the Witwatersrand are changing from traditional to modern, and in the ideal case would approximate those attitudes and values found amongst people who live and work in an industrially and economically advanced country.

Hypothesis 2.
Individual attitudinal modernity is a function of four independent variables, viz. urban-industrial work

experience, length of residence in the urban area of the Witwatersrand, standard of formal education and extent of mass-media exposure.

The hypotheses were tested using a Modernity Scale based on the work of Inkeles and Smith (1974). The literature on modernity has involved an extensive use of Modernity Scales developed by different authors. Examples are those of Lerner (1958), whose "Index of Empathy", provided a measure of personal style which would reflect attitudinal modernity, Doob (1967), Kahl (1968), Schnaiberg (1970), Armer and Youtz (1970), Lengermann (1971) and Inkeles and Smith (1974).

The most comprehensive and thoroughly tested scale is that of Inkeles and Smith. Their Overall Modernity Scale (OM Scale) has been administered to samples of 1,000 workers in six countries and the results have proved encouraging. It was decided, therefore, to adopt the Inkeles and Smith scale for use in South Africa.

Inkeles and Smith suggest that modern man can be understood in terms of his environment (i.e. urbanization, education, political participation, industrialization and mass communication) and his internalized attitudes and values.

Their scale is therefore a measure of individual attitudes and values, an attempt to measure the extent to which individuals have undergone "a change of spirit" in response to their environment.

A modern man is described by Inkeles (1966) as one who:

a)--is open to new experience, innovation and change;

b)--holds opinions on a wide range of topics outside his immediate environment, but is democratic in his acceptance of the variety of opinion;

c)--is oriented toward the present and future rather than the past;

d)--values planning;

e)--believes that man is able to dominate his natural environment i.e. efficacy;

f)--believes in calculability i.e. that the world runs according to laws which are subject to human prediction and control;

g)--is aware of the dignity of others;

h)--has faith in science and technology;

i)--believes that status and rewards should be attributed according to achievement rather than ascription.

This concept of modern man was operationalized in a long and complex interview schedule which explored 30 themes relating to the model described above, in order to develop a "general survey index score that represents the degree to which a man possesses the attitudes measured by these items" (Smith & Inkeles, 1966, p.358).

The 166-item Overall Modernity (OM) Scale of Inkeles and Smith was too long for administration in factories on the Witwatersrand. The above model was used as a guide in the selection of 75 items for the South African Modernity Scale. An additional five items were written to measure the extent of individual mass-media exposure and are concerned with the degree to which people read newspapers and listen to the radio. The scores on these items were related to modernity scores in the validation procedure. Finally biographical questions were written on educational background, urban experience, work history and region of origin.

The Modernity Scale and mass-media exposure items were scored on a four-point scale, 1 representing the "highly traditional" pole and 4 the "highly modern" pole. Of the two intermediate categories, 2 represented "fairly traditional, but with modern leanings", and 3 was "fairly modern, but with traditional leanings". Inkeles and Smith scored their items dichotomously for each of the six samples which they studied, but it was felt that account should be taken of the possibility of intermediate responses, hence the use of the four-point scoring continuum in this study.

2. THE FIRST STUDY

This schedule was administered to 201 black industrial employees drawn from eight different organisations on the Witwatersrand. There were 118 male and 83 female subjects. The mean age of the samples was 33 years, the mean education five years and the majority of the sample were concentrated in unskilled or semi-skilled occupations. The subjects had spent on average 60% of their lives in an urban area, and over 90% of their working lives had been spent in factories on the Witwatersrand.

The possible range of modernity scores was 75-300, but none of the subjects scored below 150. The mean score was 228 and scores tended to be concentrated at the higher end of the distribution. The scores appeared to be high and encompassed a limited range. An item analysis was carried out and the items rejected, on the basis of poor item reliability indices, were found to be either inaccurately coded, poorly conceptualized (particularly in terms of the translatability of certain concepts) or to encourage socially desirable responses in the modern direction.

Criterion variables expected to be related to modernity were isolated. It was hypothesized that greater time spent in the urban area, and particularly the urban work environment, would influence attitudes and values and give rise to higher modernity scores. Similarly, higher standards of education and increased mass-media exposure (as measured by scores on the five mass-media exposure items) would be positively related to modernity. Pearson product-moment correlation coefficients were calculated between these variables and the total modernity score.

The proportions of the total working life and overall life of the subjects spent in urban situations were not strongly correlated with modernity scores, the coefficients being 0,29 and 0,21 (p less than 0,05) respectively for the male sample, and -0,02 and -0,08 for the female sample (p less than 0,05).

Standard of education and degree of mass-media exposure, however, co-vary strongly with scores on the Modernity Scale, the correlation coefficients being 0,51 and 0,60 for the male sample (p less than 0,05) and 0,34 and 0,41 for the female sample (p less than 0,05) respectively. These findings support the contention that education and mass-media exposure are significant influences in the modernization process.

The findings of the first study were disappointing. We did not expect any of the subjects to fit the ideal-type of a modern man, but it was hoped that cumulative scores on these items would reflect the "degree of attitudinal modernity" within the sample population. The findings suggest that the scale is less sensitive than was hoped.

3. THE SECOND STUDY

On the basis of the first study findings 25 of the "best" items were selected for the shortened Modernity Scale. A more detailed biographical questionnaire was developed to allow us to identify an urban and semi-urban or transitional group. Once the two groups had been identified it was possible to compare modernity scores and hence say something about the discriminant validity of the shortened Modernity Scale.

The second study sample comprised 334 occupationally

low-level employees from one organisation on the Witwatersrand. The mean education was again five years, the mean age was 42 and the subjects were generally at a lower occupational level than was the case in the first study. The majority of subjects were labourers. Generally the subjects in the second study had spent shorter periods living and working in an urban area.

The possible range of modernity scores was 25-100. The mean modernity score was, 67, and the scores were well distributed over the full range. When scores were computed on these 25 items for the first study sample the mean score was four points higher and scores were clearly concentrated at the higher end of the distribution.

These findings have considerable implications, particularly since the subjects in the present study are on the whole older, less urbanized and at an occupationally lower level than those of the first study. It is suggested that the variation in responses to the items in the shortened Modernity Scale is a reflection of these differences between the two samples and, therefore, that the Modernity Scale is more suitable for application to less urbanized labourers than, for example, to highly urbanized clerks.

The modernity-related criteria employed in the first study were again adopted in the present study, viz. length of time spent in an urban area, length of time spent in an urban work environment, standard of education and degree of mass-media exposure. (Six mass-media items were used to measure the extent of the subjects' exposure to newspapers, magazines, radio and television.) Pearson product-moment correlation coefficients were calculated between these variables and total modernity scores.

The proportions of total working life and overall life of subjects spent in urban situations did not correlate with modernity scores either as strongly or in the direction anticipated. The obtained coefficients were -0,30 and 0,11 respectively. The first study coefficients were 0,29 and 0,21 for the men, and -0,02 and -0,08 for the women.

Standard of education and degree of mass-media exposure did, however, co-vary with modernity scores, the coefficients being 0,34 and 0,38 respectively. The first study coefficients were 0,51 and 0,60 for the men, and 0,34 and 0,41 for the women on these two variables. These correlations were all significant at the 5% level.

The consistently low, and sometimes negative, correlations between modernity and length of urban residence and extent of urban work experience merits further attention, particularly since Inkeles and Smith (1974) and workers in the field have emphasized the importance of the urban environment as a "school in modernity". The collection of more detailed biographical information in the second study allowed this conclusion to be tested by comparing two groups, one urban and the other transitional.

The criteria used to distinguish members of the two groups were:

1. place of birth -- urban or rural;

2. place resident for the first 15 years of life -- urban or rural;

3. length of time spent in town -- 100% or less than 100%:

4. legal status -- the urban group would be permanent by birth; the transitional group would be migrant workers;

5. place identified as home -- the urban group would see the urban areas of the Witwatersrand as home, the transitional group would not.

On the basis of these criteria 33 subjects were identified as members of the urban group, 97 as members of the transitional group. The mean modernity score of the urban group was 83,51 - whilst that of the transitional group was 63,86 - a 20 point difference which, by t-test, is significant at the 5% level.

The shortened Modernity Scale discriminates between groups of people with varying life histories, particularly amongst people at the lower occupational and educational levels. The second study confirmed the importance of education as a predictor of modernity and urban life experience is clearly an important "school in modernity". An interesting finding is that the women in both studies were more modern than the men.

4. CONCLUSIONS AND DISCUSSION

The results of the two studies are discussed in relation to the two hypotheses.

Hypothesis 1 reads: The attitudes and values of blacks who live and work on the Witwatersrand are changing from traditional to modern, and in the ideal case would approximate those attitudes and values found amongst people who live and work in an industrially and economically advanced country.

The results of the first and second studies suggest that blacks who live and work on the Witwatersrand are "becoming modern", and those at the educationally and occupationally higher levels approximate the ideal-type described in the "model of modern man".

Hypothesis 2 reads: Individual attitudinal modernity is a function of four independent variables, viz. urban-industrial work experience, length of residence in the urban area of the Witwatersrand, standard of formal education, and extent of mass-media exposure.

This hypothesis was tested by calculating Pearson product-moment correlation coefficients between measures on these four variables and modernity scores. Education and mass-media exposure correlated positively with the modernity scores in both studies. Length of urban-industrial work experience ad urban residence correlated either negatively or less strongly than was anticipated. However, in the second study the question of urban-residence was explored in greater detail by comparing two groups, one urban and the other transitional. The urban group of subjects were born in urban areas and preferred to live in an urban area, whilst the members of the transitional group were born in rural areas and disliked urban residence. The urban group had a significantly higher mean modernity score than the transitional group.

Despite the generally favourable results of the two studies, the author had doubts about the conceptual value of the "model of modern man". An examination of the model suggests three failings. The first is that the "model of modern man" does not provide a description of "traditional man". This conceptual shortcoming leads one to ignore the possibility of variations in traditional culture, behaviour and attitudes and thus perpetuates certain myths. Taking "individualism" as an example, the "model of modern man" implies that traditional people are not individualistic. Le Vine (1966), however, notes that the Ibos of Nigeria, who have had little contact with modern, urban environments, are more individualistic than the highly urbanized Hausa and Yoruba.

In South Africa one would have expected the traditional "lobola" practice (payment of cattle to the father of the prospective bride) to have died away in urban areas, but it has not, although the payment is now made in cash, not cattle. The relevance of this failing is that the conceptualization and evaluation of certain items is divorced from reality, particularly where the distinction between "traditional" and "modern man" is inaccurate.

A second problem is that by conceiving of traditional

and modern as opposites there is the underlying assumption that the two are mutually exclusive. However, Lerner (1968) states that modernization implies the acceptance of certain characteristic attitudes, and that traditional values may block this process. This assumption denies the possibility of mutual adaptation and synthesis, demonstrated among sophisticated South African blacks who, on becoming ill, consult both a modern Western doctor and a traditional diviner. Pauw (1974) notes that "ancestor beliefs have been extensively adapted to the urban and technological milieu" (p.109) and points to attempts at synthesis between indigenous traditions and Christianity as seen in the Independent Churches. Once again doubts are raised about the writing and assessment of certain items.

Finally, the concept of "modern man" is in itself ethnocentric. Peil (1972) observes that "one cannot help but be struck by the relationship between many of the attitudes characteristic of modernity and attitudes considered typical of the middle class in industrialised Western countries" (p.223). In the present model, modern people are suppposed to differ from traditional people in the area of "future planning". However, if one considers the rapidly changing political and economic structure of Africa, it is easy to appreciate that a person modern in all other respects may be very low in ability to plan for the future, particularly where this is so inherently uncertain. Here too one needs to relate ideal concepts to the reality of the social, economic and political contexts.

The criticisms of the ideal-type "model of modern man" suggest that the use of such a concept should be informed by the realities of the society or culture under consideration. It might be sensible to adopt a culturally relative interpretation of modernization based on an anthropologically informed perspective.

NOTE

The author completed the work discussed in this paper whilst employed by the National Institute for Personnel Research, Johannesburg.

REFERENCES

ARMER, M. & YOUTZ, R. Formal education and individual modernity in an African society. _American Journal of Sociology_, 1970, 76, 604-626.

Chapter 22

BRODE, J. The Process of Modernization: An Annotated Bibliography. Cambridge, Massachusetts: Harvard University Press, 1969.

DOOB, L.W. Scales for assaying psychological modernization in Africa. Public Opinion Quarterly, 1967, 31, 414-421.

DUBB, A. The impact of the city. In W.P. Hammond-Tooke (ed). The Bantu-speaking Peoples of Southern Africa, London: Routledge & Kegan Paul, 1974.

GIDDENS, A. Capitalism and Modern Social Theory: An Analysis of the Writings of Marx, Durkheim and Max Weber. Cambridge: Cambridge University Press, 1971.

INKELES, A. The modernization of man. In Myron Weiner (ed.) Modernizaton: The Dynamics of Growth. New York: Basic Books, 1966.

INKELES,A. & SMITH, D.H. Becoming Modern: Individual change in six developing countries. London: Heinemann, 1974.

KAHL, J.A. The Measurement of Modernism: A Study of Values in Brazil and Mexico. Austin: University of Texas Press, 1968.

LENGERMANN, P.M. Working class barriers in Trinidad and Tobago. Social and Economic Forces, 1971, 20(2), 151-163.

LERNER, D. Modernization. In International Encyclopedia of Social Sciences, 386-395, 1968.

LERNER, D. The Passing of Traditional Society: Modernizing the Middle East. The Free Press of Glencoe, 1958.

LE VINE, R.A. Dreams and Deeds: Achievement Motivation in Nigeria. Chicago: University of Chicago Press, 1966.

LYON, B., ROWEN, H.H. & HAMEROW, T.S. A History of the Western World. Chicago: Rand McNally & Co., 1969.

PAUW, B.A. Ancestor beliefs and rituals among urban Africans. African Studies, 1974, 33(2), 99-111.

PEIL, M. The Ghanaian Factory Worker: Industrial Man in Africa. Cambridge: Cambridge University Press, 1972.

SCHNAIBERG, A. Measuring modernism: theoretical and empirical explorations. American Journal of Sociology, 1970, 76, 399-425.

SMITH, D.H. & INKELES, A. The OM Scale: a comparative measure of individual modernity. Sociometry, 1966, 29(4), 353-377.

222

CROSS-CULTURAL DIFFERENCES IN BLIND ADOLESCENTS

A. Uba

University of Ife, Ile-Ife

Although there are now vast numbers of studies detailing cross-cultural differences in perception, cognition, attitudes, beliefs, values, etc. (eg. Triandis, 1980) there are remarkably few cross-cultural studies concerned with disabled individuals. Indeed only three studies have come to the author's attention which focus on cross-cultural differences in peoples' attitudes and behaviour towards the disabled (Sanua, 1970; Bamisaiye, 1974; Bamisaiye and Dostoor 1978/79). This study follows on from these three in that it too is concerned with documenting the differential treatment and valuing of a disabled group, the blind, in two distinct Nigerian cultural groups - the Yoruba and the Hausa. Further, this research also attempts to assess the possible consequences such differential treatment may have on the development of cognitive skills.

The Yoruba believe that should a baby be born blind, this is both indicative of wrong-doing by its parents and is a means of their punishment. Consequently Yoruba parents tend to look down with pity on their disabled blind children and are to some extent ashamed of them. Yoruba tradition also instills in individuals the tendency to keep personal misfortunes private rather than to receive sympathy that would otherwise be meted out when misfortunes are made public. In the case of blindness, however, this is problematic as a blind person cannot easily keep this misfortune to himself. For this reason, the blind person is virtually forced into an assigned role and status which greatly dictates how others will relate to him, and gives rise to the socio-cultural stigma which is attached to blindness in Yoruba culture.

There is a great contrast between this set of affairs

and that which exists in traditional Hausa culture. For example, Hausa parents tend to readily accept and respond favourably towards a blind infant. This follows from the Islamic faith which stresses the will of "Allah" (God) behind all occurrences. The disabled blind Muslim accepts his handicap as God-sent or fate, and "it is wrong to feel anything about fate" (interview with a Hausa beggar, 1982). This same religious observance also encourages liberal alms-giving as a means of securing a higher place in the Kingdom of God. Thus, most disabled Hausa blind persons gain from charitable acts. Further comments on the different sets of attitudes held by the different sections of Nigerian society concerning the disabled can be found in the work of Bamisaiye and Dostoor (1978/79).

The question now arises whether there are any significant consequences for the cognitive development of blind individuals in Yoruba and Hausa society which stem from these societal attitudinal differences. In this study an auditory task developed by the author (Uba, 1971) is used. The specific hypothesis to be tested is:

Blind Hausa adolescents will perform better than their Yoruba counterparts on an auditory task.

METHOD

Subjects

Subjects from the Yoruba ethnic group were randomly drawn from a mixed Pacelli School for Blind Children, in Lagos State, Nigeria. Thirty adolescent boys and girls were selected from primaries five and six. Their ages ranged from 15 to 16. The subjects of the Hausa ethnic group were also randomly drawn from a mixed school for Blind Children, in Gindiri, Jos, Plateau State, Nigeria. Again 30 adolescent boys and girls from primaries five and six were selected and their ages ranged from 15 to 16.

Tasks and Procedure

After the subjects were seated in a group the experimenter read out the standardized instructions to them. Then practice trials were presented during which the experimenter made sure that the subjects understood the task, and informed them of the correct answers.

The test items consisted of a letter followed by numbers. After the initial letter was given, it was followed by between one to five numbers. These numbers were used to indicate the subsequent letters in the alphabet which subjects were to recall. For example, if F354 were dictated, then the correct response would be:

I (the third letter after F), N (the fifth letter after I) and R (the fourth letter after N). That is, I N R.

After a test item was presented, on a given signal, the subjects were required to write down the letters of the alphabet corresponding to the numbers in the sequence in which the numbers were given. Precautions were taken not to give letters which might be confused in sound with numbers. The use of rough paper for computation was forbidden. No repetitions were allowed. If a mistake was made when dictating the test item, the experimenter stopped and repeated the item from the beginning. There were 15 test items with one mark for each item totally correct (2).

RESULTS

The mean and standard deviation for the 30 Yoruba blind subjects tested are $M = 6.13$; $S.D. = 1.45$. The corresponding figures for the 30 Hausa blind subjects tested are $M = 9.17$; $S.D. = 3.26$. The T-test indicates that the performance by the Hausa group is significantly better than that of their Yoruba counterparts ($t = 2.66$, d.f. = 58, $p < 0.01$).

DISCUSSION

It has been postulated that disabled adolescents in Yoruba culture are not highly motivated to act like non-disabled persons due to environmental factors which provide insufficient support for their psychological development. The present data support this belief since, on the test employed, the Hausa disabled blind group performed more accurately than did the Yoruba group. The growing concern of how specific cultural and environmental influences affect the processes of cognition has been widely studied (Cole et al., 1971; Berry, 1966; Segall et al., 1966 and Serpell, 1976). The same physical environment may have quite different functional significance for different individuals, depending on their sociocultural interpretation of the physical stimuli (Frijda and Jahoda, 1966). For instance, in traditional Hausa society wealth as such does not confer prestige but rather the socially legitimate ways of using wealth do so primarily through religious observances, that is, through pilgrimage to Mecca and liberal alms-giving (Yeld, 1960). Thus, the disabled blind beggar and the ablebodied member of Hausa society are in a relationship of mutual profit, the former because of the money he receives, and the latter through the blessings to be gained from religious observance, and increased social status acquired through charitable acts. Thus, the blind beggar has a definite social role.

Yoruba handicapped persons, in contrast to the Hausa, tend to remain within the extended family in an essentially dependent role. In some cases they are able to secure education or training of some sort which enables them to secure a job or take part in small-scale trading enterprises, but their socio-economic position is not the same as in Hausa society. The results of this study suggest that socio-cultural stigma attached to blindness in Yoruba society may have far-reaching consequences for the blind and that greater attention sould be given to these matters. A change of attitude is called for, through the education of the general public which will influence the acceptance of disabled blind adolescents in Yoruba society.

NOTES

1. With the author's approval the editors have slightly modified and shortened this paper. Readers interested in fuller details are invited to correspond with the author.

2. This test presupposes an adequate knowledge of the alphabet and that this does not vary to any great extent across the subjects being tested.

REFERENCES

BAMISAIYE, A., Begging in Ibadan, Southern Nigeria. Human Organization, 1974, 33, 197-202.

BAMISAIYE, A. & DOSTOOR, D., Socio-economic and cultural differences in attitudes to the physically handicapped in Nigeria. Nigerian Journal of Psychology, 1978/1979, 2 & 3, 84-91.

BERRY, J.W. Cultural determinations of perception. Unpublished Ph.D. thesis, University of Edinburgh, 1966.

COLE, M., GAY, J., GLICK, J. & SHARP, D.W. The Cultural Context of Learning and Thinking. New York: Basic Books, 1971.

FRIJDA, N. & JAHODA, G. On the scope and methods of cross-cultural research. International Journal of Psychology, 1966, 1 110-127.

SANUA, V. D. A cross-cultural study of cerebral palsy. Social Sciences and Medicine, 1970, 4, 461-512.

SEGALL, M.H., CAMPBELL, D.T. & HERSKOVITS, M.J. The Influence of Culture on Visual Perception. N.Y.: Bobbs-Merrill, 1966.

SERPELL, R. Culture's Influence on Behaviour. London: Methuen, 1976.

TRIANDIS, H.C. Handbook of Cross-cultural Psychology Vols. 1-6. Boston: Allyn & Bacon, 1980.

UBA, A. A Study of sex differences in attention among adolescents accepted into the Roman Catholic Schools in Lagos and Western Nigeria. Unpublished M.Phil. thesis, University of London, 1971.

YELD, E.R. Islam and social stratification in Nigeria. British Journal of Sociology, 1960, 11, 112-128.

VIETNAMESE CHILDREN AND PARENTS IN AN ENGLISH TOWN: THE REGUFEE EXPERIENCE

M. Eisenbruch

University of Cambridge

> This paper is dedicated
> to the Vietnamese refugees of
> Williamstown. The study would
> not have been possible, but
> for their humanity, trust and
> generosity.

1. VIETNAMESE REFUGEES IN AN ENGLISH TOWN: INTRODUCTION

Throughout world history, there have always been refugees. Often the victims of multiple trauma in their countries-of-origin, they comprise a vulnerable group. Usually entering social and psychological disadvantage, they also constitute a group at high risk.

In recent years, the importance of these risk and vulnerability factors has gained recognition; attempts are being made to identify an underlying process of what has been termed "refugee behaviour". Often, these studies apply Western criteria of adjustment and adaptation to the refugee group in question.

Western countries now face an escalating outpouring of refugees from Vietnam. They are being accommodated, perhaps precipitously, in several countries, including Britain. But their special needs are almost completely unknown to those concerned with their resettlement.

The present study has three objectives:

(i) to explore and define the experience of refugee family life;

(ii) to examine the impact of becoming a refugee, upon child, parent, and the child-parent unit. Some suggest that while refugee parents might be prone to develop problems, their children will find it relatively easy to adjust. Is this so?

(iii) to identify risk and vulnerability factors. Adjustment, coping and adaptation entail an interplay between the inherent vulnerability of the family in question with the social and environmental risk in which the family finds itself. Risk and vulnerability are not only objective realities for the observer, but also subjective experiences for refugee family members. The present study seeks to emphasise the actors' perspective. Particular attention is given to the refugee child's perception of his or her predicament.

The present paper focuses on the Vietnamese refugee child and family. The first case study illustrates some aspects of the refugee experience as felt by a parent, while the second takes the complementary position by a description of the child's perception of refugee life.

2. THE REFUGEE AND HIS ADJUSTMENT

2.1 THE PROBLEM: RISK AND VULNERABILITY

2.1.1 THE REFUGEE

The United Nations Convention Relating to the Status of Refugees as amended by the Protocol defines a refugee as a person who,

> "owing to well-founded fear of being persecuted for reasons of race, religion, nationality, membership of a particular social group or political opinion, is outside the country of his nationality, and is unable or, owing to such fear, is unwilling to avail himself of the protection of that country; or who, not having a nationality, and being outside the country of his former habitual residence, is unable or, owing to such fear, is unwilling to return to it."

Various operational definitions prove less than satisfactory, because they use criteria which neglect the refugees' evaluation of their own status.

Attention has been given to various aspects of Vietnamese refugee life: general background (Grant, 1979); family and community among refugees (Haines, Rutherford and Thomas, 1973); general health (Hull, 1979); physical and domestic needs (Chandanasiri, 1980); and socio-economic and occupational adjustment (Finnan, 1980; Montero, 1979;

Hirayama, 1980). The mental health of Vietnamese refugees has been examined by Aylesworth (1980), Le (1980), and Lerner (1980) in terms of their self-perceived needs. Some of the ethnomedical problems have been described in Australia (Phan My Dung, 1982), and in Britain (Philips, 1981). However, with the exception of a study of the problems of Southeast Asian children in a refugee camp (Harding and Looney, 1977), the adjustment of refugee children has been neglected.

What salient differences, if any, exist between the refugee and the non-refugee immigrant? According to Rack (1981), the refugee is a special category of migrant, who experiences physical or emotional violence. If so, then one would expect a set of consequences of such experiences of violence.

2.1.2 REACTIONS TO CATASTROPHIC TRAUMA

The impact of violence upon refugees has been considered by Krumperman (1981), in terms of psychosocial problems and consequences, and appropriate help and services to be offered.

Two responses are pertinent. Hostility, a frequent response, may be difficult to discern because the refugee may present a facade of politeness (Krumperman, 1981). This may be particularly so with Vietnamese refugees.

The second response is some form of depression, which may be developed by refugees, immediately or after arrival due to loss of home and loss of their past. This grief may become pathological and has two aspects: first, excessive anger may lead toward inappropriate and antisocial acts — recent observations of refugees note an alarmingly high incidence of criminal offences and violence; second, "survivor guilt", as described among concentration camp survivors and other similar groups (Davidson, 1981). The general experience of those working with Vietnamese refugees in the United Kingdom is that, once the wall of silence is penetrated, one discovers cases where arbitrary decisions were taken by particular family members to escape, leaving other members behind (Finlay et al., 1981). The presence of survivor guilt among Vietnamese refugees would not be surprising.

It has been argued that despite the superficial diversity between refugee groups from distinct cultures, it should be possible to identify a common underlying process, which has been termed "refugee behaviour" (Kunz, 1973; Stein, 1980).

2.2 STAGES OF THE REFUGEE EXPERIENCE

It is important to predict the sort of outcomes for refugee parents and children, not only in the immediate post-resettlement period, but also in the years and decades to follow. To date, refugee research has not been noted for building on past experience with previous waves of refugees.

The "refugee experience" has been depicted as a unitary phenomenon, with a characteristic onset, progression and possibly resolution. The type descriptions of Stein (1980) are clear examples of this approach.

Against this position, I would argue that the notion of a "unit refugee" is based on an ideal type, and has little resemblance to the actual events on the ground.

To begin with, Hitch (1981) has drawn attention to the heterogeneity of environmental risk factors. I would also add the importance of recognising the range of individual variation in vulnerabilities and in coping styles. Together, these risks and vulnerabilities will produce a range of adaptive behaviours.

Three residual characteristics may occur: guilt for lost or abandoned love ones; a sense of invulnerability through having survived; and aggresssivenesss as an outcome of guilt and invulnerability (Keller, 1975).

Various ways of representing the stages in a time-sequence have been proposed (Tyhurst, 1951; Keller, 1975; Sluzki, 1981; Hitch, 1981). The first stage has often been termed the "honeymoon period", associated with the immediate sense of relief at arrival to safety.

In the second stage, termed "decomposition or crisis", the refugee faces the realities of his lost past, his difficult present, and his uncertain future.

In the third stage, intergenerational conflicts emerge. Children reared in the host society clash with their parents, who may increasingly cherish the values of the society of origin.

The fourth stage occurs in old age. Increasing nostalgia, coupled with loss of supports, may lead to failure to cope.

It should again be emphasised that there is no "unit" refugee. Thus type descriptions of developmental stages may be useful frameworks to understand developmental process within a group of refugees; individuals vary.

The adjustment process may be separated analytically into several "tracks". It is relatively easy to identify areas such as occupational adjustment, language, residence and community pattterns and states of physical health. It is far more difficult to spot culture and identity problems, reactions to stress, relationship difficulties (both within the family and the ethnic group, and between the ethnic group and host community), and mental health and illness.

Family and social relationships may be especially brittle: the husband unable to provide; the wife forced to work; an inversion of traditional patterns. The child may be caught between two cultures (Bullivant, 1981), and may become the family mediator with the host community.

Several clusters tending towards an increase in emotional problems have been identified (Stein, 1980: 12): loneliness or isolation; changes in occupation or vocation; intergenerational conflict; problems in host-refugee relationships; and culture shock. Single refugees, those from separated families, refugees in rural areas, and others in isolated situations lacking support have also been identified as at-risk.

Despite these general indices of risk, no information is available about risk or vulnerability factors of refugee children and parents: the sort of intergenerational conflicts and the early warning signs that clinical intervention is required.

It might be expected that the refugee experience could place a strain on the child's developing sense of identity. If so, then it would be important to detect evidence that refugee children suffered a heightened sense of alienation. Indeed, alienation is a fundamental aspect of the refugee experience. The term has been used with at least five separate meanings: 1. Powerlessness - the individual supposes that he cannot influence the outcome of his situation; 2. Meaninglessness - he does not know what to believe; 3. Normlessness - he expects that socially unapproved behaviours are required to achieve given goals; 4. Isolation - he does not think the beliefs of most people in his society are worthwhile; 5. Self estrangement - he has lost pride in current life.

3. VIETNAMESE REFUGEES IN WILLIAMSTOWN

Williamstown is becoming a centre for resettlement of Vietnamese refugees.

I have become increasingly involved in two networks. The first network comprises the group of two structurally independent but functionally interrelated professional

social support groups; the second network comprises the
group of Vietnamese refugee families themselves.

I begin with the following case, which illustrates
many features of the risks, vulnerabilities and experiences
of refugee life in Williamstown.

4. A FAMILY "AT-RISK" : CASE ILLUSTRATION

4.1 THE PRESENTING PROBLEM: IMMINENT MARITAL SEPARATION

Mr Chang, 26, and his wife, 32, had arrived from
Vietnam the previous year. Their eleven-month-old
daughter had been born shortly after their arrival.
Each parent had previously been married and then
apparently divorced in Vietnam, where the children of
the first marriages remained.

Mrs Chang's two sons were cared for by the mother
of her first husband, who was detained in a Vietnamese
"re-education centre" for seven years. When he was
released, Mrs Chang suddenly received a letter offering
reunion with him and the two sons. She longed for this.
Mr Chang was willing to divorce her, on condition that
she relinquish her baby to him. She felt more strongly
drawn to her first husband and sons yet she could not
leave her baby. She became profoundly depressed and
isolated, clinging increasingly to her baby; at night,
Mrs Chang would fall asleep clutching her in her arms.

4.2 THE PROVISIONAL FORMULATION

At this stage, my interpretation of the events was
as follows. The crisis of facing the ashes of her
former marriage rising like a phoenix from her previous
life precipitated the final breakdown of the marriage;
a union apparently formed in the aftermath of the
disruption of their respective previous marriages.

Mr Chang moved out of the house. With several
close kin and friends nearby, he found relatively
little difficulty in continuing his social network. Mrs
Chang, on the other hand, found herself very isolated.
She lived in an ultra-modern block of apartments,
surrounded by trees and open space, yet devoid of
familiar people, trapped by the distance from the two
dense refugee localities, with no mode of
transportation, and with the responsibility of caring
for her daughter. Mrs Chang became increasingly
desperate. She lay awake at night, listening to the
wind blowing through the densely treed estate. She
feared the trees, for they were large and old, just
like her ancestors. She explained "When people grow
very old and then die, their spirits go into the trees.

Then there can be trouble."

Mrs Chang would eventually fall into a fitfull sleep, to be awakened with disturbing dreams. Often, there were themes involving her parents in Vietnam; sometimes she would dream of reunion, that her parents had come to her. But she was always disappointed.

4.3 CLARIFICATION: ALIENATION AND MARGINALITY

This led her to talk about her loneliness. Not only did she feel frightened at being surrounded by sinister trees; she also experienced a deep alienation from others in the neighbourhood. She complained "English people never talk. I miss being able to just knock on somebody's door and chatting with them whenever I want to. And it's too far to walk, with my baby, to meet Vietnamese."

Diffidence about her spoken English was only part of the problem: there was also the question of her self-percept as a "Vietnamese person", a "Vietnamese not in her homeland", or as a "non-English person in England". At another level, a related question was whether she regarded herself as Vietnamese, Chinese or both. According to Mrs Chang, her family had always lived in Vietnam. By contrast, her husband was clearly an ethnic Chinese, whose parents had emigrated from China to Vietnam.

When questioned about the differences between ethnic Chinese in Vietnam and "real" Vietnamese, Mrs Chang saw the two as much the same. But then she drew certain distinctions. When questioned he hated Chinese cooking; "He (present husband) hacks up the food in a wok, fries it; it's terrible." But there are other differences.

Not only did she feel cut off from the English, but to make matters worse, she felt estranged from other Vietnamese; she perceived most of them as ethnic Chinese, just like her present husband. In her words: "I can't talk to them because I don't know how to speak Chinese. So I feel embarrassed." Now that her estranged husband had departed, she had absolutely no way of communicating with the mass of the refugee community. Her sense of alienation on two fronts was massive.

"The Chinese eat, and eat, lots of rice. They eat, and eat, and eat. We in Vietnam do not eat, just two small bowls are enough (she indicated small circles with her hands). In China, they have more than we do. I know. I lived there for two months," she added.

235

The theme moved to parenting and babies. "In the old times, in Vietnam, a woman could have ten or twelve children. Now it is not allowed to have more than two. If you have one or two you would be given so and so many bowls of rice, according to whether you have one or two babies. But if you have a third child, then you get no rice at all." Mrs Chang was unaware that exactly the same restriction on family size pertained in China as well.

Mrs Chang continued her denigration of the Chinese. "The Chinese hated having little daughters. They only wanted sons to continue the family; daughters were killed after birth. We Vietnamese would not do such a thing. So what happened? They (the Chinese) killed off all their little girls. Then after a while, when the boys grew up, they found that there were no brides to be found. So they had to come down to Vietnam to find women. That's why they came."

Mrs Chang produced an airmail envelope, which contained photographs and a letter. She resumed talking about her relatives in Vietnam, particularly her father. One of the photographs showed him seated in the family home, dressed in traditional clothing. He was 77 years old, and quite deaf. Mrs Chang was quite concerned that he was unable to obtain proper help for his deafness, and asked whether she could send him a hearing aid. She was adamant that in Vietnam, audiological help was simply unavailable.

Within the context of the interview, her request seemed to have greater import than a mere wish to help her father; nor did this seem merely to be the expression of pining for her parents. But I was not to know until later, when informed of the background to her flight from Vietnam.

4.4 BACKGROUND IN VIETMAN: CRISIS AND RISK

Mrs Chang's parents were desperately poor. Her first husband was arrested, and sentenced indefinitely to a "re-education centre"; she might never see him again, and was quite powerless to intervene. Determined to make things less oppressive for her parents, she sought some way of supporting them. But there were no possibilities open to her within the war-torn country. So she decided to leave, and send them regular support from wherever she could go and work.

But it was not easy to leave Vietnam; that is, not without a good deal of gold leaf, together with a pretext for official expulsion.

Then she met Mr Chang, also separated from his spouse and children. He also wished to flee and he had the necessary gold leaf bribe. An arrangement was struck. If she would agree to "marry" him, he would pay the "bridewealth" for the two of them. They planned to divorce and go separate ways when they reached a safe destination. But there was one attached condition: Mr Chang desperately wanted another child, and she was to agree to provide one. She did not want any more children, but hoped to extricate herself from that part of the bargain. She failed. Pregnancy ensued, and her unwanted daughter, issue of a loveless, arranged marriage, was born shortly after arrival in England.

This was the key to understanding the ease with which she had dealt with the current break-up of her second marriage. Her second marriage and her young baby apparently were <u>not</u> merely precipitous attempts at reconstituting a family in a strange place, as I had previously assumed. True enough, her reaction to Mr Chang's ultimatum that she hand over their baby to him had seemed bland. But, when pressed, her eyes had clouded over with sorrow, as she experienced the pangs of anticipatory loss of the child who had unwittingly become all she had; indeed, the only person to whom she could speak in her native tongue who could understand her.

COMMENT

This case illustrates aspects of the refugee experience very clearly. There were two components to Mrs Chang's vulnerability. The first was the loss of not just one, but two families; three generations (father, husband and sons) were left behind. To this was added a strong survivor guilt. Hence, her vulnerability to depression.

Entry into a high-risk situation is quite evident. Mrs Chang's double barrelled marginality (from both host-society and the refugee community), together with her sense of continuing powerlessness and isolation led to profound alienation. This in turn fed into her depressive vulnerability, rendering her less able to reach out for social supports. These support networks are influenced by ethnicity of the person in question: it is an error to make the assumption that all Viethnamese refugees are ethnically the same.

The case illustrates how failure on the part of Western helpers to appreciate Vietnamese folk belief can lead to errors in evaluation and planning. On first blush, the Western observer might be led to think how lucky Mrs Chang had been to obtain housing in an attractive estate. Yet for her, it was particularly unfortunate. The

237

references to trees might be explicable in terms of Vietnamese belief in malicious spirits. The most dangerous spirit is "the tinh, who villagers claim use a variety of tricks to induce their intended victims to open their mouths, whereupon the tinh draws out their souls, leaving them insane. Villagers believe that the... tinh inhabit(s) great trees, often appearing as human shadows." (Hickey, 1964: 76-7).

Mrs Chang's situation is not atypical. For example, more than half of the community in Williamstown have first-degree relatives (parents, children, sibs, spouses) in Vietnam, sometimes incarcerated there, in transit camps in Malaysia or elsewhere, or in Australia. There is a significant trend toward early post-arrival marriage, remarriage and pregnancy. Some of the areas in which problems in adaptation have occurred are discussed in the following section.

5. PROBLEM AREAS IN ADAPTATION

5.1. CHILDREN: LANGUAGE AND SCHOOL

At least four-fifths of the Vietnamese refugee population in Williamstown speak some English. This has usually been learned over a short period of up to four years, during primary resettlement. The majority of the refugees are from the north and therefore are unlikely to have heard English prior to their arrival in Hong Kong, en route to the United Kingdom. Refugees from the south may have been exposed to English prior to 1975, during the period when United States forces were present.

The present study confirms that the child learns better than his parents. In some families this has produced tension when the child enjoys developing communication in English. The child's rejection of his native tongue shames the parents, who are angry and bewildered. The parents respond by haranguing the child to speak only Cantonese or Vietnamese. The parent-child rift deepens.

Schoolteachers have begun to observe behavioural, intellectual and educational difficulties, which might link with observed difficulties in the language class. Children have been described as depressed, listless, apathetic, or tearful. The opinion of coordinators and teachers has been that the special needs of these children required more specialised attention than was available. One already evident problem occurs when the child moves from the relative protection and stability of primary school to the loosely-structured secondary school. This developmental crisis has been handled poorly by some Vietnamese children. They become anxious and disorganised.

5.2 EMPLOYMENT: ORIGINAL AND CURRENT

Unemployment is a stress factor which increases the risk of failure to cope. The vulnerability of any given family will determine the extent to which its members can cope with an unemployed breadwinner. The present study has demonstrated that the Vietnamese refugee in Williamstown is disadvantaged in several respects. Without sufficient command of English, he may be badly informed of job prospects. He does not comprehend the bureaucratic form-filling and other procedures entailed in seeking work (or unemployment benefits). When attending the local Job Centre or interviews with prospective employers, he does not grasp the sort of assessment being made of him.

Instances of racial discrimination have occurred. In one case, this involved a statutory authority. A Vietnamese man attended an interview. The clerk behind the counter made a derogatory allusion to Vietnamese people. This prompted a strong response from the Refugee Resettlement Group representative who had accompanied the interviewee. Matters became heated, and the representative felt that the best thing to do was to protect her client from further embarrassment by breaking off the exchange and leaving the premises. When the matter was discussed with the Community Relations Officer, it was learned that an official complaint could be lodged only by the person who had been the object of discrimination. The employee concerned had since denied to his superiors that the incident had taken place. When the subject was gently introduced to the Vietnamese man, the representative was surprised to learn that he had perceived exactly what had happened, even though unable to understand English.

This instance exemplifies the question: despite all the good will and organisational supports which are being mobilised, what is the "hidden agenda" in refugee resettlement which impedes the acceptance and integration of the refugee into his host community?

5.3 RELIGION AND COSMOLOGY

The majority of refugees were Buddhists, a small minority Catholic. In the discussion, I shall refer to the Buddhist majority.

It is crucial to identify what is meant when informants profess to be Buddhist, and in what ways the Buddhist ideology, cosmology, ritual and way of life are passed on to children. It is already apparent that for some families, Buddhism appears to signify little more than a feeling of membership of a corporation. In such families, religious practice is nonexistent, either on a day to day basis, or on special calendric or accidental occasions. At

239

the other end of the spectrum are families who are devout Buddhists in both their adherence to ritual observance and in their general religious belief. Those homes show concrete evidence of Buddhism, parents spend time each day in worship and meditation, and children are also taught in the ways of Buddhism.

Those families at the former end of the spectrum of religious observance express less concern about their children's future religious and personal identity in their new land. Such parents combine Christmas rituals with those of the Chinese new year; they expect their children to grow up as Christians. They had no plans for their children to learn the ways of Buddhism.

This pattern formed a marked contrast with the behaviour and attitudes of families who were devoutly Buddhist. Not only were the parents themselves engaged in renewed exploration of their spiritual existence, but they also involved their children in this activity. This was explained by several informants in the following terms: during the Communist rule religious life was rapidly curtailed. Children were unable to become novices in monasteries, as had been the earlier custom. Young adults were taken away from their families, and taught that Communism was the correct creed. Only the older family members maintained the notion that they were Buddhist, and even they were not free to express this in outward ritual practice. Having fled from Vietnam, the older family members felt drawn to reestablish their links with their former spiritual life. This paved the way, and their children (by this stage themselves young parents) followed suit.

5.4 PROBLEMS IN APPRAISAL OF THE DISTURBED PERSON

It has been difficult for local professionals to accept the urgency of psychiatric emergencies when first confronted with them. In one instance, a police officer did not take action when approached with a request to intervene with a floridly psychotic out-of-control refugee, on the grounds that "that was not really abnormal behaviour for a Vietnamese." Cases are described in which acutely psychotic adults were taken from doctor to hospital, thence to other agencies, none of which acknowledged the need for emergency intervention.

Isolated single individuals with no close kin are especially at risk. Instances of major psychosis have occurred, in which these themes of alienation have figured prominently. Presentations have included paranoid schizophrenia, psychotic depression and other bizarre symptoms.

The delusional content of these episodes may also clearly be influenced by specific situational factors. One woman formerly a prominent "pro-China" communist who fled for her life after the Vietnamese switch to Russia, developed as part of her paranoid delusional system the belief that Radio Peking was transmitting messages to her. She felt quite unsafe in Williamstown, believing the KGB to be following her at every turn, accepting admission to psychiatric hospital as a safe place. It is noteworthy that in the course of this episode a whole Buddhist belief system (which previously had been eschewed) resurfaced. For the patient her illness became a combination of: (i) a real political persecution; (ii) a medical affliction and (iii) the result of straying from the Buddhist Noble Eightfold Path, with failure of "right seeing". These explanations were offered by the patient, and given graphic expression by the act of shattering spectacles, and then explaining: (i) "I can't see the KGB now, even though they are still following me"; (ii) "I must find a new way of correct seeing, to replace the distorted way I saw the world before."

Another problem is the obstacle against administering "traditional" remedies alongside standard Western treatments. Cases are reported in which the terrified or suspicious patient was unable, despite appeals and protests, to be given herbal medicines or acupuncture. Traditional remedies should be available at an early stage, when the individual first asks for them, rather than being thought of only in the midst of a subsequent florid psychosis.

Even where there is an awareness of the need for traditional remedies, access is restricted; for example, acupuncture is not available under normal circumstances on N.H.S., and the standard fee for a single treatment is seven pounds sterling, which is too expensive for most refugees.

6. THE PREDICAMENT FOR THE CHILD

Certain refugee families are in acute and chronic situations of crisis. Some parents are finding difficulty in caring for their children. Some children show symptoms of distress in the school situation, particularly noticeable on first arrival. Some children have been pressured to become like the others in the class. In several cases, headmasters are alleged to have suggested to the child that he would find things easier if he adopted an English name. Children have been placed in strange classrooms, sometimes in small rural village schools, in mid-term, without any support or follow-up. How does the child make sense of his predicament?

Chapter 24

6.1 CASE ILLUSTRATION: CHILD'S CONSTRUCTION OF REALITY

I had been visiting the Trinh family for several
months. On the occasion of one visit, Anh, aged
thirteen, began talking spontaneously about her
experience of refugee life.

She began by complaining about the cold weather.
"The weather always affects my mood. People in England
are always sad. You never really know how they feel,
though, because the grown-ups here keep their feelings
to themselves."

She looked sad as she continued, "But you can tell
how other children at school feel. They don't hide
their feelings. The girls at school don't like me,
because I'm from Vietnam. They say we're just like
animals. But I tell them "we are not monkeys! We are
human beings, just like you. We have the same hair, and
skin, and feelings, even if they don't look the same."
But they don't listen."

Anh continued: "But they say to themselves "Why
did you come to our country? You will take everything
away from us."" Asked how she knew this, Anh replied
that nobody ever said it, but they showed it on their
faces. She then asked me whether people felt the same
about Vietnamese where I came from.

Anh continued, "The food is bad here. The fish is
dried out. We came from a fishing village not far from
Haiphong. We loved the sea, and the fresh fish. All our
food had fish sauce, or fresh vegetables. Here the milk
is too rich, the meat too fat and heavy and smelly. And
the weather gives me and my family headaches." She
asked, "Do you get headaches too?"

Anh said that she would really like to leave England
for good some day. "This place is not my home, and
never will be. I am forgetting my language. Now I can
hardly speak Vietnamese or Chinese. And my little
sisters will remember even less than I do. When we were
in China, I tried to learn Mandarin, but now I can't
remember that either."

Asked where she felt at home, Anh replied, "I
would like to go back to Vietnam. But I can't. And it's
not really where I belong. My home is in China. That's
where would like to go and live."

Asked where her parents had come from, she replied
that her father had been born in China and had migrated
to Vietnam as a young man. She thought her mother's
family had always lived in Vietnam. But after some

vigorous discussion with her mother, Anh stood corrected: "I don't know why I got mixed up", she said shamefacedly. "I had thought my mother was from Vietnam, but now I find out that she was from China. Her name was Ming." She then explained how in China, a man and a woman with the same surname would not marry one another, unless one was from a "big" branch and the other from a "small" one.

Anh looked sad. "My mother feels she can't go back to Vietnam, even though we'd like to." Asked why they couldn't return, Anh replied, "There was a big war, against the Chinese. The Russians came. They promised us that if we'd fight against the Chinese, then they would give us more food. So we did. But all they gave us was bread, not rice! The Russians had fair hair, and they had white skin. Just like the English. And they couldn't speak Chinese or Vietnamese, just like the English. They were not good for us, even though they said they would be."

Anh appeared to be anxious and preoccupied. It was the week that England was at the start of an international crisis, with much media talk of war. Anh asked, "Is England going to be completely blown up? Our teacher told us that if there were to be a war, nobody would live." Anh said how frightened she felt that there would be fighting in the streets and houses around her (1). Anh remembered the fighting in Vietnam, and how scared it had made her.

Anh continued to recall life in Vietnam, "My father and mother built our house with their own hands. He was a very good builder. But he can't get work here, because he can't speak English. He will learn one day. Then he will become very very rich."

Anh continued, "My father knows how to fix things. When I get wind, my hands get paralysed because the wind goes down them. He puts burning stuff on my skin, which makes me cry. But it makes me better. He puts it between my fingers. Nobody in England knows how to do it, but he learned a little about it in China a long time ago." Her head tilted back with what appeared to be pride. I asked her why people got "wind", and why her father's remedy worked. Anh replied excitedly, "There are five causes of that!" She then stopped suddenly, looking crestfallen and solemn, "But I just can't explain them. It's too hard to, in English. I don't remember."

6.2 COMMENT

This case provides a window into the child's

perception of her refugee experience. The case also suggests areas of identity formation which might be under strain in her developmental adolescent tasks. To summarise, Anh expressed her sense of alienation, together with her confusion as to her present and future identity. Anh perceived herself as different from English children. Reciprocally, she felt that they saw her as different from themselves.

One might postulate that in her attempt to handle her sense of being different, Anh split her world into "good" and "bad". The English children persecuted her. She had to plead with them to be regarded as an equal. When this failed, she grouped English children with "cold weather" people, who were withholding and dangerous. Included in this group were the Russians, whom Anh blamed for the carnage in Vietnam. In other words, the Russians had come with false promises of help; and now, the English were offering to do good. Could they be trusted? Anh felt she would never feel at home in England. She was uncertain whether her mother was Chinese or Vietnamese. But she identified her father's healing skill with his "Chinese-ness", remembered wistfully her attempt at learning Mandarin, and expressed the desire to settle in China. Yet her pride in identifying herself as Chinese was tempered by her confusion and shame: was it legitimate to publicly display her knowledge of the Five Humours? In this case, shame won the day. Anh typifies the feelings of other refugee children, particularly adolescents. She is feeling the search for her "place of belonging". It is too early to tell whether this is the phasic grieving expression of loss of the past, or whether perhaps it could lead to persisting difficulties. Certainly some children express the wish to return to Vietnam, with or without the parents who took them away from there. Parents, too, wonder what will happen to their children in later years. As one mother explained, she and her husband had fled Vietnam for the sake of their toddler's life chances. They then realised they must prepare for the day that he might demand to return to his birthplace - a return which might not be possible. They strove to raise their child with an enduring sense of Vietnamese identity. At the same time, they felt confusion and guilt, sensing the difficulties which lay ahead, and coping with the present. As the father stated: "We lost our past. That cannot be brought back, so it's no use thinking about it. Since we cannot have a better future, that's no use thinking about either. All we can do is to get very busy with the present. That's how we can keep going. But we can't just let our child forget where he comes from, and who he is."

7. SUMMARY AND CONCLUSIONS

The entire refugee family faces the crisis of

adaptation. Stresses on various members are somewhat different. Husband and father must seek employment, mother must learn to cope with running a household in a strange place, children must enter an alien school domain. A neglected aspect of refugee research is: how do the family members cope, not only with the stress of the world outside the family and ethnic enclave; how do they cope with one another? The impact of parental disturbance upon parent-child interaction will be crucial in the case of the newly settled refugee family. It has been shown (Eisenbruch, 1982) that even mild to moderate depression may exert profound effects both upon mothering and upon the child. These internal aspects of family functioning are of no less importance than the more easily identified external ones.

The question remains: how can one detect the vulnerable refugee family, and what environmental risk factors exist? There are endless levels of analysis here, together with an endless range of variables. The quick and easy approach is to take the methodologically well-controlled experiment, in which selected variables such as unemployment, looseness of kin ties, or language difficulties are considered. While it must be admitted that this strategy yields data of high reliability, the validity of this sort of approach does little to enhance our understanding of the refugee experience. This paper has sought to explore and define factors which will be of substantive significance. It suggests that the crucial variables comprise alienation, identity confusion, responses to stress, the availability of supportive relationships within the refugee community, and the "quality" of the interactions between family members including parent and child, wife and husband.

It is too early to say what will happen to the Vietnamese refugees in the future. Health planners cannot afford to assume that problems of adjustment will "smooth themselves out" with time. Experience with very late sequelae of Displaced Person migration such as the post-1945 Polish migration, in which mental breakdown was found to occur in well-compensated individuals decades after the traumas of flight and resettlement seemed to have passed (Hitch, 1981; Jagucki, 1981), warns against such complacency. It would be equally dangerous, however, to pretend that enough is known about the refugee experience to enable effective preventive intervention at this stage. The pessimistic view would be that the damage is already done – those refugees who were sufficiently traumatised before arrival in Britain will inevitably fail to adjust. I would argue against such a position. Even though so little is known about the problem, there are some general principles which, if applied, should facilitate the recovery of the refugee from his crisis.

I would stress the relevance of crisis theory (Caplan, 1964; Wynne, 1975). Caplan has stressed the importance for individuals of constructive change, often possible only at the time of the crisis itself. Refugees cannot wait. Wynne argues forcefully that "crisis theory needs to give greater attention to disequilibrium of social systems in their own right. Earlier formulations ... emphasized individual disequilibrium. These two conceptual vantage points are necessary supplements to one another." This is the force of my argument.

Is refugee research desired? The present national policy might appear to reinforce the attitudes of a sector of the public: that the refugee "problem" will die out as the refugee becomes assimilated into the dominant society. Recent sociological and anthropological theory, together with events such as the intensifying race riots, suggest such a viewpoint to be that of The British Home Office which is winding up the refugee support services (those within its jurisdiction) two years after the peak influx. Official policy appears to state that the immediate physical difficulties entailed in resettlement will by then have been dealt with. This is correct. However, other problems take their place. Voluntary Agencies plead their case with the Home Office, emphasising the importance of maintaining offices in the field. But official policy, in the words of one senior worker, "is to pull out, stand back, and then let the normal Social Services departments cope with what comes."

I have touched upon areas of immediate concern to both policy-makers and community service organisations who deal with Vietnamese refugee communities. Although it is not yet possible to draw definite conclusions regarding details of optimal policy and service, some of the factors and processes of risk and vulnerability have been identified. Unless the impact of these aspects of refugee adjustment is given early consideration, the future adjusment of Vietnamese refugees and particularly the children may be placed in jeopardy.

NOTE

(1) Not surprisingly, she seemed unable to draw the distinction between a fleet of warships steaming to a zone eight thousand miles from Britain, on the one hand, and street fighting in her very neighbourhood, on the other.

REFERENCES

AYLESWORTH, L.S., 1980 Stress, Mental Health and Need Satisfaction among Indochinese in Colorado. Ph.D. Thesis in Psychology, University of Colorado.

BULLIVANT, B., 1981 Race, Ethnicity and Curriculum. Melbourne: MacMillan.

CAPLAN, G., 1964 Principles of Preventive Psychiatry. New York: Basic Books.

CHANDANASIRI, C., 1980 Priority Pattern of the Acquisition of Durable Household Goods of Indo-Chinese in the San Diego Area. D.B.A. Thesis, United States International University.

DAVIDSON, S., 1981 Keynote Address. Seminar on Psychosocial Problems of Refugees, University of Surrey.

EISENBRUCH, I.M., 1982 A model of depressed mothers and their children. Paper presented at 10th International Congress, International Association for Child and Adolescent Psychiatry and Allied Professions, Dublin.

FINLAY, R., ABDOUL, S. & QUY CHAU LE, LAN NG, 1981 A training programme for Vietnamese resettlement officers. Paper presented at Seminar, Psychosocial Problems of Refugees, University of Surrey.

FINNAN, C.R., 1980 The Development of Occupational Identity among Vietnamese Refugees. Ph.D. Thesis, Stanford Universty.

GRANT, B., 1979 The Boat People: an "Age" Investigation. Melbourne: Penguin.

HAINES, D., RUTHERFORD, D. & THOMAS, P., 1973. Family and community among Vietnamese refugees, International Migration Review, 15, 310-317.

HARDING, R. & LOONEY, G., 1977 Problems of Southeast Asian children in a refugee camp, American Journal of Psychiatry, 134, 407-411.

HICKEY, G.C., 1964 Village in Vietnam. New Haven: Yale University Press.

HIRAYAMA, K.K., 1980 Effects of the Employment of Vietnamese Refugee Wives on their Family Roles and Mental Health. D.S.W. Thesis, University of Pennsylvania.

HITCH, P., 1981 The mental health of refugees: Research since the Second World War. Paper presented at Seminar, Psychosocial Problems of Refugees, University of Surrey.

HULL, D., 1979 Migration, Adaptation and Illness: a Review, Social Science and Medicine, 13A, 25-36.

JAGUCKI, W., 1981 Forty years on: Problems arising later. Paper presented at Seminar, Psychosocial Problems of Refugees, University of Surrey.

KELLER, S.L., 1975 Uprooting and Social Change: The Role of Refugees in Development. Delhi: Manohar Book Service.

KRUMPERMAN, A., 1981 Psychosocial problems of violence, especially its effect on refugees. Paper presented at Seminar, Psychosocial Problems of Refugees, University of Surrey.

KUNZ, E. F., 1973 Exile and Resettlement: Refugee Theory, International Migration Review, 15, 42-51.

LE, D. D. P., 1980 Vietnamese Refugees' Perceptions and Methods for Coping with Mental Illness. Ph.D. Thesis, United States International University.

LERNER, M. 1980 Refugees: Fathers, Families and Self-Perceived Adaptation of Vietnamese in the United States of America. Ph.D. Thesis, United States International University.

MONTERO, D., 1979 Vietnamese Americans: Patterns of Resettlement and Socio-economic Adaptations in the United States. Boulder, Colorado: Westview Press.

PHAN MY DUNG, 1982 The Mental Health of Indo-Chinese Refugees. Melbourne: Mental Health Research Institute.

PHILIPS, S., 1981 Some problems in refugee resettlement in the United Kingdom, an approach from ethnomedicine. Paper presented at Seminar, Psychosocial Problems of Refugees, University of University of Surrey.

RACK, P., 1981 Introduction to seminar. Paper presented at Seminar, Psychosocial Problems of Refugees, University of Surrey, and Where do we go from here? Paper presented at Seminar, Psychosocial Problems of Refugees, University of Surrey.

SLUZKI, C.E., 1981 Migration and Family Conflict, Family Process, 18, 379-90.

STEIN, B., 1980 The refugee experience: An overview of refugee research. Paper presented at Royal Anthropological Institute, London. England, 22-24 February.

TYHURST, L, 1951 Displacement and Migration, American Journal of Psychiatry, 107, 561-8.

WYNNE, L., 1975 "Adjustment reactions of adult life" in A. M. Freedman, H. I. Kaplan & B. J. Saddock: Comprehensive Textbook of Psychiatry. New York: Williams and Wilkins.

SOCIO-ECONOMIC STATUS AND CHILDREN'S PERCEPTIONS OF MATERNAL ACCEPTANCE-REJECTION IN KOREAN-AMERICAN IMMIGRANT FAMILIES

E. C. Rohner and R. P. Rohner

University of Connecticut, Storrs

The relation between socioeconomic status (SES) and parental attitudes and behavior has long been of interest to scholars from a number of disciplines (see for example, Hess, 1970). On the whole there seems to be some agreement that, in the U.S. at least, higher SES parents (i.e., professionally employed adults with college or further education) are generally less controlling, use fewer power assertion techniques, and use more reasoning in disciplining their children than lower SES parents (i.e., unskilled or semi-skilled workers with high school or less education) (Baumrind, 1971; Maccoby, 1980). There is less agreement about differences between these two SES groups in terms of the warmth and affection parents give to their children. For example, in her recent book on social development Maccoby (1980) reported that higher SES families in the U.S. show children more affection than lower SES families. Other studies, however, do not support this assertion (Rohner & Nielson, 1979). Our own research in the U.S. and internationally, for example, shows that when SES differences in perceived parental warmth and affection do occur explanations other than simple SES per se account for the relationship (Rohner, Rohner, & Roll, 1980; Rohner, Hahn, & Rohner, 1980).

The purpose of this paper is to extend this body of research by examining the relationship between SES and children's perception of maternal warmth and affection in Korean-American immigrant families.

METHODS

Sample

As part of a nationwide study, 171 Korean-American

families in the U.S. participated in this research.
Socioeconomic status of families was defined by the current
occupation of the father: fathers whose occupational status
fell between classes 1 through 4 on Hollingshead's scale
(Hollingshead & Redlich, 1958) were classified as middle
class, and those falling between 5 and 9 were classified as
working class.

Families were recruited from among the major centers
in the U.S. where Korean-Americans have settled, including
Los Angeles, San Francisco, Chicago, and New York City.
Families with potential for inclusion in this research were
identified within each region by members of local Korean
churches, university and college communities, and
Korean-American associations. In all, 43 middle class boys,
45 middle class girls, 46 working class boys, and 37
working class girls and their mothers responded. The
Korean-American children participating in this study ranged
from 7 to 13 years of age with a mean age of ten. Fathers
and mothers were present in all but two families, where in
both cases the fathers were deceased.

Instruments and Definition of Variables

Perceived parental warmth and affection. The warmth
dimension was measured by the Parental Acceptance-Rejection
Questionnaire (PARQ) (Rohner, Saavedra and Granum, 1980)
where children are asked to respond to their perceptions of
the way their major caretaker behaves toward them in terms
of warmth and affection, hostility and aggression,
indifference and neglect, and undifferentiated rejection.
The PARQ consists of 60 statements to which the child is
asked to respond in terms of how each statement fits "the
way your mother treats you." Children responded on a
four-point scale, ranging from "almost always true," to
"never true." Details of the scales, scoring procedures,
and reports of validity and reliability of the instrument
are provided elsewhere (Rohner, Saavedra and Granum, 1980).
Each of the four PARQ scales is clarified further below.

Parental warmth and affection.--The parent-child
relationship is characterized by warmth and affection
insofar as parents give love without qualification, but not
necessarily with great demonstration. Warmth and affection
may be manifested verbally by praise, approval, and offers
of comfort or consolation. An item designed to measure
parental warmth and affection includes, "My mother makes me
feel wanted and needed."

Parental hostility and aggresssion.--Parental
hostility is an internal or emotional reaction of anger,
enmity, or resentment, whereas aggression is any overt
action which is intended to hurt soemone or something
physically or verbally. Aggressive (hostile) parents may

express themselves verbally or physically. A test item designed to measure perceived parental hostility and aggression includes, "My mother hits me, even when I do not deserve it."

Parental indifference and neglect.--Neglecting (or indifferent) parents show a restricted concern for their children's welfare or development. Neglecting or indifferent parents may be cold, unsympathetic, distant, or unconcerned about their child. Such parents tend to be both inaccessible and unresponsive to the child. A test item illustrating parental indifference and neglect includes, "My mother ignores me as long as I do not do anything to bother her."

Parental undifferentiated rejection.--This scale refers to conditions where parents are perceived as withdrawing love from the child (i.e., they reject the child), but where such rejection does not clearly reflect either aggression/hostility, or neglect/indifference, per se. A test item illustrating parental undifferentiated rejection includes, "My mother does not really love me."

Procedures

The Child PARQ and an information sheet asking about family demographics were mailed to participating research personnel in each city. Instructions were given to the research personnel regarding the distribution, completion, and collection of the questionnaires, and the researchers were directed to draw approximately half their subjects from middle class families and the other half from working class families. They were not to attempt to obtain an equal distribution by child's sex. In order to elicit full cooperation and their signatures on a Korean-language informed consent sheet, participating mothers were provided, with a comprehensive explanation in Korean of the purpose of the research.

Some families were contacted at Korean churches or other such organizations. Children completed, on the spot, the English language background information sheet. (1) Other families were reached at home and were given two weeks to complete the questionnaires. Mothers filled out the Korean language version of the background information sheets, and they were instructed to let the children complete the English language questionnaires alone and undisturbed. The return rate for the questionnaires was approximately 80 per cent for working class families and approximately 92 per cent for middle class families.

Demographic information obtained from the mothers included the child's age, sex, number of household members, occupation and education of the mother, and occupation and education of the father.

RESULTS

The first step in the analysis was to create several multiple regression equations to detect which variables could be omitted from further analysis. Children's sex, education of parents, mothers' occupation, and number of members living in the household failed to predict children's perceptions of maternal acceptance-rejection as measured by the PARQ. Thus, these variables were deleted from further consideration.

A structural model was developed in order to explain children's perceived acceptance-rejection in terms of SES. To estimate the structural coefficients of the model a regression equation was created using a simultaneous solution (Kenny, 1979). The regression of SES and age on children's perceptions of acceptance-rejection showed a significant linkage between fathers' occupation and PARQ (beta = .47(2,168) F=48.00, p <.001) after controlling for the effects of children's age. Relative to children in middle class Korean-American families, children in working class families perceived their mothers to be much more rejecting. (2)

Neither the association between children's age and PARQ controlling for fathers' occupation, nor the simple correlation between age and PARQ were significant. This reveals that older children did not percieve their mothers' overall acceptance differently from younger children. SES and children's age together accounted for 28 per cent of the variance in children's responses on the PARQ (R = .48(2,168) F=24.68, p < .001). SES alone accounted for 21 per cent of the variance in children's PARQ scores; the contribution of children's age as such was almost negligible.

DISCUSSION

Results reported here indicate that children in working class Korean-American immigrant families see their mothers as somewhat more hostile and neglecting, less warm, and overall more rejecting than children in middle class families.

Why do these working class Korean-American children experience greater rejection than middle class Korean-American children? We have no evidence to suggest that social class per se (e.g. institutionalized value differences between working class vs. middle class Korean-American families) accounts for the differences in children's perceptions of maternal warmth. Rather, differences between the two SES groups in family work

253

schedules and language fluency seem to be more salient. For example 65 per cent of the working class mothers and all of the working class fathers work long hours at jobs often requiring little or no skill or training, and providing little opportunity to learn English. Children in these families feel significantly more neglected because of this parental absence than do children in middle class families where only 15 per cent of the mothers work away from home. Mothers in the middle class Korean-American families are thereby better able to sustain the Korean value placed on the role of wife as mother.

All Korean-American children spend much of their time with English speaking peers and teachers. Through these contacts the children become fluent in English and come to identify with the dominant American culture. Working class Korean-American mothers, however, often speak English poorly or not at all, and they often continue to cling to their Korean values and customs. As a result, working class Korean-American mothers and children frequently lose their ability to commmunicate effectively with each other, and over time this communication barrier becomes associated with increasing parent-child conflict and perceived rejection.

NOTES

1. Respondents were given the choice of whether to fill out either the Korean language version of the instruments or the English language version. All children preferred to answer the English version of the PARQ, but most Korean-American mothers perferred responding to the Korean language version of the background information sheet.

2. In an absolute sense both groups of children perceived their parents to be fairly warm and accepting, though this is especially true of the middle class children.

REFERENCES

Baumrind, D. Current patterns of parental authority. Developmental Psychology Monographs, 1971, 4 (1 pt. 2).

Hess, R.D. Social class and ethnic influences upon socialization. In P.H. Mussen (Ed.) Carmichael's manual of child psychology (Vol. 2). New York, John Wiley and Sons, 1970.

Hollingshead, A.B. & Redlich, F.C. Social class and mental illness. New York, John Wiley and Sons, 1958.

Kenny, D. Structural Analysis. New York, John Wiley & Sons, 1979.

Maccoby, E. Social development psychological growth and the parent child relationship. New York, Harcourt Brace, 1980.

Rohner, R.P., Hahn, B.C. & Rohner, E.C. Social class differences in perceived parental acceptance-rejection and self-evaluation among Korean-American children. Behavior Science Research, 1980, 15, 55-67.

Rohner, R.P. & Nielson, C.C. Parental acceptance-rejection: A review and annotated bibliography of research and theory. New Haven, HRAF Press, 1979.

Rohner R.P., Rohner, E.C. & Roll, S. Perceived parental acceptance-rejection and personality organization among Mexican and American elementary school children. Behavior Science Research, 1980, 15, 23-41.

Rohner, R.P., Saavedra, J. & Granum, E.O. Development and validation of the Parental Acceptance-Rejection Questionnaire: Test Manual. In R.P. Rohner, Handbook for the study of parental acceptance and rejection. Storrs, Ct., Center for the Study of Parental Acceptance and Rejection, 1980.

DEGREE OF DEVELOPMENT AND DISTANCE AS RELATED TO MUTUAL PERCEPTIONS AND ATTITUDES AMONG STUDENTS IN SEVEN AMERICAN COUNTRIES

J. M. Salazar

Universidad Central de Venezuela, Caracas

I. INTRODUCTION

In studying the problem of intergroup relations, it is of interest to consider how external, objective variables may relate to subjective, psychological manifestations like cognitions, attitudes or orientations to other group members.

One obvious variable of this kind, when one works with national groups is geographical distance; and in fact several studies have looked into the relationship (e.g. Brewer and Campbell, 1976). Another variable closely related to this is the degree of contact between groups, which is not necessarily a function of distance and may have differential causations.

In a world characterized by heterogeneity in terms of economic and social development, it is also possible that this variable may be important. Some previous work indicates that this is so. (Brewer and Campbell, 1976, p.63; Salazar, 1981)

In summarizing explicit contradictions between theories around the problem of intergroup relations, Levine and Campbell (1972) identify three major areas of contradictions: "1.- Outgroup strength, wealth and size... 2.- Proximity and similarity... and 3.- Differential information about outgroups based on differential intergroup experience". The three variables that we have enumerated each fall into one of these areas, so it becomes interesting to explore again these relationships.

To guide us into these problem areas, special mention should be made of two important theories that may help to

257

organise findings: realistic group conflict theory and reference group theory.

Realistic group theory states, in general terms, that negative intergroup attitudes are related to experiences of conflict, derived in many cases from competition for limited resources. As this is more likely to happen in groups that are territorially near, this theory would suggest a negative relationship between distance and hostility. Although it is evident that this could be more likely to be true in primitive, tribal societies, and bound to be less important in the modern world, where competition for resources often occurs between countries that are not geographically continuous; some derivations of the theory are still worth looking at.

Reference group theory indicates the importance of, non-membership groups, of groups to which people refer, admire or overestimate. Given a world in which "progress" is given such high valuation, this theoretical orientation would suggest positive attitudes towards more developed countries.

The exploration of some of these relationships became a possibility through the organization of the Latin American Association of Social Psychology; this permitted the collection of data in seven countries in the Western Hemisphere, and the evaluation of the possible effect of distance, degree of contact and degree of development on mutual attitudes between members of different national groups.

II. METHOD

Subjects

1148 University students from: Brasil (N=124); Colombia (N=192); Dominican Republic (N=168); Mexico (N=101); Peru (N=198); U.S.A. (N=202) and Venezuela (N=199).

Instruments

In order to evaluate attitudes, we used both an "emic" and an "etic" instrument.

Our etic instrument was a semantic differential, with seven scales: good-bad; pleasant-unpleasant (simpatico - antipatico); despicable-admirable; strong-weak; small -large; slow-fast and active-passive. In the English version educated-uneducated was substituted for pleasant-unpleasant.

The emic measure was obtained by asking our subjects to indicate (on a five point scale) the degree to which it was true that members of each group possessed twelve traits; and separately also to indicate whether each one of the traits was good or bad. The list of traits was obtained in each country independently through a previous study in which open ended questions were aimed at obtaining those adjectives more commonly used in that language community to identify national groups; from those responses twelve adjectives were selected in each country. All lists were different but five traits found their way to all of them: cultured, poor, amiable, lazy and gay. The inclusion of this list of traits and their evaluation permitted us to obtain indirect measures of attitudes (Fishbein and Ajzen, 1975). The students evaluated each one of the seven groups including their own. The other variables were evaluated for each country in the following ways:

Distance was defined as the distance in kilometers between the place where the data was collected and the nearest "metropolitan" area of the respective target country. Distances were reduced to "Z" scores for each national group so as to compensate for the general position of each particular country.

Degree of Development was obtained from the judgments given by six "experts" in the area. There was a high degree of interjudge agreement, the average correlation being .89. On the basis of these judgments average ranks were calculated, which were also transformed to "Z" scores.

Degree of Contact: the questionnaire asked subjects to indicate if they had known "personally" members of each of the national groups. On the basis of these responses "Z" scores were calculated indicating different degrees of contact with each of the groups.

III RESULTS

1.- OWN GROUP VS OUTGROUP.

Using the semantic differential we observe a tendency to express a more favorable attitude towards own group, when compared with the attitude expressed to the other six groups (Table 1).

Nevertheless this is not the case when one works with the indirect (emic) measure of attitude. In this case the tendency (except in the cases of the U.S.A. and Brasil) is to express a less favorable attitude towards one's own group (Table 2).

TABLE 1

ATTITUDE (MEAN SEMANTIC DIFFERENTIAL)
TOWARDS OWN GROUP AND OUT GROUPS

	OWN($\overline{X}$)	OUT($\overline{X}$)
BRASIL	1.10	0.46
COLOMBIA	0.64	0.35
DOMINICAN REP.	1.11	0.58
MEXICO	0.86	0.51
PERU	0.52	0.56
U.S.A.	0.86	0.18
VENEZUELA	0.92	0.42

TABLE 2

ATTITUDE (INDIRECT) TOWARDS OWN GROUP
AND OUT GROUPS

	OWN($\overline{X}$)	OUT($\overline{X}$)
BRASIL	2.87	1.63
COLOMBIA	1.35	3.95
DOMINICAN REP.	5.16	8.65
MEXICO	6.25	7.85
PERU	0.79	7.70
U.S.A.	9.56	3.22
VENEZUELA	2.32	5.43

These puzzling results could mean we are measuring different things. Nevertheless the two measures are positively correlated, but weakly so. The average correlations of the subjects of each group when they evaluate the seven countries range from .33 in the cases of Peru and Dominican Republic to .54 in the cases of Mexico and U.S.A. It is justifiable to consider each measure separately and to question the equality, at least in this case, established in the "value-expectancy" model; which fits in with some current questioning of the affect-cognition relationship (Zajonc, 1980). The first of the two measures (the semantic differential) is a more affective measure; so we shall call it henceforth "affect". The second measure is more analytical and incorporates to a greater degree cognitive elements (beliefs); we shall reserve the name "attitudes" for this measure. As a matter of fact the difference is similar to the one established by Triandis (1977) between affect (A) and value of consequences (C) in his model for behavior prediction.

2.- AFFECT AND ITS DETERMINANTS.

Calculating the correlation between each one of the external variables and affect we obtain the following results:

Distance and affect = .55
Degree of development of target country and affect = -.05
Degree of contact and affect = -.61

A multiple regression of affect on these three variables yields a coefficient of determination R = .56; the "b" weights are respectively 0.39, .02, and -.47. The variables moderately predict affect, although it is evident that distance and degree of contact are the variables more highly correlated with this variable. Proximity and contact seem to be related to negative affect, which fits in with realistic group conflict theory.

3.- ATTITUDE AND ITS DETERMINANTS.

Calculating the correlation between each one of the external variables and the analytical measure of attitude we obtain:

Distance and attitude = .78
Degree of development of target country and attitude =.50
Degree of contact and attitude = -.07

A multiple regression of attitude on these three variables yields a coefficient of determination R =.69; the "b" weights are respectively: .53, .45 and -.25.

The prediction of attitude is somewhat better and again there is a significant effect of distance; there is a more positive attitude towards more distant countries; it also appears that more favourable attitude is expressed towards the more developed countries. Degree of contact in this case seems to be poorly correlated with attitude.

TABLE 3

MIRROR IMAGE PERCEPTIONS BASED ON SEMANTIC DIFFERENTIALS

	AUTO		HETERO	
	1st	2nd	1→2	2→1
BRASIL - COL.	+	+	0	+
BRASIL - D.R.	+	+	0	+
BRASIL - MEX.	+	+	+	+
BRASIL - PERU	+	+	+	+
BRASIL - U.S.A.	+	+	-	+
BRASIL - VENZ.	+	+	0	+
COL. - D.R.	+	+	0	0
COL. - MEX.	+	+	+	+
COL. - PERU	+	+	0	+
COL. - U.S.A.	+	+	0	-
COL. - VENZ.	+	+	-	-
D.R. - MEX.	+	+	+	+
D.R. - PERU	+	+	+	+
D.R. - U.S.A.	+	+	-	-
D.R. - VENZ.	+	+	0	+
MEX. - PERU	+	+	+	+
MEX. - U.S.A.	+	+	-	-
MEX. - VENZ.	+	+	+	+
PERU - U.S.A.	+	+	0	0
PERU - VENZ.	+	+	+	+
U.S.A. - VENZ.	+	+	0	-

C→C V→V C→V V→C
* 0.64/0.92/-0.34/0.07

D→D U→U D→U U→D
* 1.11/0.86/0.17/0.06

M→M U→U M→U U→M
* 0.86/0.86/-0.03/0.00

+ : more than .5
0 : .2 to .5
- : less than .2

4.- MIRROR IMAGE PHENOMENA. HOW FREQUENT?

The mirror image phenomena (Bronfenbrenner, 1961; Salazar and Marin, 1977) imply positive and similar autoimages, which are more favorable than the mutually equal and negative heteroimages. If we examine the 21 relationships using the average obtained in three semantic differential scales, the phenomena is clearly observable in three cases: Colombia-Venezuela; Mexico-U.S.A., and U.S.A.-Dominican Republic. This can be seen in Table 3. In the first two cases there exist common frontiers and there are objective work force problems; in the Dominican Republic case recent history may also account for the attitudes' pattern. A tendency toward "mirror image" phenomena in the relationship between U.S.A. and other Latin-American countries is also observed.

The evidence points out that mirror image phenomena are present in conflict situations.

5.- IDUSA. HOW WIDESPREAD?

In a previous study carried out in Venezuela (Salazar, 1981) a high percentage of subjects was observed to have attitudes towards the U.S.A. which were more favorable than those towards own country. This was interpreted as a manifestation of an ideology of dependence, contrary to an ethnocentric posture, since it implies attributing to an outgroup characteristics positively valued, and to the in-group characteristics negatively valued.

This situation is found again in all of the Latin-American countries, except Mexico where there is a tendency (although non-significant) in the opposite direction. See Table 4.

TABLE 4

DIFFERENTIAL ATTITUDES

	U.S.A. - OWN	BRASIL - OWN	MEXICO - OWN
BRASIL	4.59	-	1.11
COLOMBIA	5.30	6.33	3.70
DOMINICAN REP.	3.54	5.67	6.31
MEXICO	-2.08	4.90	-
PERU	9.26	7.01	7.52
VENEZUELA	4.69	6.05	3.42

The interpretation of this phenomenon as a manifestation of a high valuation of "progress" can be made when one calculates the same differential attitudes towards Brasil and Mexico, the most developed countries in the sample, where the same situation reoccurs. Attitude then can be said to be a function of the degree of development of the target country (which we have also found in the multiple regression): in this sense this result supports a reference group theory outlook.

Chapter 26

IV. CONCLUSIONS

In this study which started out to evaluate the effect of certain objective variables on mutual attitudes among university students of seven western hemisphere countries there is evidence of the importance of all three variables: distance, degree of contact and degree of development, yet the effects are different depending on the measure of attitude considered.

The results fit in well with Triandis' conceptualization of the determinants of behavior intention, in which there is a separation between the Affective, the Cognitive and the Normative elements. One of our measures represents the affective, another the cognitive, and although there are significant relationships between the two measures, the relationships are not strong enough to be able to predict one from the other. Furthermore in this study the external correlates of the two measures are different. Affect is correlated negatively with geographical closeness and degree of contact; a finding that fits in with realistic conflict theory. The cognitive measure also correlates with the degree of development of target country; this last finding fits in with reference group theory. It seems then that both formulations can be useful to interpret some of the facts of inter-group relations.

REFERENCES

Brewer, M. and Campbell, D.T. Ethnocentrism and Intergroup Attitudes. New York: John Wiley and Sons, 1976.

Bronfenbrenner, U. The mirror image in Soviet-American relations. A social psychologist's report. Journal of Social Issues, 1961, 17, 45-56.

Fishbein, M. and Ajzen, I. Beliefs, Attitudes, Intentions and Behavior. Reading, Mass: Addison-Wesley, 1975.

Levine, R.A. and Campbell, D.T. Ethnocentrism. Theories of conflict, ethnic attitudes and group behavior. New York: John Wiley. 1972.

Salazar, J.M. Creencias, Actitudes Nacionales e Ideologia Dependiente In Instituto de Psicologia. Contribuciones Recentes a la Psicologia en Venezuela. Caracas: U.C.V.,1981.

Salazar, J.M. and Marin, G. National stereotypes as a function of conflict and territorial proximity: a test of the mirror image hypothesis. Journal of Social Psychology. 1977, 101, 13-19.

Triandis, H.C. Interpersonal Behavior. Monterey, Calif: Brooks/Cole, 1977.

Zajonc, R.B. Feelings and thinking: Preferences need no inferences. American Psychologist. 1980, 35, 151-175.

Chapter 27

THE CROSS-CULTURAL EFFICACY OF ENTITLEMENTS IN AMERICAN AND HONG KONG CHINESE STUDENTS

P. Rosenfeld

Behrend College, Eire

R. A. Giacalone and J. T. Tedeschi

SUNY at Albany

M. Bond

Chinese University of Hong Kong

Impression management theory (Schlenker, 1980; Tedeschi, 1981) views individuals as being motivated to maintain public identities in the presence of significiant audiences. As the theory has evolved from sociologically based observations to empirically derived laboratory findings there has come an emphasis on the specific tactics that people employ to manage impressions to others.

Recent work in this field (Schlenker, 1980; Tedeschi, 1981) has described two general forms of impression management styles: defensive and offensive. Defensive impression management refers to the interpersonal strategies that people use to avoid looking bad. Offensive impression management refers to the opposite: those tactics used to gain responsibility and credit for positive consequences.

The present paper concerns itself with an offensive impression management tactic which Schlenker (1980) has called an entitlement. Entitlements are defined as verbal claims of responsibility for positive events intended to bring credit or rewards to an actor. According to Schlenker, individuals will attempt to entitle themselves to positive outcomes especially in situations where the responsibility for the outcome is unclear or ambiguous.

For example, a graduate student proposes an experimental design in a research meeting attended by her mentor and the other students in the group. A year or two later when the project is at last ready to seek publication, the graduate student is rather surprised to find that she has four co-authors. "Well, I ran some subjects," says one, "I punched the computer cards," claims another and so on with a litany of entitlement statements

266

the other students seek to claim partial responsibility for
the favorable outcome and gain the positive identity
engendered by being co-author on a prestigious research
paper.

In the current paper we describe an initial attempt to
empirically investigate the dynmaics of verbal claims for
positive events. In two studies, one conducted in the
southern United States with American college students and
the other carried out with Hong Kong Chinese students
attending the Chinese University of Hong Kong, we sought to
determine the conditions under which entitlements achieve
their goal of gaining positive identity for an actor.

In both studies, sixty female college students were
randomly assigned to one of four conditions. Each student
was provided with a booklet containing a scenario stating
that a medical research team had made an important
discovery of a cure for a serious disease. In the <u>no
entitlement</u> condition subjects were merely asked to rate
the project director and the assistant director of the
team. In the <u>entitlement condition</u> the students read that
the assistant director called a news conference and claimed
that he had the idea that led to a breakthrough. In the
<u>confirmed entitlement</u> group the assistant director's claim
was acknowledged by the project director as being
essentially true while in the <u>disconfirmed entitlement</u>
group the project director denied that the assistant
director was primarily responsible for the breakthrough.

After reading the scenarios subjects were asked to
rate the assistant director on 17 polar adjective scales.
Based on previous theoretical speculations about the
effectiveness of entitlements it was expected that ratings
of the assistant director would be more positive when he
gave an entitlement. Furthermore, confirmation of an
entitlement should increase the favorableness of the
evaluation while disconfirmation should result in a
negative impression. Given the exploratory nature of the
study, no cross-cultural differences were predicted.

Results

In order to make the data more easily interpretable
they were submitted to a principal components factor
analysis with varimax rotation. Factor scores were
generated for each subject and submitted to a 1 x 4 ANOVA.
For both the Amercian and Chinese subjects the only
significant results were obtained from the first factor
which in both cases represented a general evaluation of the
assistant director's abilities. While the pattern of
results is the same in both studies, the obtained group
differences were stronger for the American subjects. These
differences are summarized in Table 1.

TABLE 1

Mean Factor Scores for the Evaluation of the Assistant Director

Group	Americans	Hong Kong Chinese
No Entitlement	+.16 a	−.11 ab
Entitlement	+.29 a	+.07 ab
Confirmed Entitlement	+.31 a	+.39 a
Disconfirmed Entitlement	−.77 b	−.35 b

Note − Means with entirely different subscripts differ at the
.05 level. Comparisons should be made only within
cultures.

As can be seen from Table 1, rather surprisingly neither a
simple entitlement nor a confirmed entitlement resulted in
more positive ratings of the assistant director either
among American or Hong Kong Chinese students. However, when
the assistant director's entitlement was disputed, a
markedly negative impression resulted. For the American
subjects, the ratings of the assistant director were
significantly lower (p's < .05) in the disconfirmed
entitlement group than in the other three groups. For
Chinese subjects, although the patterning of means is
essentially the same as in the American data there was a
statistically significant difference only between the
confirmed entitlement group and the disconfirmed
entitlement group.

Discussion

Contrary to expectation, an entitlement for a medical
discovery, even when it was confirmed by someone else, did
not lead to a more favorable impression of the entitler
both among American and Hong Kong Chinese students.
However, we found in both cultures that entitlements can
have potential costs. That is, if an entitlement is

challenged by someone in a position of authority it may
backfire and result in a negative impression of the actor.

The failure to find more positive impressions as a
result of entitlements is problematic given that there is
ample evidence (e.g., Schlenker, 1980; Schneider, 1969)
showing that individuals in a variety of situations will
exaggerate claims regarding the possession of positive
characteristics in situations where their behavior cannot
be verified by the audience. One would assume that if such
behavior is so prevalent that it gains strength from
previous reinforcements including social approval from
others.

To clarify this difficulty we have conducted a number
of follow-up studies in the United States attempting to
ascertain when and if entitlements result in positive
impressions. The preliminary results of these studies have
once again shown that in various situations a simple
entitlement made by an actor is ineffective in gaining a
positive image. However, if the entitlement is made by
another person on the actor's behalf or if the actor goes
against the view of the group and the end result is
positive, then the entitlement results in a more favorable
impression.

To conclude, the present results conflict with
previous theoretical writings dealing with entitlements.
Indeed, we found that for both American and Chinese
students direct verbal entitlements were ineffective in
gaining an individual credit for a group product and may
actually backfire and result in negative impressions being
formed.

REFERENCES

Schlenker, B.R. Impression Management. Monterey, CA:
    Brooks/Cole, 1980.

Schneider, D.J. Tactical self-presentation after success
    and failure. Journal of Personality and Social
    Psychology, 1969, 13, 262-268.

Tedeschi, J.T. (Ed.) Impression management theory and
    social psychological research. New York: Academic
    Press, 1981.

Chapter 28

SEX TYPING OF WORK ROLES FOR CHILDREN, ADULTS AND ELDERLY: A CROSS-CULTURAL STUDY

L. Minturn

University of Colorado, Boulder

Methodology

This study is based on information on a sample of 56 societies drawn from the World Ethnographic Sample, developed by Murdock (1957). Table 1 shows the distribution of the sample societies in terms of basic economy, descent pattern, and degree of political integration. The information on work roles of the elderly is less complete than comparable information for children and adults; therefore only 32 of the 56 societies could be rated for the scales concerning the elderly.

The information was obtained and rated by students. Only files with three independent sources rated "good" to "excellent" by the Human Relations Area Files quality system were used. Scales were eliminated or refined when ratings on them were found to be unreliable. Reliability, measured by percent agreement among raters, ranged from 80% to 98% for the final scales.

Results

Tasks

Initial ratings were obtained for over 1200 tasks. Tasks done only by specialists were eliminated, and the final analysis was done on a sample of 830 tasks typically done by children and adults. Seventy-three tasks were rated for the elderly. These tasks were then grouped into 8 classes: 1. Household chores, 2. Animal Husbandry, 3. Agriculture, 4. Hunting and Fishing, 5. Transportation, 6. Construction, 7. Social Services, 8. Personal Services. Table 2 shows these eight classes, a listing of each of the 44 chores rated and the distribution of the number of societies for which each chore is cited. Household chores

270

are the most frequently mentioned task, followed by agriculture, and construction, and social services. Animal husbandry and hunting and fishing have intermediate frequencies, probably because herding, hunting and fishing societies are less frequent in the sample than agricultural societies. Transportation and personal services are the least frequent.

TABLE 1

Classification of sample by Basic economy,
Descent, and Political environment.

Basic economy	N
Hunting & Gathering	9
Fishing & Gathering	4
Seed agriculture	27
Root agriculture	9
Aboriculture	3
Pastoral & Animal Husbandry	4
Descent	
Patrilineal	26
Matrilineal	10
Ambilineal	1
Bilateral	16
Double	3
Political Integration	
Absence	1
Autonomous	26
Dependent Societies	2
Minimal States	15
Little States	6

Within cultures girls and women often perform a larger variety of duties than men and boys. Men and boys have more varied tasks for tasks across societies. The reversal is explained by looking at actual tasks: females are primarily concerned with a large number of household chores, while males are occupied with chores related to the subsistence economy and have less variety in duties. Household chores have much in common across cultures but men's tasks shift with changes in the economy, and the diversity of

271

activities is larger across societies.

This finding does not necessarily imply differential work load. Men may well work longer at fewer chores.

TABLE 2

Distribution of Tasks Performed by Typical Adults
(N = 830)

Household	N	Transportation	N
Child care	39	Canoe, sail	12
Bring fuel	40	Ride horse or camel	6
Bring water	41	Move camp	3
Cooking	49	Total	21
House maintenance	31		
Laundry	10	Construction	
Total	210	Handicrafts	64
		Major tool making	19
Animal Husbandry		Major building	37
		Mining, lumbering	4
Feed & Water	26	Total	124
Herding	14		
Clean animal or compound	3	Social Services	
Butcher, dress hides	19		
Dairy chores	8	Ritual duties	27
Total	70	Artistic performances	6
		Marketing and trading	24
Agriculture		Political activities	11
		Other maintenance	11
Clear land, plow	19	Education	10
Plant	26	Guard duty	14
Cultivating	45	Warfare	6
Harvest	24	Sell Services	4
Foodgathering	27	Total	112
Thresh, husk, winnow	14		
Grind flour	16	Personal services	
Brew, presoil or juice	7		
Total	178	Cosmetics	8
		Carry food, loads	7
Hunting and Fishing		Nurse, midwife	8
		Errands, messages	12
Hunt	39	Total	35
Trap	11		
Fish – deep water	25		
Fish – shore	4		
Total	79		

Scales

Table 3 shows the scales used in rating the classified tasks. The scale points for scale 4 are overlapping because many ethnographic reports simply refer to children doing chores without specifying the age of the children. We assumed an age range from 4 to 10 for such reports, although an age of 7 to 10 can be assumed for most tasks. If young children were mentioned we coded an age range of 4-7, older children were coded as 7-12. Since adolescence is not a clear age grade in all societies, post-pubescent persons were coded as adolescent or adult.

Note that the instructions for coding scales 9, 10, and 11 are to code for "primarily" done by one sex if it is deviant for a member of the opposite sex to perform the task. Therefore the statement that members of both sexes typically do the tasks does not necessarily indicate that both sexes do it with equal frequency, merely that it is appropriate for both sexes to do the job,

Table 4 shows the distribution of task modes in percentages.

Only one culture typically starts responsibility training at 4-7 years; on the other hand many societies do not expect responsible behavior until adolescence. The only tasks commonly expected in the 4-7 age range are running errands and carrying messages. About 26% of all tasks are not introduced until adolescence. These tasks usually require strength, involve risk, or are community oriented such as warfare or political activity. Further, about 14% of all tasks are not usually done by children at all.

Fathers teach 47% of the tasks and mothers 33%, everyone teaches 13%, with others having small percentages.

Sixty-nine percent of tasks are regular, 20% seasonal and 11% irregular. Seventy-three percent of tasks are skilled, and 27% unskilled. Eighty-four percent of tasks benefit the family and 16% the community.

Males perform 31% of the tasks as boys, 37% as men and 45% as old men. Females perform 25% of the tasks as girls, 32% as women and 48% as old women. The rise in percentage of tasks done by old men and women does not represent an increased work load; since the total number of tasks rated for the elderly is only 73, it represents a sharp decrease in the percentage of work done by both sexes.

The percent of all chores partially done by children ranged from 65% in Eurasia to 89% in Africa with the median of about 80%. Only 7 of the 56 cultures expect children to participate in less than 50% of all tasks.

TABLE 3

Scales for Work Roles

"Primarily" means that it is deviant for members of the opposite
sex to do the chore. If the chore is usually done by one sex
but may be done by both sexes without implication of deviency
rate as both sexes perform chore.

4. Age at which child is introduced to chore

    0. No answer
    1. Children 4-10 (rate only if older or younger not
       mentioned)
    2. Young children 4-7
    3. Older children 7-12
    4. Adolescent or adult

5. Identification of Teachers

    0. No answer
    1. Mothers or adult women in the household teach the chore
    2. Fathers or adult men in the household teach the chore
    3. Older children or adolescents in the household or
       community teach the chore
    4. Everyone in the household teaches the chore. (Note: Do
       not rate Point 5 unless a differentiation cannot be made
       between Points 1, 2, 3, or 4)
    5. Specialists teach the chore

6. Regularity of Chores

    0. No answer
    1. Never
    2. Not regularly
    3. Regularly
    4. Seasonal

7. Skill required to perform chore optimally

    0. No answer
    1. Unskilled, little or no training
    2. Skilled, formal instruction

8. Community imbeddedness of chore at optimal performance

    0. No answer
    1. Chore primarily benefits the agent himself
    2. Chore primarily benefits the agent and his family
    3. Chore benefits the extended kin group, entire community
       or segment thereof

9. Sex of children performing chore

10. Sex of adults performing chore

11. Sex of elderly performing chore

9, 10, 11
    0. No answer
    1. Chore not done by children or adults
    2. Primarily men
    3. Primarily women
    4. Both men and women

TABLE 4

Distribution of Task Modes in Percentages

Scale	Task N = 830
Age - Introduction	
4-7	1.8
4-10	35.0
7-12	37.3
Adolescence	25.9
Teacher	
Mother	33.3
Father	46.6
Older Child	2.2
Everyone	13.4
Specialist	4.5
Mother & Older Child	
Father & Older Child	
Regularity	
Irregular	10.9
Regular	69.5
Seasonal	19.6
Skill	
Unskilled	26.6
Semi-skilled	
Skilled	73.4
High skilled	
Community Imbeddedness	
Self	0.0
Family	84.0
Community	16.0
Sex-child	
No data	13.7
Male	31.3
Female	25.4
Both	29.6
Sex-Adult	
No data	44.4
Male	36.9
Female	32.7
Both	26.0
Sex-Elderly	
No data	0
Male	45.0
Female	48.0
Both	7.0

Chapter 28

Joint distributions of society modes. To examine
relationships between variables within societies, joint
frequency tables were constructed for society modes.

As can be seen in Table 5, sex differences appear in
the age at which children are introduced to chores. By 10
years of age girls have typically started chores in about
80% of the cultures, while only 55% expect tasks from boys.
Regular performance of chores is most frequently expected
in the middle years of childhood. There is only a slight
tendency for more skilled tasks to be introduced at a later
age than unskilled. The youngest children usually have
tasks benefiting the family; community oriented activities
are introduced to older children.

TABLE 5

Joint Distribution of Society Modes
in Percentages as a Function of Age of Child

	Age Introduced to chore			
Sex Child	4-7	4-10	7-12	Adol.
Male	5.9	49.0	35.3	9.8
Female	22.3	57.1	18.6	2.0
Both	6.8	56.9	34.7	1.6
Regularity				
Regular	12.5	39.3	41.1	7.1
Skill				
Unskilled	18.2	52.7	21.8	7.3
Skilled	18.7	46.3	24.1	12.9
Community Imbeddedness				
Self	0.0	38.4	46.2	15.4
Family	25.5	56.4	14.5	3.6
Community	4.4	43.9	39.1	13.0

Table 6 shows the breakdown by teacher. Although
teachers primarily instruct same sexed children, young
children of both sexes are taught by mothers. These tasks
that both sexes do are usually performed only by women as
adults. Fathers usually teach older boys skilled tasks
which only adult males perform. Unskilled chores are
commonly taught by mothers or older children.

TABLE 6

Joint Distribution of Society Modes in Percentages
as a Function of Teacher

	Teacher							
	Mo.	Fa.	O.C.	Peer	Every.	Spec.	Mo.&O.C.	Fa.&O.C.
Age								
4-7	66.6	17.3	4.3	0.0	8.6	0.0	4.3	0.0
4-10	40.6	27.0	8.1	2.7	13.5	2.7	2.7	2.7
7-12	41.3	48.0	0.0	2.1	4.3	0.0	4.3	0.0
Adol.	25.2	45.8	2.9	0.0	14.5	11.6	0.0	0.0
Sex Child								
Male	2.0	90.0	4.0	2.0	2.0	0.0	0.0	0.0
Female	86.0	2.0	4.0	0.0	6.0	0.0	4.0	0.0
Both	35.3	11.8	0.0	1.9	1.9	8.0	11.8	0.0
Skill								
Unskilled	54.1	17.0	5.1	0.0	8.5	1.7	11.9	1.7
Skilled	37.8	40.9	4.5	1.6	10.6	3.0	1.6	0.0

The prevalence of mothers as the teachers of young children apparently leads to greater discontinuity in the training of boys than in the training of girls (Benedict, 1938). Table 7 shows the sex typing of selected tasks for children and adults. Of the 11 tasks done primarily by girls, 8 are done by women and 3 by both men and women. All of the 11 tasks done primarily by boys are done primarily by men. However 4 of the 15 tasks done by boys and girls are done primarily by women. Table 7a presents this information in terms of the incidence of within-society change in task assignment from childhood to adulthood. The rarest change considering both sexes is a sex reversal from boy to woman or girl to man. Shifts from either boy or girl to both men and women occur with intermediate frequency and are approximately equal for both boys and girls. The largest sex difference appears in the shift from both boys and girls to men while 51% shift from both boys and girls to women. The combination of shift from boys plus both boys and girls to women vs. girls plus both boys and girls to men, tested against the theoretical shift is 7.07 significant at the .01 level.

TABLE 7

Sex Typing of Selected Tasks for Children and Adults

Tasks done by Girls	Adult assignment
Child care	w
Cooking	w
House maintenance	w
Bringing water	w
Laundry	w
Threshing and winnowing	w
Grinding grain	w
Brewing, oil pressing	b
Shore fishing	w
Marketing, trading	b
Cosmetics	b

Tasks done by Boys	
Animal care	m
Herding	m
Clearing and plowing	m
Hunting	m
Trapping	m
Deep water fishing	m
Canoeing, sailing	m
Riding	m
Tool making	m
Construction	m
Mining, lumbering	m

Tasks done by Boys and Girls	
Bringing fuel	w
Dairy work	b
Planting	b
Cultivation	b
Harvesting	b
Food Gathering	b
Shore fishing	b
Moving camp	b
Handicrafts	b
Ritual duties	b
Artistic performances	b
Education	b
Cosmetics	w
Carry loads	w
Nursing	w

w = women
m = men
b = both

TABLE 7a

Incidence of Within Society Change in Sex Typing of
Task Assignment from Child to Adult

	Boys to Women	Girls to Men	Boys to Both	Girls to Both	Both to Men	Both to Women
N = 37	3	1	6	5	3	19
$^o10$	8	3	16	14	8	51

x^2 Boy to women + both to women vs. girls to men + both men = 7.07 p<.01

TABLE 8

Joint Distribution of Society Modes in Percentages by Age and Sex

	Child			Adult		
	M	F	B	M	F	B
Regularity						
Irregular	14.5	3.7	3.8	26.6	1.9	9.4
Regular	56.3	84.9	71.1	44.9	88.2	46.2
Seasonal	29.2	11.4	25.1	28.5	9.9	44.4
Skill						
Unskilled	18.8	38.4	43.1	14.0	50.6	25.3
Skilled	81.2	61.6	56.9	86.0	50.0	74.7
Community Imbeddedness						
Self	3.7	0.0	6.4	3.6	1.9	0.0
Family	77.3	93.8	79.0	70.9	89.2	78.0
Community	19.0	6.2	14.6	25.5	8.9	22.0

These data show that boys are taught tasks done primarily by women more frequently than girls are taught tasks done primarily by men. This difference probably stems from the greater frequency of mothers as the teachers of young children. Mothers probably enlist the aid of sons for women's work when they have no daughter of the appropriate age to help them.

Task parameters vary with child-adult and male-female roles. These variations are shown in Table 8. In most societies girls and women perform tasks regularly whereas men and boys may be concerned with irregular or seasonal chores. Male tasks are more highly skilled than female in most cultures. Tasks children of both sexes do are usually regular, however tasks adults of both sexes do are about equally divided between regular and seasonal. Further tasks for children of both sexes are more likely to be unskilled than those both adults do. The difference between children and adults in chores both sexes do reflects the phenomenon discussed above. Boys often do regular unskilled tasks taught by mothers which they do not do as adults or adolescents. The difference in regularity for tasks both sexes do is solved by looking at the tasks involved. Women, but not girls, may help with heavy seasonal work such as harvesting or butchering. Males are more likely to work cooperatively than females and more likely to have community oriented chores.

Table 9 shows the percentage of tasks done by young, adult and elderly males and females, classified by type of task. The table shows that the work of the elderly shifts sharply to social and personal services. Social services account for 56% of the work of elderly men, 29% of the work of elderly women, and 25% of the work primarily done by both old men and old women. Personal services accounts for 75% of the work primarily done by the elderly of both sexes. Since Social Services rate high in community embeddedness, the percentage of work that primarily benefits the community increases with age from 25% to 39% for men, from 9% to 40% for women, and 19% to 25% for both. The increase in performance of social services for the elderly irrespective of sex is from 14% to 51% (χ^2=1483, p<.001). It seems that although the amount of work done by the elderly decreases, its benefit to the community at large increases.

Table 9 also shows that women's participation in housework takes up approximately 50% of their task load and remains constant throughout their lifetime. Men, on the other hand, do not continue their extensive participation in the subsistence ecomomy when they are elderly. Animal husbandry, hunting, fishing and trapping, and agriculture account for about 50% of the chores of boys and adult men, but only 16% of the chores of elderly men (χ^2=8.79, p<.01).

Women's participation in the subsistence economy drops from
25% to 14% of their chores returning to the level of
participation of girls. Therefore, whereas boys and younger
men contribute approximately twice as much to the economy
as do girls and women, elderly men and women are making
equal contributions.

TABLE 9

Percentage of Tasks done by Young Adult and
Elderly Males and Females: Classified by Type of Task

	Male			Female			Both Sexes		
	Ch %	Ad %	Eld %	Ch %	Ad %	Eld %	Ch %	Ad %	Eld %
Housework	1	0	8	50	44	50	10	5	0
Animal Care	14	14	8	5	7	7	11	13	0
Agriculture	11	10	4	17	18	7	26	22	0
Hunt, fish, trap	31	25	4	3	0	0	12	16	0
Transportation	10	12	0	4	3	0	3	5	0
Construction	17	22	16	12	8	7	13	15	0
Social Services	12	16	56	4	6	29	15	19	25
Personal Services	4	1	4	5	14	0	10	5	75
Number of Tasks	92	94	25	76	107	14	107	115	8

Ch = Child

Ad = Adult

Eld = Elderly

Summary and Conclusions

These data suggest that the sex typing of work roles
varies more for males than for females as a function of
age. Boys may not be introduced to their chores as early as
girls because boy's tasks are more likely to require skill,
strength and risk. Boys participate in tasks done primarily
by adult women, a condition for discontinuity in Benedict's
terms (Benedict, 1938). Furthermore, boys typically face a
shift from female to male teachers. Since men teach the
highly skilled tasks, and those are more likely to benefit

281

the community at large, this shift may be stressful for many young men. Elderly men retire more than women, in that their participation in the subsistence activities in which they participated as boys and young men is more sharply decreased than it is for women. This again may represent a discontinuity and difficult adjustment for some old men.

While males have more variability of tasks than females across societies, because their work is more closely tied to the particular subsistence of the tribe, females have more tasks to do within societies. When I first analyzed these data, I said that the colloquial phrase "Jack of all trades", should be "Jill of all trades", Girls are usually introduced to their varied, low skill jobs before adolescence. Females do virtually all the housework in virtually all societies. One does get a sense, reading the material, that the other colloquial phrase "a women's work is never done" applies universally. I am reminded of a cartoon of a housewife, in the middle of a sleepless night saying, "While I lie here, children are getting hungry, clothes are getting dirty and dust is settling on the furniture". Household chores extend throughout the lifetime and take up approximately 50% of the female work load, irrespective of age. For this reason, women do not retire to the extent that men do, even in societies not based on a salaried economy with a fixed retirement age. These findings substantiate other information indicating that the degree of identification with sex roles is firmer and easier for women than for men.

These data are relevant to the interpretation of the Barry, Bacon and Child finding that girls are trained to be more responsible than boys in over 80% of the societies they sampled (Barry et al., 1957). Since men typically hold the more responsible positions in adult societies, this finding puzzled me. I presume it is caused by the greater number of chores assigned to girls and the earlier introduction to them. If one assesses skill and community embeddedness one could conclude that boys are trained to be more responsible, since they do more highly skilled tasks, and ones which are more likely to affect persons beyond their family members.

Another finding that emerges is that both children and the elderly are valuable working members of these societies. Children participate in about 76% of the tasks of most societies, so their work is important to most of the ongoing work of their group. Elderly persons continue to participate in a variety of tasks, although their degree of participation may be reduced, particularly for men. They also assume primary importance to the community at large as specialists in social service activities. Glascock has found that societies make a distinction between the productive elderly, and persons who have become infirm and a burden to their group. He finds that the elderly only suffer substantial loss of status when they become infirm. We find frequent references for respect for the "wise old men and women of the tribes" who are valued for their skill and long term experience by younger tribal members.

I would like to conclude with two points of comparison between these societies and contemporary nation states, one concerning sex differences and the second concerning age.

First, women's participation in the subsistence economy of many societies may be higher than that reported for societies in our sample. The United Nations statistics indicate that the single, most frequent work of women is agricultural laborer. For women in third world countries, particularly Africa, this labor may be more than 25% of their task load. Similarly, women participate in the work force in a wide variety of jobs in many developed nations. The data on the high demands of housework is consistent with reports of houshold duties of women in modern nation states. American women are spending more time in housework than our grandmothers despite modern conveniences, because houses are larger, more complex in furnishing and standards are higher. The 80 hour week of working mothers has been reported in both the United States and Russia. Women's work does not vary significantly with political system.

The value of the work of both the children and the elderly has decreased in modern societies as both groups become more numerous, less productive, more expensive to maintain, and isolated from productive working in schools for the young and retirement homes for the old. Children are less valuable workers in an urban environment, in a society based on wages with child labor laws, and in societies with extensive schooling. It has been estimated that third world children, not in school, can support themselves by age 5 and subsequently contribute to the family income. Last month the U.S. government reported that it now costs $134,000 to rear an American child to age 18. College costs may add another $50,000 to this figure. While the cost of children decreases somewhat for multi-child families, it is still very high. Children in developed societies certainly do not contribute to 75% of adult tasks, rather they make additional work for their parents. Furthermore, government support for the elderly reduces the necessity of having children for "old age insurance."

Government support of the elderly, who abound in increasing numbers, as the life expectancy lengthens, places a financial burden on working adults, in addition to the taxation for public education of children. It is estimated that by the year 2000 one-third of the American population will be under 16, another one-third over 65, leaving the middle one-third supporting the young and the old. Add to this the observation of Margaret Mead that this is the first generation that attempts to teach children information that is less than one generation old, and one can see that the value of the "wise old ones" decreases markedly. They are numerous, expensive and much of their knowledge is outdated.

Most citizens may simply decry these developments and wax nostalgic about the "good old days". However, historical examination usually finds the "good old days" to be rather bad. In former times most children were uneducated and most potential elderly already dead. These conditions still prevail in many poor nations. As social scientists we are increasingly faced with the problem of maintaining the value of old and young citizens without sacrificing the education of children and the health of the elderly.

REFERENCES

Barry, H., Bacon, M.K. and Child, I.L.; A cross-cultural survey of some sex differences in socialization. Journal of Abnormal and Social Psychology; 1957, 55, 327-332.

Benedict, R. Continuities and discontinuities in cultural conditioning. Psychiatry, 1938, 2, 161-167.

Glascock, A.P. and Feinman, S.L.; Social asset or social burden: Treatment of the aged in non-industrial societies, from C.L. Fry, (Ed.), Dimensions: Aging, Culture and Health. p.913-31, New York: Praeger 1981.

Murdock, G.P.; World ethnographic sample. American Anthropologist, 1957, 664-687.

A CROSS-CULTURAL ANALYSIS OF THE DEVELOPMENT OF AGGRESSION

H. J. Kornadt

Universität des Saarlandes, Saarbrücken

I. INTRODUCTION

It is a widely known fact that cultures differ in amount and kind of aggression their members normally show. (Dentan 1968; Briggs 1957; Bateson 1941; Ataman & Savasir 1974; Gough 1965; Frost et al. 1972; Russell 1972; Lambert 1974; Whiting & Whiting 1975). But many questions have remained unsolved, not only concerning the causes of these differences, but also concerning the objectivity and the real amount of the differences reported, e.g. one does not know whether a certain test can be used as an indicator in different cultures.

To test the functional equivalence of instruments and items it is necessary not only to have enough knowledge about the cultures but also to have a consistent theoretical frame of reference. In cross-cultural aggression research such a theory should integrate various theoretical approaches and lead to hypotheses which could be tested cross-culturally.

The present study was not conducted in order only to replicate previous findings. It started from a specific motivation theory of aggression (Kornadt 1974, 1981, 1982; Kornadt et al. 1980).

The goals were: 1. To analyse those differences between cultures qualitatively within the framework of the motivation theory of aggression; this should allow us to come closer toward an understanding of the basic motivational dynamics and the interactional processes of aggression; 2. to study differences in the socio-cultural conditions for the development of aggressiveness; 3. to study the relation between those developmental conditions and individual differences in agressiveness; 4. for both aspects, the aggressiveness and the developmental conditions and processes, we assumed universals as well as culture-specific peculiarities. Both can be predicted from our motivation theory. Those assumptions should be tested. First, I will start with a very rough description of the theory, later on preliminary results of a pilot study are reported.

II. MOTIVATION THEORY OF AGGRESSION

An aggression motive is assumed to be the enduring dispositional factor for aggression, consisting of two components: approach and avoidance, called <u>aggression motive</u> and <u>aggression inhibition</u>. Aggression motive is defined by the intention of injuring or hurting somebody; aggressive inhibition by the intention not to behave aggressively, to avoid aggression.

This two-component model is important for the understanding of aggressive behavior. Low aggression is theoretically ambiguous: it can occur if the aggression is low, and also if aggression motive <u>and</u> aggression inhibition are both high. In the first case, only a few situations, in the latter many situations will be aggression relevant, but a high aggression conflict blocks overt aggressive behavior.

But this is only a very simplified view. In detail, the aggressive act consists of a sequence of different steps, wherein enduring personal factors always interact with situational conditions. Examples are the activation of anger by frustrating events, the interpretation of anger and situation, for instance as caused by bad intentions of others, the actualization of generalized goals and their application to the actual situation, or the evaluation of aggressive acts. Each of these actual steps and the enduring personal factors involved are determined by socio-cultural circumstances.

I cannot go into further details here, but I wanted to underline, that according to motivation theory:
-aggressive behavior is seen as an interaction between enduring personal factors -- motives -- and situational factors,
-the enduring aggression motive system is not seen as a simple factor or trait; at first it consists of two components, aggression motive and aggression inhibition,
-then, each of these components consists of a lot of different elements like affect, intention attribution, goals, values, and so forth,
-the aggressive act is assumed to follow some universal rules of specific motivated behavior, but also to be influenced by important cultural factors.

The motivation theory of aggression comprehends also a set of specific assumptions concerning the <u>development</u> <u>of</u> <u>aggressiveness</u> and <u>its</u> <u>individual</u> <u>differences</u>. The central point is that the aggression-motive system and its various elements have to be developed in a complex process of interaction between the individuum and its social environment. Involved are processes of affect-conditioning, cognitive structuring, evaluation and so forth.

Most interesting is the question of what the conditions are for the development of low aggressiveness. Especially whether low aggressiveness can occur at all if one agrees that there are some universal conditions contributing in every case to the development of aggressiveness, namely the biologically rooted anger reactions and some universal learning conditions in the social environment. But according to the motivation theory it should nevertheless be possible for a very low aggression motive to develop and not only highly inhibited aggressiveness. But then a whole complex pattern of developmental conditions must be given. One single factor would not be sufficient.

Such a pattern may comprehend for instance: low anger conditioning in early childhood, low reinforcement for aggression, no models for success by aggressive behavior, possibilities and incentives to learn non-aggressive alternatives to cope with frustrating events, no positive evaluation of aggression in the culture, socio-cultural factors which prevent the development of a belief in a hostile world and in the bad intentions of others as being the normal cause of frustrations (Kornadt 1981).

The theoretical background of our studies rests upon experimental and empirical work published mostly in German (Kornadt 1974, 1981, 1982).

III. DESIGN AND RESULTS OF A CROSS-CULTURAL STUDY

<u>Sample</u>

I selected three groups which seemed to be different with respect to aggressive behavior and eventually also with respect to developmental conditions but not too dissimilar in terms of other socio-cultural factors. The groups are samples from <u>Japan</u> and two other Asian groups, namely <u>Bali</u> and <u>Batak</u> in Indonesia.

The Japanese are quite often reported to be not very aggressive (Blanchard & Blanchard 1981; De Vos & Mizushima 1973; De Vos 1971; Frost et al. 1972). The Balinese are also reported as being not very aggressive (Bateson 1941) while the Batak are said to be rather aggressive.

Chapter 29

Hypotheses

We expected differences in the aggression motive
system between the cultures, in the direction mentioned
before; and we were interested in the structure of the
motive system (aggression motive versus aggression
inhibition). Subjects were young adults. Concerning child
rearing and socio-cultural conditions relevant for the
development of aggressiveness we expected differences
between the cultures also in accordance with the theory.
Subjects were young adults and parents of young children.

Then we did not want to rely only on intercultural
comparison with its methodological pitfalls. Therefore we
also selected different subgroups within each culture,
which can be assumed to be different in aggression: that
is, at the one hand, more traditional versus more
modernized people, and at the other hand, boys versus
girls. The whole design is as follows (Table 1):

TABLE 1

CROSS-CULTURE RESEARCH ON AGGRESSION: OVERVIEW*

| | | Adolescents | | Parents | |
		Girls	Boys	Mothers	Fathers
BATAK	trad.	(45) 14	(45) 15	(8) 2	(9) 2
	mod.	(45) 15	(40) 15	(14) 4	(12) 4
BALI	trad.	(39) 15	(56) 15	(13) 7	(14) 7
	mod.	(25) 15	(70) 15	(14) 7	(15) 8
JAPAN	trad.	(17) 17	(28) 28	(16) 16	(16) –
	mod.	(242) 5	(248) 5	(10) 10	(10) –
GERMANY	mod.	(35) –	(35) 98	(8) 4	(8) 4

* This table contains the numbers of TATs (adolescents) and
  interviews (parents) that have been scored as yet. The highest
  number taken in a respective culture for data processing of
  questionnaires is added in brackets.

The data were collected by three kinds of instruments:
questionnaires, TAT and interviews. The most important
instrument is a special aggression-TAT constructed and
tested carefully on the basis of the theory. The TAT

consists of eight pictures with four degrees of aggression relevance. The scoring system consists of theory-related formal categories, which can be applied to different culture-specific contents. Therefore, we believe the TAT to be especially useful in cross-cultural studies. Moreover, its advantage is to have separate scores for the aggression motive and the aggression inhibition.

The questionnaires and semi-structured interviews were mostly adapted from other authors (Taylor 1965, Bottenberg 1975).

Results

Let's start by looking at the global aggression scores obtained in differen cultures. Figure 1 shows that there are differences, and that they are in accordance with the general hypotheses: In the n-Aggr. score the Japanese should be lowest and the Batak highest, as they indeed are.

But low n-Aggr. score is ambiguous: it can result from low aggression motive as well as from high aggression and inhibition scores (high conflict). One must ask what here is the case, and we were especially interested in that kind of motive-structure. Therefore we compared the total aggression scores (Figure 2). As can be seen from this figure the pattern of scores is similar; the Japanese scores are lowest. One would expect them to be high in the case of conflict between "inhibition" and "conflict".

These results show that low aggression motive can occur, as it does in the case of Japan. But of course there are some problems of reliability and validity of the scores, especially in the intercultural comparison. But if we find differences also between the intra -cultural subgroups according to our assumptions, then this would support the validity of the data. Such differences would be interesting also with respect to developmental conditions in traditional and modernized societies. Figures 3 and 4 show the differences we found between the groups we considered to be more traditional versus more modernized.

The next question deals with the developmental conditions. Here we have a lot of data, not always and not yet completely analysed. We selected some of them which seemed theoretically interesting. We wanted to know whether the same conditions and processes in all cultures are connected with high versus low aggressiveness, as predicted by our Western based theory. We have data available from four different sources: retrospective questionnaire and interview data from the adolescents and interview and questionnaire data from parents. In many variables, we found differences between the cultural and subcultural groups.

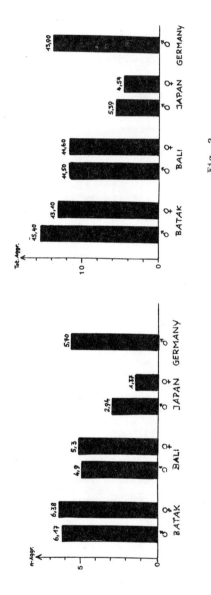

Fig. 2

TAT-Total-Aggr. Scores in Different Cultures

Fig. 1

TAT-n-Aggr. Scores in Different Cultures

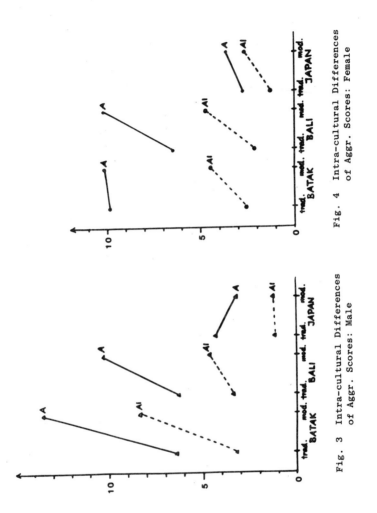

Fig. 3 Intra-cultural Differences
of Aggr. Scores: Male

Fig. 4 Intra-cultural Differences
of Aggr. Scores: Female

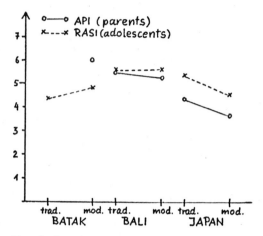

Fig. 5 Developmental Conditions: Comparison
of Data from Adolescents and Parents
- Verbal Punishment, Boys/Mother

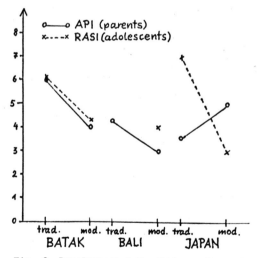

Fig. 6 Developmental Conditions: Comparison
of Data from Adolescents and Parents
- Love Withdrawal, Girls/Mother

Chapter 29

Some of the theoretically more interesting variables, such as physical punishment and love withdrawal, were chosen for further analysis.

Then we wanted to know whether the child rearing data reported by the parents are in correspondence with the data retrospectively reported by the adolescents. As a rough indicator for such a correspondence we used the direction of differences between traditional and modern groups.

As Figures 5 and 6 show, we found some similarities. Therefore it seems not to be unjustified to draw conclusions about developmental factors effective within a given socio-cultural group.

Then we come to the question, whether there are general trends of relationship between developmental conditions and aggressiveness in all cultures. As a first approach we calculated mean scores of selected child rearing variables for each cultural subgroup and their correlation with the n-Aggr. sores.

According to the theory we assumed frustrating conditions like unfriendliness, negligence, hostility as facilitating aggressiveness and a warm emotional relation and security as impeding aggressiveness. As an example Table 2 shows some results.

TABLE 2

CORRELATIONS BETWEEN PERCEIVED
CHILD REARING (RASI) AND TAT-n-AGGR.
(means of all cultural groups)

ADOLESCENTS	physical punishm.	psych. reward
male by father	.76	.16
by mother	.82	-.50
female by father	.10	-.92*
by mother	.74	-.86*

In fact there seem to exist such general relationships. They are in line with the theory and with other findings (Allen 1972; Pepitone, 1979).

But looking for universals in the process of aggression motive development is only one of our goals. We

293

are just as much interested in developmental conditions, which may be culture-specific, and in related peculiarities of the motive-structure.

We analysed our data in order to find qualitative peculiarities. As mentioned before we expected those specialities not so much in single variables, but rather in complex patterns.

By studying the content of the interviews we got indeed the impression that such a culture-specific pattern in child rearing may exist in East Asia, especially in Japan. It may perhaps be called "silent socialization", that is influencing a child
- <u>not</u> so much by explicit means as verbal praise or punishment, material rewards, expressed affection by pointing to norms, and evaluating of behavior;
- <u>but</u> much more indirectly by forms of non-verbal behavior, by mere intimating feelings of affection, anger, disappointment, thereby enhancing empathy and guilt feelings in the child.

It is hard to objectify such a pattern of interaction by usual psychological instruments - even by direct observation. But we will try to pursue the idea further.

Another approach for getting information about cultural peculiarities was a cluster analysis of the questionnaires. I can mention only a few examples of the results. In child-rearing: e.g. in some Asian cultures strict control by parents cannot have the same meaning as in Western cultures. In Western cultures it is obviously understood as a sign of mistrust, hostility and rejection. In Indonesia it seems to be a sign of care and affection. For instance, in all Indonesian groups items like:
He/She had a lot of rules that I had to obey.
He/She controlled everything that I did.
seem to indicate aggression impeding conditions instead of aggression enhancing as in Germany (Bottenberg 1975). On the other hand, in Japan a behavior of mothers seems to be related to aggression enhancing conditions, which is in Germany obviously a sign of mother's affection and care. For instance:
She often gave up her plans to do something with me. Comparable results of the cluster analysis of the aggression-questionnaire indicate that there may be culture-specific peculiarities in the aggression motive structure as well.

IV. CONCLUDING REMARKS

Our data seem to support hypotheses derived from the motivation theory of aggression:

294

-that there can be developed a <u>low</u> <u>aggression</u> <u>motive</u>,

-that there are some <u>universal</u> <u>processes</u> in the development of the aggression motive, so that in different cultures the same basic conditions are responsible for low and high aggressiveness,

-that there may be also certain <u>culture-specific</u> forms of child rearing and culture specific <u>characteristics</u> in the aggression motive structure.

For the next step of the study we shall try to improve the instruments in order to assess more precisely the culture-specific characteristics as well as the universals. That is we have to deal with the problem of functional equivalence of the indicators, and to avoid irrelevant differences in meaning.

We hope to analyse the functional relationships in behavior development in more detail, in order to finally understand the conditions of the development of low aggressiveness.

REFERENCES

ALLEN, M.: A cross-cultural study of aggression and crime. Journal of Cross-Cultural Psychology 1972, 3, 259-271.

ATAMAN, J. & SAVASIR, Y.: Interpretation of situations leading to aggressive behavior by Turkish children: A cross-cultural study. In: De Wit, J. & Hartup, W.W. (eds): Determinants and origins of aggressive behavior. The Hague: Mouton 1974, 481-488.

BATESON, G.: The frustration-aggression hypothesis and culture. Psychological Review 1941, 48, 350-355.

BLANCHARD, D.C. & BLANCHARD, R.J.: Violence in Hawaii. A preliminary analysis. Unpublised manuscript. University of Hawaii. Honolulu 1981.

BOTTENBERG, E.H.: Aggressivität und perzipierte elterliche Erziehungsstile. Schweizerische Zeitschrift für Psychologie 1975, 34 (2), 129-140.

BRIGGS, J.L.: The origins of nonviolence: Inuit management of aggression (Canadian arctic). In: Montagu, A. (ed) Learning non-aggression. The experience of non-literate societies. Oxford: Oxford University Press 1957, 21, 343-348.

DENTAN, R.K.: The Semai. A nonviolent people of Malaya. New York: Holt, Rinehart & Winston 1968.

DE VOS, G.A.: Deviancy and social change: a psychocultural evaluation of trend in Japanese delinquency and suicide. In: Smith, R.J. & Beardsley, R.K. (eds): Japanese culture. Its development and characteristics. New York: Johnson Reprint Corporation 1971, 153-171.

DE VOS, G.A. & MIZUSHIMA, K.: Delinquency and social change in modern Japan. In: De Vos, G.A.: Socialization for achievement: Essays on the cultural psychology of the Japanese. Berkeley, Ca.: University of California Press 1973, 327-368.

FROST, B.P., IWAWAKI, S. & FOGLIATTO, H.: Argentinian, Canadian, Japanese and Puerto Rican norms of the Frost self-description questionnaire. Journal of Cross-Cultural Psycholoy 1972, 3, 215-218.

GOUGH, H.G.: Cross-cultural validation of a measure of asocial behavior. Psychological Reports 1965, 17, 379-387.

KORNADT, H.-J.: Toward a motivation theory of aggression and aggression inhibition. Some considerations about an aggression motive and their application to TAT and catharsis. In: De Wit, J. & Hartup, W.W. (eds); Determinants and origins of aggressive behavior. The Hague: Mouton 1974, 567-577.

KORNADT, H.-J.: Development of aggressiveness. A motivation theory perspective. Paper presented at the NATO ASI "Aggression in Children and Youth". Maratea, Italy 1981.

KORNADT, H.-J.: Aggressionsmotiv und Aggressionshemmung. 2 Bde. Bern: Huber 1982.

KORNADT, H.-J., ECKENSBERGER, L.H. & EMMINGHAUS, W.B.: Cross-cultural research on motivation and its contribution to a general theory of motivation. In Triandis, H.C. & Lonner, W. (eds): Handbook of Cross-cultural psychology. Basic processes, Vol. 3. Boston: Allyn & Bacon 1980, 223-321.

LAMBERT, W.W.: Promise and problems of cross-cultural exploration of children's aggressive strategies. In: De Wit, J. & Hartup, W.W.: Determinants and origins of aggressive behavior. The Hague: Mouton 1974, 437-459.

PEPITONE, A.: On the universality of psychological theories: a cross-cultural study of judgements of aggression. In: Eckensberger, L.H., Lonner, W.J. & Poortinga, Y.H. (eds): Cross-cultural contributions to psychology. Lisse: Swets & Zeitlinger 1979, 121-130.

RUSSELL, E.W.: Factors of human aaggression. A cross-cultural factor analysis of characteristics related to warfare and crime. Behavior Science Notes 1972, 4, 275-307.

TAYLOR, S.: The relationship of expressed and inhibited hostility to psychological activation. University of Michigan. Ann Arbor 1965.

WHITING, B.B. & WHITING, J.W.: Children of six cultures: A psycho-cultural analysis. Cambridge: Harvard University Press 1975.

THE IMPACT OF POLITICAL AND SECTARIAN VIOLENCE IN NORTHERN IRELAND

L. McWhirter

Queen's University, Belfast

The Northern Ireland conflict is deeply rooted and highly complex but it embraces two underlying problems. One concerns external relations between Ireland and Great Britain and the other concerns internal relations between the two major community groups in Northern Ireland, Protestant and Roman Catholic. The conflict - known euphemistically as the "troubles" - thus involves both political and sectarian violence.

The centuries-old divisions between Protestants and Roman Catholics extend beyond religious differences to encompass historical and cultural diversity. The sectarian conflict also reflects the large extent to which religion and politics coincide in Northern Ireland. Ireland and Great Britain are two neighbouring islands (off the coast of Western Europe). Great Britain, which is traditionally Protestant, consists of three countries, England, Scotland and Wales. Ireland is traditionally Catholic. After centuries of violent conflict between Ireland and Great Britain, Ireland was divided in 1921. The north-eastern part of Ireland, with its Protestant majority, retained the existing links with Great Britain and became known as Northern Ireland. The rest of the island of Ireland eventually attained political independence as the Republic of Ireland with 26 counties and a predominantly Catholic population. While the majority of Protestants wish to uphold the current political status of Northern Ireland and to retain their British identity, most Catholics aspire to severing the ties with Great Britain in favour of a reunited Catholic Ireland. The present spate of violence, the longest episode in Ireland's troubled history, dates from 1968. Towards the beginning of the present "troubles" attempts by the police and army to control Protestant loyalist violence were a predominant feature.

298

The mid 1970s were characterized by sectarian conflict between Protestants and Catholics. Since then the most evident theme is the struggle between the forces of the British government and Catholic republican paramilitary groups, particularly the Provisional IRA. The main regions of violence have been the urban areas of Belfast and Londonderry and the rural area surrounding the border between Northern Ireland and the Republic of Ireland, with variations between those regions in relative intensities of the violence and its form and target. In Belfast, for example, the incidence of explosions, from 1969 to 1977, directed at classical targets (police, army, government personnel and installations, public transport, utilities, communications, etc.) is less than expected in relation to the overall incidence while that of economic and sectarian targets is greater than expected. Similarly, there have been fewer police and army deaths but more sectarian killings (Murray, in press).

In world terms, the absolute statistics relating to Northern Ireland "troubles" (e.g., nearly 2,500 deaths in over 14 years) are hardly momentous. Furthermore, more people have died violently on the roads in Northern Ireland than due to the "troubles". Indeed, although the road death toll for 1981 was the lowest since 1968, it was still more than twice the number of deaths due to the civil strife.

In spite of these positive comparisons, it is difficult for anyone anywhere in Northern Ireland to totally escape from the "troubles". Northern Ireland is a very small land mass (about 13,500 square kilometres) with a population of only 1.5 million which is composed of small tightly-knit communities. In addition, although much of the country has been untouched by overt violence, media coverage of acts of violence is widespread.

THE RESEARCH

While there have been attempts to apply social psychology to an understanding of the conflict, most of the "psychological" interest in the "troubles" has focused on the effects of sectarian division, intergroup conflict and strife upon the people of Northern Ireland, particularly the children and adolescents.

Early studies by American psychologists (e.g., Doob and Foltz, 1973; Fields, 1973) produced controversy while adding little to knowledge or understanding. Initial reports of the consequences of direct exposure to rioting, shooting and bombing (e.g., Lyons, 1973; Fraser, 1973) were based on the atypical experiences of psychiatrists working largely in Belfast. These psychiatric studies testified to the resilience of the children, in that the observed

299

nightmares, enuresis and phobias appeared to be generally short-lived. Furthermore, it was children who were in some way already psychologically vulnerable who were the most likely to manifest psychiatric symptoms.

The attitudes of children to violence were assessed by Russell (1974) in a large-scale sociological survey. The data suggested that over half of primary schoolboys (aged 7 to 11) and two-thirds of secondary schoolboys (aged 12 to 16 years) approved of violence for political ends. Those who believed most strongly in political violence, however, were not necessarily those who approved of general vandalism. The validity of these results, though, is thrown in doubt because it is possible that the boys had been cued to give stereotyped group responses rather than individual opinions. It is also likely that the youngest children in the sample may not have fully understood the lengthy questionnaire.

A much more rigorous study carried out as part of major curriculum review project, but reported somewhat briefly (Ungoed-Thomas, 1972), concerned patterns of relationships among Northern Irish adolescents (N=1257). Use of the open-ended critical-incident technique, concerning "good", "bad" and "difficult" situations (apparently without controlling for order effects), revealed that the pupils were preoccupied with violence, as well as concerned about their families, and that they experienced social difficulties with strangers.

The first experimental study on the effects of the "troubles" on Northern Ireland children (Jahoda and Harrison, 1975) demonstrated that strong negative evaluations of the out-group were expressed by both Protestant and Catholic children living in a strife-torn part of Belfast as early as six years of age. Their data also showed that in 1973 when children were asked to identify ambiguous objects almost one-third of a group of six-year-olds and three-quarters of a group of 10-year-olds perceived at least one object as a bomb in sharp contrast to a group of Scottish children where such perceptions were virtually non-existent. However, one must not overlook the possibility in this study of the experimenter cueing the Belfast children by explicitly using the names of areas in the city renowned for conflict and violence.

The fist major programme of psychological research on the conflict (Cairns, 1980) was developmental in emphasis. Not surprisingly, perhaps, it focused on ethnic discrimination using perspectives derived from American research. The series of studies utilized ingenious disguised experimental procedures adapted from cognitive psychology and it also served to highlight the need to use ecologically valid tasks and revealed the difficulties inherent in naively translating perspective from one culture to another (McWhirter and Trew, 1981; McWhirter and Gamble, 1982).

Whithin the last few years there has been a growing interest in the continuing strife. Resident psychologists have tended to be more circumspect in their research on Northern Ireland children than "visiting" academics have been and current work is also more methodologically rigorous than the early studies (McWhirter, in press a). The two main lines of recent research on the effects of the "troubles" relate to anti-social behaviour (see Harbison & Harbison, 1980), especially involvement in terrorist-type offences (e.g., Curran, 1982), and to social awareness (e.g. McWhirter and Trew, 1982; McWhirter, in press b,c).

Recent research on social awareness

From a psychological viewpoint, subjective interpretations are more important than the objective situation, but two studies by Cairns, Hunter and Herring (1980) have clearly illustrated the influence of local television news coverage. Two groups of children exposed to Northern Irish television, one from an area on the west coast of Scotland which can receive only Northern Irish television (N=93), were compared with a control group from an urban area in Scotland which cannot receive Northern Irish television (N=48). Younger Scottish children (5- to 6-year-olds) within Northern Ireland's television range made much more mention of bombs and explosions in making up stories about ten ambiguous pictures than their Glasgow counterparts, and were every bit as aware as their Northern Irish counterparts of bombs and explosions. The pattern was similar in essays about "the News" written by 7- to 8-year-olds. This research also showed how temporal changes in the levels of violence can be reflected in the thinking of Northern Irish children. The second study, which was carried out when the number of explosions had decreased, produced fewer allusions to bombings.

After 14 years of the present "troubles" it might be suggested that "abnormality" has now become "normality", at least in a statistical sense (McWhirter and Trew, 1981), and that as the political and sectarian violence continues habituation is taking place. If this is true, and personal experience testifies to its likely truth, then violence should no longer be a prominent feature in the spontaneous thinking of the young people of Northern Ireland.

It was this hypothesis which instigated the ongoing programme of research on social awareness in young people in Northern Ireland presently being carried out in Queen's University in Belfast. For ethical reasons most of the studies to date have used disguised and/or open-ended procedures (Trew and McWhirter, 1982). One such technique involves the embedding of target words which are potentially distressing into a word-definition test supplemented by more probing questions presented casually as if incidental to the main assessment session. Using this technique to investigate ideas about death held by Belfast children (N=200) aged between 3 and 16 years, McWhirter, Young and Majury (1982) found that pre-school children living in an area of the city which had witnessed a high level of violence had a more mature concept of death (in a Piagetian sense) than their age mates living in a relatively peaceful district. Overall, 29 per cent made possible references to the Northern Ireland conflict by citing murder, killings, shootings, or explosions but only 5 per cent made unambigous specific allusions to local violent events. Indeed, the general causes of death were attributed more often to sickness (54 per cent) than to violence (46 per cent) or accidents (40 per cent) and, at a more specific level, just as frequently to heart disease (30 per cent) and to old age (29 per cent) as to explosions or shootings (29 per cent), and more often to road accidents (26 per cent) and cancer (10 per cent) than to specific local violence (5 per cent). These perceptions surprisingly accurately reflect the total objective situation as given by the Registrar General's statistics for deaths in Northern Ireland.

Another popular procedure used in attempts to assess the salience of violence in children's spontaneous thinking about their social world continues to be the essay technique. As part of a large cross-cultural study, Hosin and Cairns (1980) asked a group (N=425) of Protestant children aged 9 and 12 years, from peaceful areas of Northern Ireland, to write an essay entitled "My country". Word counts revealed that for both age groups by far the most frequently cited categories were homeland, geography and climate, important people of the country, and violence. At neither age did violence predominate.

Interested in the public image of Belfast compared to children's (and adult's) experience of living there, McIvor (1982) asked 7- and 11- year-olds (N=957) from different districts of Belfast to write an essay entitled either "Belfast" or "Where I live". Children from each area were assigned randomly to one condition. Analyses by theme showed that overall 28 per cent cited violence compared with 80 per cent for geographical information and 83 per cent for self related material. Although twice as many from the strife-prone areas mentioned anti-social behaviour (19%) - vandalism, joy-riding, gang fights, etc. - than from the more peaceful districts (9%), there were no statistically significant differences between locations in terms of incidence of conflict related themes - Protestant-Catholic relations, sectarian or political violence, army, police, law and order. Themes related to the conflict were, however, more prevalent in the description of Belfast (45%) than in the account of where the children lived (10%).

These data suggest that the television image of Belfast colours the way the children see it and that the violence has perhaps become mentally compartmentalised so that a cue such as Belfast, with its violent media image, is needed before the door to the compartment is opened.

In the light of this finding it is interesting to note what children in Northern Ireland make of the term "violence" itself. Essays (McWhirter, 1982a) on the topic by 9- and 12- year-olds living in different areas of Northern Ireland revealed that 19 per cent appeared not to know the meaning of the word. Amongst those who showed at least a vague idea (N=517) there was a low level of awareness of sectarian conflict or hostility (5%) but a greater reflection of area variations in the extent and nature of the violence, similar to the temporal variation found by Cairns et al. (1980). The children from strife-prone areas in Belfast cited more Northern Ireland type of violence - stoning, rioting, shooting, bombing, throwing petrol bombs, intimidation, etc.-(71%) than those living in a peaceful provincial town (58%). In view of the nature of the conflict over the last few years it was not unexpected that location also interacted with religion; the Catholic children from the troubled area made more references to Northern Ireland violence (80%) than the Protestant children living in the neighbouring area of West Belfast (60%) and Catholic children from the peaceful region (58%). Overall, while the children are certainly aware of violence in Northern Ireland and its violent image (65% overall made reference to Northern Ireland violence), their conceptions were very global and embraced much more than the "troubles": 60 per cent described general universal acts of violence which were either unspecific - bullying, kidnapping, killing, etc. - or occurred somewhere other than Ireland. However they interpreted the term, two-thirds spontaneously condemned it.

Recent Research on Anti-social Behaviour

Violence and aggression may be undesirable modern world-wide phenomena - in addition to being predominant features of both children's fiction and television fiction - but one significant result of the present prolonged period of civil unrest in Northern Ireland has been a level of very serious crime unprecedented in the troubled history of Northern Ireland. It is noteworthy that, in spite of appalling social conditions, Northern Ireland has traditionally been a region of relatively low levels of crime and delinquency, and serious crime more particularly. For example, at no time during the 1960s, prior to 1969, did the total number of murders reach double figures.

The rate of increase of the official crime figures for Northern Ireland over the ten years from 1969 to 1978 (120 per cent) is twice the rate for England and Wales, but the number of indictable offences known to the police in Northern Ireland is still only two-thirds the rate in England and Wales. In contrast, recent criminological research suggests that a greater proportion of juvenile offenders in Northern Ireland engage in serious offending than in England and Wales. Offences associated with political violence and terrorism, however, constitute a relatively small proportion of all known offences in Northern Ireland. The extent of young people's involvement in the political violence may appear considerable but the vast majority of juvenile indictable offences are, in fact, crimes of dishonesty. Moreover, the increased level of juvenile deviance is seen to be closely associated with particular urban areas which have been exposed to extremes of both socio-economic deprivation and civil unrest. In such beleagured communities it is not surprising that young people are drawn into what is the "norm" for their area.

Indeed, there is some evidence that those who have become involved in the violence are quite normal in the psychological adjustment sense, or even above the psychological and personal norm. In one analysis of people on trial for terrorist crimes in 1975, a group of researchers (Boyle et al., 1976) found that overall, in terms of socio-economic background, employment status and previous criminal history, the defendants were broadly representative of the communities, both Protestant and Catholic, from which they came. There is no psychological evidence that those who have been involved in terrorist-type activities are clinically disturbed, but there do appear to be important personal differences between juvenile "scheduled" (terrorist-type) offenders and "ordinary" delinquents. A small-scale study by Elliott and Lockhart (1980) showed that, despite similar socio-economic and family backgrounds and similar reconviction rates, juveniles charged with terrorist-type offences and sent to the assessment centre, were older and more intelligent with higher educational attainments than "ordinary" delinquents. The "scheduled" offenders were also less prone to physical illness or accidents in childhood and were less likely to have been referred for psychiatric help or to have had a history of truancy. Completion of the Jessness Inventory of Deviant Attitudes by a sample of juvenile "scheduled" offenders (Curran, 1982) revealed them to be lower on the scale of manifest aggression than a control group of "conventional" delinquents. On the other hand, the terrorist offenders were more "socially maladjusted" than a

sample of secondary schoolboys. Curran interprets the
finding of lack of abnormal attitudes of aggression and
alienation as contrary to many of the assumptions in the
literature on political terrorism and suggestive of
inadequate or disturbed socialization.

One likely factor which may account for the law
abiding nature of Northern Ireland society, and the
relative containment of crime, is the strength of churches'
influence and the fundamentalist religious values espoused
by both Protestants and Catholics in Northern Ireland
(Rose, 1971). Another is the essentially traditional nature
of Northern Irish society in which positive
characteristics, which have been lost elsewere, are
maintained - strong family support, allied to people having
a place in the community and an identification with it
(Beloff, 1980).

CONCLUSIONS

Clearly much more psychological research on the impact
of the "troubles" on the people of Northern Ireland is
needed, both on the intra-Northern Ireland level and on a
cross-cultural basis. Three obvious and important gaps
which exist in the current corpus of research work are:
one, clinically oriented, stress-related studies; two,
studies on the ideologies of the young (McWhirter, 1982b);
three, studies on the effects of conflict on the normal
everyday social behaviour of young people (McWhirter, in
press d). There must also be a greater explicit recognition
of possible task demands and researcher bias (McWhirter,
1982c) and of the very real difficulties involved in
assessing potentially sensitive information, particularly
when children are the subjects. Although low-intrusive
measures may be ethically desirable it is possible that
they may be too superficial to reveal the "true" level of
consciousness, knowledge and understanding of violence -
and its highly complex causes - in the young people of
Northern Ireland. Criminal statistics are also notoriously
unreliable. In conclusion, however, recent studies do
converge to produce a coherent picture which suggests that
relative "normality" seems to prevail in Northern Ireland -
though within the now well established framework of
political and sectarian violence.

Chapter 30

REFERENCES

Beloff, H., A place not so far apart. In J. & J. Harbison (Eds.), A Society under Stress. Somerset: Open Books, 1980.

Boyle, K., Chesney, R. & Hadden, T. Who are the terrorists? New Society, 6 May, 1976.

Cairns, E., The development of ethnic discrimination in children in Northern Ireland. In J. & J. Harbison (Eds.), A Society under Stress. Somerset: Open Books, 1980.

Cairns, E., Hunter, D. & Herring, L. Young children's awareness of violence in Northern Ireland: The influence of Northern Irish television in Scotland and Northern Ireland. British Journal of Social and Clinical Psychology, 19, 3-6, 1980.

Curran, D. D. Juvenile offending, civil disturbance and political terrorism - A psychological perspective. In L. McWhirter & K. Trew (Eds.), The Northern Ireland Conflict: Myth and Reality. Ormskirk: G. W. & A. Hesketh, 1982.

Doob, L. W. & Foltz, W.J. The Belfast workshop: an application of group techniques to a destructive conflict. Journal of Conflict Resolution, 17, 489-512, 1973.

Elliott, R. & Lockhart, W.H. Characteristics of scheduled offenders and juvenile deliquents. In J. & J. Harbison (Eds.), A Society Under Stress. Somerset: Open Books, 1980.

Fields, R.M. A Society on the Run: A Psychology of Northern Ireland. Harmondsworth, Penguin, 1973.

Fraser, M. Children in Conflict. London: Martin Secker & Warburg, 1973.

Harbison, J. & Harbison, J. (Eds.) A Society Under Stress Somerset: Open Books, 1980.

Hosin, A. & Cairns, E. Political consciousness in children in Northern Ireland. Paper presented at the British Psychological Society Annual Conference, Aberdeen, 1980.

Jahoda, M. & Harrison, S. Belfast children: some effects of a conflict environment. The Irish Journal of Psycholgy, 3, 1-19, 1975.

Lyons, H. A. Violence in Belfast - a review of the psychological effects. Public Health, 87, 231-238, 1973.

McIvor, M. Social and environmental awareness of Belfast children. Ongoing Doctoral study, University of Belfast, Private Communication.

McWhirter, L. Northern Irish children's conception of violent crime. The Howard Journal, 21, 167-177, 1982a.

McWhirter, L. Yoked by violence together: Stress and coping in children in Northern Ireland. Community Care, 4 Nov. 14-17, 1982b.

McWhirter, L. The meaning of violence for Northern Ireland children. Paper presented at the congress of the International Association for Child and Adolescent Psychiatry and Allied Professions, Dublin, 1982c.

McWhirter, L. The Northern Ireland "Troubles": Current developmental perspectives. Bulletin of the British Psychological Society, in press, a.

McWhirter, L. Awareness of conflict: Socialization and stress in Northern Ireland children. In L. McWhirter & K. Trew (Eds.), The Northern Ireland Conflict: Myth and Reality. Ormskirk: G.W. & A. Hesketh, in press b.

McWhirter, L. Growing up with the "troubles". In A.P. Goldstein & M. Segall (Eds.), Aggression in Global Perspective. New York: Pergamon Press, in press, c.

McWhirter, L. Looking back and looking forward: An inside perspective. In J. Harbison (Ed.), Children of the Troubles Belfast: Stranmillis College, in press, d.

McWhirter, L. & Gamble, R. Development of ethnic awareness in the absence of physical cues. The Irish Journal of Psychology, 5, 109-127, 1982.

McWhirter, L. & Trew, K. Social awareness of Northern Ireland children. Bulletin of the British Psychological Society, 34, 308-311, 1981.

McWhirter, L. & Trew, K. Children in Northern Ireland: A lost generation? In E.J. Anthony & C. Chiland (Eds.), Children in Turmoil - Tomorrow's Parents. Yearbook of the International Association for Child Psychiatry and Allied Professions. Vol. 7. Chichester: Wiley, 1982.

McWhirter, L., Young, V. & Majury, J. Belfast children's awareness of violent death. British Journal of Social Psychology. 1982 (in press).

Murray, R. Patterns of violence. In L. McWhirter & K. Trew (Eds.), The Northern Ireland Conflict: Myth and Reality. Ormskirk: G.W. & A. Hesketh, in press.

Rose, R. Governing without Concensus: An Irish Perspective. London: Faber & Faber, 1971.

Russell, J.L. Socialization into Conflict. Ph.D. Thesis, University of Strathclyde, 1974.

Trew, K. & McWhirter, L. Conflict in Northern Ireland: A research perspective. In P. Stringer (Ed.), Confronting Social Issues. London: Academic Press, 1982.

Ungoed-Thomas, J.R. Patterns of adolescent behaviour and relationhips in Northern Ireland. Journal of Moral Education, 2, 76-81, 1972.

TOWARD A GLOBAL STRATEGY FOR RESEARCH ON AGGRESSION

M. H. Segall

Syracuse University, New York

The ultimate goal of the research with which I am concerned is to understand why humans behave aggressively and violently. That they do so is beyond doubt. That they do so to different degrees, in different manners, and for a variety of different reasons is also clear. At the same time, there may well be some universal features of human aggression. The pan-cultural similarities <u>and</u> the cross-cultural differences in aggressive behavior together comprise the puzzle which we must confront.

What we must try to do is identify as many as possible of the various factors in the natural and man-made environments of humans which might influence, in reliable ways, their behaviors relating to conflict, aggression, and violence. These ecocultural factors comprise the context in which such behaviors occur. These factors are distributed in a dazzling variety of ways across human habitats. They include features of the habitats themselves (like climate and terrain) plus many other factors (like economic systems, political structures and socialization practices), some correlated with environmental features and some which cut across them. In an overall research strategy, this large set of ecocultural, contextual factors, singly, in combination, and very likely in interaction with each other, must comprise our independent variables.

Following the suggestions of the anthropologist/psychologist team, Robert L. and Ruth Munroe (Munroe and Munroe, 1980), we think of culture as dissected into numerous, separable (ablbeit often correlated) contextual factors, including basic institutions, subsistence patterns, social and political organizations, languages, social rules governing interpersonal relations, divisions of labor by sex, age or other dimensions, population density, dwelling styles, and more, so many more that an exhaustive list of such independent variables is impossible.

All those anthropologists and cross-cultural psychologists who pursue hologeistic research in the tradition of Murdock (1957, 1967) and Naroll (1973), among others, employing either coded ethnographies like the Standard Cross-Cultural Sample (Murdock and White, 1969) or the Human Relations Area Files (Barry, 1980) or systematically coordinated multiple-site field work (Whiting, 1963) in order to test universal hypotheses about human behavior, employ variables like those enumerated above. In all such work, behavioral differences across cultural groups are related to one or more (and it is almost always more) variables like presence or absence of, or degree of presence of, some specific contextual factor. And so it must be in our work on aggression.

A Conceptual Framework

Assuming that we are confronted with facts about aggression that reveal reliable behavioral differences between human groups and that our objective is to relate them to the kinds of variables listed here, it is useful also to have an overarching conceptual framework about how human behavior changes over time and, by implication, comes to differ over space. I find that framework most cogently expressed in Donald Campbell's evolutionary epistemology (1977). Campbell's view of behavioral development at the individual level (and of change at the social level as well) is a model based on (but not identical with) contemporary theories of biological evolution. It is a model which emphasizes random variation and selective retention, tending toward adaptiveness in a circuitous manner and only in the long run.

If we have reason to believe that some behavior related to aggression is culturally influenced, we still have to ask, "In what way might this particular behavior, which we find in this/these particular place(s) be adaptive?" In this formal respect, we must think like biologists and ask, "What do we know about the eco-cultural contexts of the groups for which behavior A prevails and those of the groups for which behavior A-prime prevails that makes each of those behaviors fit the contexts in which they are found?"

This conceptual framework which we have adopted is in tune with a growing eco-cultural emphasis in cross-cultural psychology, as is found, for example, in Berry's (1975) perspective wherein most complex human behaviors and the cultural recipes for them are cumulatively selected for their adaptive character and are transmitted

inter-generationally by social processes, including
socialization and enculturation, rather than by genetic
adaptations.

The Nature-Nurture Controversy

Because aggression is our topic, it may be necessary
to be very explicit about where we stand on the question of
genetic determination, particularly since we have just
emphasized our interest in processes that parallel natural
selection. As is well known, human aggression is widely
thought to have a genetic basis. It may well be that this
is the single most popular view. It certainly is among
laypersons. And over the past few decades many scientists
have written works which have restored respectability to
it. However, in accord with most students of aggression, we
do not find the aggression-instinct arguments, in any of
the several versions which have appeared in recent years
(e.g., Lorenz, 1963; Ardrey, 1966; Morris, 1967; Storr,
1968; Wilson, 1975; Lumsden and Wilson, 1981), at all
compelling.

The mere fact of differences across societies in
degree, form, and concomitants of aggressive behavior is an
overwhelming problem for instinct theorists and
sociobiologists. I doubt that they are equipped to solve it
by remaining within their theoretical frameworks. And I
will not try to do it for them.

As I have noted elsewhere (Segall, 1981), genetic
hypotheses and learning hypotheses, as competing
alternatives, both must ultimately be assessed in the light
of their competence in pointing to systemic fit. While we
find learning more plausible than biological evolution as
the mechanism that provides that fit for aggression, we
nonetheless acknowledge that only when the adaptiveness of
the aggressive behavior is accounted for can that behavior
be said to be understood. So, in the end, our criterion for
success is the same as the sociobiologist's or the instinct
theorist's. Like them, we have to explain aggression
wherever it occurs, in whatever form. We have to show how
it fits its setting. But, unlike some instinct theorists,
we do not ever have to claim that aggression is "good".
Functional, yes, in the sense that a given degree or kind
of aggression fits other features of a particular
eco-cultural setting, but good for the aggressors or for
their victims? Absolutely not! Only instinct theories or
other frameworks which employ hydraulic system metaphors
force their adherents into that morally repugnant and
scientifically indefensible stance.

I turn now to a project, carried out with my colleague
at Syracuse University, Arnold Goldstein, that constitutes
a first step toward the kind of research program that the

311

foregoing strategic consideration requires.

We set out in this project to take a global perspective on human aggression. By this we meant two things -- to examine aggression wherever in the world it occurs, and to view aggression as an array of behaviors that probably relate, in varying degrees, to a large number of factors -- ecological, cultural, social, economic, physiological, and psychological -- in complex interaction with each other. To pursue this two-fold objective, we sampled a number of contemporary societies in which local experts provided discursive accounts of features of aggressive behavior and the setting for that behavior.

Most of them are large, complex contemporary societies, in nearly every case a modern nation state. Six of these are western Eurpoean nations, from Finland in the north, to Italy in the south, with Ireland, France, Germany, and Holland also in this category. Three are eastern European or middle-eastern, viz; Hungary, Turkey, and Israel. Five are located in Asia -- China, Japan, India, Hawaii, and New Zealand, two in Latin America -- Brazil and Peru, and one in Africa -- Nigeria, and one in North America -- the United States. This geographic categorization could, of course, be different; Hawaii, though located in Asia, is actually one of the United States of America, but a large portion of the population of Hawaii is ethnically Asian. Israel, though located in the middle east, has a majority Jewish population that is largely of recent European origin. But its middle eastern location is obviously a fact that has critical implications for matters pertaining to aggression in Israel. New Zealand, treated here as Asian, might also be thought of as European, since it has an overwhelmingly Anglo-Saxon population. So, the foregoing categorization is somewhat arbitrary. We use it primarily to indicate the geographic range of coverage provided by our collaborators.

Their contributions range not only geographically, but substantively as well. Nearly all -- but not all -- present facts regarding aggressive behavior, both individual and collective, in the nations, or regions, covered. Many -- but again, not all -- describe research on aggression that has been done by compatriate scholars. Several provide very rich historico-socio-contextual accounts. Some emphasize analyses at a micro level, others stress more macro analyses.

There are certain topics that show up in most of the contributions, like crime statistics and socialization emphases. Other topics show up in several areas wherever relevant, such as terrorism and political violence; while some topics are treated either uniquely or only in a few contributions, like vigilante activities.

Theoretical emphases also vary across the eighteen
contributions, reflecting intellectual trends that are
themselves imbedded in the cultural contexts which are of
primary concern in this volume (Goldstein and Segall,
1982). For example, the ideas of Henri Laborit (cf.
Laborit, 1978), the French biologically-oriented student of
human aggression, are discussed critically in the analysis
of recent experiences with armed acts of self defense by
individual citizens in France, but his ideas are not
mentioned in any other contribution. Psychoanalytic
approaches are referred to in several. Instinct approaches
are frequently mentioned, but usually dismissed as
unhelpful. Most often, but not always, the contributors
employ one or another version of social learning theory
(e.g. Bandura, 1971), and many also find reason to refer to
the frustration-aggression hypothesis.

So, the picture presented in the 18 chapters of our
report (Goldstein and Segall, 1982) is somewhat
kaleidoscopic, rather than global in the sense of
"comprising a gestalt." If there is an overarching
generalization that emerges, however, it is that aggression
clearly varies in form and function in ways that reflect
the cultural context in which it is shaped, manifested, and
controlled.

Moreover, an overwhelming impression that one must
gain from the bulk of accounts contained in this volume is
that child-rearing antecedents must loom large in any
framework that attempts to explain human aggressive
behavior. It cannot be understood except as a complex
product of the experiences that human beings have while
growing up, wherever in the world they happen to be born.

This overarching generalization subsumes numerous
others which may be derived from, and are consistent with,
the pictures provided by the contributors to this volume.
Among these, the following are the most provocative.

1. Aggression is predominantly "masculine" behavior.
Males tend to commit most of the aggressive acts described
by our contributors. The availability of male role models
and the behavior they display for emulation by their
children is clearly implicated in the traits acquired by
their children, particularly their sons. The nature of the
relationships between the sexes during adulthood, which
varies across societies, contributes both positively and
negatively, to the probability that aggression will be
encouraged, emulated, and otherwise learned. In certain
cases, a kind of compensatory machoism, of which displays
of aggressive behavior will be a salient feature, will be a
likely product of the way men relate to women and the way
parents in turn relate to their children.

2. The structure and function of societies matters greatly. The ability of "states " to provide for the needs of their citizens, to approach equity in the distribution of resources, to minimize stresses and frustrations, and to gain the respect and support of their citizenry affects the probability of both individual and collective aggression.

3. The role of certain forms of socially-sanctioned aggressive "outlets" like body-contact athletic contests, e.g., soccer and rugby, may be, to the embarrassment of catharsis theory, to set the stage for and serve as a trigger for, non-socially sanctioned violence. Similarly, post-war periods do not seem generally to be characterized by declines in internal violence.

4. The degree of cultural or ethnic homogeneity/ heterogeneity of a society does not predict very well the degree of aggression within the society. The nature of the culture(s) seems to be much more critical.

5. Punitiveness, either within families or in social institutions such as criminal justice systems, may very well enhance aggressive behavior. At least, the chapters contained in the volume provide no evidence that punitiveness reduces aggression.

6. For most of the societies described in the volume, punishment of crime is more prevalent than efforts designed to prevent it. While a movement away from the death penalty and other extreme forms of punishment may be discerned and while efforts to control the availability of guns are under way in many countries, aggression control is still most often and most widely thought of in terms of after-the-fact reactions rather than prevention.

7. There is a disconcerting gap between the perceptions of the causes and consequent means of reducing aggression held by scholars on the one hand and the citizenry of nearly all of the nations in which the scholars do their research. Popular beliefs about aggression are profoundly more pessimistic, in that they tend to treat aggression as inevitable and demanding punitiveness. Ironically, even if the scholars are right in their relative optimism, they will not be proven right until they somehow succeed in changing the perceptions of the public, for those public perceptions and beliefs necessarily contribute to self-fulfilling prophecies that will serve to maintain aggression at higher levels than would otherwise be the case.

These few generalizations, and several others that may be gleaned from the volume, do not comprise a complete answer to the question of why humans aggress in the ways and to the extent which they do. To understand aggression and its antecedents, and to be in a position to prescribe programs and policies to reduce it, requires an ongoing research program to which the volume may serve as both an introduction and an inspiration. The generalizations derivable from it we offer, then, not as answers, but as hypotheses. We and the colleagues who joined us in the present effort will surely continue to search for hypotheses that are latent in our collective knowledge of aggression in the various societies in which we live. We invite others to do the same. Together we must pursue research on human aggression that is designed within a global framework, research that seeks details about the complex process whereby we humans, through our cultural creations, make subsequent generations, in each of the ecocultural settings in which they will dwell, more or less aggressive than those of us who preceded them.

REFERENCES

Ardrey, R. The Territorial Imperative. New York: Atheneum, 1966.

Bandura, A. Social Learning Theory. New York: General Learning Press, 1971.

Barry, H. III. Studies Using the Standard Cross-Cultural Sample. In Barry, H. III, and Schlegel, A. (Eds.), Cross-Cultural Samples and Codes. Pittsburgh: University of Pittsburgh Press, 1980. Pp. 445-458.

Berry, J.W. An ecological approach to cross-cultural psychology. Nederlands Tijdschrift voor de Psychologie , 1975, 30 ,51-84.

Campbell, D.T. Descriptive Epistemology: Psychological, Sociological, and Evolutionary. William James Lectures, Harvard University, 1977.

Goldstein, A.P. & Segall, M. H. (Eds.), Aggression in Global Perspective. Elmsford, New York: Pergamon Press, 1982.

Laborit, H. The biological and sociological mechanisms of aggression. International Social Science Journal, 1978, 30, 727-794.

Lorenz, K. On Aggression. New York: Harcourt Brace Jovanovich, 1963.

Chapter 31

Lumsden, C.J. & Wilson, E.O. The Coevolutionary Process. Cambridge, Mass: Harvard University, 1981.

Morris, D. The Naked Ape. New York: McGraw-Hill, 1967.

Munroe, R. L. & Munroe, R. H. Perspectives Suggested by Anthropological Data. In Triandis, H. C. & Lonner, W. (Eds.) Handbook of Cross-Cultural Psychology, Boston: Allyn & Bacon, 1980, 253-317.

Murdock, G. P. World ethnographic sample. American Anthropologist, 1957, 59, 664-687.

Murdock, G.P. Ethnographic Atlas. Pittsburgh: University of Pittsburgh Press, 1967.

Murdock, G.P. & White, D.R. Standard cross-cultural sample. Ethnology, 1969, 68, 329-369. Reprinted in Barry, H. III & Schlegel, A. (Eds), Cross-Cultural Samples and Codes. Pittsburgh: University of Pittsburgh Press, 1980. Pp.3-43.

Naroll, R. Holocultural Theory Tests. In Narroll, R. & Naroll, F. (Eds.), Main Currents in Cultural Anthropology. New York: Appleton-Century-Crofts, 1973. Pp. 309-384.

Segall, M.H. On the search for independent variables in cross-cultural research. Paper presented at the Human Factors Panel, N.A.T.O. Conference, Kingston, Ontario, August, 1981.

Storr, A. Human Aggression. New York: Atheneum, 1968.

Whiting, B.B. (Ed.) Six Cultures: Studies of Child Rearing. New York: Wiley, 1963.

Wilson, E.O. Sociobiology. Cambridge, Mass.: Harvard University Press, 1975.

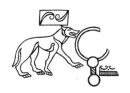

EMPLOYEE ABSENTEEISM: A CROSS-CULTURAL PERSPECTIVE

A. Aziz

University of Petroleum and Minerals, Dhaaran

Absenteeism is one of the most important determinants of organizational effectiveness. It results in considerable loss of man-days in organizations around the world, and influences productivity in both the developing and developed countries. But in order to control absenteeism, its meaning and the causal factors must be properly understood. The absence behavior may be caused by a number of personal, organizational and extra-organizational factors. The surrounding culture in which the organization exists may also be responsible for voluntary or involuntary absence from work on the part of the employee. Therefore, the absence behavior, like any other organizational behavior variable, may also vary from culture to culture. The assumption that behavior in organizations may be influenced by socio-cultural environments has given rise to theoretical models (Farmer & Richman, 1964; Negandhi & Eastafen, 1965), and is supported by empirical evidence related to some of the organizational behavior variables. Empirical research can be found on cross-cultural differences in preference for a leadership style (Sadler & Hofstede, 1972; Haire, Ghiselli & Porter, 1966; Bass, 1968a,b; Thiagarajan & Deep, 1969; and Barrett & Franke, 1969). Other variables which have been studied across various cultures include the role of needs in employee motivation as explained by Maslow's (1954) theory of Hierarchy of Needs (Haire, Ghiselli & Porter, 1966; Sirota & Greenwood, 1971; Slocum, Topichak & Kuhn, 1971). The validity of Herzberg's theory (Herzberg, Mauser & Synderman, 1959) has also been empirically tested in different cultures (Herzberg, 1965; Yadov, 1965; Simonetti & Weitz, 1972). Similarly different studies have compared life goals of managers from different countries (Alexander et al., 1970; Haire, Ghiselli & Porter, 1966; Heller & Porter, 1966; Barrett & Ryterband, 1968; Lazarus & Barrett,

317

1970). McClelland (1961 & 1969) has studied achievement motivation across different cultures.

The research on absenteeism has also been done in different cultural settings, but it seems that no attempt has been made so far to bring such research studies together. Perhaps many such research studies are not reported in professional American and European journals published in the English language. Specially the research done in developing countries seems to be inaccessible. For the purpose of this paper an attempt was made to collect research evidence through on-line search facility. While searching through five different data bases, whenever the term "developing countries" was used with the key word "absenteeism", the search yielded no results. Most of the research on absenteeism which is available has been done on U.S. samples. Table I presents factors investigated in absenteeism research in countries other than the U.S.A. It is evident that there are very few research studies from other countries which have investigated cultural or environmental factors. The cross-cultural comparison between research findings from different countries becomes a difficult task.

There are various reasons for scarcity of cross-cultural research on absenteeism. Unlike some other organizational behavior variables on which cross-cultural research is available, there is a large variation in operational definitions of absenteeism used in different settings. It may be differently defined in different organizations, industries and countries. This leads to the use of a wide variety of measures to determine absenteeism for an employee or an organization. Some of such measures used, for example, include the total number of days lost, the frequency of absence, absence due to sickness and unauthorized absence. The use of absenteeism as a dependent variable is a highly controversial issue (Smulders, 1980; Hammer & Landau, 1981). Similarly there is no standardized instrument or questionnaire available to ascertain the causes of absenteeism. In addition, till very recently, there has been no systematic theory of absenteeism. The first serious attempt was made by Steers and Rhodes (1978) to integrate various research studies and to present an attendance model. In cross-cultural research on other organizational variables discussed above, either the same questionnaire or adapted forms were used on samples from different countries.

Absenteeism research, in general, lacks an emphasis on cultural or environmental factors. This is true of research on both samples from the USA as well as from other countries. The research efforts have been directed more towards investigating the relationship of absenteeism to personal, job environment and organizational factors. But

TABLE I

Absenteeism Research in Different Countries
Excluding U.S.A.*

Country and Factors	Investigators
Argentina	
Travel distance	Knox, 1961
Canada	
Job satisfaction, Job involvement	Vroom, 1962
France	
Length of work week, Job level, Age, Travel distance, Sex	Isambert-Jamati, 1962
India	
Anxiety	Sinha, 1963
Sweden	
Job satisfaction, Wage rate, Satisfaction with a) pay equity b) supervision c) human relations ability d) co-workers e) work itself, Technical and organizational skills of Supervisor.	Lundquist, 1958
Job or Socio-technical redesign	World Week Report, 1977
United Kingdom	
Job satisfaction, Satisfaction with the company, Participation in decision making.	Nicholson et al., 1977 b
Satisfaction with a) pay b) promotion c) supervision d) work itself and e) co-workers	Nicholson et al., 1976 Nicholson et al., 1977 b
Work Unit Size, Sex	Kerr et al., 1951
Overtime	Buch and Shimmin, 1959; Gowler, 1969; Martin, 1971
Unemployment Level	Behrend, 1951 and 1953; Crowther, 1957
Tenure of Service	Nicholson and Goodge, 1976; Nicholson et al., 1977 a
Family Size, Marital Status	Nicholson and Goodge, 1976
Travel Distance	Hill, 1967; Martin, 1971; Nicholson and Goodge, 1976
Financial Responsibility	Buch and Shimmin, 1959

* This table is based on Rhodes, S. R. and Steers, R. M.
Summary Tables of Studies of Employee Absenteeism
(Technical Report No. 13, University of Oregon, 1977)

the most influential theme in absenteeism research has been to consider it as a form of withdrawal behavior. According to this hypothesis it is assumed that an employee stays away from his job because of unmet expectations. It is the dissatisfaction with the job which is responsible for absence on the part of the employee. Job satisfaction is, therefore, negatively related to, and is considered as one of the most important determinants of, absenteeism. Earlier reviews of the literature (Brayfield & Crockett, 1955; Herzberg et al., 1959; Porter & Steers, 1973) supported the withdrawal model of absenteeism. An overemphasis on this model is perhaps one of the most important reasons for the lack of studies focusing on extra-organizational factors.

The withdrawal model of absenteeism has been recently criticised. Nicholson et al. (1976) have discussed the reasons for the popularity of the belief in this hypothesis among social scientists as well as managers. They have also analyzed 29 studies and their own data taken from 16 different organizations to show that the concept of absenteeism as a "pain reductive" response is "naive, narrow and unsupportable" (p. 735). Similarly Muchinsky (1977) showed that out of 32 relationships between various factors of satisfaction and absenteeism, only 18 are negative (in support of the hypothesis), 13 are insignificant and one reverse i.e., positive. Other later empirical studies also show a similar trend (Ilgen & Hollenback, 1977; Dittrich & Carrell, 1979; Cheloha & Farr, 1980; Spencer & Steers, 1980; Watson, 1981).

It can be clearly seen that such an approach to understand the causes of absenteeism has no place for extra-organizational factors. The role of the needs of an employee should be given due emphasis in research, but it should not be limited to intra-organizational factors. The immediate work environment is not independent of the organizations's external environment. Similarly, an employee's needs and their satisfaction is not dependent only on his relationship to the organization. This assumption is a very narrow interpretation of Maslow's (1954) theory of needs. As pointed out by Nicholson et al. (1976), the assumed relationship between job satisfaction and absenteeism is influenced by "Human Relations school's oversimplistic prescriptions" (p. 728). Even if it is possible to obtain empirical support for this concept of absenteeism, it may not necessarily hold true in all cultures. The importance attached to various needs is highly influenced by culture (Slocum et al., 1971; Schaupp, 1978), specially when a comparison is made between industrially advanced and developing nations. In developed countries a worker may attach higher importance to his job, and his expectations from life may center around it. Developed countries or western culture encourage achievement (McClelland, 1961) while traditional societies emphasize affiliation (Kakar, 1971). In other words, for an employee in a traditional society, social relationships outside the organization may be as important as his job.

A broader view of absenteeism should include the cultural or environmental factors. The present study suggests a "dual commitment" model to explain absenteeism. It assumes that absenteeism does not always arise out of frustration from unmet expectations. It is not always a negatively motivated behavior. To be absent from work may be a positively motivated decision, influenced by an employee's commitments outside the organization, independent of his commitment to the job or the organization. It may be a result of approach-approach conflict rather than an avoidance behavior.

An employee's extra-organizational commitments may be social or financial in nature. Part of his financial and social needs may be fulfilled by the job and the organization, but the other part is fulfilled by the social and cultural environment. The model is explained further through focusing on Indian workers as an example.

India is fast developing as an industrialized country, but at the same time it inherits from the past a traditional society. The phenomenon of industrialization is changing the life pattern of the average person.

The workers in large Indian organizations, specially, manufacturing organizations, are usually from rural or traditional families, with the minimum required or no education. They are an integral part of the their family together with being members of formal or informal groups in the organization. They have high commitments to their families (which means more than wife and children, including parents, brothers, sisters and sometimes even cousins or distant relatives), for various reasons: a) The family has a highly stable structure with its own sources of income in the form of business or agricultural land; b) the cultural and social relationships are developed and maintained by the family and not by the person himself. The family provides a worker with high financial security. It is something on which he can always depend, with or without a job. In case the worker's pay is sufficient for meeting only routine expenses, the family finances may help to celebrate special occasions like birthdays, festivals etc., more lavishly. Often the worker may be drawing finances from the family source of income for routine expenses too. If the work place is far away from the town of the permanent or family home of the worker, often the worker's wife and children may be staying, permanently or temporarily spending months, at the permanent home where the expenses are borne by the head of the family. This suits the worker financially and otherwise. He makes

occasional trips to the home town during the holidays and
other occasions. Irrespective of being near or far from the
family, a worker will like to be considered as one of its
active members. He would like to take part in the efforts
of the family in carrying out the agricultural activity or
the business, irrespective of the fact that his wife and
children are living with him or with his parents or
relatives in the home town. This does not only make him
eligible for taking monetary help in the hour of need, but
it also ensures inheritance of the family property or land
at a later stage. This link is a reminder of his claim to
such assets, lest he is forgotten and his claims are
ignored. The family encourages this kind of arrangement. A
worker's participation in the family business or
agricultural activity is possible by absenting from the
organization for the required period of time, even if it is
more than his sanctioned leave. A worker in such cases
would absent himself from the organization, irrespective of
his being satisfied or dissatisfied with the job or the
organization. In fact, in many cases, the worker does not
have many expectations from the job or organization. The
job may be sometimes a source of supplementing the family
income, but the prime motivation for having a job in the
organization may be social benefits.

The job, for a worker in the organization, may mean an
elevated social status for himself and for the family in
the community. The people in the community may look upon it
as a worthwhile occupation and it may be a distinction for
the person to work for an organization. It means the source
of the person's esteem is still the community of which,
through his family, he is an integral part. The community
needs the presence of this person on every important social
occasion, including marriages and festivals. The reasons
for absence from his job for a worker could also be the
social demands by the community on his time. The worker
respects these demands for fear of social ostracization and
for the desire to expect reciprocal participation of others
in his family functions. This is a social reality for him.

The "dual commitment" model may apply to a variety of
situations. The nature of the socio-cultural environment
may chanage across different cultures. In western
countries, the extra-organizational commitments may be
different from those in developing countries. But in any
case, there can be extra-organizational commitments for an
employee, which are attractive enough to result in
absenteeism. When it is assumed that an employee withdraws
from the organization, it is by no means necessary to look
for reasons within the organization. The reasons may also
be located in the outside environment. Therefore, it is
worthwhile to explore the socio-cultural environment for an
understanding of the causes of absenteeism. The present
empirical study was conducted within the framework of this

"dual commitment" model.

EMPIRICAL STUDY

The empirical study reported here was conducted in a medium-sized process industry near Delhi in India. The organization was facing the problem of absenteeism, in spite of the fact that the service conditions offered by it were much more attractive than those offered by other industrial organizations around the area. Therefore it was necessary to make a comprehensive study of the causes of high absenteeism rates. Informal discussions with the supervisors and workers led to the belief that investigating personal and organizational factors may not reveal the real causes of absenteeism. It pointed out a need to include extra-organizational factors.

Since Delhi has climatic extremes and the nature of work in the organization required considerable amount of manual labor, it was considered necessary to explore some of the physiological factors. Personal and organizational factors which had been shown through empirical research to be related to absenteeism were also included in the study. Thirty-one factors included in the study were classified under the following five categories: (a) Physiological factors; (b) Personal factors; (c)Job content factors; (d) Job environment factors; and (e) Extra-organizational factors.

METHODOLOGY

The Sample: The sample of the study was drawn from male blue-collar workers of a medium-sized process industry near Delhi. The total number of workers in the organization was 1450, out of which an initial sample of 252 workers was drawn through random sampling methods. On the basis of attendance records of these 252 workers a final sample of 128 workers was drawn, which consisted of the following two groups, as per the criteria defined below:

Poor workers (N = 64) – These workers were absent from duty for 12% or more of the scheduled working days during any two of the three preceeding years. This group of workers was thus away from work more than its leave entitlement.

Regular workers (N = 64) – These workers were present on duty for 90% or more of the scheduled working days during any two of the three preceeding years. This group of workers was thus away from work during a year for fewer days than entitled to by the leave rules.

Method of Data Collection: The records of the workers as

maintained by the organization were the first source of data. The number of days of absence and leave, gross earnings, overtime earnings and past medical history at the time of joining were some of the indices directly taken from the official records. Other factual and attitudinal data was collected through interview method. This method was adopted in view of the low literacy level of the workers who were not expected to respond to a questionnaire. The interviews were based on a pre-designed schedule consisting of multiple choice type structured questions. Some dummy questions were also included to camouflage the basic purpose of the study. No direct reference was made to absenteeism either in the schedule or verbally during the interview. The interviews were conducted by two "management trainees" who were on training with the organization for a period of two months during the summer vacation from an academic institution where they were studying. In an effort to establish the reliability of the information obtained through interviews, the two interviewers were asked to interview the same five workers. Since there was no possibility of deriving a summated score on the basis of the interview schedule, and hence quantitatively calculating the reliability, a comparison of responses was made between the data obtained by the two different interviewers. The difference between the responses of the five workers did not exist in respect to the factual questions, while in case of attitudinal questions the difference did not go beyond one response category.

ANALYSIS, RESULTS AND DISCUSSION

The data was collected from two groups of workers defined above as "Poor" and "Regular" in attendance, and was initially coded in the form of contingency tables. Tetrachoric Correlation Coefficients were calculated (Guilford & Fructer, 1973, p. 303) which are given in Table II, with their level of significance (Guilford & Lyons, 1942). Table II also gives the number of respondents for each factor. Even though the final sample used in the study was 128, the response for each factor was not available for all the respondents.

Physiological Factors: Past medical history of a worker related to any major illness or ailment reported by him at the time of recruitment. Chest expansion, blood pressure and pulse rate, weight and height were taken at the time of recruitment. Body weight and height ratios were calculated according to medical norms and the deviations from these norms were used for the purpose of analysis.

Chest expansion and pulse rates are positively related to absenteeism rates. The expectation was that chest expansion would indicate a good physique and would be

324

TABLE II

Tetrachoric Correlation Coefficients between
Physiological, Personal, Job Content, Job
Environment and Extra-organizational
Factors and Absenteeism

	FACTORS	N	r_t
Physiological Factors			
1.	Past Medical History	65	-.185
2.	Chest Expansion	102	+.376*
3.	Blood Pressure	108	-.185
4.	Body Weight and Height Ratio	110	-.505**
5.	Pulse Rate	109	+.335*
Personal Factors			
6.	Age	118	-.195
7.	Tenure of Service	118	+.270*
8.	Education	118	-.115
9.	Family Size	112	+.225
10.	Additional Family Liabilities	118	+,035
11.	Personal Savings	118	-.050
Job Content Factors			
12.	Skill Level	118	+.295*
13.	Perceived Physical Effort	118	-.165
Job Environment Variables			
14.	Difficulty in Securing Leave	116	-.105
15.	Fake Medical Certificate Submission	114	.225
16.	Fairness in Disciplinary Action	117	-.205
17.	Job Security	116	-.425**
18.	Intention to Stay	118	+.035
19.	Knowledge about the Organization and its Products	106	-.325
20.	Relatives Employed in the Organization	118	-.505**
21.	Mode of Payment[a]	118	.755[b]**
22.	Overtime Earnings	118	-.405**
23.	Gross Earnings	118	-.405**
24.	Side Occupation Income	118	+.215
Extra-Organizational Factors			
25.	Size of Agricultural Land	118	+.335*
26.	Extent of Help Given in Agricultural activity	78	+.335
27.	Income from Agricultural Land	75	+.295
28.	Community[a]	113	.485[b]**
29.	Degree of Urbanization	116	+.205
30.	Distance from Permanent Home	118	-.215
31.	Transport Facility	118	-.145

* p < .05
** p < .01
a See text for categories used
b Direction of relationship not shown

negatively correlated with absenteeism. The results can not
be easily explained. It is however understandable that the
pulse rate is positively associated with absenteeism.
Higher pulse rates may indicate anxiety which has been
found to be positively related to absenteeism in other
empirical research (Sinha, 1963; Bernardin, 1977). Body
weight and height deviation from medical norms is
negatively correlated with absenteeism. It means that those
who have normal ratios are higher on absenteeism. It is
again difficult to advance a logical explanation for this.
Maybe the nature of the work requires a person to be more
"weighty" than normal under existing weather conditions.
This is not an explanation but only an hypothesis for
further research. Again the direction of deviation has not
been taken into account. It is possible that by avoiding
confounding between positive and negative deviations the
true relationship can be studied.

There is no empirical research on physiological
factors available to provide a direct comparison with the
findings of this study. This category of factors seems to
be neglected in absenteeism research. The results of the
present study, however, indicate it to be a promising area
for further investigation in the case of heavy manual jobs
in unfavourable weather conditions.

Personal Factors: From six personal factors only tenure of
service is significantly correlated with absenteeism. The
correlation coefficient is positive. Even though there is
some empirical support for this finding it is contrary to
expectations, and contradicts the results of a number of
research studies. Most of the research studies have used
the explanation given by Hill and Trist (1955) for positive
relationships between tenure and absenteeism, even though
there is no empirical proof of it. According to them,
tenure gives the opportunity to a worker to learn the
"absence culture". The present study shows that skill
level, as one of the job content factors, is also
positively related to absenteeism. It seems that as a
worker spends more years in the organization he develops
confidence in his abilities and employability elsewhere,
and therefore he can afford to absent himself from the
organization. A positive relationship between skill level
and absenteeism supports this explanation. Another
explanation may be the increasing monotony of the job with
increasing years of experience. This assumption is
supported by the fact that samples used in some of the
studies showing a positive relationship, including the
present study, consist of blue collar workers (Hill &
Trist, 1955; Martin, 1971; Baumgartel & Sobol, 1959) while
a number of studies which show a negative relationship
(Metzner & Mann, 1953; Waters & Roach, 1971 & 1973;
Bernardin, 1977; Garrison & Muchinsky, 1977; Spencer &
Steers, 1980) used samples of white collar workers. It is

expected that blue collar jobs induce higher absenteeism in accordance with the research findings that task repetitiveness is positively related to absenteeism (Killbridge, 1961). The relationship between absenteeism and tenure is, however, inconsistent (Muchinsky, 1977) and unstable (Fitzgibbons and Moch, 1980).

The assumption that financial liabilities directly or indirectly exert pressure on the individual to avoid absenteeism is, by and large, proved to be wrong. Factors like family size, additional family liabilities and personal savings are not related to absenteeism. However, a negative relationship between paying rent for living accommodation and absenteeism supports the assumption.

Age and education are not related to absenteeism. Both of these factors are supposed to raise expectations of reward from the organization (Steers & Rhodes, 1978). Age has yielded mixed results, while education is not found to be related to absenteeism in other empirical research in female while collar workers (Waters & Roach, 1971 & 1973; Weaver & Holmes, 1972).

Job Content Factors: Skill level is positively related to absenteeism, which is a finding in contradiction to many other research studies (Baumgartel & Sobol, 1959; Isambert-Jamati, 1962; Waters & Roach, 1971 & 1973; Herbiniak & Roteman, 1973; Garrison & Muchinsky, 1977). Like tenure, skill level perhaps makes the person more confident of his employability outside the organization. In fact, acquiring a certain skill level may induce a person to look outside the organization for better opportunities. Higher absenteeism may only be a prelude to leaving the organization.

Lack of relationship between perceived physical effort and absenteeism is perhaps indirect evidence against the withdrawal model which assumes that it is the work situation which drives a person away from the job. Indirect empirical support is provided for the present findings by lack of relationship between satisfaction with physical conditions of work and absenteeism (Waters and Roach, 1971 & 1973).

Job Environment Factors: Job security, relatives as co-workers, mode of payment, overtime and gross earnings are all negatively correlated with absenteeism. But other job content factors are not related to absenteeism.

There are no studies available directly showing a relationship between job security and absenteeism, but research on tenure has indicated that absenteeism is higher among short service employees (Baumgartel & Sobol, 1959; Behrend, 1959; Knox, 1961).

Job security should lead to higher commitment to the organization which, in turn, should reduce absenteeism. But the present findings show that both intention to stay and knowledge about the company and products are not significantly related to absenteeism. However, another similar factor, "relatives employed in the organization", has a significant negative correlation with absenteeism. But relatives working in the organization is not the same as satisfaction with co-workers, which has been shown to be negatively related to absenteeism among similar samples (Metzner & Mann, 1953; Nicholson et al., 1976; Nicholson et al., 1977b). Some of these workers include those who helped their relatives to get employment with the same organization, thereby earning for the workers higher esteem in the family. For those workers who get jobs through such influence, the security of the job is higher. Both types of workers should have positive attitudes towards the organization.

The other job environment factors which are negatively related to absenteeism are financial. Gross earnings are negatively related to absenteeism in the present study, even though earlier research largely shows a lack of relationship between these variables (Steers & Rhodes, 1978 p. 397). There are studies showing that overtime earnings are positively related to absenteeism (Gowler, 1969; Martin, 1971), but our results show a negative relationship.

A positive relationship between overtime and absenteeism has been interpreted to be rewarding absenteeism. This assumption is perhaps not true for our sample. For Indian workers, money is important, as shown by the negative relationship between the mode of payment and absenteeism. In this factor, two types of wage rates were compared. One, type A, included wages either on "per day" basis or on the basis of "group output", while the other, type B, was based on piece work by the individual. The correlation coefficient is highly significant, indicating low absenteeism to be associated with type A. It shows clearly that an individual wants a more secure and safer wage system rather than a risky system. This may be a highly culturally biased phenomenon. McClelland (1961) has shown that Indians are low on need achievement.

Side occupation income as a factor is not found to be related to absenteeism, contrary to the expected positive relationship. There are reasons to believe that a number of respondents did not want to disclose the fact of having a side occupation.

Extra-organizational Factors: The size of agricultural land owned by the family and the extent of help given in

328

agricultural activity are negatively related to absenteeism. These factors are, as such, interrelated. Since a number of workers belonged to families with agricultural land, it was hypothesized that a worker would take time off from work to help in agricultural activities. The assumption that the reasons for helping the family could also be financial is not however supported, because there is no relationship between the income from agricultural land and absenteeism. There are two reasons for this. Firstly, the help in agricultural activity is given because of the social rather than the monetary value attached to the relationship between the worker and the family. Secondly, the assessment of income from land by the worker can hardly be accurate. The material benefits from agricultural activity, for example, living expenses of the wife and children and expenses at special occasions, are not easily quantifiable. In all such cases the worker does not directly receive money. If the total financial benefit from the family to the worker is calculated, the relationship with absenteeism may come out to be positive and significant.

The community is defined by the Caste System. Different communities are represented in the employees of the organization. For our analysis we included a special community A (name of communities are omitted) and other communities forming group B. The community A was compared with others specially in view of their customs. Members of this community are supposed to perform some rituals in social and religious functions. This role is a symbol of prestige and cannot be allowed to be drifted away to other communities. It also means money apart from social significance. The relationship between absenteeism and membership in this community is significant. A higher number of members of this community A form the "poor" attendance group, or in other words have higher absenteeism.

CONCLUSIONS

The empirical study shows that physiological, job environment and extra-organizational factors are prominently related to absenteeism. The person, financial rewards and his socio-cultural environment provide the main determinants of absenteeism. From among these, physiological and socio-cultural factors have been conspiciously neglected in absenteeism research, presumably because of heavy pre-occupation of researchers with the job satisfaction-absenteeism hypothesis. The "dual-commitment" model suggested in this study derives support from empirical results. But further research, focusing on socio-cultural factors relevant to a given culture, needs to be done. It is suggested that such research need not necessarily be promoted at the cost of research on other determinants of absenteeism, including job satisfaction. A balanced approach in order to understand the causes of absenteeism must be followed.

Absenteeism research across various cultures should be promoted. For this purpose, standardized indices of measuring absenteeism and reliable and valid questionnaires to ascertain the causes of absenteeism must be developed. Dissemination of absenteeism research within and across cultures also needs to be improved.

REFERENCES

Alexander, R.A., Barrett, G.V., Bass, B.M., & Ryterband, E.C. Empathy, Projection and Negativism in Seven Countries. Technical Report No. 35 (Corrected). Rochester, N.Y.: Management Research Center, University of Rochester, August, 1970.

Barrett, G.V. & Franke, F.H. Communication Preference and Performance: A Cross-Cultural Comparison. Technical Report No. 29. Rochester, N.Y.: Management Research Center, University of Rochester, August, 1969.

Barrett, G. V. & Ryterband, E.C. Cross-Cultural Comparisons of Corporate Objectives on Exercise Objectives. Paper presented at 76th annual convention, American Psychological Association, September, 1968, San Francisco, California.

Bass, B.M. A Preliminary Report on Manifest Preferences in Six Cultures for Participative Management. Technical Report No. 21. Rochester, N.Y.: Management Research Center, University of Rochester, June, 1968a.

Bass, B.M. When Planning for Others. Technical Report No. 20. Rochester, N.Y.; Management Research Center, University of Rochester, 1968b.

Baumgartel, H. & Sobol, R. Background and organizational factors in absenteeism. Personnel Psychology, 1959, 12, 431-443.

Behrend, H. Absence under Full Employment. Monograph A3. Birmingham, England: Birmingham Studies in Economics and Society, University of Birmingham, 1951.

Behrend, H. Absence and labour turnover in changing economic climate. Occupational Psychology, 1953, 27, 69-79.

Behrend, H. Voluntary absence from work. International Labour Review, 1959, 79, 109-140.

Bernardin, H.J. The relationship of personality variables to organizational withdrawal. Personnel Psychology, 1977, 30, 17-27.

Brayfield, A.H. & Crockett, W.H. Employee attitudes and employee performance. Psychological Bulletin, 1955, 396-424.

Cheloha, R.S. & Farr, J.L. Absenteeism, job involvement and job satisfaction in an organizational setting. Journal of Applied Psychology, 1980, 65, 467-473.

Dittrich, J.E. & Carrell, M.R. Organizational equity perceptions, employee job satisfaction, and departmental absence and turnover rates. Organizational Behavior and Human Performance, 1979, 24, 29-40.

Farmer, R.N. & Richman, B.M. A model for research in comparative management. California Management Review, 1964, 7, 55-68.

Fitzgibbons, D. & Moch, M. Employee absenteeism: A multivariate analysis with replication. Organizational Behavior and Human Performance, 1980, 26, 349-372.

Garrison, K.R. & Muchinsky, R.M. Attitudinal and biographical predictors of incidental absenteeism. Journal of Vocational Behavior, 1977, 10, 221-230.

Gowler, D. Determinants of the supply of labour to the firm. Journal of Management Studies, 1969, 6, 73-95.

Guilford, J.P. & Fruchter, B. Fundamental Statistics in Psychology and Education. New York: McGraw-Hill, 1973.

Guilford, J.P. & Lyons, T.C. On determining reliability and significance of a tetrachoric coefficient of correlation. Psychometrika, 1942, 7, 243-249.

Haire, M., Ghiselli, E.E. & Porter, L.W. Managerial Thinking: An International Study. New York: John Wiley, 1966.

Hammer, T.H. & Landau, J. Methodological issues in use of absence data. Journal of Applied Pschology, 1981, 66, 574-581.

Heller, F.A. & Porter, L.W. Perceptions of needs and skills in two national samples. Occupational Psychology, 1966, 42, 1-13.

Herbiniak, L.G. & Roteman, R.M. A study of the relationship between need satisfaction and absenteeism among managerial personnel. Journal of Applied Psychology, 1973, 58, 381-383.

Herzberg, F. The motivation to work among Finnish supervisors. Personnel Psychology, 1965, 18, 392-402.

Herzberg, F., Mausner, B. & Synderman, B. The Motivation to Work. New York: John Wiley, 1959.

Hill, J.M. & Trist, E.L. Changes in accidents and other absences with length of service. Human Relations, 1955, 8, 121-152.

Ilgen, D.R. & Hollenback, J.H. The role of job satisfaction in absence behavior. Organizational Behavior and Human Performance, 1977, 19, 148-161.

Isambert-Jamati, V. Absenteeism among women workers in industry. International Labour Review, 1962, 22, 431-444.

Kakar, S. The theme of authority in social relations in India. Journal of Social Psychology, 1971, 84, 93-101.

Killbridge, M. Turnover, absence and transfer rates as indications of employee dissatisfaction with repetitive work. Industrial and Labour Relations Review, 1961, 15, 21-32.

Knox, J.B Absenteeism and turnover in an Argentine factory. American Sociological Review, 1961, 26, 424-428.

Lazarus, S. & Barrett, G.V. National Clusters of Manager's Life Goals. Technical Report No. 44. Rochester, N.Y.: Management Research Center, University of Rochester, 1970.

Martin, J. Some aspects of absenteeism in a light engineering factory. Occupational Psychology, 1971, 45, 77-91.

Maslow, A. Motivation and Personality. New York: Harper and Row, 1954.

McClelland, D.C. The Achieving Society. New York: Free Press, 1961.

McClelland, D.C. Motivating Economic Achievement. New York: Free Press, 1969.

Metzner, H. & Mann, F. Employee attitudes and absences. Personnel Psychology, 1953, 6, 467-485.

Muchinsky, P.M. Employee absenteeism: A review of literature. Journal of Vocational Behavior, 1977, 10, 316-340.

Negandhi, A. R. & Eastafen, B.D. A research model to determine the applicability of American know-how in differing cultures and/or environments. Academy of Management Journal, 1965, 8, 309-318.

Nicholson, N., Brown, C.A. & Chadwick-Jones, J.K. Absence from work and job satisfaction. Journal of Applied Psychology, 1976, 61, 728-737.

Nicholson, N., Wall, T. & Lischeron, J. The predictability of absence and propensity to leave from employee's job satisfaction and attitudes towards influence in decision making. Human Relations, 1977b, 30, 499-514.

Porter, L.W. & Steers, R.M. Organizational, work and personal factors in employee turnover and absenteeism, Psychological Bulletin, 1973, 80, 151-176.

Sadler, P.J. & Hofstede, G.H. Preferences and perceptions of employees of an international company in different countries. Mens en Onderneming, 1972, 26, 43-63.

Schaupp, D.L. A Cross-Cultural Study of a Multinational Company: Attitudinal Responses to Participative Management. New York: Praeger Publishers, 1978.

Simonetti, S.H. & Weitz, J. Job satisfaction: Some cross-cultural effects. Personnel Psychology, 1972, 25, 107-118.

Sinha, A.K.P. Manifest anxiety affecting industrial absenteeism. Psychological Reports, 1963, 13, 258.

Sirota, D. & Greenwood, J.M. Understanding your overseas work force. Harvard Business Review, 1971, 49, 53-60.

Slocum, J.W. Jr., Topichak, P. & Kuhn, D. A cross-cultural study of need satisfaction and need importance for operative employees. Personnel Psychology, 1971, 24, 435-445.

Smulders, G.W. Comments on employee absence/attendance as a dependent variable in organizational research. Journal of Applied Psychology, 1980, 65, 368-371.

Spencer, D.G. & Steers, R.M. The influence of personal factors and perceived work experiences on employee turnover and absenteeism. Academy of Management Journal, 1980, 23, 567-572.

Steers, R.M. & Rhodes, S.R. Major influences on employee attendance: A process model. Journal of Applied Psychology, 1978, 63, 391-407.

Thiagarajan, K.M. & Deep, S.D. A Cross-Cultural Study of Preferences for Participative Decision making by Supervisors and Subordinates. Technical Report No. 33. Rochester, N.Y.: Management Research Center, University of Rochester, September, 1969.

Waters, L.K. & Roach, D. Relationship between job attitudes and two forms of withdrawal from work situation. Journal of Applied Psychology, 1971, 55, 92-94.

Waters, L.K. & Roach, D. Job attitudes as predictors of termination and absenteeism: Consistency over time and across organizations. Journal of Applied Psychology, 1973, 57, 341-342.

Watson, C.J. An evaluation of some aspects of the Steers and Rhodes model of employee attendance. Journal of Applied Psychology, 1981, 66, 385-389.

Weaver, C.N. & Holmes, S.L. On the use of sick leave by female employees. Personnel Administration and Public Personnel Review, 1972, 1, 46-50.

Yadov, V.A. The Soviet and American worker. Soviet Life, January, 1965.

DIMENSIONS OF NATIONAL CULTURES IN FIFTY COUNTRIES AND THREE REGIONS

G. Hofstede

Institute of Research on Intercultural Co-operation, Delft

In my book "Culture's Consequences" (Hofstede, 1980), I have analysed paper-and-pencil scores on questions about values, by employees of subsidiaries of one large multinational business corporation in 40 countries. The questions were part of an employee attitude survey cycle that took place twice, once in the period 1968-'69 and once in 1971-'73. The total survey material consisted of over 116,000 questionnaires in 20 languages, but for the country comparison I used about 31,000 questionnaires from the 1967-'69 survey round and 41,000 from the 1971-'73 round. The number of respondents per country varied from 37 (Pakistan) to 4691 (France) in 1967-'69 and 58 (Singapore) to 7907 (Germany) in 1971-'73. In 1967-'69, six countries were missing entirely (Hong Kong, Portugal, Singapore, Taiwan, Thailand, and Yugoslavia); in 1971-'73, four other countries were missing (Chile, India, Italy, and U.S.A.). See Hofstede (1980: 411). So 30 countries were actually surveyed twice.

Calculating four indices for forty countries

From one country to another, I compared matched samples of employees in seven different occupations, giving equal weight to each occupational category, regardless of the actual number of respondents in it. The occupations were two categories of managers, two categories of college-level professionals, two categories of skilled technicians, and one category of administrative personnel (op.cit.: 73). I only used the data for an occupational category if there were at least eight respondents in it. I only used the data from a country if at least four occupational categories reached this minimun of eight respondents in at least one of the two survey rounds (1967-'69 or 1971-'73). Missing data were extrapolated from

the available data according to a set of extrapolation
rules based on minimum expected error (op.cit.: 73). In
this way, I could use the data from 40 countries having
larger subsidiaries of the multinational corporation.

The purpose of my analysis was to explore the
structure of consistent differences in mean values scores
among countries. For each values question considered, I
therefore computed a mean score for each country (following
the matching procedure for respondents described above). I
averaged between the 1967-'69 and 1971-'73 survey rounds. I
did this after testing whether the ranking of country mean
scores on the question concerned was sufficiently similar
in both survey rounds, that is, whether the country
differences proved stable over this time . If not, I
eliminated the question (op.cit.: 74). I was finally left
with 32 values questions for which I had mean scores on my
40 countries. I factor analysed the 32 variables, 40 cases
matrix and, after orthogonal rotation it yielded three
factors, together explaining 49% of the variance in mean
values among countries. I call this an ecological factor
analysis because it uses the mean scores of countries as
variables and not the scores of individual respondents.

The three factors found corresponded to dimensions of
differences among countries, which I had identified before
in an eclectic way and by theoretical reasoning. In fact,
my earlier eclectic analysis of the data had yielded four
dimensions, of which two were intercorrelated so that they
loaded on the same factor in the ecological factor
analysis. For good theoretical reasons (see below), I kept
treating them as two separate dimensions.

The four dimensions which I found in the country mean
values scores for the 40 countries are the following:

Power Distance, that is the extent to which the members of
a society accept that power in institutions and
organizations is distributed unequally.

Uncertainty Avoidance, that is the degree to which the
members of a society feel uncomfortable with uncertainty
and ambiguity, which leads them to support beliefs
promising certainty and to maintain institutions protecting
conformity.

Individualism, which stands for a preference for a loosely
knit social framework in society in which individuals are
supposed to take care of themselves and their immediate
families only; as opposed to Collectivism, which stands for
a preference for a tightly knit social framework in which
individuals can expect their relatives, clan, or other
in-group to look after them, in exchange for unquestioning
loyalty.

336

<u>Masculinity</u>, which stands for a preference for achievement, heroism, assertiveness, and material success; as opposed to <u>Femininity</u>, which stands for a preference for relationships, modesty, caring for the weak, and the quality of life. In a masculine society, even the women prefer assertiveness (at least in men); in a feminine society, even the men prefer modesty.

Each of the forty countries has been given an Index score on each of the four dimensions. The Index scores for Power Distance and Individualism are negatively correlated (r = -.67) and these are the two dimensions that load on the same ecological factor. They deal, however, with conceptually different issues (inequality versus the degree of integration of individuals with others). Both dimensions are correlated (with opposite signs) with the national wealth of the countries. If we control for national wealth, Power Distance and Individualism are no longer correlated. This justifies maintaining them as separate dimensions.

Although the four dimensions were found by comparing the values of matched respondents within the same multinational organization, in my book I have been able to validate them against about 40 other quantitative studies of values and value-related indices across countries, by other researchers on other material (op.cit.: 326-329), so I consider them as valid indices of elements in the national culture of at least the middle classes in these countries. They touch upon basic issues facing any human society and to which a society has found its own answers from a range of possibilities (Inkeles and Levinson, 1969: 447; Hofstede, 1980: 47).

If this is true, it should be of great interest to expand this research in order to cover countries not included in the list of forty, and eventually to arrive at a world-wide atlas of work-related value systems. However, data on the values of matched samples of respondents across a number of countries are hard to get at.

<u>Expanding the data base to fifty-three units</u>.

The most obvious source of additional data was the employee attitude survey data bank of the multinational corporation that supplied the initial data. It contained data for 67 different country codes (Hofstede, 1980: 62) of which 27 had been excluded for not meeting the minimum criterion of at least eight respondents for at least four out of seven particular occupational categories in at least one survey round. This minimum criterion had been chosen arbitrarily but on the basis of traditional data reliability considerations: it led to a minimum sample size for the smallest country of 58. If a population can be considered homogeneous as to the phenomena studied, a sample of 50 provides reasonable reliability which hardly improves if we increase the sample further. However, samples below 50 are not immediately unreliable. In a detailed study (Hofstede, 1975:16) I showed that the rank correlation of two sets of scores on 15 values (work goals) in a two-week test-retest-stability experiment attained a minimum of .75 with samples of 10 respondents, .88 with 20 respondents, .97 with 30, and .98 with 62. As what we are interested in are the relative scores of values, this suggests that samples of about 20-30 respondents can still be used. I therefore went back to the multinational corporation data bank to look at the 27 countries initially excluded. Their number of respondents are listed in Figure 1.

It unfortunately turned out that the tapes at the "HERMES" corporation containing the original data were lost. Hardcopy output data books were available with answer distributions for categories of employees with eight or more respondents. For the smaller subsidiaries, only few occupational categories reached this minimum (also including some not used in the original analysis); however, there was always a country total data print out with all categories of employees added. An exception were the Arab-speaking countries of the Middle East for which the data book with the 1967-'69 survey round data was lost entirely; only regional totals, not subdivided by country but subdivided by occupational categories, were available in another data book. For the African countries, besides country data (often with very few respondents), East African and West African regional totals were also available. Figure 1 shows, besides the number of respondents, the numbers of employee categories for which data were available.

The selection of the countries for further analysis was made on the basis of:

(1)   the number of respondents;

(2)   the number of survey rounds for which data were available - two preferred over one;

(3)   the number of separate categories for which data were available - every category allowing an independent estimate of the country's cultural dimension scores.

Based on these three criteria, I decided to perform the additional analysis for ten countries (the numbers 1 through 10 in Figure 1) and for the three regions: Arab-speaking countries, East Africa, and West Africa. I did try to retrieve the data for a number of the other countries but they usually had to be based on a single

Figure 1
Data in the "HERMES" data bank not used in the first analysis

Country	Code	Total respond-ents	1967 - '69		1971 - '73	
			Respond-ents	Cate-gories	Respond-ents	Cate-gories
1. Uruguay	URU	133	86	5	46	4
2. Guatemala	GUA	99	68	4	31	2
3. Indonesia	IDO	91	43	3	48	4
4. Panama	PAN	81	56	2	25	2
5. Costa Rica	COS	75	52	3	23	3
6. Equador	EQA	73	42	3	31	3
7. Jamaica	JAM	73	44	2	29	2
8. Malaysia	MAL	72	27	1	45	1
9. El Salvador	SAL	70	43	1	27	1
10. South Korea	KOR	56	-	-	56	5
11. Honduras	HOD	25	-		25	1
12. South Vietnam	VIE	24	-		24	2
13. Trinidad	TRI	22	-		22	1
14. Ghana	GHA	21	-		21	2
15. Dominican Republic	DOM	20	-		20	1
16. Nicaragua	NIC	20	-		20	1
17. Bolivia	BOL	19	-		19	1
18. Zambia	ZAM	19	-		19	1
19. Nigeria	NIG	17	-		17	1
20. Neth. Antilles	NAT	16	-		16	1
21. Kenya	KEN	12	-		12	1
22. Bahamas	BAH	8	-		8	1
23. Lebanon	LEB	*	*		23	1
24. Kuwait	KUW	*	*		11	1
25. Lybia	LYA	*	*		10	1
26. Egypt	EGY	*	*		-	-
27. Iraq	IRQ	*	*		-	-
Regions (country combinations):						
Arab-speaking countries (Egypt, Lebanon, Lybia, Kuwait, Iraq, Saudi-Arabia, United Arab Emirates)	ARA	141	62	7	79	6
East Africa (Kenya, Ethiopia, Tanzania, Zambia)	EAF	46	-		46	4
West Africa (Ghana, Nigeria, Sierra Leone)	WAF	43	-		43	3

* Data tape and data books with individual country data were lost. Only data book with total region data (ARA) available.

Country codes correspond to Hofstede, 1980: 62

figure from a data book table with too wide a confidence interval to make sense. An additional problem in the small subsidiaries is the presence of expatriates among respondents. Responses were codified by country of location, not by the nationality of the respondents, so the answers by expatriates cannot be identified. However, in the larger subsidiaries the HERMES corporation employs virtually no expatriates, and even if there are a few their influence on the total sample will be numerically insignificant - like one foreigner in a group of fifty nationals. However, the small subsidiaries in the Third World countries employ expatriates for managerial and specialist jobs much more often; and, say, six foreigners in a group of twenty nationals do seriously affect the results.

So the decision was taken to add to the original forty countries ten more countries and three multi-country regions - which makes for a total of fifty-three units.

Data treatment and results

The data retrieval consisted of extracting from the data books (1), for each available category of employees, the answers for the questions that make up the four dimensions indices:

- 3 questions for the Power Distance Index (PDI; see Hofstede, 1980: 103);
- 3 questions for the Uncertainty Avoidance Index (UAI; see op.cit.: 164);
- 14 questions for the joint calculation of the Individualism Index (IDV) and the Masculinity Index (MAS; see op.cit.: 241).

The country scores in the original analysis of forty large subsidiaries were each computed as a mean of 2×7 occupational category scores (2 survey rounds, 7 occupations - see earlier in this paper). Missing data were relatively few and were made up by extrapolated estimates (op.cit.: 73). If a country participated in only one survey round, its country score was computed as the mean of 1×7 occupational category scores, but corrected with 0.5 of the mean shift on this question across all other countries, between the first and the second survey round.

For the present extension of the analysis, the need for extrapolation of missing data was much larger. Rather than $2 \times 7 = 14$ scores per question per country, there were at maximum 13 scores (ARA) but generally fewer than 7: for MAL and SAL there were only 2 each. For extrapolation, a table of "total world" data was used, which showed the "total world" means for each of the 7 occupational categories in each of the 2 survey rounds, as well as the mean of these 14 means. For each country, the available data were compared to the corresponding "total world" data; a mean difference between country data and corresponding "total world" data was computed; and this difference was added to or subtracted from the "total world" mean of means to arrive at the best estimate of the true country score.

The Power Distance Index (PDI) and the Uncertainty Avoidance Index (UAI) were simply computed from the country scores on 3 questions each according to their formulas. For the other two indices (IDV and MAS), a more complicated calculation was necessary. First, for each country, the scores for 14 questions (work goals, see op.cit.: 403-404, question A5-A18) had to be standardized, that is transferred into standard scores (distances from their common mean divided by their common standard deviation; op.cit.: 78, 80). The standard scores thus obtained had to be transposed into a new set of standard scores, using as a basis the work goals factor analysis for these 14 goals across the original 40 countries (op.cit.: 299). Then, the new standard scores had to be multiplied by IDV and MAS factor scores and added (op.cit.: 300). The sums were finally transposed into IDV and MAS scores through multiplying by 25 and 20, respectively, and adding 50 (op.cit.: 299).

Figure 2 lists the results of the computations. The new countries and regions have been added to the group of 40 countries analysed before. The countries (not the regions) have been ranked on each of the four dimensions, so that rank 1 = low, rank 50 = high. For the three regions, I show in Figure 2 the rank level at which they would fall in the 50-country table, but the regions have not participated in the ranking itself (after all, they are not countries).

Testing the validity of the newly added data

It can be tested relatively easily whether the new data fit the structure I found in the earlier 40-country data. For this purpose, I have first checked the Index score intercorrelations across 53 units versus 40 units (Figure 3).

The pattern of intercorrelations does not change at all. There remains a highly significant correlation between PDI and IDV (from -.67 to -.68) and weaker correlations between UAI and IDV, and UAI and PDI. The new data are, therefore, quite in line with the existing data, in spite of the fact that the four dimensions were derived from the original 40 countries' data alone.

Figure 2

Value of the four indices for fifty
countries (with rank numbers) and three regions

Country	Abbrev-iation	Power distance		Uncertainty avoidance		Individu-alism		Masculinity	
		Index	Rank	Index	Rank	Index	Rank	Index	Rank
Argentina	ARG	49	18-19	86	36-41	46	28-29	56	30-31
Australia	AUL	36	13	51	17	90	49	61	35
Austria	AUT	11	1	70	26-27	55	33	79	49
Belgium	BEL	65	33	94	45-46	75	43	54	29
Brazil	BRA	69	39	76	29-30	38	25	49	25
Canada	CAN	39	15	48	12-13	80	46-47	52	28
Chile	CHL	63	29-30	86	36-41	23	15	28	8
Colombia	COL	67	36	80	31	13	5	64	39-40
* Costa Rica	COS	35	10-12	86	36-41	15	8	21	5- 6
Denmark	DEN	18	3	23	3	74	42	16	4
* Equador	EQA	78	43-44	67	24	8	2	63	37-38
Finland	FIN	33	8	59	20-21	63	34	26	7
France	FRA	68	37-38	86	36-41	71	40-41	43	17-18
Germany (F.R.)	GER	35	10-12	65	23	67	36	66	41-42
Great Britain	GBR	35	10-12	35	6- 7	89	48	66	41-42
Greece	GRE	60	26-27	112	50	35	22	57	32-33
* Guatemala	GUA	95	48-49	101	48	6	1	37	11
Hong Kong	HOK	68	37-38	29	4- 5	25	16	57	32-33
* Indonesia	IDO	78	43-44	48	12-13	14	6- 7	46	22
India	IND	77	42	40	9	48	30	56	30-31
Iran	IRA	58	24-25	59	20-21	41	27	43	17-18
Ireland	IRE	28	5	35	6- 7	70	39	68	43-44
Israel	ISR	13	2	81	32	54	32	47	23
Italy	ITA	50	20	75	28	76	44	70	46-47
* Jamaica	JAM	45	17	13	2	39	26	68	43-44
Japan	JAP	54	21	92	44	46	28-29	95	50
* Korea (S.)	KOR	60	26-27	85	34-35	18	11	39	13
* Malaysia	MAL	104	50	36	8	26	17	50	26-27
Mexico	MEX	81	45-46	82	33	30	20	69	45
Netherlands	NET	38	14	53	18	80	46-47	14	3
Norway	NOR	31	6- 7	50	16	69	38	8	2
New Zealand	NZL	22	4	49	14-15	79	45	58	34
Pakistan	PAK	55	22	70	26-27	14	6- 7	50	26-27
* Panama	PAN	95	48-49	86	36-41	11	3	44	19
Peru	PER	64	31-32	87	42	16	9	42	15-16
Philippines	PHI	94	47	44	10	32	21	64	39-40
Portugal	POR	63	29-30	104	49	27	18-19	31	9
South Africa	SAF	49	18-19	49	14-15	65	35	63	37-38
* Salvador	SAL	66	34-35	94	45-46	19	12	40	14
Singapore	SIN	74	40	8	1	20	13-14	48	24
Spain	SPA	57	23	86	36-41	51	31	42	15-16
Sweden	SWE	31	6- 7	29	4- 5	71	40-41	5	1
Switzerland	SWI	34	9	58	19	68	37	70	46-47
Taiwan	TAI	58	24-25	69	25	17	10	45	20-21
Thailand	THA	64	31-32	64	22	20	13-14	34	10
Turkey	TUR	66	34-35	85	34-35	37	24	45	20-21
* Uruguay	URU	61	28	100	47	36	23	38	12
U.S.A.	USA	40	16	46	11	91	50	62	36
Venezuela	VEN	81	45-46	76	29-30	12	4	73	48
Yugoslavia	YUG	76	41	88	43	27	18-19	21	5- 6
Regions:									
* East Africa	EAF	64	(31-32)	52	(17-18)	27	(18-19)	41	(14-15)
* West Africa	WAF	77	(42)	54	(18-19)	20	(13-14)	46	(22)
* Arab Ctrs.	ARA	80	(44-45)	68	(24-25)	38	(25)	53	(28-29)

* New data

Figure 3

Correlations Among the Four Indices

Pair of indices	Across 40 countries [a]	Across 53 units
PDI x UAI	.28 * ***	.23 * ***
PDI x IDV	-.67	-.68
PDI x MAS	.10 *	.06 **
UAI x IDV	-.35	-.33
UAI x MAS	.12	-.03
IDV x MAS	.00	.08

a   From Hofstede, 1980: 316

Significance levels:

   * .   05-level
  ** .   01-level
 *** .   001-level

Secondly, I validated against external data. The highest correlation of any of the four Indices with any of a set of seven economic, geographic and demographic indicators is a .82 correlation between the Individualism Index IDV and national wealth (1970 GNP per capita; see op.cit.: 86, 330). Figure 4 shows a new plot of IDV against GNP/capita, for 50 countries (the corresponding plot for 40 countries is Figure 5.4 in op.cit.: 232). The regions have been left out because countries within the regions vary in GNP per capita. The correlation $r_{IDV,GNP}$ increases from .82*** for 40 countries to .84*** for 50 countries. The regression line rotates slightly: from IDV = .16 GNP + 24 to IDV = .18 GNP + 19 which means a clockwise rotation around a point IDV = 64, GNP = 250 (that is about the position of FIN). So the new data confirm and even reinforce the relationship between wealth and Individualism (op.cit.: 231 ff) which was a rather fundamental finding of the earlier study.

A final validation test is the clustering of the new data with the old. Figure 5 reproduced the "dendrogram" of the clustering of the forty countries according to their scores on the four indices together (Fig 7.11 in op.cit.: 334). Figure 6 is a new "dendrogram" of the fifty-three units(2)). Although the order of the clusters and of the countries within them shifts somewhat, the composition of the clusters remains largely the same. From the original 40 countries, only Iran (IRA) shifts from cluster 4 to cluster 5.

Figure 4. Individualism Index (IDV) versus
1970 national wealth (per capita GNP) for fifty countries

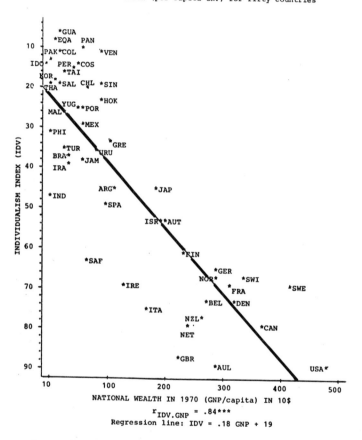

$r_{IDV.GNP} = .84***$
Regression line: IDV = .18 GNP + 19

For country abbreviations see Figure 2

Figure 5.   Cluster Analysis of 40 countries

PROGRAMME YHAK (H. Forst, Cologne and F. Vogel, Kiel)
DENDROGRAM, WARDS METHOD.   Variables: PDI, UAI, IDV, MAS

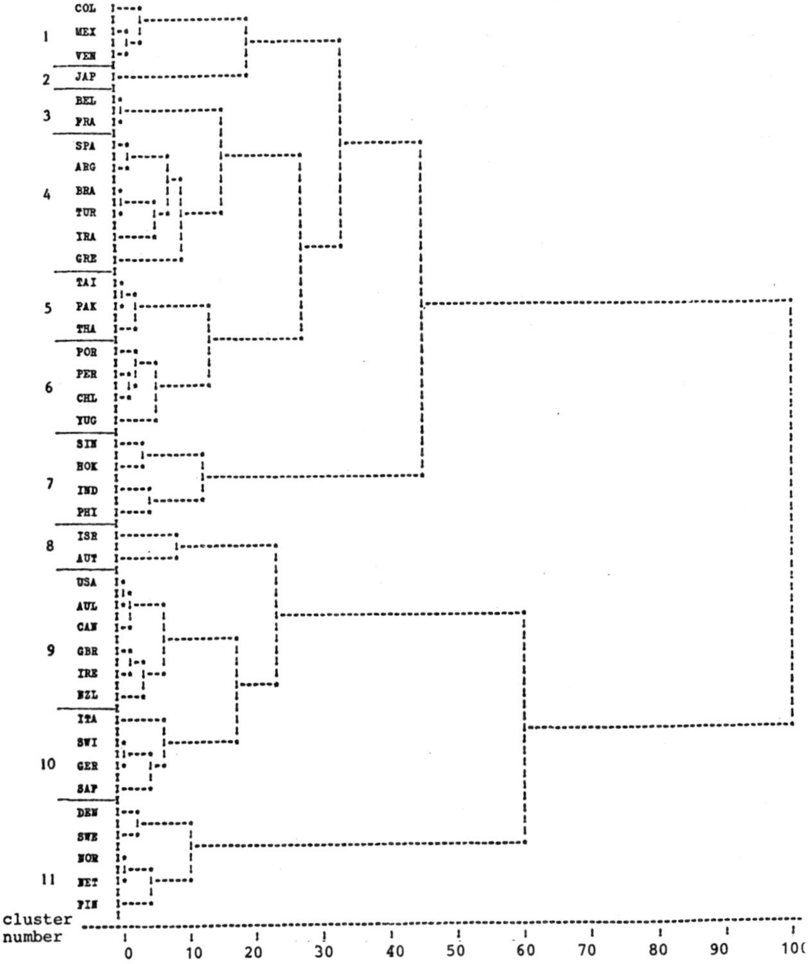

ERROR SUM OF SQUARES IN PER CENT OF TOTAL

For country abbreviations see Figure 2.

345

Figure 6. Cluster Analysis of 53 countries and <u>regions</u>

PROGRAMME YHAK (H. Forst, Cologne and F. Vogel, Bamberg)
DENDROGRAM, WARDS METHOD. Variables: PDI, UAI, IDV, MAS

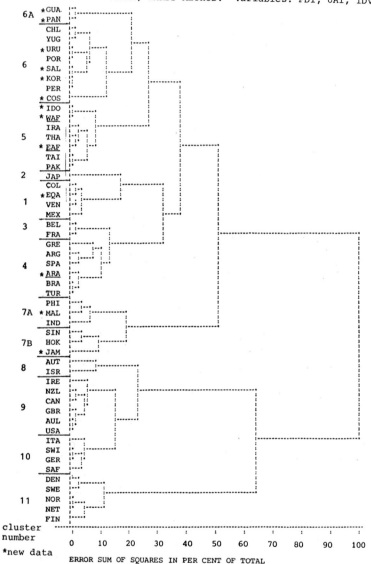

ERROR SUM OF SQUARES IN PER CENT OF TOTAL

For country abbreviations see Figure 2.

As far as the new units go:

- Equador joins neighbouring Colombia in cluster 1.
- The Arab-speaking countries join Turkey in cluster 4.
- Both East Africa and West Africa show up in cluster 5; so does Indonesia which thus joins the other Asian countries, Iran, Thailand, Taiwan and Pakistan (two Muslim, two Buddhist).
- The Central American countries, Guatemala and Panama, form a new cluster with as its closest neighbour cluster 6 which contains the other Central American countries, Salvador and Costa Rica, as well as Uruguay which joins Portugal, Peru and Chile. South-Korea does not show up with the other Asian countries but also joins cluster 6.
- The former cluster 7 splits into two parts; in one, Malaysia joins India and the Philippines; in the other, Jamaica shows up with Singapore and Hong Kong. All group 7A and 7B countries are former British or U.S. colonies.

In looking at these clusters it should be stressed again that the computer that made the clustering did not receive any input on the countries' geographical position and/or history; it clustered purely on the numerical value of the four index scores. Thus there are cases in which geographically/historically unrelated countries show up in the same cluster, like Brazil (BRA) and Turkey (TUR), but the remarkable thing is that this happens so seldom. The new data show also some examples of this (KOR, WAF, EAF), but again relatively few. The face validity of the clusters after adding the 13 new units (Figure 6) is as good as before (Figure 5).

The three validity tests used suggest that there is no reason to assume that the new data for 13 units are unreliable or invalid.

Discussion: culture patterns

The new data, and in particular their clustering in Figure 6, allow conclusions about culture patterns in a number of areas not, or less extensively, covered by my previous research: Latin America, the British West Indies, East Asia, Africa and the Arab World.

Latin America: data were obtained for four of the seven Central American states. From these, Costa Rica scores unexpectedly low on Power Distance (Figure 2: lower than any other Latin country). It nevertheless remains a marginal member of cluster 6, with El Salvador. In Figure 7 I have listed the Index scores for all 13 Latin American countries in my sample, with Portugal and Spain for comparison. They are remarkably close together on Uncertainty Avoidance (high score range 67-101), which fits with their common Catholic Christianity, and on

Individualism (very low to medium, score range 6-46). On Power Distance, except for the low score (35) of Costa Rica, they are also together (medium to high, score range 49-95). There is, however, a wide range across the Latin American countries on Masculinity (21-73). We see that the clustering of Latin American countries in Figure 6 (third column in Figure 7) is mainly based on differences in Masculinity. Cluster 6 and 6A are feminine clusters, cluster 4 is a medium cluster, and cluster 1 is a masculine cluster. The feminine countries tend to be the smaller ones (second column in Figure 7). This cultural trait may well have played a role in history (when the Latin American independence was established in the early 19th century) in causing these countries to remain separate and small, and vice versa smallness may have reinforced Femininity. I earlier showed Femininity to be associated with "small is beautiful" (op.cit.: 284, 292). In the feminine countries, we can expect sizable groups with sympathy for a welfare state which looks after the weak and poor. Historical events in Portugal, Uruguay, Peru and Chile and now in El Salvador bear this out. This orientation meets with little sympathy among the majority in the masculine U.S.A.

Figure 7   Index Scores of 13 Latin American Countries (in order of Masculinity Index Scores) compared to Portugal and Spain

Country	Population [a]	Cluster number [b]	Power Distance	Uncertainty Avoidance	Individualism	Masculinity
Costa Rica	2	6	35	86	15	21
Chile	10	6	63	86	23	28
Guatemala	5	6 A	95	101	6	37
Uruguay	3	6	61	100	36	38
Salvador	4	6	66	94	19	40
Peru	14	6	64	87	16	42
Panama	1	6 A	95	86	11	44
Brazil	93	4	69	76	38	49
Argentina	23	4	49	86	46	56
Equador	6	1	78	67	8	63
Colombia	22	1	67	80	13	64
Mexico	51	1	81	82	30	69
Venezuela	10	1	81	76	12	73
Portugal	10	6	63	104	27	31
Spain	34	4	57	86	51	42

[a] In millions, 1970 figures according to World Bank Atlas
[b] See Figure 6

The masculine countries, Equador, Colombia, Mexico and Venezuela, can be associated with "machismo" and "Marianismo" (op.cit.: 289). The origins of the differences in Masculinity in Latin America must be sought in history. Both Portugal and Spain score relatively feminine (Figure

7). The Latin American cultures were formed in the 16th century by a merger between native Indian cultures and Spanish-Portuguese settler cultures, strongly influenced by military and political events (Gibson, 1966: 135). Masculinity in Mexico may have been inherited from the Aztecs, while the Maya culture (Guatemala) and Inca culture (Peru) were probably more feminine.

The British West Indies: I only have data for Jamaica, which shows a unique configuration of values which I had not met yet: extremely low Uncertainty Avoidance, a Power Distance score which is low for a Third World country but an Individualism score which is high, and very high Masculinity. I would expect a similar pattern to show up for Barbados and the British Leeward Islands. With these, Jamaica shares a unique cultural past. Originally inhabited by Arawak Indians, Jamaica was colonized by Spain in 1509. The Spaniards started to import African slave labour to replace the Indians who were soon extinct. The British conquered the island in 1655 and drove out the Spaniards. They then imported African slaves on a large scale (Dunn, 1972: 165). Jamaica became independent in 1962, with a population of 2 million people of whom about 95% is of African descent. There is a romantic desire for return to Africa which finds its expression in the Rastafarian movement (Barrett, 1977: 81 ff).

Figure 8

Index Scores of Jamaica Compared to a Number of Other Countries and Regions

Country/region	Power Distance	Uncertainty Avoidance	Individu-dialism	Masculin-ity	Sum of Score difference with Jamaica
Jamaica	45	13	39	68	-
Great Britain	35	35	89	66	84
English America (Canada, U.S.A.)	40	47	86	56	98
West Africa	77	54	20	46	114
Spain	57	86	51	42	123
Spanish America [a]	70	86	20	48	137

[a] Mean of 12 countries: ARG, CHL, COL, COS, EQA, GUA, MEX, PAN, PER, SAL, URU, VEN

Figure 8 compares the Index scores of Jamaica to Great Britain, the other English American countries in my sample (Canada and U.S.A.), and to West Africa, from where the Jamaicans came. As a parallel, it also compares the scores of Spain to those of Spanish America. As a broad generalization we can conclude from Figure 8 that Jamaica

349

relates to Britain as Spanish America relates to Spain. If
we remember that national wealth relates to Power Distance
and negatively to Individualism and that both Jamaica and
Spanish America (on average) are much poorer than the
mother country, we can expect differences between ex-colony
and mother country on these two dimensions. Taking these
into account, we recognize in Figure 8 an "English culture"
configuration of low P.D., low U.A., high IDV and high MAS
versus a "Spanish culture" configuration of higher P.D.,
high U.A., lower IDV and (on average) lower MAS. The
comparison with West Africa in Figure 8 shows Jamaican
culture to be closer to British and English American
culture than to West African culture (right hand column).
On P.D. and IDV, Jamaica positions itself between Britain
and West Africa but this reflects its economic development
level; on the non-economically influenced dimensions of
U.A. and MAS, Jamaica is more like Britain than like West
Africa. The slaves, in spite of a highly exploitative
slavery system were culturally programmed by their masters
(Dunn, 1972: 151; Barrett, 1977: 216). The "Ethiopianism"
in Jamaica (desire for Africa, see Barrett, 1977: 68ff) is
not based on present-day cultural proximity.

Figure 9

Index Scores of 12 Asian countries (in order
of Uncertainty Avoidance Scores)

Country	Cluster number [a]	Power Distance	Uncertainty Avoidance	Individu- alism	Masculin- ity
Singapore	7 B	74	8	20	48
Hong Kong	7 B	68	29	25	57
Malaysia	7 A	104	36	26	50
India	7 A	77	40	48	56
Philippines	7 A	94	44	32	64
Indonesia	5	78	48	14	46
Iran	5	58	59	41	43
Thailand	5	64	64	20	34
Taiwan	5	58	69	17	45
Pakistan	5	55	70	14	50
South Korea	6	60	85	18	39
Japan	2	54	92	46	95

[a] See Figure 6

East Asia: the countries added to the list are South
Korea, Malaysia and Indonesia. In Figure 9, I summarize the
Index scores for 12 Asian countries (all except those near
the Mediterranean). The 12 countries are relatively close

together on Individualism (low to medium, score range
14-48), and Power Distance (medium to high, score range
54-104). The range is wider on Masculinity but this is
mainly due to Japan; except for Japan (95) the score range
is 34-64 which is much closer than we find for the Latin
American counties. There is, however, a very wide range
among Asian countries on Uncertainty Avoidance, from 8
(Singapore, rank number 1) to 92 (Japan, rank 46) In the
cluster analysis of Figure 6, the Asian countries are
divided over 5 clusters (second column in Figure 9) and it
is evident from Figure 9, that the clustering follows in
fact the Uncertainty Avoidance scores (unlike in Latin
America where we saw in Figure 7 that it follows the
Masculinity scores). Again unlike Latin America, Asia is
very heterogeneous in terms of religion and philosophy,
with Islam (Sunni and Shia), Buddhism (Theravada and
Mahayana), Hinduism, Taoism, Shinto, Confucianism,
Zoroastrianism, and Christianity (Catholic and various
kinds of Protestantism). Religion and Uncertainty Avoidance
are related (Hofstede, 1980: 181).

The Chinese city states and (ex-) British colonies,
Singapore and Hong Kong, show the lowest Uncertainty
Avoidance but high Power Distance: an extreme "family"
model of organizing (op.cit.: 319) with centralized
personal authority but few rules: a highly flexible,
pragmatic, opportunistic value system. This fits with the
Chinese tradition of management by wisdom but without
abstract principles and without a system of law
(Fitzgerald, 1966: 130). The next in order of U.A. are
Malaysia, India and Philippines, with very high Power
Distances and not as collectivist as most other Asian
countries.

The religious composition of their populations is
mixed and there is no dominant state religion. Indian
Hinduism is particularly undoctrinaire. Again the "family"
model of organizing prevails. Being larger and politically
more complicated than the Chinese city states, these
countries are more bureaucratic. The next and largest
cluster contains the Muslim states of Iran and Pakistan,
predominantly Muslim Indonesia, and Buddhist Thailand and
Taiwan. These countries tend to show somewhat lower Power
Distances but are (except Iran) extremely collectivist and
more feminine than most of the previous countries. Islam is
an uncertainty avoiding religion, although not as much as
Catholic Christianity. Buddhism is more uncertainty-
avoiding than Hinduism. The Collectivism in these countries
probably has older cultural roots than Islam or even
Buddhism, being rooted in the very ancient family culture
of these countries. It is remarkable that Pakistan scores
quite differently from India: more equalitarian (lower
P.D.), more collectivist, more uncertainty avoiding. Both
countries stem from the same base population of the Indian

subcontinent; whether the Pakistani values were instilled by Islam or whether the subgroups with those values adopted Islam is a matter of speculation. The most feminine-scoring country is Thailand. Thai boys learn not to fight back to a brutish opponent (Benedict, 1946: 147). Taiwan, formerly part of China, nevertheless scores much higher on Uncertainty Avoidance than Singapore and Hong Kong. It is possible that Singapore and Hong Kong really reflect a subculture of migrant Chinese traders under British colonial conditions, while a complex society with agricultural roots like Taiwan reflects a different subculture, less flexible and more bureaucratic. In this case, China itself can be expected to score more like Taiwan. Or, Taiwan's period of occupation by Japan (1895-1945) can have played a role.

Highest on Uncertainty Avoidance are South Korea and Japan, the former collectivist and rather feminine, the latter half-way towards Individualism and highly masculine: the samurai ethic (Befu, 1971: 32). There is an extensive literature on Japan, less on Korea. The Uncertainty Avoidance in Japan is not so much expressed in religious behaviour. Japanese are great borrowers of foreign ideas, scientific as well as religious, although the Japanese version of e.g. Buddhism is so far from its Chinese model to be almost unrecognisable (Moore, 1967: 294). Claiming absolute truth for an idea is not the Japanese way. However, the Japanese in their social settings fear the unforeseen, the unexpected: they strive for a thoroughly known world (Benedict, 1946: 27, 28, 286). They partly achieve predictability through a rigid system of ranking people (more rigid than in China: see Nakane, 1973: 30). They are uncomfortable abroad (op.cit.: 141 ff), even if their foreign business is successful.

Extraordinary economic success is reported not only for Japan but now also for Singapore, Hong Kong, Taiwan, and South Korea. It appears that with different levels of Uncertainty Avoidance, East-Asian societies can be equally successful under the present world conditions. Economics has no explanation why East-Asian countries are so successful, whereas, for example, Latin American countries, starting from a similar or even more favourable economic base line, remain stagnant. A cultural or mixed economic/cultural explanation is much more promising, as the Newly Industrializing Cultures of the Far East all share certain cultural influences, for example from Buddhist religion and Confucian philosophy. These do not mean, however, one single culture pattern for all these countries: Figure 9 shows a variety of culture patterns on the four dimensions. Exactly what in given culture patterns leads to economic success under the present circumstances demands more research.

Africa and the Arab world: the new data are at the bottom of Figure 2. The clustering in Figure 6 places both African regions with a number of Asian countries and the Arab-speaking countries with Levantine Greece and Turkey. Uncertainty Avoidance is fairly low in Africa while Power Distance is higher which again suggests a "family" model of organizing, combined with strong Collectivism and moderate Femininity. The Arab region shows medium Uncertainty Avoidance (like other Islamic countries) and quite high Power Distance, medium Individualism and a middle position on the Masculinity/Femininity scale. Between the Arab countries and Israel, there is a wide gap on Power Distance; on the other dimensions, they are not too far apart.

Discussion: Methodological issues

The expansion of the data base has shown that even with numbers of respondents as low as about 40, country data were generated that have good face validity and satisfy various tests about their fit into the structure of the existing data. The framework of four dimensions has held up as a meaningful reference frame for interpreting differences in measured values among countries. The data added have contributed to our insight into communalities and differences of value patterns in different parts of the world, like in Latin America and East Asia.

There remain, however, large areas on the map not covered by the present research. Firstly, the Eastern European countries other than Yugoslavia; then, China itself; then other African countries, so that a more detailed map of African values can be drawn. Out of the "HERMES" questions I have extracted a "Values Survey Module" (Hofstede, 1980: 419-422; now available in an improved 1982 version) which can be used in surveying other samples of respondents. I have already received data from Chinese managers, and data from managers and professionals in Ivory Coast are forthcoming. The problem is that these samples are obviously not matched with the original "HERMES" samples so that it is difficult to find out what part of the score differences found are due to occupation and organization effects and what part to nationality. It is better, if possible, to duplicate the research on matched samples of respondents on several (at least 2) countries, at least one of which is also in the HERMES set, so that the new data can be "anchored" to the existing ones. With "anchored" data, I hope to expand towards the goal of a world-wide atlas of work value systems.

NOTES

(1) The extraction and data handling were done by Mr. Albert Lonink; the data processing by the computer department of Twijnstra Gudde International, management consultants.
(2) Produced again through the kind help of Professor Dr. Klaus Brockhoff of Kiel University and his computer staff.

REFERENCES

Barrett, L. 1977 The Rastafarians: Sounds of Cultural Dissonance. Boston: Beacon Press.

Befu, H. 1971 Japan: An Anthropological Introduction. Tokyo: Charles E. Tuttle.

Benedict, R. 1946 The Chrysanthemum and the Sword: Patterns of Japanese Culture. New York: New American Library.

Dunn, R.S. 1972 Sugar and Slaves: the Rise of the Planter Class in the English West-Indies, 1624-1713. New York, W.W. Norton & Company.

Fitzgerald, C.P. 1966 A Concise History of East Asia. Harmondsworth Mddx., England: Pelican.

Gibson, C. 1966 Spain in America. New York: Harper Colophon.

Hofstede, G. 1975 The Stability of Attitude Survey Questions, in Particular Those Dealing with Work Goals. Working Paper 75-45 Brussels: European Institute for Advanced Studies in Management.

Hofstede, G. 1980 Culture's Consequences: International Differences in Work-Related Values. Beverly Hills CA.: Sage.

Inkeles, A. & Levinson, D.J. 1969 "National Character: The Study of Modal Personality and Sociocultural Systems". In G. Lindzey and E. Aronson (Eds.), The Handbook of Social Psychology, Second Edition, Vol. 4. Reading MA.: Addison-Wesley, 418-506.

Moore, C.A. 1967 "Editor's Supplement: The Enigmatic Japanese Mind". In C.S. Moore (Ed.), <u>The</u> <u>Japanese</u> <u>Mind</u>: <u>Essentials</u> <u>of</u> <u>Japanese</u> <u>Philosophy</u> <u>and</u> <u>Culture</u>. Tokyo: Charles E. Tuttle, 288-313.

Nakane, C. 1973 <u>Japanese</u> <u>Society</u>. Harmondsworth Mddx., England: Pelican.

INTERPERSONAL CONSTRUCT SYSTEM AND WORK STYLES OF INDIAN MANAGERS

U. Kumar

Indian Institute of Technology, Kanpur

S. B. Saxena

H. A. L. Bangalore

One of the issues which continues to evoke and sustain interest among social scientists is that of understanding and predicting managers' style of functioning in an organization. In the early phase of problem development, leadership studies, especially effective leadership styles, provided some guidelines for it. Democratic and participative styles were generally considered desirable, an endorsement which reflected the tacit influence of the researcher and the subjects' belief systems about how people ought to act. Nonetheless, many elaborations and refinements of leadership styles have emerged from more recent studies where interactive aspects of the person, situation, and task factors have been taken into account.

Cognitive theorists were not long in bringing out studies on attitudes and values and their impact on executive styles. For instance, Guth and Tagiuri (1965) presented a number of examples and case studies illustrating ways in which personal values influenced choices of corporate strategies. Graves (1970) tried to justify the signifiance of studying the value system on the ground that it influenced managers' perceptions of people, situations and problems.

The importance of developmental experiences for later distinctive styles was not lost on social learning theorists or psychoanalytically inclined psychologists. For instance, Runyon (1973) studied the interaction between management styles and employee personality by assuming that generalized expectancies are acquired through early reinforcements. Psychoanalytically inclined theorists were quick to observe the comparability between ego's management apparatus within the personality and the manager's attempt at managing the external environment. Managerial styles were the outcome of the ego's processes regulating the exchange between the inner and the outer worlds of the individual. Thus a focus on the managerial styles became a focus on the interface between the internal and the external worlds. The quality and characteristics of this exchange in the adult understandably had its genesis in the developmental experiences during the formative years (Zaleznik, 1966).

Addressing himself to the same issue, England (1968) developed a theoretical model for predicting managerial behaviour by elaborating the differential impact of value sub-systems. Simultaneously, empirical studies (Haire, Ghiselli & Porter, 1966; Negandhi & Prasad, 1970) noting the variation in the styles of managers in different countries gave an additional complexity to the belief value hypothesis.

In addition, cultural theorists noted the impact of developmental patterns and organizational structural constraints which accompanied differences in culture (Khandwalla, 1980).

Statement of the Problem:

In presenting a paradigm of relationship in the Indian setting, Kumar and Singh (1978) proposed a typology of behaviour patterns with possible implication for managers. They proposed a construct system of the manager which was defined as his "interpretative system" (Kelly, 1955) employed to give meaning to the events in the world.

In developing their viewpoint, they suggested that early socialization experiences of the Indian child in the Hindu joint family led him to develop two major constructs for interpreting and predicting people-related events. These constructs were labelled as a sense of identification with and belonging to the family and a sense of obligation to it. The identification-with-family construct labels people as close, similar and belonging to the same group. These people are perceived as one's own in that one relates to them closely and responds to them with concern. Nurturance and warmth underlie such interpersonal relationships. The other category groups those people together who are outside the inner circle of one's affection. They are placed in one's life space but there is usually little or no sense of belonging or kinship feeling for them.

The obligation constuct elicits a sense of personal indebtedness and responsibility to behave in the socially expected ways with people. This indebtedness legitimizes a highly personalized ethics in relationships. This is the template of the personal, one of the poles of the

357

obligation construct in which the actor relates to other on the basis his personal orientation of what he can expect from and give to the other. The contrasted end of the construct is the impersonal pole. Herein, in the absence of emotional gratitude and obligations, it is a sense of duty which dictates relationships. There is a compulsion to do what is dictated by tradition and a feeling of binding to discharge one's duty.

The combination of the above dichotomized constructs yielded a four-fold typology of constructs regarding people. By allowing perceptual and interpretive differentiation this typology helps classify people in four categories (Table 1).

TABLE 1

Dominant Pattern of Anticipation in Human Interactions

Sense of Obligation

		Personal	Impersonal
		Personal own	Impersonal own
Sense of Family Identification	Own	Familial behaviour	Role behaviour
		Group 1	Group 2
		Personal other	Impersonal other
	Other	Supportive behaviour	Explorative behaviour
		Group 4	Group 3

According to the authors, dominant responses expected in each category were as follows:

Personal Own (Group 1)
Responses expressing responsibility, nurturance, unconditional belonging, dependency and emotional attachment. Dominant mode of interaction: familial behaviour.

Personal Other (Group 2)
Responses expressing adherence to a mutually accepted code of ethics and a binding to do one's duty, irrespective of personal likes or dislikes. Dominant mode of interaction: conventional behaviour.

Impersonal Other (Group 3)
Responses in this category are undifferentiated. The existing situation determines the nature of interactions. Dominant mode of interaction: exploratory/undifferentiated behaviours.

Impersonal Own (Group 4)
Responses displaying expressive behaviour, mutual liking and respect unencumbered by a sense of duty. Dominant mode of interaction: supportive behaviour.

With this frame of reference in view, the major question was then just this: Can one predict the management styles of Indian managers on the basis of their identification-with-the-family and their sense of obligation. With the delineation of dominant styles of relating to people, it seemed appropriate to extend these categories to the Indian manager's place of work where distinct relationships with authority, peers and subordinates appeared to be a realistic arena for validating these assumptions.

Thus the independent variables selected for the study were the two major constructs, namely, the sense of identification-with-the-family and the sense of obligation. Operationally, sense of obligation was treated as a person-non-person orientation. It was the dimension of non-instrumental versus impersonal concern for the other. The former implied very personal relationship while the latter focussed on the functions of the other in the relationship.

The dependent variables were four management styles each associated with one of the four groups. It was proposed that:

(i) The Personal Own Group with dominance on familial behaviour would display paternalistic/power oriented style. It would be characterized by strong, firm, protective orientation coupled with personal power to punish and reward subordinates and a demand for personal loyalty and obedience from them.

(ii) The Personal Other Group with dominance on conventional behaviour would display role/bureaucratic style in organizations. This comprised impersonal but correct behaviours related to responsibilities and duties of the position. Power would be exercised through the enforcement of standards and procedures and respect for contracted obligations.

(iii) The Impersonal Other Group with undifferentiated behaviours would display task orientation. With no predisposition to regard people in any specific manner, they would be guided by the demands of the situation more than by their own compulsions. The behaviours thus expressed would focus on skill, competence and commitment to the organization.

(iv) The Impersonal Own Group with supportive behaviour as dominant behaviour would respond to the needs and values of others with an equally strong commitment to their growth and development. These individuals were likely to further those collaborations which were personally satisfying and stimulating.

These propositions were put to an empirical test in the study.

METHOD

This study had a two-by-two experimental design.

1. Sample:

Out of the 90 managers who returned the mailed questionnaire only 80 managers were selected for the study. Majority of the subjects (N=60) were employed by the government owned aeronautical industry located in different parts of the country. The remaining 20 managers were drawn from another large comparable government enterprise engaged in the production of heavy electrical machinery.

The mean age of these 80 middle level managers mostly professionally qualified engineers (76.2%) was 38 years (+/- 8.87) years. Scientists, finance and personnel managers made up the remaining number. The salary scales of two organizations were comparable placing these managers in the professional middle class category.

2. Measures:

(a) Family Identification and Belongingness Questionnaire (FIBQ) This questionnaire was specially constructed to assess the intensity of the respondent's attachment and his identification with the family. Only fifteen items were considered in the final version. It contained items such as "children should be trained to develop strong emotional bonds with the members of the family" and "one can be closer to friends than to the members of one's family".

These items elicited agreement or disagreement on a four point scale. The items were controlled for a response bias and social desirability. The higher the score, the higher the identification and belongingness expressed toward the family. Using the Cronbach (1941) formula the reliability coefficient of this scale was 0.955.

(b) People Orientation Scale (POS) This questionnaire, also specially constructed for the study, consisted of 15 items measuring respondents' degree of gratification derived from relating to people. Items, such as, "when free, I like to spend my time alone" and "I like to do things with people rather than by myself" were included. Subjects recorded their agreements or disagreements as true or false. A reliability coefficient of 0.997 was obtained by using the Cronbach formula (1941).

(c) Managerial Styles Questionnaire (MSQ) This questionnaire instructed the respondents to rank four statements which characterized their management style from the most true to the least true as represented by each statement. The scale consisted of fifteen items and the ranking preferences were always between "authority", "role", "task", "self growth" styles of management. For instance, the following set of statements represents one such group of choices presented to the managers for purposes of ranking.

A good member of the organization gives first priority to:

(i) Personal demands of the boss   authority

(ii) Duties, responsibilities and
requirements of his role and
to the customary standards
of personal behaviour   role

(iii) Requirements of the task for
skill ability, energy and
material resources   task

(iv) Personal needs of the
individuals involved   self growth

This questionnaire was given under two other instructional sets as well. These sets required the respondents to state their organization's preference (as perceived by them) and their own ideological preference for each style. Thus three sets of information were finally available on this questionnaire, namely, manager's characterization of his own style in day-to-day functioning, his statement of personal ideology and finally, his perceptions of his organization's preference for these. Rank preferences were obtained on all three sets.

3. Procedure:

Two hundred and seventy booklets each comprising five questionnaires presented in a counterbalanced order were mailed to the heads of division in the two companies with a covering letter from the Dean R. & D., requesting these heads to distribute these to their managers. The managers were instructed to mail their questionnaires directly to the researchers. Ninety questionnaires were returned in time to be considered for the study.

On the basis of the scores obtained on the FIBQ and the POS, only 80 managers qualified to represent the four classifications of managers. Four subgroups were identified on the basis of the two median scores which provided the cut-off points for this fourfold classification.

On the measures of dependent variables, for each instructional set, the rank preferences for each style were given weights and aggregated over all items for the final score. The highest first preference alternative was considered as the dominant style and the weighted aggregate of ranks was considered the most representative style of the manager.

RESULTS

I. Procedural Checks on Assumptions

Correlation coefficients between managers' scores on the FIBQ and the POS was near zero ($r = -0.044$). Thus the assumption that these two questionnaires assessed different psychological dimensions of the managers was confirmed. The validity of these questionnaires was accepted at the face value of the items.

The classification of managers into four categories on the basis of their median scores on the FIBQ and POS was further analysed to ascertain if any relationship existed between other sociological demographic factors and the four subgroups. Significant differences were observed between managers of groups 2 and 4 ($t = 2.63$; $p < .05$) and between those in groups 3 and 4 ($t = 2.65$; $p < .05$). In both cases, the managers in group 4 were younger than the other group by four to eight years. The mean age of group 4 managers was 34 years +/- 7.91. This difference in age was accordingly reflected in differences in length of work experience as well.

II. Chi-Square Analysis of Dominant Ranks Assigned to Styles on the Managerial Style Questionnaires.

   Managers' responses on the MSQ were analysed separately for each of the three instructional sets, which elicited organizational ideology, manager's personal belief system and manager's patterns of behaviour manifested in his day-to-day functioning in the organization. With the number of first preferences accorded to each of the styles two chi-square analyses were computed to ascertain differences, if any, between the groups and within a group. Tables 2 and 3 present the findings obtained on three MSQ sets.

TABLE 2

Differences within a group for first preferences of allocated styles on three instructional sets on MSQ

	Organization Ideology		Managers Ideology		Perception of practice	
	Chi-Value	Signi-ficance	Chi-Value	Signi-ficance	Chi-Value	Signi-ficance
Group 1	4.4	NS	4.8	NS	23.8	.001
Group 2	7.60	NS	13.20	.01	34.2	.001
Group 3	5.00	NS	7.00	NS	19.4	.001
Group 4	6.00	NS	6.00	NS	8.2	.05

TABLE 3

Differences between groups on four styles of managements

	Organizational Ideology		Managers Ideology		Perception of practice	
	Chi-Value	Level of signi-ficance	Chi-Value	Level of signi-ficance	Chi-Value	Level of signi-ficance
Power	5.8	NS	4.8	NS	23.8	.001
Role	7.6	NS	13.2	.01	34.2	.001
Task	5.0	NS	61.6	.001	19.4	.001
Growth	6.0	NS	10.8	.02	8.2	.05

(A) <u>Organizational Ideology</u>:

The dominant view expressed by the manager provided the data for analyses. On both analyses, that is, differences between groups in styles and differences in styles in a group, no significance was obtained. The managers, it is thus assumed, did not perceive their organizations professing any dominant ideology by giving distinct priority to any particular pattern of behaviour.

(B) <u>Individual Belief System</u>:

The chi-square values were significantly different between groups in the first preferences assigned to three managerial styles, namely, role, task and self growth. No differences appeared between groups on power. Differences in style within a group appeared only in group 2 where role/bureaucratic style was predominant. No significance was observed within the remaining three groups.

(C) <u>Self Perception of Style</u>:

It was in this set that all analyses were significant. Significant chi-square values were obtained on all four styles when group differences were computed. Significant differences were also obtained between styles within a group. The hypotheses stated earlier were thus confirmed. These results confirmed the anticipated findings.

III. <u>Chi Square for Weighted Preferences Aggregated on Style</u>.

Computing chi-square values from weighted frequencies not only reconfirmed some of the earlier findings obtained from the analysis of dominant priority but also revealed additional findings (see Table 4). Differences in style between t and within the groups pointed to organizational preferences for role/bureaucratic style ($=16.82$, p ` .001, df=3). Style was consistently perceived to be the least preferred organizational style.

On manager's personal viewpoint about desirability of styles, differences between groups now also included power style ($=14.28$, p`.001, df=3).

On the self description of styles, again all computations were significant, even more so than obtained on the predominant response analysis.

Briefly then, these results revealed an overall emphasis on bureacratic/role style in the ideology of the organization and indicated a clear correspondence between the personal belief system and the practice of certain styles for a particular group. On the whole, the

TABLE 4

Aggregated weighted style preferences of managers.

Style	Group 1			Group 2			Group 3			Group 4		
	MSQ_1^a	MSQ_s^b	MSQ_3^c	MSQ_1	MSQ_2	MSQ_3	MSQ_1	MSQ_2	MSQ_3	MSQ_1	MSQ_2	MSQ_3
P	53	50	71	44	35	34.5	55	28	35	54	32	43
R	61	54	40	63	66	87.5	54	53	60	60	46	52
T	52	60	47.5	61	65	53.5	54	70	69	48	60	62
S	27	36	27.5	32	34	24.5	26	42	36	35	62	45

$^a MSQ_1$ = Organization Ideology

$^b MSQ_2$ = Manager's Ideology

$^c MSQ_3$ = Manager's perception of his own actions

self-growth style was least preferred ideologically by the organization in all groups, but ideologically preferred along with task orientation by group 4 managers only. Generally, the ideological preference of managers was basically for task orientation for all four groups with an additional bias for bureaucratic style by group 2 and self-growth by group 4. Self-description of style varied in each group as expected despite organizational ideological priority for role/bureaucratic styles.

DISCUSSION

The purpose of eliciting managers' perceptions of organizational "ideology" regarding styles was mainly to ascertain conditions in which the managers worked. Habibullah & Sinha (1980) found meaningful patterns between management styles and climate factors, suggesting an existence of a state of partially balanced reciprocal relationship between the climate of an organization and the use of leadership styles. Therefore, obtained condition of uniformity among managers in this respect provided a useful measure of control.

A clear agreement among managers in attributing role/bureaucratic style as the preferred one is not an unexpected finding. The managers were drawn from the government managed organizations. Moodie (1968) observed that Brahmanical culture of India and the value system of the British civil administrators were so alike that it was inevitable for bureaucratic values to be deeply entrenched in the functioning of the government.

Curiously enough the belief systems of managers were differentiated enough from their perceptions of their organizational ideology to give distinct preference to task orientations, with additional bias for role/bureaucratic functioning for Personal Other group and for self growth style for Impersonal Own group.

In the characterization of their day-to-day styles of functioning, significant differences clearly emerged in the direction anticipated by the study.

Personal Own Group

This group, differentiated on the basis of high belongingness to family and high person orientation, characterized itself unequivocally as practising power oriented style. It is stereotypically considered to be the leadership style of managers in India (Meade, 1967; Barrett and Bass, 1970) where cultural idealization of authority (Kakar, 1971) is undefensively accepted. It is this style that Negandhi and Prasad's study (1971) on management practices found most prevalent in the Indian organizations studied by them.

This power oriented style had particular usage here. It is not equated with the obverse of democratic functioning nor is it authoritarian in the conventional use of the term. It is paternalistic, wherein it is assumed that the activities of the subordinates are very much like those of children and they must be strictly watched over. It is more akin to authoritative style which is characterized by firm control and benign concern.

Personal Other Group

These managers were classified on the basis of high family identification and impersonal obligation in dealing with people. Taylor (1948), commenting upon the Hindu social organization, stated:

"Hindu joint family discourages decision of any matter of importance by the individual himself and puts a premium on conformity. So deeply is this attitude ingrained that an orthodox Hindu normally feels that a decision taken on his personal responsibility is likely to be ipso facto wrong. It, therefore, tends to prevent the development of habits of personal decision as core of character formation (p. 5)."

Due to this emphasis on traditions and convention, management style is likely to depend upon rules and regulations. There is a strong cultural support for power being vested in the position and not in the person. Such managers usually administer by interpreting procedures and regulations. Operating on the basis of convention, managers may take cover under precedence and rules.

This group's uniformity in responses, preferring bureaucratic/role style for all three questionnaires, namely, organizational ideology, personal ideology and characterization of personal styles in practice, possibly indicates an undifferentiated use of the constructs to fit diverse situations.

Impersonal Other Group

These managers, classified on the basis of low scores on both joint family and person orientations, characterized themselves as task oriented. One assumes that both these factors enable such individuals to arrange conditions of work which minimize feeling and attitudes. Such individuals acknowledged and engaged people but at the level of task directed activity rather than personality and feelings (Zaleznik, 1966). Since ego rewards to task oriented individuals related to work performance and gratification from achievement, it offsets limited gratification from warmth and friendship of work associates. However, the ego weakness of this type of manager centred around the need to defend themselves against displays of intimacy in others and their own deep-rooted passive wish for such an intimacy, that occasionally emerges in their own personality (Zaleznik, 1966).

Impersonal Own Group

Low family identification and high people orientation managers did not fully support the hypothesis on dominant set of responses but received support when aggregated responses were considered.

It was conjectured that high people orientation made them invest their effort and find gratification in relating to people. They look for supportive environment and learn from others in achieving their goal. Argyris (1964) also pointed out that self fulfilment could be achieved by receiving information on feedback from others as to how they saw them, and how they affected them. Furthermore, their low bonds of attachment to family and to tradition facilitated exploration beyond their surroundings.

The responses of this group of managers were variable. The rationale underlying the classification of this group needs to be reconsidered in the light of the above finding. In the present study there is no way to know how the age factor, on which these managers differed from two other groups, affected the findings. Jaggi (1978) reported relationship between length of work experience and styles of management in his study.

Briefly, the significance of this study lies in the easy identification of styles which managers are likely to manifest in an organization. Fairly reliable predictions about managerial behaviours can be made from feelings of family belongingness and a sense of obligation.

Even though this study is recognised to be a preliminary effort at validating some propositions of a conceptual framework (Kumar and Singh, 1978), nevertheless, there is adequate evidence that the constructs of sense-of -family-identification and sense of obligation may well become reliable predictors of Indian managers' behaviour patterns in work organizations. This study thus underscores that there is a need to understand the Indian styles of management in the Indian context so that we grasp what Khandwalla stated as "Management in our backyard."

Further research in the area needs to focus on other related factors and in incorporating refinement of methodology. The self perceived attributes of the managers become more meaningful if supported by objective criteria.

368

Also developmentally, some empirical relationship between the variables of early experience and later management styles will substantiate the premise which led to the formulation of these constructs.

This study has cross cultural implications for research. The two constructs in the study seem to rest on the foundation of rural society where family and kin relationships have dominance and where low social and occupational mobility confine people to a limited geographical areas (Kumar and Singh, 1978). It may be useful to test if some similarities exist in later functioning as managers in these cultures where rural and urban affiliations are strong.

In conclusion, it may be stated that despite preponderant concern with climate factors of the organizations determining managerial behaviors, the role of personality variables influencing executive behaviour in organizations cannot be minimized in such studies.

REFERENCES

ARGYRIS, C. Integrating the Individual and the Organization. N.Y.: John Wiley, 1964.

BARRETT, V. and BASS, M. Comparative surveys of managerial attitudes and behavior. In J. Boddewyn (Ed), Comparative Management Teaching and Research-proceedings of the Comparative Workshop. N.Y.: University Press, 1970.

CRONBACH, L.J. The reliability of ratio scores. Educational Psychological Measurement, 1941, 1, 269-278.

ENGLAND, G.W. Personal value system of American managers. Academy of Management Journal, 1968, 10, 53-68.

GRAVES, D. Management Research - A Cross-cultural Perspective. Amsterdam: Elsevier, 1970.

GUTH, W. and TAGIURI, R. Personal values and corporate strategies. Harvard Business Review, 1965, 123-132.

HABIBULLAH, A.H.M. and SINHA, J.B.P. Motivational climate and leadership styles. Vikalpa, 5, 1980, 85-93.

HAIRE, M., GHISELLI, E.E. and PORTER, L.W. Managerial Thinking: An International Study. N.Y., John Wiley, 1966.

JAGGI, P.L. Management leadership styles in Indian work organizations. Indian Manager, 1978, 9, 139-55.

KAKAR, S. The theme of authority in social relations in India. Journal of Social Psychology, 1971, 84, 93-101.

KELLY, G. The Pycology of Personal Constructs. New York: Norton, 1955.

KHANDWALLA, P. Management in our backyard. Vikalpa, 5, 1980, 173-184.

KUMAR, U. and SINGH, K.K. The interpersonal construct system of an Indian manager: A determinant of organizational behaviour. Management International Review, 1978, 18, 49-59.

MEADE, R.D. An experimental study of leadership in India. Journal of Psychology, 1967, 72, 35-45.

MOODIE, R.D. Brahmanical Culture and Modernity. Bombay: Asia Publishing House, 1968.

NEGANDHI, R., and PRASAD, B.S. Comparative Management. N.Y.: Appleton Century Crofts, 1971.

RUNYON, K.E. Some interactions between personality variables and management styles. Journal of Applied Psychology, 1973, 57, 288-294.

TAYLOR, W.S. Basic personality in orthodox Hindu culture patterns. Journal of Abnormal and Social Psychology, 1948, 43, 3-12.

ZALEZNIK, A. Human Dilemmas of Leadership, N.Y.: Harper & Row, 1966.

DISTRIBUTIVE BEHAVIOR IN A FEMININE CULTURE

R. Nauta

Rijksuniversiteit Groningen

1. Introduction

In studying the relation between cultural differentiation and the way people allocate rewards and punishments for distinct contributions in performing a group task, Bond et al. (1981) found that, contrary to their original expectations, collectivist cultures do not emphasize the importance of maintenance contributions. It was expected that collectivistic cultures, because of the value put on group harmony, cohesiveness and solidarity, would be more equitable in the distribution of rewards. In more general terms this hypothesis could be formulated as: those members who contribute more to the culturally relevant outcomes of the group will receive more rewards.

In its formulation concerning the egalitarian relation between rewards and instrumental inputs in an individualistic culture, this general hypothesis was confirmed. The complementary formulation concerning the equitable relation between rewards and socio-emotional inputs in a collectivistic culture, however, was not.

In the collectivistic culture of Chinese Hong Kong, rewards for both task and maintenance contributions were distributed in an egalitarian manner. This was compared and related to the distribution of rewards in the more individualistic culture of the U.S.A. In discussing these results, Bond et al. (1981) suggest that, on second thoughts, not the collectivistic-individualistic dimension of cultural differentiation, but the masculine-feminine dimension (cf. Hofstede, 1980) might be more relevant for the egalitarian or equitable distribution of rewards for socio-emotional contributions to group functioning and task performance.

371

Feminine societies are not concerned with the formal characteristics of harmony and solidarity, but stress the importance of the material, substantial outcomes of warmth and support in relationships and performance. Feminine societies positively value co-operation but negatively value advancement, recognition and challenge relative to more masculine cultures. Given these value priorities, it is probable that research subjects in a more feminine culture would emphasise the socio-emotional contributions towards the functioning of the group project, while subjects from more masculine cultures would emphasise instrumental task contributions.

To assess this possibility, the format and design of the Bond et al. (1981) study was replicated in the Netherlands. This culture is very similar to the United States on all of Hofstede's (1980) dimensions except for masculinity, where it is one of the most feminine. Differences with Hong Kong society are related to the individualistic-collectivistic and feminine-masculine dimension. The Chinese culture of Hong Kong is more collectivistic and masculine.

2. Design of the study

Students from the Netherlands were asked to read a scenario describing a group member who made high, medium or low instrumental task and socio-emotional contributions towards a group project for a university course. Subjects then rated their perceptions of, and behavioural intentions towards, this target person (TP). In total, 123 male and female students participated in the study. They were at random given one of the scenarios. At least 11 subjects answered questions related to each one of the scenarios. Students were recruited via introductory courses in psychology and from libraries and canteens in the University of Groningen.

3. Results

3.1 Structure of rewards

To analyse the structure of behavioural intentions and person perceptions, a principal component factor analysis was run on each of the two groups of dependent variables. Those factors with an eigen value greater than 1.0 were rotated to a non-orthogonal simple structure. The resulting pattern with regard to behavioural intentions shows a sharp distinction between "competence rank" (grade assignments) on the one hand, and "intimacy of relationships" on the other (cf. Table 1).

TABLE 1

Structure of Rewards : Intentions

	Netherlands		Hong Kong/U.S.A.[1]	
	I[2]	II	I	II
Letter grade assigned to TP	0.93		0.91	
Percentage grade assigned to TP	0.89		0.84	
Choice of TP as future task group member	0.36	0.65	0.85	
Choice of TP as study group partner	0.43	0.50	0.82	
Choice of TP as friend outside working groups		0.60	0.46	0.65
Discussion with TP of grade assigned him (her)		0.37		-0.81

[1] Results for Hong Kong/U.S.A. adapted from Bond et al. 1981.

[2] Loadings smaller than |0.30| are omitted.

This distinction between rank and relation, between performance evaluations and judgements about personal attractiveness and likeability, is far more clear-cut in this study than in that of Bond et al. (1981). For Dutch students, one's willingness to co-operate and be friends with a target person is independent of an evaluation of the TP's task performance and personal competence. Or in other words: in the sample of Dutch students, perceived competence (as expressed in rank and grade) does not seem to influence the degree of co-operation or friendship. For Chinese and American students, however, there is a distint connection between these concepts of rank (performance, competence) and relation (co-operation, friendship). While in the more masculine societies work relationships are based on task contributions and performance evaluations, in the more feminine culture of the Netherlands people like to

work with friends, unconcerned about the positive or
negative results of such a co-operation in terms of task
goal achievements of project outcome.

The concept of friendship is also different in
masculine and feminine societies. In Hong Kong and the USA
a more restricted interpretation of friendship seems to be
maintained (cf. Table 1). In such an interpretation there
is no place for work and work relationships. The masculine
interpretation of friendship is more privatised - friends
are confined to the private, non-work sphere of life.
Friends, in this conception, cannot be confronted with an
open declaration and discussion of (in)competence.

In a masculine society one tries to evade hierarchical
relationships with friends. Or, alternatively, friendship
relationships are only made with those who are of the same
competence level. In that case a discussion of (differences
in) competence is irrelevant, unnecessary and, if
undertaken, will end the relationship. In the Netherlands,
however, one prefers to work with friends. And in this work
relationship questions of competence and task performance
can be discussed. The proverb: "It is my friend who shows
me my failures," shows the embeddedness of this open,
discursive concept of friendship in Dutch culture. However,
because of their non-instrumental base - i.e. friends are
chosen not primarily for their utility in terms of task
performance, but on the basis of personal attraction and
mutual liking - friendship relations may, paradoxically, be
instrumental for solving problems in task co-operation and
project contribution. This more open and supportive
character of personal relationships seems to be a distinct
characteristic of feminine cultures.

The factor structure of person-perception is rather
similar to the one found in Bond et al. (1981). One factor
is related to the impression of task skills (competence),
the other factor is related to the impression of
maintenance skills (friendliness) (cf. Table 2). Both
factors constitute a manipulation check for variations in
TP input. In this sample, friendliness is related to the
independent variables by the equation:
$$F = 1.18***M + .28T - .15MT + Constant.$$
Competence is related to the independent variables by the
equation:
$$C = .14M + .97***T - .06MT + Constant.$$
The coefficient of the maintenance input (M) and the task
input (T) respectively is significant (p<.001). In these
regression equations the independent variables are assumed
to be continuous.

TABLE 2

Structure of Rewards : Evaluations

	Netherlands[2]		Hong Kong/U.S.A.[1]	
	I	II	I	II
Likable-unlikable	0.86		0.87	
Goodnatured-irritable	0.78		0.92	
Kind-unkind	0.82		0.89	
Cooperative-uncooperative	0.74		0.82	0.36
Persevering-quitting		0.66		0.74
Productive-inefficient		0.72		0.89
Responsible-undependable				0.85
Competent-incompetent		0.88		0.91

[1] Results from Hong Kong/U.S.A. adapted from Bond et al. 1981.

[2] Loadings smaller than | 0.30 | are omitted.

3.2 Determination of intention

Both behavioural rewards (competence grading and intimacy relationships) are influenced by the degree to which the TP contributes on both input domains. Competence grading (rank) is related to the independent variables by the equation:

Rank = 63***T + .46*M + .03MT + Constant.

Both task inputs and maintenance inputs are significantly related to the rank and competence grading attributed to the TP (respectively $p < .001$ and $p < .05$). Both kinds of inputs explain also distinct contributions to the amount of variance explained in the rank criterion, when using a hierarchical regression analysis. However the grade assigned to the TP seems to be more influenced by the task-related contributions than by the socio-emotional maintenance contributions. In this respect the Dutch sample does not seem to be different from the USA and HK samples. In these cultures too, performance related ranking (subordination - superordination) is associated with both task and maintenance contributions (cf. Table 3; Bond et al. 1981, p. 9-10).

TABLE 3

Relations between Rewards and Contributions

Rewards	Equation
Competence rank/ subordination superordination	NL 0.63***T + 0.46*M + 0.03MT + K HK 0.72***T + 0.63***M − 0.02MT + K USA 0.21***T + 1.10***M − 0.16MT + K
Intimacy/ intimacy of relationship	NL 0.45λT + 0.64*M − 0.12MT + K HK −0.02T + 0.34*M − 0.14MT + K USA 0.02T + 0.69*M − 0.11MT + K
Friendliness/ Impression of maintenance skills	NL 0.28T + 1.18***M − 0.15MT + K HK 0.16T + 0.56***M − 0.02MT + K USA 0.20T + 1.21***M − 0.06MT + K
Competence/ Impression of skills	NL 0.97***T + 0.14M − 0.06MT + K HK 1.02***T + 0.27M + 0.09MT + K USA 0.81***T + 0.12M + 0.09MT + K

K : constant
λ : p<0.10
* : p<0.05
** : p<0.01
*** : p<0.001

In contrast with the USA and HK cultures however, in the Dutch sample intimacy rewards are also influenced by both maintenance and task contributions. Thus, although there is a sharp distinction, behaviourally, between grade awarded and intimacy allowed, both can be exchanged as a reward for task and maintenance contributions. Apparently, in evaluating performance, people take into account the socio-emotional contributions to group functioning, as well as direct instrumental task contributions. Parallel to the more open definition of friendship in feminine cultures, grade and rank - as purely competence related rewards - are not only determined by task contribution but also by socio-emotional contribution. Similarly, intimacy rewards are not only determined by maintenance contributions but also by instrumental task inputs. This plural and pluriform determination of rewards in a feminine culture is not an artefact of the character of the rewards in question (as is perhaps a possibility in the case of the determination of subordination - superordination rewards in a masculine society - cf. Bond et al. 1981, p. 9-10), but seems to be a genuine effect of cultural orientation.

The differentiation between masculine and feminine

cultures operates not only through differences in reward
structure, but does also affect the connection between
rewards and contributions. While the collectivistic-
individualistic dimension seems to be relevant for matters
of degree in relation to the reward strategy, the
masculine-feminine dimension is related to differences in
kind with regard to the rewarding process.

3.3 Men and women in a feminine culture

There is no difference in distributive strategy
between male and female students in the Dutch sample.
Neither main effects nor interaction effects significantly
differ between the male and female sub-samples. So there is
more reason to suppose that the specific relationships
between and within rewards and contributions, found in this
research, are an effect of culture than that they should be
attributed to the different sexual composition of the Dutch
sample. The effects of sex were analysed in a manner
suggested by Cohen and Cohen (1975). In a hierarchical
regression analysis, a significant contribution (i.e.
addition) of the interaction of one of the main independent
variables with sex (coded as a dummy-variable) to the
explained variance in the criterion above the amount of
variance already explained by the main effects would
suggest a significant effect of sex. This was not the case.

4. Discussion and conclusions

4.1 Distribution of inputs

As in the study of Bond et al. (1981), it is clearly
established that the behaviour of group members can be and
will be evaluated in terms of their contribution to the
performance of the group task and the functioning of the
group. As such there is a strong resemblance to leadership
studies in which the leader's behaviour is evaluated on
these same dimensions - instrumental task-orientated
behaviour and socio-emotional support. There is no reason
to suppose that these two, or indeed any, leadership
behaviour dimension is exclusively relevant for describing
the behaviour of leaders. This paper supports the idea,
already noted in the literature, that these dimensions are
important for the behaviour of both leaders and followers.
Of interest might be further research into the question of
how the distribution of task and socio-emotional inputs
among group members is related to the structure and process
of authority and decision-making. The cultural
differentiation of reward structure and rewarding process,
especially between masculine and feminine cultures, may
explain one of the mechanisms influencing the culture-bound
conditions for participative management (Hofstede, 1980).

4.2 Salience of rewards

If one would compare the results of the three samples together (HK, USA, NETH.), disregarding the differences in the detail of the reward structures, the following broad hypothesis could be formulated: - The more feminine a culture, the more egalitarian the distribution of competence rewards. This hypothesis is based particularly on the comparison of results in the Dutch sample and in the USA sample. Given the salience of competence rewards in both these individualistic cultures, one could argue that the more feminine characteristics of the culture act to subdue an exaggeratedly equitable distribution of competence rewards, not because of a more general trend towards moderation in distributing resources in order to preserve working relationships between members differing in competence, as in the collectivistic culture of Chinese Hong Kong, but because recognition of excellence, and precedence, as such, is negatively valued in a feminine culture.

A second hypothesis follows from the comparison between the Hong Kong and the Dutch samples: - The more feminine the culture, the more equitable the distribution of intimacy/relation rewards.

The distribution of rewards seems to be of primary relevance for the collectivistic-individualistic dimension of cultural differentiation. Collectivistic cultures are moderate on distributing rewards. Differences in status and rank between people are kept small. Solidarity and harmony are accentuated. Individualistic cultures attach great importance to matters of precedence and rank, be it as a result of individual achievements in the sphere of task performance or of contributions in the domain of socio-emotional support.

The importance attached to the substantial nature of rewards seems to be of primary relevance for the distinction between feminine and masculine cultures. Given the characteristics of these societies (Hofstede, 1980a, b), competence rewards, especially if performance related, are expressive of dominant cultural values in a masculine society, while intimacy and relationship rewards seem to be more salient in feminine societies. The more equitable distributive strategy in relation to intimacy rewards in feminine societies might be a reflection of the importance attached to co-operation and friendship in these cultures. A more equitable distribution of competence rewards might similarly represent the salience of excellence and achievement in masculine societies. However, characteristics of both dimensions may interact at any given cultural position, either strengthening or weakening the main effects. In the case of the Dutch sample, for instance, the equitable way in which intimacy rewards are distributed would be predicted by both the feminine and individualistic character of its culture. Similarly, the strongly equitable way in which competence rewards are distributed by American students would be predictable on the basis of the individualistic and masculine characteristics of their culture. The distributive strategies of Chinese Hong Kong students are more ambiguous. The Hong Kong Chinese are less outspoken than American students in distributing competence rewards because their culture is masculine but collectivistic. They are less equitable than Dutch students in distributing intimacy rewards because their culture is masculine and collectivistic.

These suggestions about the relations between cultural differentiation and the distribution of rewards are the result of a test of the hypothesis suggested by Bond et al. (1981, p.13) that there is a relation between masculinity-feminity of culture and the weighting of different contributions in rewarding behaviour. In order to test these suggestions, empirical relationships between data from different cultures should be analysed together within one design. Michael Bond is presently supervising such an analysis, using the data from this research and the data on which the paper by Bond et al. (1981) is based.

4.3 Culture and behaviour

Cultural differentiation seems to be more relevant for behavioural intentions than for evaluations of personality. This might argue for a behaviourally based interpretation of culture (cf. Nauta, 1982).

4.4 Differential effects of culture and reward

Although there is some effect of culture on reward structure, differences in distributive strategy seem to be more influenced by type of reward than by differences on cultural dimensions. In future research the interaction between type of culture and type of reward should be taken into account. Hypotheses about the effect of culture should be formulated with respect not only to specific contributions but also to particular rewards.

Chapter 35

REFERENCES

Bond, M.H., Kwok Leung and Kwok Choi Won, The impact of task and maintenance contributions on reward distribution: How does cultural collectivism operate? Paper, Chung Chi College, Chinese University of Hong Kong, 1981.

Cohen, J. & Cohen, P., Applied Multiple Regression Correlation for the Behavioural Sciences. Hillsdale, N.J., Erlbaum, 1975.

Hofstede, G., Culture's consequences: International differences in work-related values. Beverley Hills: Sage Publications, 1980a.

Hofstede, G., Motivation, leadership & organisation: Do American theories apply abroad?" Organisational Dynamics, 1980b, 9, 42-63.

Nauta, R. Motivation & Behaviour. Assen, Van Gorcum, 1982. (in Dutch).

COMMENT

W. J. Lonner

Western Washington University, Bellingham

The four papers in this section deal with a variety of topics. But even with this variation among so few papers a thread of commonality is evident.

Two of the papers (by Hofstede and Nauta) have the Hofstede imprint and are culture-comparative. While those by Kumar and Aziz address certain parts of the Indian scene only and do not rely on any specific framework. Readers of these two papers can make judgments concerning how generalizable to other cultures their results are.

Kumar and Aziz rely on measures developed exclusively for their own use, with no apparent desire to have them blossom into more widely usable devices. Kumar, influenced by both psychodynamics and some basic components of social learning theory, investigated the "interpretative system" of Indian managers. Her four-fold typology reflects a belief that early interpersonal experiences are predictive of stylistic differences among managers in India. To test these assumptions, three paper-and-pencil measures were developed, and data from 80 managers were analyzed. One has to worry about how one interprets convincingly the complexities emerging from the partitioning of just 80 people into 4 groups and assessing their responses to home-made measures. Despite these concerns, Kumar's closing comments imply that a few aspects of her conclusions may well be generalizable across cultures. One of these is that family interrelationships are dominant in shaping managerial behavior when there is low social and occupational mobility; perhaps the organization serves as a family surrogate. Until this sort of sweeping relationship is looked into on a greater scale, Kumar's heavily method-bound results will have to be accorded culture-relative status.

Aziz's paper concerning absenteeism in one "medium-sized" plant near Delhi contains some colorful cultural background material. It also contains some informative comments on absenteeism research -- the type of research which itself is apparently absent from the literature -- and is evidently unique as a study of absenteeism designed to have cross-cultural implications. But by itself it is not cross-cultural, nor need it be at this stage. The sample of 128 workers was split in half. One group of 64 was termed "poor workers" (absent 12 per cent or more of the time), and the other 64 comprised a group of "regular workers" (on duty 90 per cent of the time). Each participant was interviewed, and other data were gathered as well. The data were analyzed by χ^2 and correlational procedures. Aziz's discussion of the pattern of relationships makes interesting reading. His call for the development of standardized indices of absenteeism (hopefully separating groups of "poor" and "regular" workers by more than a mere 2 per cent difference in job attendance, which was done in the present study) and reliable and valid questionnaires to measure absenteeism both within and across cultures is a good prescription.

Hofstede is a reliable contributor to the cross-cultural literature, especially in the industrial-organizational area. His massive and impressive HERMES data, seemingly limitless in what may be done with it, is currently one of the "hottest shows in town." It may set the stage for years to come. The sheer volume of the data, the potential for more data collection, and the uses to which the data can be put are reminiscent of the impact that Charles Osgood has had with his semantic differential technique. Hofstede even mentions his desire to construct a "world wide atlas of work-related value systems." To my knowledge, only Osgood and Murdock have had the necessary data base, and the courage, to mention "atlas" with respect to their cross-cultural data bases. But Hofstede's data base is very different from Osgood's, and probably can never match the flexibility and utility of his methods. Responses to questionnaires, after all, do have their limitations. We should nevertheless welcome this new report on the expanding data base, up to 53 from the original 50 countries.

The remaining paper in the section, Nauta's, is a good example of the uses to which the HERMES data can be put. The convenient collectivistic-individualistic dimension (not one of Hofstede's 4 factors), used in Asia by Bond and others, is replaced by the masculine-feminine dimension (which is one of the dimensions extracted from the HERMES data). Instead of a "logical" contrast on the former dimension (simply Hong Kong and the United States, for example), a three-way contrast on the latter dimension was made by adding The Netherlands (a "feminine" culture, according to Hofstede's ecological factor analysis). Like all the rest, Nauta's paper was interesting and generally easy to follow. I must admit, however, that it contained some rather cumbersome reasoning in places. For example, in the first paragraph of section 4.2 the following hypothesis is presented: "The more feminine a culture, the more egalitarian the distribution of competence rewards." In one of the very next sentences this completely clear and

testable   hypothesis is then tested in an ad hoc fashion by
using 80 words and more than a few commas. The sentence   is
nicely   constructed,   but I had to read it several times in
an attempt to sort things out. I'm afraid I still have not.

COMMENT

D. Munro

University of Zimbabwe, Harare

Perhaps the first task of a commentator is to draw out the common theme which links the papers in a symposium but which is not evident from their titles. Due to the difficulties of bringing together cogent topics in such a small conference, this might not at first seem an easy task, but a claim I would like to make is that these papers represent a healthy trend towards cultural relativism in the study of work and other values, and away from the naive view, propagated by American texts, that universals have all but been positively identified.

Hofstede, in his 1980 book and various papers, is bidding to provide a theoretical nexus into which further cross-cultural work value studies could fit. He is likely to succeed in this, if for no other reason than that there is no other model, based on empirical evidence, which offers any competition; nor is one foreseeable, given the expense of establishing a comparable data base. Consequently, it is important that the theory stands up to every possible check of its validity, though this is not the proper place to undertake such an evaluation.

Hofstede has presented us with an extension of the main body of his research, using less reliable data, and has been able to show that the theory stands up virtually perfectly against his original criteria. It could be that an impediment to the general acceptance of the theory will be this very perfection, particularly in view of its degree of reliance on highly processed data. But it is difficult to see how these problems can be avoided in the formulation of a wide-spectrum theory, which must compress a mass of complex information, both qualitative and quantitative, and collected in varied circumstances; Hofstede's accounts of how this was done shows due attention to the details of the statistical steps and an awareness of sources of error. The theory must also mesh in a plausible way with observations of behaviour in the target cultures, and the historic and economic factors which have contributed to their present states; here there is much more room for debate among social scientists, but no theory of similar scope could avoid such a debate. It remains to be seen whether the theory has offered rigorous enough predictions of behaviour in cultures of different standings on the four main value dimensions for it to be tested and linked to variables or theories more local in scope; Hofstede has pointed to the formidable research task required. Even more critical tests of the relativistic basis of the Hofstede model will involve examining whether the mutual perceptions of members of different cultures can be accounted for (1). This is an important practical issue for the world, and of great theoretical interest to cross-cultural psychologists who are divided about the value of such inclusive theories. At the national and more immediately practical level an interesting question is whether the same factor structure will hold if we compare subgroups within nations, or individuals within subgroups, using either exploratory or procrustean factor analysis. There seems a reasonable chance of this, and of the model being useful in accounting for inter-group and inter-organizational behaviour. Hofstede's existing data may yet yield some of these answers.

Nauta's naturalistic experiment shows one of the ways in which further progress could be made in testing the Hofstede model. Perhaps because I have never lived in Holland, I found it difficult to grasp some of the detailed observations of evaluative behaviours there. This reminds me that a taxonomic system for social behaviours would be helpful, and perhaps essential for personality and value theory to be dragged out of the endless swamp of verbal and conceptual quicksands in which it struggles. Even better would be a thorough-going system-theory analysis of the mental states and behavioural processes which are involved.

Kumar's paper is representative of a genus of studies in which India is perhaps leading the field of third-world psychologists, wherein truly indigenous ideas and concerns are investigated by using established research methods. Until the centre of gravity of psychology moves away from America and West or North it will continue to be important that third-world scientists establish their credentials by doing technically good work, in the course of which they will have a chance to bring non-western ideas to the attention of international psychology. But even more difficult, and important, is the task of bringing new ideas to the attention of the managers of organizations. As Kumar mentions, their attitudes and practices have been moulded by the coincidence of values of colonial bureaucrats and indigenous power groups (in India and many third-world nations) and a major issue in development studies is how they may now be changed to respond to the needs of wider societies in which they function. Kumar's study illustrates the links which exist between the self-perceived styles of managers and their styles in the wider context of family and community. This finding shows that we should be cautious in assuming that radical social engineering efforts could bring quick results.

It is of interest to note that the personal construct system which Kumar & Singh had proposed for Indian managers is not an exotic one, but is quite similar to systems which have been proposed in the Western world for both organizational behaviour and socialization practices. While this may reflect the continuing cultural dominance of western viewpoints, it should encourage those who seek universals among human values, and it moves the task of the psychologists towards the ethnographic study of local semantic links. But we should also be asking Kumar and Hofstede to explicate the links between their construct systems.

Aziz takes a more mundane concern of organizational psychology internationally, absenteeism from the formal work environment. His approach to economic behaviour considers the goods and services provided by the total community rather than the formal organization alone, and the costs and obligations owed to that wider community. This reflects a move to a less narrow view of work behaviour than has been typical of industrial psychology to date, a view which is influenced by modern economic and sociological analyses. In view of that, a sociological analysis of the meaning of absenteeism in the Indian context would have been helpful to give coherence to the psychologist's findings.

Finally, to my opening remarks about the value of a cultural-relative perspective in psychology should be added the point that applied social psychology is also time-relative. In a profound sense our findings are ephemeral, the incremental components of the psychologists' contribution being the research methodology, our conceptual systems, and our methods of disseminating findings to those who are in a position to utilize them constructively and timeously. Our talents in the last area lag behind those in the first two, though success may be critical to the advance of psychology in the third world. I hope that society at large will begin to feel the impact of work such as it is contained in these four papers.

NOTE

(1) Metatheorists might also ask whether the theory can recursively account for its own construction of reality. If so, it follows

CULTURAL COMPARISON ON DECISION-MAKING UNDER UNCERTAINTY

G. N. Wright

City of London Polytechnic

L. D. Phillips and A. Wisudha

Brunel University, London

Previously, Phillips and Wright (1977) and Wright, Phillips, Whalley, Choo, Ng, Tan and Wisudha (1978) found cultural differences in probabilistic thinking between Asians and the British. British students were found to adopt a more finely differentiated view of uncertainty, both verbally and numerically, than students from Hong Kong, Malaysia and Indonesia in response to uncertain situations. For numerical probabilities assigned to almanac questions, the British were much better "calibrated" than the Asian students. For an individual to be perfectly calibrated for every event assessed .XX probability of occurrence, XX% of all events so assessed should be correct. Whatever numerical assessments the Asian groups gave (except for 100 per cent assessments) they were right roughly 50 per cent of the time. The Asian student groups were also more extreme in their probability assessments, giving many more 100 per cent responses than the British, although this extra confidence was not reflected in the realism of these 100 per cent assessments.

Generally, the British tend to view uncertainty in terms of degrees of probability which are fairly well calibrated. Wright and Phillips (1980) have called this style "Probabilistic Thinking". Asians, on the other hand, tend to view the world in terms of certainty or total uncertainty, any elicited probabilites tend to be poorly calibrated. Wright and Phillips have labelled this style "Non- Probabilistic Thinking".

There are individual and group differences, in degree, within each culture but these alternative ways of dealing with uncertainty outweigh any within-culture effects of subculture religion, occupation, arts/science orientation or sex (Wright and Phillips, 1980). Within British culture,

Wright and Phillips (1979) have found that the tendency to respond in terms of certainty (100 per cent probabilities) and be poorly calibrated with these extreme assessments is linked to the authoritarian personality.

What are the implications for decision-making of these two cognitive styles? For Asians, is the Subjective Expected Utility model of decision-making, which is based upon subjective probabilities, poor as even a first approximation? Can cultural differences in performance be found on decision-making tasks measuring other aspects of probabilistic processing?

The present study attempts to answer these questions by comparing the performance of British and Asian student samples on a wide range of decision tasks. These tasks measure set to obtain probabilistic information, probabilistic planning, attitude toward risk, portfolio choice in investment, acceptance of a normative axiom of decision theory, probability revision where the normative impact of probabilistic information can be quantified, and subjective value of probabilistic information.

How would a probabilistic thinker perform on these tasks? We would expect such a person to take a probabilistic rather than non-probabilistic view when confronted with uncertainty, to value information that could reduce uncertainty, to revise probabilities in light of new information, to be less prone to violate the normative axiom, to take account of future uncertainties when making plans, and to show no bias for certain over uncertain events just because the former are certain. On the other hand, the non-probabilistic thinker would translate uncertainty into yes-no or don't know terms, would put little value on fallible information, show little revision of probabilities when fallible information is presented, be prone to violation of the normative axiom, make plans on the basis of best guesses, and be biased towards options with certain consequences.

Generally, then, throughout the tasks certain choices or acts can be seen as indications of probabilistic thought while other choices or acts can be seen as indications of non-probabilistic thought. Insofar as these two cognitive styles are adopted consistently by British and Asian students, respectively, cultural differences in performance should be observed.

METHOD

A detailed description and documentation of the psychometric properties of the battery of questionnaires utilized in this study, and summarized below, is given in Wright (in press). Indices of internal consistency or test-retest reliability, where appropriate, were shown to be acceptably high in each case, for a British sample.

Instruments

Decision Scenarios

In two problems a decision-maker faces uncertainty about future events, one concerning a business investment, the other oil exploration and drilling. The respondent is asked to write a summary of what he or she would do if faced with the decision situation and why he or she would do it.

Responses on the decision scenario were divided into four categories: (a) act now/take a gamble; (b) don't act because of uncertainty; (c) act only if information obtained is considered conclusive; (d) find out more information before acting, even though this information may not be conclusive.

Two independent judges coded the subjects' responses on each of the problems. Disagreement between judges on the categorizations were resolved by subsequent discussion.

We expect probabilistic thinkers to choose (a) or (d), non-probabilistic thinkers to select (b) or (c). To be classified as a probabilistic thinker a respondent must give some indication that he or she has assessed the degree of uncertainty inherent in the decision. A non-probabilistic thinker would, we believe, either be discouraged by the uncertainty or try to obtain perfectly diagnostic information.

Probabilistic Planning

This problem describes the manufacture of "Zylene" by making and combining a series of compounds whose production is probabilistic. The respondent has to estimate how long it takes to manufacture Zylene and its constituent compounds and to describe how to manufacture Zylene in the quickest possible time.

"Best guess" and "longest time" estimates were coded and subjects were categorised into those who recognised that the "longest time" could be infinity and those who did not. Descriptions of how to manufacture Zylene in the quickest time were categorised into those who recognised that attempts to manufacture each of Zylene's constituent compounds could be undertaken simultaneously and those who proceeded serially. Probabilistic thinkers would realize that the longest time would be infinity and that the time to Zylene's production could be decreased by simultaneous manufacturing attempts. Two independent judges categorized responses. There were no disagreements.

"Risk" Problems

Kogan and Wallach (1960) investigated the relationship between judgemental confidence, expressed in terms of a subjective probability that an event will occur, and attitude toward risk. They found that low confidence was associated with a negative evaluation of risk-related concepts such as "risk" and "stock market". However, in a later study Wallach and Kogan (1961) found no evidence that subjects who made more confident and extreme probability assessments, where no payoffs were involved, were also more risky in their decision-making behaviour. These investigators concluded that "attempts to conceptualize various judgemental processes in decision and risk terms must be considered premature" (Wallach and Kogan, 1961: 35). Summarizing this research, Kogan and Wallach (1967) noted that a view of judgemental confidence in terms of a boldness and conviction is only one possible interpretation and that judgemental confidence may also be interpreted as a denial or inability to cope with uncertainty. They concluded that:

> ...there are two alternative conceptualizations of judgemental confidence and extremity, which we might label as cognitive risk and desire-for-certainty. The former proposes a reflective process in which extremity and confidence represent a cognitive-judgemental counterpart of risky decision-making. The latter conceptualization proposes a compensatory process in which extremity and confidence express a need to overcome underlying feelings of uncertainty and caution (p.204).

Our definition of non-probabilistic thinking with its emphasis on response to judgemental situations in terms of uncertainty has obvious analogies with Kogan and Wallach's interpretations of judgemental confidence. However, our definitions of decision styles are empirically based and make no reference to underlying psychological mechanisms. The similarities and differences between our own and Kogan and Wallach's conceptualizations will be discussed later, for the moment we note that it is possible to consider the relationship between judgemental styles shown on tasks involving pure uncertainty and tasks containing utility attached to possible outcomes.

We adopted three problems from Wallach and Kogan (1961). In these problems the respondent is given a choice between a "sure thing" and a risky option with two possible consequences, one worse than the "sure-thing" and one better. The respondent is asked to choose a probability for the better consequence so that the risky option becomes as good as the "sure-thing". The probability given by the respondent was coded for each problem, and the mean probability across the three problems was calculated.

Although utilities for each of the consequences in the problems will vary from one respondent to the next, we expect that non-probabilistic thinkers will tend to choose the certainty option whereas probabilistic thinkers would be more likely to act on probabilistic information.

Portfolio Choice

This problem is an investment decision where the respondent has to invest 10,000 pounds, or equivalent sum, in shares which have different interest rates and probabilities of the total loss of money invested. The actual amounts invested were 10,000 pounds, 50,000 dollars and 10,000,000 rupiah for the British, Malaysian and Indonesian samples, respectively. These amounts are roughly equivalent in terms of buying power and exchange rates. Two values were computed from this problem:

(1) the total amount invested on the share with no chance of loss but a low interest rate;

(2) the overall expected value of the portfolio investment.

Expected value of the portfolio is a maximum when the whole amount to be invested is placed on the share which has the highest interest rate but which also has the highest probability of the loss of money invested.

Someone who is a non-probabilistic thinker will, we hypothesize, not act on probabilistic information even though to do so will maximise expected value. On the other hand, a probabilistic thinker will utilise information to maximise expected value.

Test of a Normative Axiom of Decision Theory

We included Ellsberg's (1961) problem as used by Slovic and Tversky (1974) to test Savage's (1954) Independence Principle (SIP), also called the sure-thing axiom. This principle asserts that, "if two alternatives have a common outcome under a particular state of nature, then the ordering of the alternatives should be independent of the value of that outcome". Respondents on Ellsberg's problem were asked to imagine an opaque bag containing ninety balls. Thirty of the balls are red, the remaining sixty are black or yellow in unknown proportions. One ball is to be drawn at random from the bag. Table 1 shows the possible actions and payoffs in situation A and situation B. The respondent's task was to indicate his or her preference between Act 1 and Act 2 <u>and</u> between Act 3 and Act 4.

Respondents were classified into those choosing in accordance with SIP, i.e., choice of acts 1 and 3 <u>or</u> 2 and 4; those choosing to avoid the ambiguous probabilities which must be inferred by a symmetry argument, i.e., acts 1 and 4; and those choosing by neither of these principles, i.e., acts 2 and 3.

We expect fewer violations of SIP among probabilistic thinkers than non-probabilistic thinkers.

TABLE 1

Ellsberg's Test of Savage's Independence Principle

		30	60	
		red	black	yellow
Situation A				
Act 1.	Bet on red	£10	nothing	nothing
Act 2.	Bet on black	nothing	£10	nothing
Situation B				
Act 3.	Bet on red or yellow	£10	nothing	£10
Act 4.	Bet on black or yellow	nothing	£10	£10

Probability Revision

We included a Bayesian probability task using the urns and balls paradigm (after Phillips and Edwards, 1966), which has the advantage of assuming no prior statistical knowledge, but used three non-symmetric binominal data-generators in an attempt to remove the possibility of inappropriate strategies contaminating our measures of probabilistic processing (Marks and Clarkson, 1972). Respondents were instructed to imagine three bags each containing one hundred poker chips. One bag contained predominantly red poker chips, one bag contained predominantly blue poker chips whilst the final bag contained an equal amount of red and blue poker chips. The predominant colour was allocated as a 60-40 and 70-30 basis. Three sequences of ten successive draws, with replacement, were taken from one of the data generators. Bayes' theorem did not consistently favour one data generator over another within a sequence of draws and the Bayesian posterior odds over the thirty draws were never greater than 3.5. to 1. Two measures were computed from this task:

(1) After each draw the data generator favoured by Bayes' theorem was noted and the number of times the respondent favoured a different data generator was counted.

(2) The log-likelihood deviation (D) of the subject's assessed probability from the Bayesian probability associated with the chosen urn at a particular draw. This is defined as:

$$D = \log \frac{B}{1-B} - \log \frac{P}{1-P}$$

where B = the Bayesian probability associated with the chosen urn at a particular draw and P = the subject's assessed probability of the same urn at the same draw. For a very "conservative" person the log likelihood deviation would be high and negative. We expect probabilistic thinkers to be more nearly Bayesian in their probability revision than non-probabilistic thinkers. This prediction is derived from the finding of poor performance shown by non-probabilistic thinkers on calibration tasks involving the assessment of static probabilities.

Value of Probabilistic Information

In this task the respondent can win 10,000 pounds or equivalent sum, by guessing which one of the three bags, each containing different proportions of red and blue marbles, has been chosen by the experimenter. He or she can guess for nothing or see 10, 50 or 100 marbles drawn, with replacement, from the bag for a price. The respondent is asked what is the maximum price he or she would pay for the information.

This task came immediately after the Bayesian Revision task. We expect that fewer non-probabilistic thinkers pay for samples in the problem than probabilistic thinkers.

SAMPLES

The data reported here is a comparison of British university students (N=40) attending University College, London, Malaysian students (N=194) attending the University of Malaysia, and Indonesian students (N=84) attending the University of Indonesia.

We further subdivided the Malaysian samples into Malay

Malaysians (N=62), Indian Malaysians (N=65) and Chinese Malaysians (N=67) since Wright and Phillips (1980) had found some subcultural differences on their original probabilistic thinking tasks. All subjects were paid 1.50 pounds (or equivalent sum) for voluntarily participating in the experiment.

PROCEDURE

Each participant was first asked to read a brief statement of the general purpose of the experiment. The statement discussed decision-making in general and made no reference to probabilistic thinking. The participant was then given the Decision Problem questionnaire which contained the problems in the order given under "Method". Finally, each participant was given a personal inventory which asked for such information as age, sex, race, course followed, and so forth.

The British were given the English version of the questionnaire and the Indonesians an Indonesian version. The Malaysians had a choice of translation of their questionnaire: English, Malay, Chinese or Tamil. All non-English versions of the questionnaire had been translated from the English using the back-translation method (after Brislin, 1970).

RESULTS

Task-by-Task Analysis

Throughout this section the major interpretation of the results will be placed on comparisons between the performance of the British students and the Asian students, as a whole. We have no specific predictions about differential performance on our tasks between the Asian student samples.

On the first decision scenario problem, a higher proportion of the Chinese Malaysians gave probabilistic responses than the British (78% as opposed to 55%, respectively). On the second problem the British gave a higher proportion of probabilistic responses than the Malay Malaysians (93% as opposed to 73%, respectively). Otherwise, there were no differences between Asian student samples and the British students. Clearly, Asian students are, on the whole, just as likely to respond probabilistically to the decision scenarios as the British students. The higher proportion of probabilistic responses for all groups given to the second problem can perhaps be explained by the nature of the second problem which explicitly stated that probabilistic information, in the form of seismic soundings, was available.

On the probabilistic planning problem, a much higher proportion of the British noted that the longest possible time to Zylene's manaufacture could be infinity than did either of the Asian student groups (35% as opposed to an average of 4.5%, respectively). This finding is completely compatible with our predictions. No differences were found between the Asian student groups.

Similarly, a higher proportion of the British students noted that the time to Zylene's eventual production could be decreased by simultaneous manufacturing attempts than did either the Indonesian students, the Indian Malysian students or the Malay Malaysian students (58% as opposed to 37%, 25% and 35%, respectively). However, no difference emerged between the British students and the Chinese Malaysian students.

On the Risk problems and Portfolio Choice problem, differences between the British and Asian samples did emerge but these were not as strongly directional as we predicted. On the Risk problems the mean probability given by the British students was lower than that of the Indonesians and both the Chinese and Indian Malaysians, but not the Indian Malaysians. The result is, generally, in accordance with our hypothesis; Asians tend to choose the certainty option.

On the Portfolio Choice problem, although the British placed less money on the share with no chance of loss but a lower interest rate than did the Indonesians, no other differences emerged between the British sample and the other Asian samples. The overall expected value of the portfolio investment was similar across all groups. Clearly there are no major differences between the Asian and the British on propensity to take risks with money.

A higher proportion of the Indonesian and Malay Malaysians chose in accordance with a normative axiom of decision theory, Savage's Independence Principle, than did the British students (50% and 39% as opposed to 20%, respectively). This finding is contrary to our prediction that there should be fewer violations of SIP among probabilistic thinkers than non-probabilistic thinkers. However, strong differences in the predicted direction did emerge from comparisons of the student samples on the two measures of ability to revise probabilistic opinion. The British students agreed with Bayes' theorem as to the chosen data generator more often than either of the Asian student samples. Similarly, the British were more normative in the degree of opinion placed on the Bayes'-favoured data generator than either of the Asian groups.

On the value of information problem, a higher proportion of the British students indicated willingness to

buy information compared to the Indonesian and Indian
Malaysian students (48% as opposed to 17% and 22%,
respectively).

Generally then, from the task-by-task analysis, the
overall result is a variation of cultural difference with
the task, leading to the conclusion that task influences on
the expression of probabilistic thought are strong.

Within-Task Analysis

This analysis involved the computation of Goodman and
Kruskal's (1954) lambda index of association strength for
the categorical data, and correlation coefficients for the
interval level data.

On the two decision scenario problems, no association
was found between probabilistic and non-probabilistic
responses for any of our five samples. Within individual
tasks the results are more positive and in line with the
psychometric data presented by Wright (in press). On the
probabilistic planning problems the three "best guess"
estimates gave a mean intercorrelation of .57, .65, .24,
.61 and .60 for the Malay Malaysians, the Indian
Malaysians, the Chinese Malaysians, the Indonesians and the
British, respectively. Similarly, the three "longest time"
estimates gave mean intercorrelations of .59, .89,.32, .82
and .76. The final "best guess" estimate for Zylene's
production gave intercorrelations with the final "longest
time" estimate of .69, .59,.88, .56 and - .04.

On the three "Risk" problems, the mean inter-problem
correlation was.40, .41, .26, .32 and .31 for the Malay
Malaysian, Indian Malaysian, Chinese Malaysian, Indonesian
and British students, respectively. These results suggest
that responses to the problems within the cultures share
some variance in common.

On the portfolio choice problems, the intercorrelation
between the total amount invested in the share with no
chance of loss but a low interest rate and the overall
expected value of the investment were -.76, -.73, -.67,
-.43 and -.73 for the Malay Malaysians, Indian Malaysians,
Chinese Malaysians, Indonesians and British, respectively.
This result was entirely in accordance with our
predictions.

On the probability revision problems, the number of
times the respondent favoured a different data generator to
that specified by Bayes' theorem was correlated with the
log-likehood deviation of the subject's assessed
probability from the Bayesian probabilities. This
intercorrelation was -.85, -.53, -.44, -.71 and -.56 for
the Malay Malaysians, Indian Malaysians, Chinese Malaysians

and British, respectively. The results indicate that the choice aspect of the task was consistent with probabilistic assessment.

Between-Task Analysis

Again, we computed Goodman and Kruskal's (1954) lambda index of association strength for the categorical data and correlation coefficients for the interval data. We also made mean comparisons of the interval level data obtained from our subjects on the basis of the nominal categorizations used on some tasks, in order to look for the maximum possible number of inter-task associations.

In all cases between-task analysis produced non-significant results, although some of the mean comparisons were abandoned due to very small sample sizes of one set of scores from a dividend set.

DISCUSSION

Intercultural and intracultural differences in tendency to adopt a probabilistic or non-probabilistic style of response to a wide variety of decision problems involving probabilistic processing have clearly been demonstrated. However, these differences are not systematic and are certainly not as directionally pronounced as the earlier work of Phillips and Wright (1977), Wright et al. (1978) and Wright and Phillips (1980) would predict.

In support of our predictions, the British showed more evidence of probabilistic planning and Bayesian probability revision than the Asians. The results of the planning comparisons are in accordance with Redding (1980), who has observed that:

> The practice of planning in the West ... is founded upon scientific extrapolations ... econometrics and forecasting techniques are relied upon... it is frowned upon to rely on guesswork ... The Chinese ... world ... rests on ... an almost pre-ordained view of the future. In this context the future is not seen as being "for calculation" ... Even success is taken as having been pre-determined...In Chinese business, planning is rudimentary...Within Western planning behaviour are two elements that are especially related to time. The first is programming, which determines a correct sequence of activities through time. The second is scheduling which places the activities in defined periods of time ... organising into the future is not highly developed in Chinese business (Redding, 1980, p.144).

However, the predicted differential performance on

measures of: set to obtain probabilistic information, attitude towards risk, portfolio choice in investment, acceptance of normative axiom of probabilistic decision theory, and subjective value of probabilistic information were not systematic and, in some cases, were contrary to our hypotheses.

Results of the within-task analysis showed evidence of intra-task reliability on all but responses to the two-problem component of the decision scenarios. The evidence is fairly strong for good intra-task reliability across the cultures studied here.

In personality psychology three main theoretical positions describe the individual and his interaction with the environment. Personologism advocates that stable intra-organismic constants such as traits or cognitive styles are the main determinants of behavioural variation (e.g. Alker, 1971). Situationism emphasises environmental (situational) factors as the main sources of behavioural variation (e.g. Mischel, 1973). Interactionism, a synthesis of personologism and situationism, implies that the interaction between these two factors is the main source of behavioural variation (e.g. Endler, 1975).

One empirical approach to the problem of isolating the sources of behavioural variation has been to use correlational studies employing a sample of individuals, a sample of situations, and a dependent variable that is an indicator of some underlying trait. Given that the measurements of the dependent variable are perfectly reliable, correlation coefficients of unity support personologism. As Ekehammer (1974) points out, high correlation coefficients are seldom found and the interactionist view shown by low, but non-zero, correlations is often supported. Zero correlations, as we obtained, favour situationism.

The lack of between-task associations obtained in the present study supports an interpretation that probabilistic and non-probabilistic thinking may be strongly situation specific rather than the result of a consistent, culturally determined, cognitive style expressed across situations.

In earlier studies, Slovic (1962, 1964) found no relationship between various questionnaire risk-taking measures, including those of Kogan and Wallach, and measures derived from a preference for long shots in hypothetical bet situations similar to the Portfolio investment problem used here. Slovic (1962) concluded that:

> The implications of the present study for the existence and measurement of a general risk-taking trait are (a) none or only a few of the variables

analysed actually measure the trait, or (b) willingness to take risks may not be a general trait at all but rather one which varies from situation to situation within the same individual (Slovic, 1962, p.70).

The lack of association between the measures derived from our tasks leads us to similar conclusions. A consistent personality trait of risk aversion, or desire-for-certainty, on these tasks would have resulted in a strong association between responses which fell in categories (b) or (c) on the Decision Scenario problem with choice of the certainty options in the risk problems and also with investment of a large proportion of money on the share with no chance of loss on the Portfolio choice problem.

None of these risk-taking measures was related to any degree to our other measures of probabilistic and non-probabilistic thinking, which were themselves not significantly intercorrelated or categorically associated. Responses on the latter tasks are not readily interpretable in terms of Kogan and Wallach's (1967) desire-for-certainty construct and so our findings of little association between the risk-aversion or desire-for-certainty measures, and the measures derived from our other tasks which do not involve utility considerations, cannot be taken as a test of their conceptualization.

Studies of organisational decision-making have also tended to favour situationism. For instance, Frank Heller and his colleagues have made close investigation of the influence of the decision-making task upon the type of decision-making undertaken. Heller, Drenth, Koopman and Rus (1977) note that most studies of decision-making in organisations assume that participative behaviour is most appropriate in all decision situations and that this is associated with increased job satisfaction. However, these researchers have identified a "substantial variety of decision styles used by managers in every sample investigated. The decision styles varied with level of organisation, type of decision, skills and qualifications of staff etc. " (Heller et al., 1977, p.570).

Using samples of managers in Britain and Germany who were questioned about their decision-making style in twelve different decision situations, Heller and Wilpert (1977) were led to conclude that:

The findings show that senior, experienced and presumably successful managers do not use the same decision method in all circumstances. A manager will use a "democratic" method on one occasion and an "autocratic" one on another. The terms democratic and autocratic are really inapplicable because they pretend to describe personality whereas our findings suggest that the situation or task is the real differentiator (Heller and Wilpert, 1977, pp.77-78).

Heller and Wilpert's conclusions tend to confirm those of Vroom and Yetton (1973). Interestingly, Heller and Wilpert's matched sample of German and British managers shows similar responses on a decision situation analysis.

The major conclusion from the present study is that set to obtain probabilistic information, probabilistic planning, attitude toward risk, acceptability of an axiom of decision theory, ability to revise opinion in a normative manner and valuation of probabilistic information are virtually unrelated. This finding indicates that our alternative decision-making styles cannot account for performance on the tasks utilised in this study. Similarly the lack of a systematic series of low, but still non-zero, correlations argues against the interactionists' view of decision-making. The evidence seems to favour situationism.

REFERENCES

Alker, H.A. Relevance of person perception to clinical psychology. Journal of Consulting and Clinical Psychology, 1971, 37, 167-176.

Brislin, R.W. Back-Translation for Cross-Cultural Research. Journal of Cross-Cultural Psychology, 1970, 1, 185-216.

Ekehammar, B. Interactionism in personality from a historical perspective. Psychological Bulletin, 1974, 81, 1026-1048.

Ellsberg, D. Risk, Ambiguity and the Savage Axioms. Quarterly Journal of Economics, 1961, 75, 643-649.

Endler, N.S. The case for person-situation interactions. Canadian Psychological Review, 1975, 16, 319-329.

Goodman, L.D. and Kruskal. W.H. Measures of association for cross-classifications. Journal of the American Statistical Association, 1954, 49, 732-765.

Heller, F.A., Drenth, P.J.D., Koopman, P. and Rus, V. A longitudinal study in participative decision-making. Human Relations, 1977, 30, 567-587.

Heller, F.A. and Wilpert, B. Limits to participative leadership: Task, structure and skills as contingencies - A German-British comparison. European Journal of Social Psychology, 1977, 7, 61-84.

Kogan, N. and Wallach, M.A. Certainty of judgement and evaluation of risk. Psychological Reports, 1960, 6, 107-213.

Kogan, N. and Wallach, M.A. Risk taking as a function of the situation, the person and the group. In T.M. Newcom (ed) New Directions in Psychology III, New York: Holt Rinehart and Winston, 1967.

Marks, D.F. and Clarkson, J.K. An explanation of Conservatism in the bookbag and pokerchips situation. Acta Psychologica, 1972, 36, 145-160.

Mischel, W. On the empirical dilemmas of Psychodynamic approaches: Issues and alternatives. Journal of Abnormal Psychology, 1973, 82, 335-334.

Phillips, L.D. and Edwards, W. Conservatism in a simple probability inference task. Journal of Experimental Psychology, 1966, 72, 346-354.

Phillips, L.D. and Wright, G.N. Cultural differences in viewing uncertainty and assessing probabilities. In H. Jungermann and G. de Zeeuw (eds). Decision Making and Change in Human Affairs, Dordrecht: D.Reidel, 1977.

Redding, G. Cognition as an aspect of culture and its relation to management processes. Journal of Management Studies, May, 1980, 127-148.

Savage, L.J. The Foundations of Statistics. New York: Wiley, 1954.

Slovic, P. Convergent validation of risk-taking measures. Journal of Abnormal and Social Psychology, 1962, 65, 68-71.

Slovic, P. Assessment of risk taking behaviour. Psychological Bulletin, 1964, 61, 330-333.

Slovic, P. and Tversky, A. Who accepts Savage's Axiom? Behavioural Science, 1974, 19, 368-373.

Vroom, V. and Yetton, P. Leadership and decision-making. Pittsburgh Pa; University of Pittsburgh Press, 1973.

Wallach, M.A. and Kogan, N. Aspects of judgement and decision making: Inter-relationships and changes with age. Behavioural Science, 1961, 6, 23-36.

Wright, G.N. Decision-making - Cognitive style or task specific behaviour? In Bonarius, G. van Heck and N. Smid (eds) Personality Psychology in Europe. London: Lawrence Erlbaum Associates (in press).

Wright, G.N. and Phillips, L.D. Personality and probabilistic thinking; An exploratory study. British Journal of Psychology, 1979, 70, 295-303.

Wright, G.N. and Phillips, L.D. Cultural variation in probabilistic thinking: alternative ways of dealing with uncertainty. International Journal of Psychology, 1980, 15, 239-257.

Wright, G.N. Phillips, L.D., Whalley, P.C., Choo, G.T.G., Ng, K.O., Tan, I and Wisudha, A. Cultural differences in probabilistic thinking. Journal of Cross-Cultural Psychology, 1978, 9, 285-299.

CHANGING EXPECTATIONS OF THE FUTURE

J. Louw

University of Transkei, Umtata

South African society is characterized by rigidity as
well as instability: rigidity via an administrative system
of social differentiation by race; and instability due to
the fact that the existing system of social relationships
is placed under severe stress. The social instability is
easily noticeable via the conspicuous disagreements between
the various social groups concerning the country's future.
Consequently, there is a multiplicity of ways of thinking,
producing conditions under which anxiety and speculation
about the future of South African society as a whole are
rife. The situation resembles Mannheim's (1979) breakdown
of the "unitary world-view", where divergent modes of
thought manifest themselves, and the same world appears
radically different to different observers. Since social
antagonism in South Africa takes on the form of a struggle
on the issue of racial discrimination, one would expect a
breakdown of the unitary world-view to occur along racial
lines.

Stating that there can be few societies where doubt
about the future is more intense than in South Africa,
Danziger (1963) invited South African students from
different race groups to write future histories of the
country. The aim was to investigate how future orientations
would be distributed among the different social groups.
These future histories were classified into five
orientations: Conservative, Technicist, Catastrophic,
Liberal and Revolutionary. (Brief descriptions of these
orientations are given below. For a full description,
consult Danziger, 1963, 68-69). Twenty years later, Du
Preez, Bhana, Broekman, Louw and Nel (1981) replicated
Danziger's study, finding changes as well as similarities
over time. This study is an extension of Du Preez et al.'s
study, broadening the data-base as far as black students

403

are concerned. Three sets of comparisons are made in this paper:

(i) Du Preez et al.'s comparison between their results and Danziger's;

(ii) a comparison of the views of black students only, as obtained by Danziger, Du Preez et al., and the present study; and

(iii) a comparison between Du Preez et al.'s group of white English-speaking students and the two groups of black students of the present study in terms of the probability and value of the different future orientations.

Comparison 1 : Du Preez et al. (1981) and Danziger (1963)

Method and sample

Du Preez et al. asked first year psychology students at five South African universities in 1981 to write an essay on the future of South Africa, using Danziger's original instructions. The five universities, together with the racial groupings they represented, were: University of Cape Town (white English-speaking); University of the Western Cape ("coloured"); University of Stellenbosch (white Afrikaans-speaking); University of Durban-Westville (Indian); and University of Transkei (black). A total of 1387 essays were scored for future orientation.

A few explanatory remarks concerning the make-up of the sample are necessary here. The Population Registration Act No. 30 of 1950, as amended, divided the South African population into basically white, "coloured" (2) and black (at first called Native, later on Bantu) people. Coloured and black persons might be further subdivided acccording to their ethnological groups (Horrell, 1978). Universities are racially segregated : the Extension of University Education Act No. 45 of 1959 provided "for the establishment, management and control of separate university colleges for Bantu persons and for non-white persons other than Bantu persons." (The Open Universities in South Africa and Academic Freedom, 1974, p.9). (3) The University of the Western Cape therefore serves mainly the Cape Coloured, Cape Malay and Griqua sub-groups within the general "coloured" population group. The University of Durban-Westville is for the Indian population group, another sub-group within the general group designated as "coloured" (Horrell, 1978). The promotion of Bantu Self-Government Act No. 46 of 1959 recognized eight national units of black people; Du Preez et al's group of black students was predominantly from the Xhosa-speaking people. The University of Transkei was established in 1977. Although it does not discriminate on the basis of race, colour or national origin in admission of students, its student population is predominantly Xhosa-speaking.

Results

The results from the different universities (Du Preez et al.) are presented in Table 1 with Danziger's results in parenthesis. All numbers have been rounded.

TABLE I

Percentage frequency of various types of historical orientation in essays from different social groups (Danziger's (1963) results in parenthesis).

	White (Afrikaans)		White (English)		Indian		Black		Coloured *
Conservative	8	(30)	13	(20)	9	(8)	6	(13)	2
Technicist	8	(38)	4	(13)	8	–	16	(1)	8
Catastrophic	23	(19)	40	(32)	–	(2)	7	(5)	5
Liberal	30	(4)	15	(19)	19	(49)	34	(23)	19
Revolutionary	9	–	20	(2)	64	(31)	25	(46)	66
Unclassified	21	(10)	8	(14)	–	(10)	12	(12)	1
	n= 372		n= 360		n= 120		n= 211		n= 134

* not included in Danziger's study

Discussion

Both white groups have moved away from a Conservative orientation towards a greater emphasis on change: English-speakers remain predominantly Catastrophic, with an increased emphasis on a Revolutionary orientation; while Afrikaans-speakers are increasingly Liberal and Catastrophic in their orientation.

The modal orientation of the Indian sample is Revolutionary, with Liberal a poor second. This is a reversal of the order found in Danziger's study. A very similar picture emerges from the Coloured sample at the University of Western Cape.

405

The most surprising result is the reversal of the 1963
finding, that Revolutionary was modal among black students,
followed by Liberal. In subsequent discussions with these
students, this finding was probed. More than half of the
sample indicated that they were cautious in what they
placed on paper, since they were suspicious of the use that
might be made of their essays. A similar conclusion could
be reached from the Universtiy of the Western Cape sample,
where only 25% (134) of the Psychology I class handed in
their essays. This suspicion is not surprising to find in
as politically tense a society as South Africa (see for
example Welsh, 1975).

Comparison 2 : Views of four groups of black students

The present study was undertaken one year after Du
Preez et al.'s investigation. It probed the possibility
that the distribution of the five orientations among black
students might have been a once-only occurence, perhaps due
to the peculiar position of the University of Transkei in
the South African situation.

Method and sample

Three major problems concerning the use of essays as a
method of investigating future orientation emerged from Du
Preez et al.'s study. It is time-consuming to write,
scoring is tedious and reliability has to be constantly
checked, and it does not distinguish between what is
thought probable to happen and what is preferred. Du Preez
et al., in a second part of their study, developed a
questionnaire aimed at avoiding these problems. In this
questionnaire, the five models of the future were described
as follows:

Conservative:
Though the pattern of society may be temporarily
disturbed, things will remain very much as they are at
present. Traditional policies will be maintained and power
will not change hands to any marked extent, because there
is a basic equilibrium in the system.

Technicist:
The main changes in society will be technological and
material. The technological transformatioh of society by
new inventions and processes is the most fundamental form
of change and progress.

Catastrophic:
Social violence and destruction are inevitable, with
little prospect of recovery. Things will go from bad to
worse. There is no way out of the present deadlock and
there is little that anyone can do about it.

Liberal:
Change will be relatively gradual and smooth as reforms are initiated within the political system. Enlightened self-interest will lead people to negotiate a society which is different from and better than the one in which we now live.

Revolutionary:
The only way in which change can be brought about is by violence, since there are irreconcilable conflicts between different interest groups. Strategic foresight and planning by individuals and by groups of individuals who are prepared to intervene is necessary to overthrow the regime and introduce a new social order.

Each model is followed by a rating of its probability and a rating of its value, using the semantic differential technique.

At the beginning of 1982 this questionnaire was administered to Psychology I students at the University of Transkei and the University of the North. The latter was established to serve mainly students of the Sotho, Pedi, Venda, Tswana, and related language groups (Horrell, 1978) It is nearly twenty years older than the University of Transkei, and has a history of student unrest and revolt against the racially differentiated education system.

As in Du Preez et al.'s study, students were invited to participate in a study of the way in which they saw the future of South Africa. Anonymity was guaranteed, and students were told that they could remove their completed questionnaires if they wished. A white lecturer administered the questionnaire at the University of Transkei, and a black lecturer at the University of the North. The time required for administration was approximately fifteen minutes.

A total of 172 questionnaires were returned at the University of Transkei, and 263 at the University of the North. In both cases, it represented more than 80% of the class present.

Results

Table II shows the rank-order of the five historical orientations obtained from four groups of black students: Danziger (1963), the University of Transkei (Du Preez et al., 1981), the University of Transkei (1982), and the University of the North (1982). The data are given in rank-order form only, since part of it was obtained via essays, and part of it via questionnaires.

TABLE II

Rank-order of various types of historical orientation of black students

	1963 (Danziger)	1981 (Du Preez et al)	1982 (Transkei)	1982 (North)
Conservative	3	5	5	5
Technicist	5	3	1	1
Catastrophic	4	4	4	4
Liberal	2	1	2	3
Revolutionary	1	2	3	2
	n=84	n=211	n=172	n=263

Discussion

The most obvious change over time as far as these groups are concerned is the movement towards a Technicist orientation. The Revolutionary option is generally seen as the second most likely to occur (the 1982 Transkei sample is the exception). The ranking of Catastrophic has remained constant, while Conservative is now consistently ranked as the least likely possibility for the future.

Comparison 3 : Probability and value of future orientations as perceived by white English-speaking and black students.

Du Preez et al. predicted that, if a distinction is made between what people expect to happen and what they prefer to happen, one might find a convergence in perceptions of probability among various groups, which might be absent from their evaluations. This section tests this prediction by comparing white English-speaking and black students. It also allows for a comparison of the views of two groups of black students.

Method and sample

The sample consisted of the black students at the University of Transkei (N=172) and the University of the North (N=263) to whom the questionnaire was administered in 1982, and the 100 white English-speaking students at the University of Cape Town whom Du Preez et al. used in the second part of their study.

Results

A table showing the mean ratings of probability and
value of the future orientations is given below (Table
III). The orientations are in order of magnitude from most
to least probable and from most highly valued to least
valued on a seven-point scale.

TABLE III

Mean ratings of probability and value of future orientations by different groups

PROBABILITY					VALUE				
U C T (1981)		TRANSKEI (1982)		NORTH (1982)		U C T (1981)		TRANSKEI (1982)	NORTH (1982)
Rev.	4,8	Tech.	5,6	Tech.	5,7	Lib.	6,1	Tech. 5,4	Lib. 5,7
Cat.	4,4	Lib	5,0	Rev.	5,3	Tech.	4,0	Lib. 5,2	Tech. 5,6
Tech.	3,7	Rev.	4,4	Lib.	4,8	Rev.	3,2	Rev. 3,9	Rev. 4,6
Lib.	3,1	Cat.	4,3	Cat.	4,5	Con.	2,6	Con. 3,5	Con. 2,8
Con.	2,6	Con.	3,5	Con.	3,0	Cat.	2,9	Cat. 2,9	Cat. 2,4
n= 100		n= 172		n= 263					

Discussion

The data in Table III show clearly the value of
distinguishing between the probability and value of the
five orientations. English-speaking whites think
Revolutionary and Catastrophic change most likely, but they
rate Liberal and Technicist change as most valuable. Black
students in Transkei view Technicist and Liberal change to
be most likely and most valuable. Black students at the
University of the North regard the Technicist and
Revolutionary options as most likely, but the Liberal and
Technicist as most valuable. One therefore finds a
convergence in black and white perceptions of the value of
the five orientations, but an absence of convergence in the
likelihood that changes will come about like that. This is
contrary to Du Preez et al.'s expectations. White
English-speaking students have a more "pessimistic"
expectancy of the future. But it might also mean that they
have a different attitude to the changes that blacks may
see as Liberal or Technicist. The latter possibility is
clearly outside the scope of the present study, but might
be a fruitful question for further investigation.

The high probability as well as value ratings given to
the Technicist orientation by both groups of black students

are somewhat surprising. In Du Preez et al.'s study this
orientation was only placed third in terms of likelihood,
while in Danziger's group it received the lowest rating
(Table I). Black students in Du Preez et al.'s and the
present study have consistently showed more of a Technicist
orientation than the other population groups (Tables I, II
and III). When one compares for example the white
Afrikaans-speaking groups of Danziger and Du Preez et al.,
one finds that the Technicist orientation has shifted from
most likely to least likely over twenty years' time.

Upon closer examination of the <u>distribution</u> of the
ratings given by the black students (data for white
students not available), a lack of consensus on some of the
orientations becomes apparent. Although there was a
tendency to agree on the probability and value of some of
the orientations, there was disagreement on some others.
Disagreement was indicated when almost half of the students
gave an orientation (e.g. Conservative probability) a very
low rating, while the other half gave the same orientation
a very high rating. Agreement was indicated when most of
the ratings were at one end of the scale, either very low
or very high. In general, students used the extreme ends of
the scale much more than the middle. This in itself could
be an indication of the intensity of involvement in these
issues.

There was some consensus about:

(i) the probability and value of Conservative (both
low);
(ii) the probability and value of Technicist (both
high);
(iii) the value of Catastrophic (low); and
(iv) the value of Liberal (high).

There was less consensus concerning:

(i) the probability of Catastrophic;
(ii) the probability of Liberal; and
(iii) the probability and value of Revolutionary.

In other words, there were quite obvious
disagreements within one race group on how probable and how
valuable certain options for the future were. Lack of
consensus occurred mainly in the two future orientations in
which violence was involved. While the description of the
outcome of the Catastrophic orientation was such that few
people would really value it, the subjects were divided on
the probability and value of the Revolutionary model. The
disagreement on the likelihood of the two violent models
probably affected the rating of the likelihood of the
Liberal option as well.

Conclusion

The above-mentioned results suggest that there are other variables apart from race operating here. One strong possibility to account for these within-groups differences is class distinction, cutting across race differentiation. The uneven class composition of the South African race groups is a well-established fact. To investigate this possibility, however, sampling procedures will have to be extended. Almost all subjects in the three studies discussed in this paper were first-year students. No attempt can therefore be made to view them as representative of their respective population groups.

However, as far as student groups are concerned, all three studies show differences in future orientations between the main race groups. Among these groups, one therefore does find a breakdown of the "unitary world-view", although the black and white English-speaking groups showed a convergence in the value they placed on the five orientations (Table III). Mannheim claimed a privileged position for the intelligentsia, namely that they have a special freedom to synthesize a more objective world-view, relatively free from specific group interests. Danziger's results did not support this position. If one accepts that first-year students are part of the intelligentsia, the findings of the present study partially support Danziger. The students surveyed by Du Preez et al. and the present study could synthesize a more "objective world-view" as far as their evaluation of future orientations is concerned, but not for their probability. To what extent this will hold true for groups other than students is still on open question.

The findings of the three studies compared in this paper could be summarized as follows:

(i) Important changes did occur in the future orientations of South African students over a period of twenty years;
(ii) Different race groups still construct different futures for South Africa, often not as stereotypical expectations would have it;
(iii) It is advisable to distinguish between the probability and value of different models of the future;
(iv) White English-speaking and black students tend to converge in the value they placed on the five future orientations, but not in their probability; and
(v) Differences do exist within race groups, making a simplistic interpretation of how "blacks" or "whites" think highly dubious.

. NOTES

(1) The author is grateful to Peter du Preez of the University of Cape Town and Nico Cloete of the University of Transkei for their comments on an earlier draft of this paper, and to Prof. A.G. le Roux of the University of the North for his assistance.

(2) Since this Act, with its amendments, is one of the cornerstones of the apartheid system, the majority of Coloured and Black persons find this classification offensive. The inverted commas are used to reflect this, and are implied throughout this paper where reference is made to a specific racial classification.

(3) Students of all racial groups could (and continue to be able to) study by correspondence at the University of South Africa. (See also editor's note below.)

Editor's Note

It was the editor's (J.B.D.) impression during his visit to South Africa that a large number of "non-white" students is admitted to "white" universities, especially so in those disciplines in which insufficient facilities exist in the "non-white" institutions. In some areas, notably in engineering, special tuition is provided within "white" institutions for students from other cultural groups. He also understands that the Medical School of the University of Natal in Durban (a "white" university) admits solely "non-white" students. The situation is therefore more complex than the above summary of legal points may lead someone unfamiliar with the country to believe.

REFERENCES

Danziger, K. Ideology and utopia in South Africa: A methodological contribution to the sociology of knowledge. British Journal of Sociology, 1963, XIV, 59-76.

Du Preez, P.D., Bhana, K., Broekman, N., Louw, J., and Nel, E. Ideology and utopia revisited. Social Dynamics, 1981, 7 (1), 52-55.

Horrell, M. Laws affecting race relations in South Africa 1948-1976. Johannesburg: South African Institute of Race Relations, 1978.

Mannheim, K. Ideology and Utopia. An introduction to the sociology of knowledge. (Translated by E. Shils). London: Routledge and Kegan Paul, 1979.

The Open Universities in South Africa and Academic Freedom 1957-1974. Cape Town: Juta, 1974.

Welsh, D. Social research in a divided society: The case of South Africa. Social Dynamics, 1975, 1 (1), 19-30.

TOWARDS PARTNERSHIP FOR RELEVANT RESEARCH IN THE THIRD WORLD

J. B. P. Sinha

A.N.S. Institute, Ptana

The present symposium is part of the effort to show the relevance of psychology for national development, despite the doubts about the inadequacy of the theories (Jahoda, 1973, 1980; Zaidi, 1979) and methods (Diaz-Guerrero, 1977; Sanford, 1965) available in the developed countries. There is also a growing expectation that psychologists from the developed and the developing countries would work as equal partners (Kelman, 1968; Sinha, D. 1982), however unequal and varied their resources are (Ayman, 1981; Triandis, 1980). The progress on both counts is not unimpressive, but not quite satisfactory either.

Over twenty years back, the concept of development and the resource superiority in the west imposed on the third world psychologists a relationship which since then has evolved from the stage of pure subordination through restlessness and unrootedness into a phase which might turn out to be relatively more collaborative. The purpose of this paper is to take a brief historical account of the process of this evolving relationship which also tends to change the concept of development itself. The paper is based on the Indian experiences, but the perspective developed here may have some relevance to the third world in general.

The Early Years

In the fifties, national development was taken as synonymous with economic development which was, naturally, the domain of economists. There was, however, a realization among the economists themselves that the economic development of the newly independent nations in the third world did not obey the simple formula of saving,

414

investment, and growth because of the interfering effects of the unique socio-cultural features of the traditional societies (Rostow, 1952, 1960; Lewis, 1955). Hence a number of "Marshall Plans" (e.g. Hagen, 1962; Hoselitz, 1954; Inkeles & Smith, 1974; McClelland, 1961; McCelland & Winter, 1969; Parsons, 1960; etc.) were called upon to clear the ground for the economic laws to function. Nash (1963), while organizing a special issue of the Journal of Social Issues on Psycho-cultural Factors of Asian Economic Growth, identified three types in them. The first type abstracted the general features of the developed economy and prescribed them as the ideal to be emulated by the undeveloped countries. The second approach recommended the diffusion of western skill, knowledge, values, and technology which in turn were expected to transform the traditional societies into the modern ones. Nash himself preferred an approach of process analysis whereby the varieties in the traditional societies were to be mapped with a view to identify "the sources of resistance and vulnerability to modernization" (p. 4) which then can place a society somewhere on a continuum of modernity. The essence in all three approaches remained the economic growth for which the traditional societies were to be modernized in one way or the other.

The same ethos was permeating the Ibadan (Nigeria) Conference (December 29, 1966 - January 5, 1967) on Social Psychological Research in Developing Countries. Hefner and DeLamater (1968), who edited the special issue of the Journal of Social Issues, introduced the theme: "The problems faced by the developing countries of the world are numerous and of critical importance. These problems include those of industrialization and economic development, of changing traditional social institutions such as stratification and power mechanisms so that they facilitate rather than inhibit modernization and of providing percentages of citizens with an education that teaches the economic and social skills required to assuming rewarding roles in a changing society (p.1; my underlining)." Kelman (1968), who organized the conference, was much more receptive to the fact that the forces of development, although more pronounced in the developing countries, were a "world problem" and that even the west had the problems of development because of the pockets of poverty amidst affluence, absence of integration of ethnic and cultural minorities, and the occurences of conflicts and violence. He, therefore, appealed for the interdependence of psychologists from the developed and the developing countries because "the problems that we wish to investigate and the detailed knowledge of the nature of these problems and their social and cultural context reside in the developing countries. On the other hand, the human and material resources for investigating these problems are more fully developed in the industrialized nations where

trained research personnel, accumulated research
experience, research facilities, and research funds are far
more readily available (pp.18-19)." While Kelman was
accurately describing the realities as they existed in the
sixties and to some extent even today, this agenda for
interdependence disclosed inadvertently what was then
recognised as the "scientific temper": acting on something
(persons or objects) in order to produce what the actor
considers desirable outcomes whereby the actor is somehow
presumed to be superior to the targets or beneficiaries. In
such a temper, it was not so difficult to overlook that
part of Kelman's observation in which he credited the
psychologists of the developing countries with "the
detailed knowledge of the nature of these problems and
their social and cultural context". It was indeed easy to
initiate change programmes of ethnocentric nature (Zaidi,
1979) with a missionary zeal for: inculcating achievement
motivation (McClelland, 1961; McClelland & Winter, 1969),
modernization (Inkeles & Smith, 1974), innovation
acceptance (Rogers, 1962), participative management
(Bennis, 1966), etc. in countries such as India.

In the early sixties, the psychologists in India were
just not prepared for any meaningful partnership with their
western counterparts. They were methodologically weak
(Sinha, J.B.P., 1971) or preoccupied with the study of
personality characteristics and attitudes of individuals
and were quite oblivious to their social context (Sinha, D.
1966; Sinha, J.B.P. 1971). Many joined the missionaries in
a mercenary spirit with a view either to advance the
career, to enhance status, or to gain international
visibility. The genuine partnership, which Kelman (1968) so
fervently advocated, was conspicuous either by its absence
(except for a few exceptions, e.g., Jacob, 1971) or by its
lifeless presence. There were a few sparks of indigenous
insights or findings which were not quite congruent with
the prevailing western notions. For example, Pareek (1968)
wanted to add extension motive (concern for other people
and society) to the Need for Achievement (n-Ach) before it
could be conducive to development. Singh (1967) effectively
repudiated Weber's contention that Hindu culture is a
barrier to economic development. Ganguli (1964) reported
that the majority of managers and workers preferred
autocratic organizational climate. D. Sinha (1969) did not
find any basic difference in the motivational pattern of
the economically developed and undeveloped villages. Such
insights or leads, in the absence of sustained efforts and
theories, could not develop into viable alternatives to
examine the Indian realities. On the contrary, the imported
models of development took the Indian researchers away from
the research ideas which otherwise might have struck roots
in the Indian soil. Neither did the models themselves
benefit significantly beyond their replications. As a
result, Indian psychology witnessed a fairly large number

Chapter 40

of studies in the sixties which, by and large, were
replicative, misleading, and irrelevant (Nandy, 1974;
Sinha, D., 1972; Sinha, J.B.P., 1971).

The Changing Perspective

What seemed to be strikingly missing in these studies
was the "Indianness" (Sinha, J.B.P., 1971 p. 1252) - a
spirit or vitality which grows out of researcher's
sustained encounters with the socio-economic context. The
western models of development were embedded in the western
values and concept of development where "individual" was
and still is the agent as well as the recipient of social
change. Triandis (1971) aptly described the profile of such
an individual: "Modern man is apparently open to new
experiences; relatively independent of parental authority;
concerned with time and planning; willing to defer
gratification; he feels that man can be the master over
nature, and he controls the reinforcements he receives from
his environment, he believes in determinism and science; he
has a wide cosmopolitan perspective, he uses broad
ingroups; he competes with a standard of excellence, and he
is optimistic about controlling his environment." This was
the model of man which had emerged out of the western
rational, secular, individualistic, and impersonal
orientations which themselves were the concomitants of
technological revolution and the growth of natural science.
This was the model of man that McClelland, Inkeles, and
others wanted to transplant in India as a precondition for
her economic growth. To a large extent, the model has
managed to persist in the western studies on development.
Triandis (1982), while integrating the studies conducted in
the sixties and seventies, has identified a list of the
following behaviours which are believed to lead to economic
development: planning, concern for time and for the future,
willingness to defer gratification, accuracy of keeping
appointments, assembling many elements of production into a
coordinated system, interpersonal trust, eagerness to
cooperate with others on the basis of role rather than
familiarity with others, small power distance, moderate
risk taking, self-control, and hard work. The overlap with
the 1971 profile is obvious. Furthermore, Triandis does
allow "individual" to remain the focus of development.

It is hard to argue that these behaviours are not
relevant for economic growth or that the individual does
not count in a country's development. Indeed, Triandis has
placed the individual in the inter-locking systems of
social and environmental factors and has carefully traced
the linkages between the three. His familiarity with some
of the developing countries and his years of experience in
organizing the Handbook of Cross-Cultural Psychology have
led him to formulate an internally consistent model which
may account for parts of the realities particularly in the

417

industrialized and urbanized sectors of the developing countries such as India.

Some of us, however, felt uncomfortable with the model. J.B.P. Sinha (1968), for example, showed that in a limited resource condition, striving for excellence often turns into competition for monopolizing and hoarding resources which interfere with optimal resource allocation and utilization. As a result, while a few individuals might maximize their achievement, the aggregate achievement suffers. The individuals also experience interpersonal friction and mutual distrust. What is needed most in a resource limited condition is the need for cooperation and coordination which are coeval of altruism (Sinha & Pandey, 1970) or need for extension (Pareek, 1968). A supportive view was advanced by Mehta (1978) who distinguished social n-Ach from the individual n-Ach and concluded that it is the former which leads to development.

Such critical appraisals were often accompanied by searches for indigenous concepts and processes. It was, for example, reported that Indians prefer dependency relationship (Pareek, 1968; Sinha, 1970), they appreciate an authority which is nurturant (Kakar, 1971; Sinha, J.B.P., 1980) - and respond to the subordinate's need for personalized and dependency relationships. In the seventies, a large number of such studies were conducted which either tried to discover the cultural roots of our social behaviour or to create a data base which might be later used for theorizing. A typical feature of many of these studies was the tinge of a negative self-image which led us to list "what-we-are" in terms of "what-we-are-not". We realized rather slowly that our efforts to identify indigenous concepts and processes were surreptitiously guided by the very western perspective which we were trying to disown. For example, studies on dependency were meant to fashion strategies to cultivate autonomy and competence. Nurturance of a superior was to be utilized for fostering a fraternal type of participative relationship. Studies on the socialization of an Indian child either reflected our concern for the growth of competence and autonomy, etc., or were directed to relate the patterns of family interactions to the psychological differentiation of the child (Sinha, D., 1981). Such examples can be piled up where the implicit theory of western origin either determined the range of our research and did not allow us to go very far or distracted us from the core issues which might have otherwise provided greater impetus to our research activities.

One such issue is the emphasis on social group and collective in contrast to the individual (Sinha, D., 1980a). In the west, the image of the pre-industrialized child - "happy, blissful, and prototype of the beatic angels" (Nandy, in press, p. 17) was changed into a physically, emotionally, and morally weak entity which stands in-between the animal and the human, and hence needs to be <u>reared-up</u> under the hyper-masculine culture of the Protestant ethic (Nandy, 1981). On the contrary, the Indian child is <u>nurtured</u> by the whole family to develop a collective orientation which he carries wherever he goes (Kakar, 1978). A typical example of this collective orientation is villager's style of life. One is struck by the everlasting consultations among them about the sowing time, seeds, cropping pattern, use of fertiliser, etc. In fact not a single decision whether it concerns farming or household issues such as the marriage of sons and daughters is made individually. I often used to wonder why can't they take initiative, plan their own activities, and decide on their own the affairs which concern them. It took some experiences in a village to understand that the pattern of land distribution, collective living, continuous social interactions over generations, scarcity of material resources, and the socialization processes have created a system of inter-woven socio-economic structures and inter-dependent relationships where individual initiative is at a discount. It is neither satisfying nor functional, unless the whole village economy and social system are re-structured which does not seem to be a feasible proposition. On the other hand, villagers' collective life styles have not prevented them from adopting innovations in farm practices. At places the quickness with which they mobilize their resources at least for social and religious purposes could be a pointer to us.

It is also a common experience of behaviour scientists in India that highly competent "modernized" individuals in the work organizations are often totally isolated and completely neutralised by the persons who work around them. Despite their drive and hard-working styles, they remain "islands" and their influences do not "cascade" into the rest of the organization, unless they mobilize the persons around them. Although the evidence is not conclusive, it is strong enough to suggest a possibility that <u>an effective way of human resource mobilization in India is to focus on the social groups and collectives as the instruments of change.</u> The Japanese are known to dissolve their individuality into their work group and to prefer harmony and cohesiveness over individual initiative and technical competence. They have still been able to adopt the modern technology and to cultivate positive work values. Cherns (1974) is probably right that modern technology and organizations are not necessarily antithetical to traditional social systems and an integration of the two is not quite improbable. Each culture, however, will have to explore the range of technologies available to it and the extent of "looseness" in its social systems in order to find a flexible balance between the two. Elsewhere J.B.P. Sinha (1982) has observed that the Indian collectives, in contrast to the Japanese, are internally differentiated and hierarchically structured with individuals as the nodes who respond more to personalized communications. If that - good or bad - is the reality, the change strategy will have to be directed to the key individuals embedded in the collectives (not such located in the society) who then can mobilize the collectives for development. Their efforts are indeed to be directed to the developmental tasks but only through the collectives.

An Emerging Concept of Development

Our search for an alternative route to development has been encouraged by a couple of new pieces of evidence which has been made available recently. For example, massive evidence has accumulated to prove that material affluence beyond a point may not lead to better quality of life either for individuals or social aggregates. The widespread instances of violence, drug abuse, divorce, alienation, and self-estrangement in materially affluent groups in the east as well as in the west are the warning signs that economic development does not subsume the full sense of development which literally means "de-envelopment", i.e., unfolding of potentials and the eradication of constraints which prevent the potentials from their full bloom. Neither can we visualize development in any sense of the term unless the basic needs of food, shelter, health, and education of people are reasonably satisfied. If affluence beyond a point desensitizes us to others, acute poverty dehumanizes even to a more alarming extent. It seems then that economic development has a curvilinear relationship with human development.

There is also conclusive evidence that the economic development, which is based on the principle of control over the environment in order to exploit the natural resources, has caused pollution, to the extent which, if not remedied, can threaten human survival. The alternative being suggested is to make peace with the environment. That is, to develop with rather than at the cost of the environment. The logical corollary for man is to grow with the social groups and collectives rather than to strive for personal excellence which might alienate him from the persons around him. The core value then becomes harmony rather than control, and the focus shifts from the individual to his relationships with his social collectives and environment. Zepke et al. (1981) have nicely outlined the profile of this approach to development:

> "It aims at promoting social harmony and balance in the ecosystem by limiting personal ambition, low consumption of goods and renewable energy, and

the establishment of small scale, self-sufficient communties. Provision of basic human needs is a community responsibility. The possible outcomes would be a dispersed society with cooperative communities, slow pace of life, less demarcation between work and leisure, little trade, less material comfort, and increased identification with neighbouring Pacific island nations" (Ng, 1982, pp. 4-5).

A group of social scientists (e.g. Cherns, 1982; Emery & Trist, 1973; etc.) have further elaborated the profile by providing a package of new values, socio-economic systems, educational and occupational structures, and life styles which would characterize the post-industrial society in the west. The core theme in their approach is to restore to man his collectivity where he actually belongs, and let the system of overlapping groups and collectives plan, conduct, and monitor their internal activities with minimally critical interventions from outside. The structure within such "autonomous groups" is rather fluid with roles and positions changing hands in the spirit of participation, group decision making, and sharing.

Watching from a developing country such as India, which has yet to complete its industrialization and modernization, the double revolutions of the west inspire hope as well as awe. We, with our 80 per cent populations in villages, over 60 per cent of people below the poverty line, and about 70 percent illiterate, often wonder: how to catch up with the west, how to avoid following blindly the steps of the west, and how to take an alernative route to development which is not entirely contingent on the material affluence on the scale currently available in the west. Probably, "simple aesthetic living within forseeable future" (Thaper, 1966, p. 3) is what development should mean to us.

Srinivasan and Bardhan (1974) have stated that there is a "growing realization in both developing and developed countries that the fruits of rapid economic growth, where achieved, have not reached the poor and to some extent, growth has even accentuated their problems" (p. v). The planning has to reverse this process by suggesting measures to provide the basic minimum amenities of food, housing, medical care, and schooling to all. Comforts, to the extent that they might contribute to quality of life, are to be sought after, but will have to follow the principle of equitable distribution. The emphasis is on providing opportunities helping men with integration into social groups and collectives through which they can actualize themselves and can create pro-social institutions. It is not the striving for excellence but for extension (Pareek, 1968) which is made to play the key role.

Scope for Policy Research

Once development is detached at least partially from
its economic mooring and anchored into the processes of the
individual's integration into his social groups and
collectives which assume responsibilities for all round
growth of individuals as well as the health of the
collectives, psychologists can stop playing second fiddle
by either preparing ground for or healing the wounds of
economic development.

They can collaborate with other social scientists as
equal partners in defining development, identifying its
indicators, designing social institutions and relationships
and planning strategies for national development. Such a
pivotal role would bring psychologists into the arena of
policy research where their absence has been too
conspicious for too long. Reviews of literature, for
example, in India, reveal a wide range of micro-level
analyses and solutions of problems regarding education,
health, farm practices, organizational development, mental
health, etc. which are credited to psychologists (Sinha,
D., 1980b). Yet the micro-level studies have failed to
yield a global holistic picture of development which can
stimulate macro-level analyses of aggregate data for policy
planning. Policy research requires larger data bases
pertaining to specific long and short term social problems
caused by factors which are the domains of a variety of
disciplines and sectorial (e.g. political, linguistic,
religious, ethnic, etc.) interests.

Hence the solutions also reflect the power politics
within and between the social scientists, policy makers,
and administrators. Rubbing shoulders with them for
privileges, power, visibility, and a significant say in the
designing of the future and simultaneously incurring the
risk of failure in public accountability (Shimmin, 1981) is
the challenge that confronts psychologists today.

The most appropriate entry point for psychologists in
policy research seems to be the planning of hierarchically
and vertically arranged overlapping collectives which are
to assume responsibilities for developmental activities.
While the internal management and planning within the broad
policy guidelines are to be the primary concern of a
collective, its coordination with other collectives will
have to be taken care of by a chain of coordinating bodies
drawing members from the concerned collectives and groups
which will decide the policy issues and will provide the
guidelines for the implementation of decisions. The
decision making has to be decentralized for the local
issues and centralized for policy guidelines and
coordination. The technology has to be graduated
accordingly. Psychologists' crucial role is also to develop

a system of identifying the nodes within collectives and to help them with strategies of group mobilization. A good deal of research has been conducted to find out how the local and group identities centred around the local issues can be integrated into regional and eventually national identity.

Agenda for Partnership

The picture developed above is in no way complete. It neither gives us a full view of the future, nor indicates the detailed way to go about it. It is at best an agenda for research by the psychologists from the developed and the developing countries. The configuration attempted here draws from the experiences of both worlds and seems to have relevance for all of us. The contents of development or the order of priorities have to be different, but the process of designing, demarcating, and arranging social interactions in a system of overlapping social, religious, ethnic, and work groups and collectives may be culturally invariant. Group mobilization by individual level forces is probably the area where third world psychologists can significantly contribute. The western theories, methods, and concepts may be inadequate, but our constructive mutual confrontation may be the best source of inspiration and stimulation. It is not chance that the most active psychologists in the third world are those who have been exposed for a reasonably long duration to western psychology.

I am tempted to go a step further and reproduce Kelman's (1968) third recommendation on which we have yet to act:

".... it is necessary to develop mechanisms of mutual exposure and two way research, which will allow social scientists from developing nations to observe various aspects of industrialised societies and their problems and to contribute to the understanding of their dynamics - just as social scientists from industrial nations come to observe and analyse the developing societies" (p. 20).

REFERENCES

Ayman, I. (1981) Psychology in developing countries. International Review of Applied Psychology, 30, 401-406.

Bennis, W. (1966) Changing Organization. Bombay & New Delhi: McGraw Hill.

Cherns, A.B. (1974) Traditional values and modern organizations in developing countries. Paper presented to the International Association of Applied Psychology, Montreal.

Cherns, A.B. (1982) The contribution of social psychology to the nature and function of work and its relevance to societies of The Third World. Paper presented at the UNESCO/IUPS Conference, Edinburgh.

Diaz-Guerrero, R. (1977) Editorial response. IACCP Newsletter, 11, 4-6.

Emery, F.E. & Trist, E.L. (1973) Towards a Social Ecology. London & New York: Plenum.

Ganguli, H.C. (1964) Structure and Process of Organization. Bombay: Asia Publishing House.

Hagen, E.E. (1962) On the Theory of Social Change: How Economic Growth Begins. Homewood, Illinois: Dorsey Press.

Hefner, R. & DeLamater, J. (1968) National development from a social psychological perspective. Journal of Social Issues, 24 1-5.

Hoselitz, B.F. (1954) Sociological approach to economic development. Paper presented to the International Congress of Studies on the Problems of Underdeveloped Areas. Milan: Museo Nazionale della Scienza e della Tecnica, pp.19-42.

Inkeles, A. & Smith, D. H. (1974) Becoming Modern. London: Heinemann.

Jacob, P.E. (ed) (1971) Values and Active Community. New York, Free Press.

Jahoda, G. (1973) Psychology and the developing countries: do they need each other? International Social Science Review, 25, 461-474.

Jahoda, G. (1980) Has social psychology a distinctive contribution to make? Paper presented at the Conference on Psychology & Developing Countries, University of Lancaster.

Kakar, S. (1971) Authority patterns and subordinate behaviour in Indian organizations. Administrative Science Quarterly, 16, 298-307.

Kakar, S. (1978) The Inner World: a Psycho-analytic Study of Childhood & Society in India. New Delhi: Oxford University Press.

Kelman, H.C. (1968) Social psychology and national development. Journal of Social Issues, 24, 9-20.

Lewis, W.A. (1955) Theory of Economic Growth. London: Allen & Unwin.

McClelland, D.C. (1961) The Achieving Society. New York: Van Nostrand.

McClelland, D.C. & Winter, D.G. (1969) Motivating Economic Development. New York: Free Press.

Mehta, P. (1978) Work motivation in Indian public sector: Some conceptualisation. Paper presented at the seminar on Alienation, Efficacy Motivation and Employee Participation at the National Labour Institute, New Delhi.

Nandy, A. (1974) The non-paradigmatic crisis in Indian psychology: Reflections on a recipient culture of science. Indian Journal of Psychology, 49, 1-20.

Nandy, A. (1981) Reconstructing childhood: A critique of the ideology of adulthood. Lecture delivered at Tsukuba University, Japan.

Nandy, A. (in press) The psychology of colonialism: Sex and age in the idiom of political inequality in British India. In A. Beteille (ed.) Aspects of Inequality. New Delhi: ICSSR.

Nash, M. (1963) Introduction: Approaches to the study of economic growth. Journal of Social Issues, 19, 1-5.

Ng, S.H. (1982) Power, values and alternative developments in New Zealand. Paper presented to the 20th Congress of the International Association of Applied Psychology, Edinburgh.

Pareek, U. (1968) A motivational paradigm of development. Journal of Social Issues, 24, 115-122.

Parsons, T. (1960) Structure and Process in Modern Societies. New York: Free Press.

Rogers, E.M. (1962) Diffusion of Innovations. New York: Free Press.

Rostow, W.W. (1952) The Process of Economic Growth. New York: Norton.

Rostow, W.W. (1960) The Stages of Economic Growth. A Non-Communist Manifesto. Cambridge: Cambridge University Press.

Sanford, N. (1965) Will psychologists study human problems? American Psychologist, 20, 192-202.

Shimmin, S. (1981) Applying psychology in organizations. International Review of Applied Psychology, 30, 377-386.

Singh, A.K. (1967) Hindu culture and economic development in India. Conspectus, 1, 9-32.

Sinha, D. (1966) Psychology in the arena of social change. Presidential address to the Section of Psychology & Education, Indian Science Congress, Chandigarh.

Sinha, D. (1969) Indian Villages in Transition. New Delhi: Associated Publising House.

Sinha, D. (1972) Industrial Psychology. In S.K. Mitra (ed). A Survey of Research in Psychology. ICSSR, Bombay Popular Prakashan, pp. 175-237.

Sinha, D. (1980a) Collective as the target: a new perspective to research on prosocial behaviour. Paper presented to the International Conference on Development and Maintenance of Prosocial Behaviour at Polish Academy of Science, Warsaw.

Sinha, D. (1980b) Applied psychology and problems of national development. Paper presented at the Conference on Psychology & Developing Countries, University of Lancaster.

Sinha, D. (ed.) (1981) Socialization of the Indian Child. New Delhi: Concept Publishing House.

Sinha, D. (1982) Cross-cultural psychology: a view from the Third World. Presidential address at the 6th Conference of the International Association for Cross-Cultural Psychology, Aberdeen.

Sinha, J.B.P. (1968) The n Ach/n Co-operation under limited/unlimited resource condition. Journal of Experimental Social Psychology, 4, 233-246.

Sinha, J.B.P. (1970) Development Through Behaviour Modification. Bombay: Allied Publishers.

Sinha, J.B.P. (1971) Methodology of problems oriented research in India. Paper presented to the International Association of Applied Psychology, Liège, Belgium.

Sinha, J.B.P. (1980) The Nurturant Task Leader. New Delhi: Concept Publishing House.

Sinha, J.B.P. (1982) Socio-technical determinants of work values: A research proposal. A.N.S. Institute of Social Studies, Patna, India.

Sinha, J.B.P. & Pandey, J. (1970) Strategies of high n Ach persons. Psychologia, 13, 210-216.

Srinivasan, T. N. & Bardhan, P. K. (eds) (1974) Poverty and Income Distribution in India. Calcutta: Statistical Publishing Society.

Thaper, R. (1966) A design for living, a design for development. Paper presented at the UNESCO International Round Table on Jawaharlal Nehru. New Delhi: India International Centre.

Triandis, H.C. (1971) Some psychological dimensions of modernization. Paper presented at the International Association of Applied Psychology, Liège, Belgium.

Triandis, H.C. (1980) Reflections on trends in cross-cultural research. Journal of Cross-Cultural Psychology, 11, 35-58.

Triandis, H.C. (1982) Toward a psychological theory of economic development. Paper presented at UNESCO/IUPS Conference, Edinburgh.

Zaidi, S.M.H. (1979) Applied cross-cultural psychology: Submission of a cross-cultural psychologist from the Third World. In L. Eckensberger, W.S. Lonner, & Y. H. Poortinga (eds.) Cross-Cultural Contributions to Psychology. Amsterdam: Swets & Zeitlinger.

Zepke, N. et al. (1981) Context for Development: Clarifying Values. Wellington: P.D. Hasselberg.

FACES IN CROSS-CULTURAL PERSPECTIVE

J. W. Shepherd

University of Aberdeen

The human face is a stimulus of great social significance. From the earliest months of life, the human infant's reaction to faces is different from that to other stimuli. For example, infants are disturbed by a totally immobile real face, but not by other immobile stimuli. Within these early months the infant also learns to distinguish its mother's face from other people's and well within the first year learns to discriminate new faces from those seen before, (see Carey, 1981 for review).

Philosophers and scientists have for centuries acknowledged the special importance of the face, though for most of this time their efforts were directed at using the face as a means of assessing character and temperament. The failure to establish any empirical relationship did little to interfere with the use of the face for this purpose, and it is ironical that one of the greatest pioneers of the psychological study of the face and particularly of cross-cultural studies, Charles Darwin, very nearly failed to make his celebrated voyage on the Beagle because the Captain of that vessel objected to the shape of his nose. "He doubted", wrote Darwin, "whether anyone with my nose could possess sufficient energy and determination for the voyage," (Keynes, 1979).

The search for the key to character in the face has now abated, and interest has turned to other aspects of the face. I want to mention three of these.

First, the face is the most important vehicle for the expression of emotion, and there is a century of research, beginning with Darwin, which has analysed the nature of these expressions, and of the ability of others to recognise the emotions being expressed.

Second, we use the face as our principal means of distinguishing people. The ability to recognise someone as the person we saw yesterday is a vital skill in everyday life, and one, which I have mentioned, we begin to acquire from our earliest days. Indeed, such is our facility at recognising faces that it has been argued by some though not generally accepted, that there must be a specific face-processing mechanism in man specially evolved for that purpose (see Ellis, 1981 for review).

Third, in virtually all societies the face, and particularly a woman's face, is one element, and an important one, in physical attractiveness. Until quite recently, psychologists generally paid little attention to this fact, regarding it, it seems, as a somewhat trivial matter compared with the study of more fundamental factors in attraction. Yet the importance of physical attractiveness in everyday life is clear from the fortunes being made by the cosmetic industry, and from empirical findings that social mobility of working class girls is correlated with physical attractiveness. Darwin, as we shall see, as long ago as 1871 drew attention to the importance of physical attractiveness in sexual selection.

I shall allude only briefly to emotional expression, because, although it is the area in which there has been most cross-cultural research, it is not a topic on which we have conducted work in Aberdeen. One of the questions which exercised investigators of this topic was whether patterns of facial expression of emotions were universal throughout mankind, or whether each society developed its own conventions as it would in language, so that members of different societies would learn only the convention appropriate to that culture.

Over the past 15 years a number of cross-cultural studies of the recognition of emotions has been carried out, initiated by Izard (1971) and by Ekman and Friesen (Ekman 1973). These have usually made use of photographs of posed expressions of emotions, in which an actor is asked to produce the expression associated with a particular emotional state. From a large number of such photographs, those are selected on which Caucasian subjects show highest agreement on what emotion is being expressed. Ekman and Friesen, for example, asked people from five different cultures to judge the emotions being expressed in such a series of pictures, and found a high degree of agreement from culture to culture. The interpretation of these results as evidence of universals in facial expression is not, however, completely justified. It could be argued that these posed expressions are cultural conventions, and that the common judgements across cultures are due to diffusion of these conventions through the cinema and other visual arts. What is needed is evidence from a culture uncontaminated by contact with Western media. Ekman and Friesen succeeded in collecting data from two isolated tribes in New Guinea - the Fore and the Dani. In these studies they found considerable agreement between the judgements of the pre-literate people and the literate Western observers for posed expressions by Western actors.

In addition, Ekman and Friesen collected a set of video tapes of New Guinea men posing emotional expressions in response to stories. When these video tapes were shown to American students, there was again considerable agreement in the judgements except for surprise and fear, which tended to be confused, as indeed they were by the New Guinea people when judging American poses.

Studies in other cultures have also found evidence for cultural generality in facial expression of emotion and in recognition of emotion - or at least of the limited number of emotions which have been studied, although the circumstances in which particular emotions will occur or be displayed will be dependent upon specific cultural rules.

Communication of emotions is only one function of the face. In everyday life the face is the main basis on which we distinguish one person from another. Such is the importance of the face as an index of personal identity that it is used in official documents as well as in informal settings to establish that a person is who he claims to be. Identity cards and passports normally include the bearer's photograph, and it is assumed that a stranger will be able to match the photograph with the bearer, even if there have been changes to the face. In fact, our impressions of faces we have seen are so robust that the faces can withstand massive loss of information and still remain recognizable.

The ability to recognize faces develops from early childhood. For the most part, the faces we experience in acquiring this skill are characteristic of members of our own culture. In the case of Western Europeans we know that certain parts of the face and head are more important than others as a basis for identifying faces. Hair style, face shape and the upper part of the face are particularly salient (Shepherd, Ellis and Davies, 1981). It is not necessarily the case that the same features would be of equal importance in cultures where the physical racial type is different. For example, hair colour and texture may not be as distinctive among non-European as among European people.

There is a popular notion that members of a race different from one's own all look alike -- and all look very different from one's own race. The work of, among others, Malpass and of Goldstein in the U.S. has shown that white people there show poorer recognition performance for faces of blacks and Japanese than they do for their own race (Malpass and Kravitz, 1969; Chance et al., 1975). With black subjects, however, the effect is less consistently found. The asymmetrical nature of these differences raises difficulties of interpretation since blacks are a minority in the U.S. (though not necessarily in their city of residence) and may therefore be exposed to, and have to learn to discriminate among, white faces more than white people do among black faces.

Shepherd, Deregowski and Ellis (1974) therefore set out to test for a cross-cultural, cross-race effect in face recognition by comparing the performance of young Scots soldiers and women with those of black Rhodesian soldiers and women. In this case for both Scots and Rhodesians the other race constituted a minority in their society. The method used was a standard procedure in recognition memory. First a set of photographs of target stimuli, 10 African and 10 European faces, were shown to subjects. Then after a delay of 24 hours, these same stimuli were shown randomly mixed in with the same number of photographs of new faces. The subjects' task was to indicate which of these photographs were old (had been seen before) and which were new.

In this study we used the signal detection measure d', which combines correct identification of old photographs and false identification of new photographs as our index of recognition accuracy. The results, illustrated in Figure 1, showed that both races, Africans and Europeans alike, were better at recognizing faces of their own race than of the other race.

One might account for these results in terms of differential experience. People learn to distinguish among and remember people of their own race because they see them more often and see more of them than they do of members of a minority race. If this were so, one might expect progressive rise in performance with age of subjects, both for own race and for other race faces. Of course performance on other race faces might still be inferior to that on one's own race, but with increased experience associated with age, there should be some improvement in other race recognition.

As a test of this, Deregowski and Shepherd compared the performance of 10 year old children, 13 year old children and adults in Salisbury, Rhodesia, and Aberdeen, Scotland. The children in Salisbury were attending schools in the city, and were all black Africans, though with some contact with whites. The adult African subjects were students at the University of Rhodesia in Salisbury, where about half of the students were white. The children in

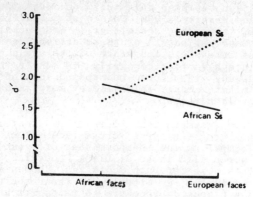

Figure 1. Recognition performance of African and European subjects on African and European faces.

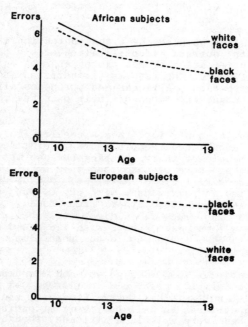

Figure 2. Errors (misses and false alarms) for African and European subjects at three age levels with white and black faces.

Aberdeen were all white, and attended primary and secondary schools in the city where the population is overwhelmingly white. The adults were students at the University of Aberdeen where there are only a very few black students.

On any simple differential experience hypothesis one would predict a superior performance for the adults of each race over the children, and particularly on own race faces. There should also be improvement with age for other race faces which might be more marked for African adult subjects given their experience of whites, compared with the Scottish experience of blacks.

The procedure for the experiment was similar to that of the previous experiment, except that slides were used, and the results can be seen in Figure 2. It is clear that the expected improvement with age for own race faces occurs with the African subjects but for other race faces there is no discernable increase in performance scores for age 10 to adulthood. With the Scottish subjects a similar pattern occurs with improvement in own race faces, but no improvement on other race faces. This suggests that recognition of other race faces is not simply a matter of experience of faces of that race but that the development of the ability to recognize own race faces may interfere with adequate processing of other race faces, an idea already suggested by Goldstein and Chance (1980).

Further support for this notion could be claimed from another study conducted by Deregowski with members of the Rhodesian police. This was a racially integrated police force whose members were concerned with the enforcement of law among the people of all racial communities. This duty might be regarded as providing an incentive for members of the force to learn to distinguish and remember members of the other races as well as those of their own race. However, when tested for memory for faces, both black and white policemen show a strong other race effect. If simple exposure to members of the other race were the basis for learning to discriminate among them, one would expect the white Rhodesian police to be relatively better at remembering black's faces than would Scottish undergraduates who would have limited experience of black people. Yet the performance of white Rhodesian policemen is very similar to that of the Scots, as shown in Figure 3.

Why is it that the adults in a particular culture were superior to children in recognizing own race faces but not other race faces? And adults of the same race but with different levels of experience of other race faces did not differ in recognition performance for that race? One notion, which has been previously explored by Malpass (1975), is that we develop a set of generalised images or prototypes relating to the most frequently occurring events, in this case faces, in our environment. It is likely that we have at the centre a modal or typical notion of what we imagine a face to be and that other faces we encode are related in some way to this prototypical face.

We may also form prototypes for less common classes of face, such as those of other races, but these are likely to involve dimensions or attributes different from those appropriate for our own race.

The implication of this is that the prototype developed for recognizing faces of our own racial group is inappropriate for other racial groups. It may be, for example, that the features we use to discriminate among members of our own race are different from those required for other races.

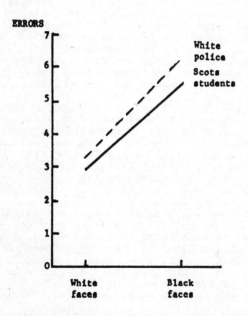

Figure 3. Errors (misses and false alarms) for white African police and white Scots students on white and black faces.

As a first approach to testing this notion, we used a free response procedure to explore prototypes. We envisaged a race prototype for a particular racial group as being a prototype or stereotype of the "typical" member of that group. If people are asked to describe a face they will mention various features, and qualifiers for these features e.g. long hair, big nose, round face. People of all races have the same features – they all have eyes, a nose, a mouth, skin, but the qualifiers or characteristics of these features vary – "black" people have dark skins, "white" people fair skins. If people of all races were subsumed under a single schema, one would expect features to be mentioned with similar frequency, but that the qualifiers for these features would vary from race to race. However, if different schemata are involved one would expect different features to be mentioned.

In one of our Aberdeen studies, British men and women were asked to write a detailed physical description of the face of a typical man from each of four "racial" groups: a black African, a Japanese, a Pakistani and a Northern European. I should stress that these descriptions were carried out without any visual aids in the form of photographs or drawings. The free descriptions were coded into the frequency with which various features were mentioned as for example, skin colour, eye colour, eye shape, hair texture etc. The relative frequency with which each feature was mentioned could be compared across the four target groups.

The relative frequency with which particular features were mentioned within racial groups may be taken as one index of the relevant salience of these features in the prototype subjects may have of these faces.

Table 1 shows the relative frequency with which features were mentioned for each racial prototype. For descriptions of Northern Europeans, face or head shape accounted for 24 per cent of the features mentioned, while skin colour accounted for 22 per cent. In the description of an African, however, these two features together accounted for only 22 per cent of the total, while hair texture or length accounted for 19 per cent and nose shape for 17 per cent.

It seems then, that in the racial physiognomic prototypes of these Western European subjects, different features are salient according to the particular prototype being described. As a measure of the relative similarity of the prototypes we ran correlations on the frequencies with which features were mentioned across the three other race groups. The correlations ranged from 0.91 for the European-Pakistani comparison to 0.60 for the African-European, and 0.57 for the African-Japanese correlation.

As another source of relative similarity of prototypes, we used the results of a rating task we gave to another group of subjects. Instead of writing a free description of their racial "prototypes" these subjects were asked to provide ratings on a set of empirically derived face description scales. From these ratings a profile similarity score was derived for each pair of prototypes for each subject.

The order of profile similarity for these prototype ratings was correlated with that for the free descriptions. The resulting correlation was 0.99. The two forms of prototype assessment based upon different subjects, different modes of response and different similarity index thus came up with similar results.

In a second study (Shepherd and Deregowski, 1981), we approached the question cross-culturally. The question posed was whether members of different racial and cultural groups would use different features to make discriminations among faces of strangers, and whether this would vary with the race of the target faces.

Table 1

Relative frequency with which specific features

were mentioned in "prototype descriptions".

(Percentages of column totals)

| | Prototype | | | |
	N-EUR	AFR	JAP	PAK
skin colour	22	10	13	17
eye colour				12
nose	10	17		
lips		12		
hair colour	13		12	17
hair texture/length		19		14
face/head shape	24	14	13	20

The stimuli we used were coloured full face photographs of head and shoulders of 30 African and 30 European women. The African women were from a northern mining town in Zambia and were employees or wives of employees of the mining company. They ranged in age from about 20 to 50 years. The European women were employees or wives of employees of Aberdeen University, comprising post graduate students, cleaners, secretaries and wives of academic staff.

Subjects were male and female students from the University of Rhodesia and the University of Aberdeen. The procedure was to present a triad of faces to the subject and tell him or her that two of the photographs were more similar to each other than they were to the third. The subject was asked to identify the odd face and describe in what respect the other two were more similar. This was repeated for five triads with different faces in each triad.

When five attributes had been elicited, Ss were asked to rate all 30 of the faces in the stimulus set on all 5 attributes. For some subjects the faces were all of African women, while for others the faces were all European.

On the basis of the ratings, similarity measures were computed between all pairs of photographs for each subject, and these were analysed using the INDSCAL programme for multidimensional scaling. This enables the many similarity measures between the stimuli to be represented in a few dimensions. In this case a four-dimensional solution was adopted.

Because we cannot inspect the disposition of stimuli in 4 dimensions all at once, we try to interpret the dimensional structure by correlating the coordinates of the stimuli on these dimensions with some external measures on the stimuli. In the present case the external measures were ratings by an independent group of subjects on a set of scales based on the most frequently occurring attributes.

If we look at the multiple correlation coefficients in Table 2 we can see to what extent variance on each scale is explained by the scaling dimensions. Scales for attributes with high multiple correlations are important aspects of the judgements made by subjects. Low correlations indicate scales of little significance in this case.

Table 2

Multiple correlations between coordinates on INDSCAL

dimensions and rating scales (decimal point omitted)

	African faces	European faces	European + African faces
dark - light hair		96	82
long - short hair		94	83
straight - curly hair		80	79
large - small eyes			
round - slit eyes			
broad - narrow nose	82		
long - short nose	76		79
thick - thin lips			
round - oval face	75		
fat - thin face	81	78	
smooth - rough skin	73	75	75
dark - light skin	90		93
old - young		94	
feminine - masculine	81	75	
smiling - scowling	86		80

Comparing the multiple correlations for African faces and European faces, it appears that subjects use different attributes. For African faces the highest correlations are for skin colour, nose breadth, fatness of face, expression and femininity. For European faces the highest are hair colour, hair length, hair texture, age and femininity.

These results seem to indicate that different facial features are used for discriminating among African faces and among European faces. To test whether African and European subjects differed in their use of these features the individual subject weights on each dimension were examined. This enables one to see the extent to which each subject gives more weight to one dimension than to another.

If African and European subjects differed in the attributes they used, we would expect their weights to differ across the various dimensions, but this was not the case with racially homogeneous sets of stimuli.

In another part of the experiment the same procedure was carried out but in this case the stimuli comprised 15 African and 15 European faces. The highest multiple correlations in this case were associated with colour, length and texture of hair, colour and texture of skin and nose length. The first dimension polarised the faces from the two races, with no overlap. On the other dimensions, attributes other than race were used and the faces from the two races overlapped. In this case the distribution of subject weights differed markedly for African and European subjects. European subjects were overwhelmingly weighted on dimension 1 while African subjects were equally divided across the four dimensions.

This rather surprising result seemed to indicate that European subjects were more sensitized to physical racial distinctions than were the Africans.

One possible reason for this might have been that the African subjects had much more contact with whites than the Europeans had with blacks. The Africans were at a racially mixed University where black and white students were in almost equal proportions. The European subjects were at a University with a very few black students in a part of Great Britain with a minute black minority.

Our next study was conducted with 10 year old children and 14 year old children in Europe and Africa. The European children were Polish children in Gdansk; the African children were schoolchildren in Salisbury, Zimbabwe. Neither racial group would have had much direct experience with members of the other race. The task for these children involved making similarity judgements among a set of 10 coloured photographs, 5 of white women and 5 of black women. The procedure was to select one of the 10 pictures at random, and to ask the child to select from the remainder the picture that looked most similar to the target picture. With the most similar one removed he was then asked to select the most similar one from the remainder of the pictures, and so on until each picture had been compared.

Another target was then selected and the procedure was repeated until all faces had been used as a target. Each child thus produced a matrix of rank ordered similarity judgements for each face in the set to every other face. These were used as input for the ALSCAL scaling programme, with separate analyses being carried out for Polish and for African children. Two dimensional solutions were adopted for each group. The two questions we asked were i) did both groups use race as a major basis for discriminating between the two races in their ordering of the stimuli along the coordinates; ii) was there agreement between the children from the two races in their ordering of the stimuli along the dimensions.

The answer to the first question was an unequivocal affirmative. The first dimension for both groups of children was one which produced a clear division between black and white faces. To test whether the children used similar criteria in discriminating among the faces on both dimensions the two solutions were correlated. These produced a correlation of 0.90 for the first dimension and 0.83 for the second dimension.

These experiments point to the conclusion that discrimination among African and among European faces involves different physical features, or, we might say, requires different prototypes. However it also appears that African adults and children as well as European adults and children can make use of the same appropriate prototype for each racial category of face.

The development of different facial prototypes in different cultures might be expected to lead to cross-cultural differences in other judgements about faces. One kind of judgement frequently made about faces is beauty or physical attractiveness, particularly in relation to female faces.

According to some authors (e.g. Morris, 1977) there is a link between sexual signals and attractiveness. The dilation of the pupil which occurs with arousal, including sexual arousal, is said to enhance attractiveness.

The face is also said to contain features which mimic the male and female genitalia. These have developed as a result of the evolution of the face to face mode of copulation in the human species (Morris, 1977). Thus the fleshy lips of the female, unique to humankind, are supposed to mimic the labia of the vulva, while the bulbous end of the nose in men is a mimicry of the penis (a notion familiar to Freudians).

On the whole, academic analyses of facial beauty have not drawn attention to these explicitly sexual aspects of the face, but, in the west at least, have stressed the classical values of proportion. The English Victorian ideal is described in a treatise on beauty in women by Alexander Walker who wrote in 1836 of the ideal of a small mouth with a heart shaped upper lip, large eyes and rounded and plump cheeks.

It is widely assumed that standards of female attractiveness vary widely from one culture to another. Surveys of anthropological reports on sexual preferences, such as those by Darwin (1871) and by Ford and Beach (1952), have stressed the disparities between cultures in what they regard as desirable. If we disregard the gross differences in preferred body form and consider only the face, we find a wonderous variety. Some admire large eyes, others insist they should be small; a light complexion is admired among some dark skinned people, while others regard it as a disfigurement; white regular teeth are widely admired, but others blacken their teeth, while some people file their teeth to a point to enhance their attractiveness.

Darwin argued that one of the reasons for variations among races in physical appearance was a preference in each race for those characteristics which distinguish them from other races.

However, one anthropologist, Donald Symons (1979), has suggested that standards of physical attractiveness may not be as variable or arbitrary as many claim. There may exist what he calls innately discernable attributes which universally reflect a high reproductive value. He mentions specifically, good health, for which a good complexion might be a sign, and relative youth.

In addition to these universals he claims there is another preference mechanism related to a tendency to detect the population mean, and to prefer those features which approximate that mean, so that some of the cross-cultural variations in standards of attractiveness may be a product of racial differences.

As a preliminary approach to these questions of the cross-cultural commonality or culture specific criteria of attractiveness we asked our subjects in our scaling studies in Scotland and Africa to rank the stimuli in order of attractiveness.

As a result we had from both races of subjects attractiveness rankings for African faces, European faces and the set of African and European faces. We began by correlating the rankings of the African subjects with those of European subjects. For African faces the correlation was 0.66, and a similar correlation of 0.66 was obtained for the European faces. Both of these correlations are significant at the 0.1 per cent level, but they do not indicate perfect agreement. It seemed possible that there were some aspects common to the judgements of both races of subjects, but that there may be some differences in the features they used in making their judgements. We therefore correlated the attractiveness rankings with the ratings we had obtained on a number of features of the faces. Table 3 summarises the significant correlations resulting from this analysis. If we examine the correlation for the African faces, it is clear that the highest correlations occur on the same features for both races of subject, but there are differences on one or two features. African subjects appear to give greater emphasis to a pale skin than do Europeans, while the Europeans have higher correlations than the Africans for shape and size of eyes. For both groups of subjects, however, age, skin texture, and femininity are the most salient attributes.

With the European faces also there is much in common between the judgements of the two races of subjects, although eye size and hair style appear to be of more importance for European subjects than for Africans.

Table 3

Correlations between beauty rankings and

ratings on physical features

	Race of face					
	African		European		Afric + Euro	
	Race of subject					
	Afr	Eur	Afr	Eur	Afr	Eur
dark - fair hair					34	
straight - curly hair				47		
large - small eyes	36	64	34	63	36	
round - slit eyes	31	62		34	33	
thick - thin lips	-40					
smooth - rough skin	68	57	74	62	36	34
dark - fair skin	-50					
old - young	-52	-57	-64	-76		
feminine - masculine	81	76	49	55	37	42

When we turn to the combined sets of African and European faces, we found that the correlation between the two sets of attractiveness rankings was lower than for the homogeneous groups of faces, being 0.43, which is statistically significant, but reflects less correspondence in the rankings. One might expect a lower correlation, indeed a negative correlation, if each group of subjects were showing an own race bias. To test for this own race bias we computed for each subject an own race preference score based upon the number of own race faces he assigned to ranks above the median rank for the set. We then tested the deviation of this own race score from the score expected if both races were judged randomly. The European Ss had a small but non-significant trend towards an own race preference, but the African Ss have a trend towards an other race preference. It was clear, then, that neither race of subjects had a strong own race preference as a basis for attractiveness judgements. Other features, in this sample of faces, were more important; a smooth skin and a generally feminine appearance.

The absence of an own race preference was a bit surprising, particularly for European subjects who had shown such sensitivity to racial attributes in their similarity judgements. However, it could be that we were dealing with young adults who were also sensitive to sexually relevant cues such as skin texture and general femininity, in judging attractiveness. For pre-adolescent children these cues might be less evident and consequently one might get a stronger own race preference among these. The Polish and African children we used for our scaling study, who were 10 years old and 14 years old, were also asked to rank the faces on attractiveness. A measure of own race preference was derived in the same way as for adult subjects, though in this case based on a smaller set of faces. For the 10 year olds in both groups there was an own race preference, though this was significant only for the Polish children. There was generally less consistency among the African children in their rankings compared with the Poles, and this may in part account for the non-significance of the trend. Nevertheless, the correlation between the ranking of the Poles and the Africans was -.66 (significant at the .05 level). Neither group of 14 year olds showed any own race preference, indeed the Polish 14 year olds actually had a significant other race preference, the two sets of rankings correlating +.40. These results provide tentative support for our hypothesis that own race preferences in attractiveness judgements will be found among children but that with maturity other cues will be utilised in such judgements.

In sum, the faces of people in different cultures differ in their physical characteristics. These differences affect the facility with which people can remember the faces of people from other races, and are also related in some ways to the perception of attractiveness. The exploration of these differences may shed some light on the processes involved in face memory and on facial attractiveness. The discovery of commonality among cultures, as in recognition of emotion and evaluation of attractiveness, can also be used to assess certain universal processes in human judgement and behaviour.

REFERENCES

Carey, S. (1981) The development of face perception in G.M. Davies, H.D. Ellis and J.W. Shepherd, (eds.) Perceiving and remembering faces. London: Academic Press.

Chance, J., Goldstein, A.G. and McBride, L. (1975) Differential experience and recognition memory for faces. Journal of social psychology, 97, 243-253.

Darwin, C. (1871) The descent of man and selection in relation to sex. London: John Murray.

Ekman, P. (1973) Cross cultural studies of facial expression in P. Ekman (ed.) Darwin and facial expression. London: Academic Press.

Ellis, H.D. (1981) Theoretical aspects of face recognition in G.M. Davies, H.D. Ellis and J.W. Shepherd (eds.) Perceiving and remembering faces. London: Academic Press.

Ford, C.S. and Beach F.A. (1952) Patterns of sexual behaviour. London: Eyre and Spotiswoode.

Goldstein, A.G. and Chance, J.(1980) Memory for faces and schema theory. Journal of psychology, 105, 47-59.

Izard C.E. (1971) The face of emotion. New York: Appleton.

Keynes, R.D. (1979) The Beagle record. Cambridge: Cambridge University Press.

Malpass, R.S. (1975) Towards the theoretical basis of understanding differential face recognition. Paper presented at the meeting of the Midwestern Psychological Association, Chicago.

Malpass, R.S. and Kravitz, J. (1969) Recognition for faces of own and other race. Journal of personality and social psychology, 13, 330-334.

Morris, D. (1977) Manwatching. London: Jonathan Cape.

Shepherd, J.W. and Deregowski, J.B. (1981) Races and faces: a comparison of the responses of Africans and Europeans to faces of the same and different race. British journal of social psychology, 20, 125-133.

Shepherd, J.W., Deregowski, J.B. and Ellis, H.D. (1974) A cross-cultural study of recognition memory for faces. International journal of psychology, 9, 205-212.

Shepherd, J.W., Ellis, H.D. and Davies, G.M. (1981) Studies of cue saliency in G.M. Davies, H.D. Ellis and J.W. Shepherd (eds.). Perceiving and remembering faces. London: Academic Press.

Symons, D. (1979) The evolution of human sexuality. Oxford: Oxford University Press.

INDEX

The references in the index are to chapters and
not to pages. In the body of the volume chapter numbers are shown in the top right hand or left hand
corners of the pages.

447

ALREADY PUBLISHED

CROSS-CULTURAL PSYCHOLOGY.

Readings in Cross-Cultural Psychology. Proceedings of the inaugural Meeting of the International Association for Cross-Cultural Psychology held in Hong Kong, August 1972. Edited by J. L. M. Dawson and W. J. Lonner.
1974. XVIII + 398 pp.   ISBN 0 85656 114 2

Applied Cross-Cultural Psychology. Selected Papers from the 2nd International Conference of the International Association for Cross-Cultural Psychology, Kingston, Ont., August 6 – 10, 1974. Edited by J. W. Berry and W. Lonner.
1975. 340 pp., 5 figs.   ISBN 90 265 0214 1

Basic Problems in Cross-Cultural Psychology. Selected Papers from the 3rd International Conference of the International Association for Cross-Cultural Psychology, Tilburg, July 12 – 16, 1976. Edited by Y. H. Poortinga.
1977. VIII + 380 pp.   ISBN 90 265 0247 8

Cross-Cultural Contributions to Psychology. Selected Papers from the 4th International Conference of the International Association for Cross-Cultural Psychology, Munich, July 28 – August 5, 1978. Edited by L. Eckensberger, W. Lonner and Y. H. Poortinga.
1979. X + 442 pp.   ISBN 90 265 0300 8

Diversity and Unity in Cross-Cultural Psychology. Selected Papers from the 5th International Conference of the International Association for Cross-Cultural Psychology, held in Bhubaneswar, India, December 28, 1980 – January 1, 1981. Edited by R. Rath, H. S. Asthana, D. Sinha and J. B. H. Sinha.
1982. VI + 374 pp.   ISBN 90 265 0431 4

Expiscations of Cross-Cultural Psychology. Selected Papers from the 6th International Conference of the International Association for Cross-Cultural Psychology, held in Aberdeen, July 20-23, 1982. Edited by J. B. Deregowski, S. Dziurawiec and R. C. Annis.
1983.   ISBN 90 265 0450 0

DAWSON, J. L. M., G. Blowers and R. Housain (Eds.), Perspectives in Asian Cross-Cultural Psychology. Selected Papers of the First Asian Regional Conference of the IACCP, 19 – 23 March 1979.
A central concern of this Conference was the ways in which psychology can assist in the solution of important social problems in Asia. The implications for psychological research for the problems of national integration, economic development, population control, pollution control, mental health, interpersonal cooperation across ethnic boundaries were discussed.
1981. X + 198 pp.   ISBN 90 265 0359 8

To be ordered from:
SWETS PUBLISHING SERVICE
347 b, Heereweg
2161 CA LISSE, The Netherlands

In USA and Canada please order from:
C. J. HOGREFE, INC.
P.O. Box 51
Lewiston, NY 14092, USA